Administrative Law
Textbook

17th edition

Michael T Molan
BA, LLM (Lond), Barrister
Head of Law, South Bank University

HLT Publications

HLT PUBLICATIONS
200 Greyhound Road, London W14 9RY

First published 1979
17th edition 1995

© The HLT Group Ltd 1995

ISBN 0 7510 0541 X

British Library Cataloguing-in-Publication.
A CIP Catalogue record for this book is
available from the British Library.

Acknowledgement
The publishers and author would like to
thank the Incorporated Council of Law
Reporting for England and Wales for kind
permission to reproduce extracts from the
Weekly Law Reports.

Printed and bound in Great Britain

Contents

Preface

HLT Textbooks are written specifically for students. Whatever their course they will find our books clear and concise, providing comprehensive and up-to-date coverage. Written by specialists in their field, our textbooks are reviewed and updated on an annual basis.

In addition to the usual updating that we undertake each year for this book, we have added a new chapter called 'Recent Cases'. This chapter includes the most significant cases that have occurred in the last year. In order to assist the student extracts from the judgments and commentary, where appropriate, have been included. In many instances these cases highlight new interpretations of particular facets of existing law.

Knowledge of recent cases is extremely important for those studying for their examinations. It demonstrates not only an active interest in the law as it develops, but also the dynamic nature of the law which is constantly adapting to changing social and economic trends.

The Administrative Law textbook is designed for use by any undergraduates who have Administrative Law within their syllabus. It will be equally useful for all CPE students who must study Administrative Law as one of their 'core' subjects.

In addition those studying for certain professional examinations, such as the Institute of Legal Executives, will find this textbook gives them sufficient information for their appropriate examinations in Administrative Law.

This latest edition of the *Administrative Law Textbook* assesses the impact of all the key decisions reported during 1994, notably the House of Lord's ruling on the scope of public interest immunity in *ex parte Wiley*; and the continuing liberalisation of locus standi, as evidence by decisions such as *ex parte Greenpeace, ex parte World Development Movement Ltd* and *ex parte Equal Opportunities Commission*. Other decisions noted include *Mercury Energy Ltd* (reviewability of commercial undertaking), *ex parte Dallaglio* (rule against bias), and *ex parte Fewings* (green politics).

The law is stated as of 31 December 1994.

Table of Cases

Table of Statutes

1

Introduction to Administrative Law

1.1 Introduction

There has never been any serious doubt that administrative law is primarily concerned with the control of power. With the increase in the level of state involvement in many aspects of everyday life during the first 80 years of the twentieth century, the need for a coherent and effective body of rules to govern relations between individuals and the state became essential.

It should be noted at the outset, by any student of the subject, that administrative law is a constantly evolving subject, and to date the object of developing the above mentioned body of coherent rules has not yet been achieved. The subject has developed rapidly during this century, however, and since 1945 the judiciary have contributed massively to the creation of something approaching a 'law' governing relations between individuals and state agencies.

A brief survey of this textbook will reveal that the topic essentially falls into two sections. First, consideration is given to the various administrative agencies that have been created by Parliament, such as local authorities, public corporations and tribunals, and to various administrative devices, such as delegated legislation, and the local public inquiry. Secondly, consideration is given to judicial review: the control exercised by the courts over the actions (and failure to act) of the administrative bodies.

There are many approaches that can be taken to the subject. Whilst it is traditional to concentrate on the case law, it should be remembered that there are many administrative law problems that do not come before the courts because of the

1

provision of some statutory remedy, lack of funds for litigation, delay in applying for relief, or because the jurisdiction of the courts has been ousted by statute. In those cases that do reach the courts, the outcome of the decision is not always what was hoped for. (For example, see *Padfield* v *Ministry of Agriculture* [1968] AC 997.)

1.2 Does administrative law exist?

Bearing in mind that there are a considerable number of learned texts devoted to the subject, the above question might seem redundant, but it does have a serious purpose.

Administrative law suffered for many years from the after-effects of Dicey's denial of its existence. Writing in *The Law of the Constitution* in 1885, Dicey rejected the concept of administrative law, claiming it had no place in the British constitution. His reason for doing so was his adherence to the principle of the rule of law; to his mind everyone should be equal before the law and subject to it. He feared that the development of administrative law would involve the evolution of a special body of rules and principles giving administrative agencies privileges in litigation against the private individual, resulting in a situation whereby they became a law unto themselves.

His justification for these views came from comparison with the French droit administratif, and his assumption that the French administrative courts, including the Conseil d'Etat, must be biased in favour of the administration, against the interests of the individual.

Today, this view of administrative law is largely discredited. The French system, although fundamentally different from our own, has many features from which English administrative law could learn. For example, it has a developed system for compensating individuals who suffer financially from the actions of public officers. As Professor Wade points out (Administrative Law 6th ed p27):

'The reality is that the French Conseil d'Etat is widely admired and has served as a model for other countries.'

The result has been that, during this century, administrative law has had to struggle to develop an identity. In many ways it has emerged as a branch of law more due to necessity than conscious design. The promotion of the welfare state, introduction of much more stringent planning controls, and increased licensing of various professions has necessitated the development of a body of rules and principles which go some way towards regulating the way in which the various administrative agencies involved in the above mentioned tasks, perform their functions. Hence the development of rules of fair procedure, and the reasonableness principle.

A remaining problem, however, especially since the House of Lords' decision in *O'Reilly* v *Mackman* [1983] 2 AC 237, is the question of classification. The real problem is that no clear division has ever been made between the two, partly at least thanks to Dicey's influence. Most would say that administrative law should be classified as 'public law' because it is generally concerned with relations between individuals and state agencies, rather than between private individuals, but this does not satisfactorily dispose of the matter. Many of these agencies, such as local planning authorities or rent tribunals are dealing with individual property rights; many licensing bodies regulate the manner in which an individual should pursue his chosen profession; some administrative agencies even determine questions affecting personal liberty. Can it truly be said that such 'rights' are a matter of public law? Where an individual only has a right because he has been given it by Parliament, such as entitlement to income support, then it may be more sensible to regard it as a matter of public law; but many examples could be put forward where it would be exceedingly difficult to choose. Similar difficulties arise in trying to assess the status of various bodies. Are the BBC, the universities, the National Trust, or the Law Society public or private bodies?

It is because administrative law has developed sporadically over the last 50 years, instead of being established as a separate body of rules along the lines of the French system, that these difficulties persist.

The uninitiated reader may be forgiven for asking why the public/private dichotomy is of any significance. The answer would be that in many areas, notably the procedure for applying for judicial review, and also litigation in negligence, an individual may be denied the remedy he seeks and possibly deserves, simply because he has failed to correctly classify the respondent body, or issue of law, as public or private.

For the moment, however, it is heartening to note that senior members of the judiciary themselves confess to some difficulty with the public/private dichotomy.

In *Davy* v *Spelthorne Borough Council* [1983] 3 All ER 278 Lord Wilberforce stated (at p285):

> 'The expressions "private law" and "public law" have recently been imported into the law of England from countries which, unlike our own, have separate systems concerning public law and private law. No doubt they are convenient expressions for descriptive purposes. In this country they must be used with caution, for, typically, English law fastens not on principles but on remedies. The principle remains intact that public authorities and public servants are, unless clearly exempted, answerable in the ordinary courts for wrongs done to individuals ... we have not yet reached the point at which mere characterisation of a claim as a claim in public law is sufficient to exclude it from consideration by the ordinary courts of law; to permit this would be to create a dual system of law with the rigidity and procedural hardships for the plaintiffs which it was the purpose of recent reforms to remove.'

The matter is considered in more depth in Chapter 11.

1.3 Historical perspective

Professor Wade has written, of administrative law, that:

> 'The spread of the tree still increases and it throws out new branches, but its roots remain where they have been for centuries.' (Administrative Law 6th ed p17):

For our purposes, the historical development of administrative law can be dealt with in three periods.

Pre-1688

Most administrative functions would have been carried out by justices of the peace. They were supervised by judges of assize, who carried out the instructions of the Crown. Real control was centralised in the Privy Council, acting through the Star Chamber. Some features of modern day administrative law existed, for example the principles of natural justice, administrative agencies, the prerogative remedies of certiorari, prohibition and mandamus.

Given the relationship between Parliament and the Crown that obtained during this period, however, no direct comparison with present day administrative law is really possible.

1688–1900

Fundamental in importance to the development of administrative law were the Civil War and the Revolution of the seventeenth century, which resulted in a massive shift in power from the Crown to Parliament, and a change in the supervision of administrative agencies.

The Court of King's Bench took over the function of supervising Justices of the Peace and similar bodies by means of granting the prerogative orders of mandamus, prohibition and certiorari.

During this 200-year period, more and more administrative agencies came into existence, being provided with statutory powers to perform various tasks, such as commissioners of sewers, local boards of works, and school boards. In exercising its supervisory jurisdiction over these and Justices of the Peace, the judges of the King's Bench began to gradually develop the doctrine of ultra vires; the theory that if one of these bodies purported to act outside the scope of its power, its acts would be quashed.

Until 1888 Justices of the Peace continued to play a significant role in the carrying out of administrative tasks, but from that year, many of their functions were transferred to local authorities. Obviously the supervisory jurisdiction of the High Court extended to these new bodies.

With this superficial historical analysis we have now reached the end of the nineteenth century, and one can clearly see the foundations being laid for the system as it exists today. It must not be forgotten, however, that life in England at that time was very different. There was no developed welfare state system. There were a comparatively small number of administrative agencies. Generally, there was much less state involvement in the lives of ordinary citizens, and consequently, less administration and bureaucracy.

> 'Until August 1914 a sensible law-abiding Englishman could pass through life and hardly notice the existence of the State, beyond the post office and the policeman.'
>
> (A J P Taylor)

Administrative law was barely recognised as a branch of legal study.

1900 to the present day

The legal system found itself singularly unprepared to deal with the changes that occurred during the first half of this century. Administrative law simply did not develop fast enough to deal with the problems created by the enactment of a whole raft of regulatory legislation. For the first time massive inroads were being made upon personal liberty in areas such as: housing, education, employment, pensions, health, planning, manufacture of goods and pursuit of livelihood. It was due to the absence of proper legal controls that many citizens began to become concerned at the powers of the new bureaucracy. The courts during the early part of this century did little to solve the problem: see *Local Government Board* v *Arlidge* [1915] AC 120.

Due to the increasing complexity of governing the country, government ministers were making increasing use of delegated legislation in order to introduce significant new measures (see Chapter 2). This led to the Report of the Committee on Ministers' Powers of 1932, which went some way to rectifying problems of uncontrolled power, but in many other respects, such as its discussion of public inquiries, it served only to highlight the problems that existed at that time.

A legitimate question to ask at this point would be, what of the judiciary? What was their contribution? The answer would have to be that during this period, judicial control over administrative action had largely fallen into abeyance. A contributing fact was undoubtedly the Second World War. The courts deferred almost without question to the wishes of the executive during this period, working on the principle that during a time of national emergency it would be wrong for the courts to intervene and hamper the exercise of executive discretion. Decisions such as *Liversidge* v *Anderson* [1942] AC 206 are illustrative of this.

The real problem for administrative law arose from the fact that the judiciary seemed to suffer from the effects of this war-time restraint, and in the period immediately following 1945 they continued to limit the scope of their control.

A number of decisions, dealt with at more length in the appropriate chapters, illustrate the point. In *Racecourse Betting Control Board* v *Secretary for Air* [1944] Ch 114, the Court of Appeal held that there was no power in a supervisory court to quash a decision for error of law on the face of the record; in *Duncan* v *Cammell Laird & Co* [1942] AC 624, the House of Lords allowed the Crown very wide powers to suppress evidence in litigation on the ground that its production was against the national interest; in *Nakkudu Ali* v *Jayaratne* [1951] AC 66, the Privy Council held that the revocation of a licence upon which an individual depended for his livelihood was an administrative act and did not attract the protection of the rules of natural justice.

A parallel development was the increased use of the tribunal, as an alternative to the court, as a means of resolving disputes between individuals and state agencies, and inquiries, to resolve disputes over planning matters.

There was widespread dissatisfaction with the operation of both these administrative devices, which resulted in the Report of the Committee on Administrative Tribunals and Inquiries (the Franks Report) in 1958. A more detailed account of this is to be found in Chapters 6 and 7. It suffices to say here that the very fact a report was thought necessary at all is indicative that all was not well with the system, and further, that much of the committee's recommendations were subsequently enshrined in the Tribunals and Inquiries Acts 1958, 1971 and, most recently, 1992. This resulted in a tangible improvement in the proceedings of both tribunals and inquiries.

In many ways, this last mentioned development was responsible for a marked change in judicial attitude that took place during the 1960s. It was as if it had been made clear that the administrative process could be controlled by suitable rules and principles, with the result that the judiciary re-asserted themselves as the traditional supervisors of the administrative agencies.

To some extent old established concepts such as the ultra vires doctrine and the rules of natural justice were revitalised. On the other hand judicial activism also resulted in the development of new heads of review, for example, 'acting on no evidence': see *Secretary of State* v *Tameside Metropolitan Borough Council* [1976] 3 WLR 641.

As Professor Wade put it:

'In the 1960s the judicial mood completely changed. It began to be understood how much ground had been lost and what damage had been done to the only defences against abuse of power which still remained.' (Administrative Law 6th ed p19)

Through a number of 'landmark' decisions – such as *Ridge* v *Baldwin* [1964] AC 40; *Padfield* v *Minister of Agriculture* [1968] AC 997; *Secretary of State* v *Tameside Metropolitan Borough Council* [1976] 3 WLR 641; *Anisminic* v *FCC* [1969] 2 AC 147; *O'Reilly* v *Mackman* [1983] 2 AC 237; *CCSU* v *Minister for the Civil Service* [1984] 3 All ER 935; *R* v *Panel on Take-overs and Mergers, ex parte Datafin* [1987] 2 WLR 699 – the position has been reached where most members of the judiciary would agree with Lord Denning's comment in *Breen* v *AEU* [1971] 2 QB 175 at page 189:

'... it may truly now be said that we have a developed system of administrative law'.

Lord Diplock has remarked that these developments are the greatest achievements of the English courts in his lifetime.

Whilst the contribution of the judiciary cannot be overstated, it must be remembered that they have developed administrative law very much along their own lines of thought and policy. There are many who feel that the sum total of this combined judicial effort is less than wonderful. There are areas where the courts have been slow to intervene and exercise their rediscovered power. Students, trade unionists, the homeless, immigrants and deportees to name a few, are categories of persons who may have reason to regard themselves as being 'short changed' by the courts when applying for judicial review.

As indicated in the introduction to this chapter, it should be borne in mind that administrative law is a living subject, and the process of development and refinement goes on, as Lord Denning observed:

'In the present century the Government has concerned itself with every aspects of life. We have the Welfare State and the Planned State. The Government departments have been given much power and in many directions. They set up tribunals and inquiries. They exercise unfettered discretion. They regulate housing, employment, planning, social security and a host of other activities. The philosophy of the day is socialism or collectivism.

But whatever philosophy predominates, there is always a danger to the ordinary man. It lies in the fact that all power is capable of misuse or abuse. The great problem before the Courts of the 20th century has been: In an age of increasing power, how is the law to cope with the abuse or misuse of it?'

What Lord Denning would not have perhaps foreseen is that during the 1980s and early 1990s the political landscape would be redrawn, with the result that deregulation and privatisation are now key factors determining the thrust of the legislative programme. What are the consequences of this for administrative law? In one sense, if there is a reduction in the number of administrative agencies, there is less for the courts to supervise, and the importance of administrative law diminishes (assuming of course that one subscribes to the traditional theory that it is concerned with the control of public power). Where powers and functions are transferred from the public sector to the private sector, the courts can either revert to applying the principles of private law to newly privatised bodies, or extend the principles of administrative law to the private sector. This issue may be of considerable significance in relation to the liability in negligence of private bodies providing services such as water, prisons, and telecommunications. It is submitted that the role of administrative law is increasingly becoming one of providing some residual means of control over private bodies: see *R* v *Panel on Take Overs and Mergers, ex parte Datafin* (above), or *R* v *Advertising Standards Authority Ltd, ex parte The Insurance Service plc* (1989) The Times 14 July.

1.4 Constitutional perspective

Two very basic constitutional principles underpin much of administrative law.

Parliamentary sovereignty

Parliament, as the ultimate law-making body, can in theory make or repeal any law it wants. The judges cannot question the validity of primary legislation, and can only challenge subordinate legislation on limited grounds.

The judiciary clearly have no choice but to apply primary legislation where required, although it may be possible for them to render its provisions nugatory by means of tortuous reasoning: see *Anisminic* v *FCC* [1969] 2 AC 147.

Consequently, when a primary statute creates a new administrative agency and gives it new wide-ranging powers, the courts cannot question the validity of the body itself, or the purposes for which it was created. By means of the second principle mentioned below, however, some control is possible.

The rule of law

The twentieth century has seen the introduction of the philosophy that the state is primarily responsible for remedying social and economic evils by means of legislation and the activities of administrative authorities. The state now supervises almost every aspect of a citizen's life 'from the cradle to the grave'. Matters such as housing, education, employment, health, pensions and planning are all now regulated by the state. Even by 1887 Maitland had noted:

> 'We are becoming a much-governed nation, governed by all manner of councils and boards and officers ... exercising the powers which have been committed to them by modern statutes.'

In 1922 Lord Sumner in *R* v *Nat Bell Liquors Ltd* [1922] AC 128 summarised the way in which the courts reviewed and controlled this vast new body of administrators:

> '... supervision goes to two points: one is the area of the inferior jurisdiction and the qualifications and conditions of its exercise; the other is the observance of the law in the course of its exercise'.

The clearest and most forceful philosophical justification of the doctrine of the rule of law is to be found in F A Hayek, *The Road to Serfdom* (1944):

> '... stripped of all its technicalities this means that government in all its actions is bound by rules fixed and announced beforehand – rules which make it possible to foresee with fair certainty how the authority will use its coercive powers in given circumstances, and to plan one's individual affairs on the basis of this knowledge'.

At its most basic, therefore, the doctrine of the rule of law means that everyone must act within the confines of the law. When applied to an administrative agency created by statute, this means that the agency must act within the confines of its enabling Act. In other words the agency must not act 'ultra vires'.

The courts will ensure compliance with the enabling Act in two ways: firstly, by ensuring that an administrative agency keeps within the limits of its power as laid down in its enabling Act. If an Act empowers an agency to award compensation of up to £500 and it purports to award an individual £600, then it has exceeded the express limits upon the powers laid down by statute. Anyone with 'sufficient interest' can apply for judicial review requesting an order of certiorari to quash the decision. Secondly, the courts can impose implied limits on power. They will 'read in' certain limitations upon an agency's statutory powers, for example, it must not act unfairly or unreasonably. If on an application for judicial review the courts are satisfied that one of these implied limits has been exceeded, then again the result will be that the administrative body will be held to have acted ultra vires, and its decision may be quashed.

Diagrammatic summary

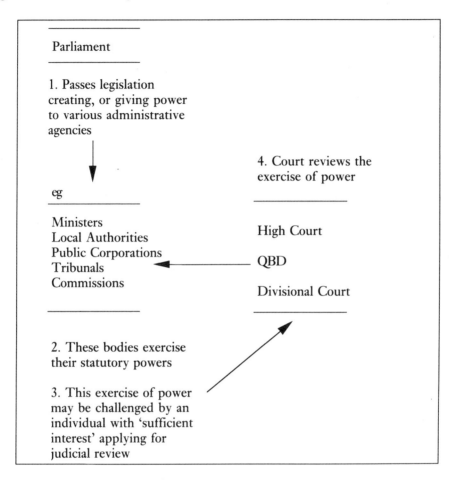

Parliament

1. Passes legislation creating, or giving power to various administrative agencies

eg

Ministers
Local Authorities
Public Corporations
Tribunals
Commissions

4. Court reviews the exercise of power

High Court

QBD

Divisional Court

2. These bodies exercise their statutory powers

3. This exercise of power may be challenged by an individual with 'sufficient interest' applying for judicial review

Political reality

The granting of judicial review is at the discretion of the courts, and there may be situations where they decline to intervene, even though an ultra vires action may have taken place: see *R* v *Home Secretary, ex parte Hosenball* [1977] 1 WLR 766.

The granting of remedies is discretionary, so that even where judicial review is allowed, the conduct of the applicant may be such that a remedy is denied.

There may be situations where the courts decline to intervene, for example to quash a minister's decision, relying instead on the principle of ministerial responsibility and the fact that he will be answerable to Parliament for his actions. This is particularly the case where what is being challenged is not so much the legality of the actions taken by a minister, but more the legality of the policy upon which the action is based. The fact that ministerial action has been approved by

Parliament may also inhibit judicial intervention: see *Nottinghamshire County Council v Secretary of State for the Environment* [1986] 1 All ER 199 where the House of Lords had to consider a challenge to the action of the Secretary of State, under the Local Government Planning and Land Act 1980, in issuing 'expenditure guidance' which had a directly restraining effect on local authorities' spending. Before the guidance could take effect it required the approval by resolution of the House of Commons. The authorities challenged the Secretary of State's guidance on the ground, inter alia, that it was unreasonable as contravening the principles expounded in the judgment of Lord Greene MR in *Associated Provincial Picture Houses Ltd v Wednesbury Corporation* [1948] 1 KB 223, 229, the leading authority concerning the basis for a challenge to an administrative decision on the ground of unreasonableness. Lord Scarman stated (at 247):

> 'The submission raises an important question as to the limits of judicial review. We are in the field of public financial administration and we are being asked to review the exercise by the Secretary of State of an administrative discretion which inevitably requires a political judgment on his part and which cannot lead to action by him against a local authority unless that action is first approved by the House of Commons ... I cannot accept that it is constitutionally appropriate, save in very exceptional circumstances, for the courts to intervene on the ground of "unreasonableness" to quash guidance framed by the Secretary of State and by necessary implication approved by the House of Commons, the guidance being concerned with the limits of public expenditure by local authorities and the incidence of the tax burden as between taxpayers and ratepayers. Unless and until a statute provides otherwise, or it is established that the Secretary of State has abused his power, these are matters of political judgment for him and for the House of Commons. They are not for the judges or your Lordships' House in its judicial capacity. For myself, I refuse in this case to examine the detail of the guidance or its consequences. My reasons are these. Such an examination by a court would be justified only if a prima facie case were to be shown for holding that the Secretary of State had acted in bad faith, or for an improper motive, or that the consequence of his guidance were so absurd that he must have taken leave of his senses.'

1.5 How it all fits together

Acting ultra vires

As the diagram on page 9 indicates there is a triangular relationship between the courts, parliament and administrative agencies. Further, in 1.4 (above), under 'The rule of law', the nature of acting ultra vires was explained; this needs to be considered in a little more detail here.

Express limits on power
Some of these will be mandatory, breach of which always results in action being declared to be ultra vires; other express limits are regarded as merely directory, failure to follow them precisely will not usually invalidate administrative action.

Implied limits on power
Remember that these are the limits 'read in' by the courts. These could be: unreasonableness, acting on irrelevant considerations, failing to take into account relevant considerations, acting on no evidence, acting for an ulterior purpose, acting on bad faith, acting unfairly or taking action disproportionate to that required.

Transgressions under express or implied limits on power will result in a body's decision being amenable to judicial review because it has acted ultra vires.

Conversely, if a body acts 'intra vires', that is, within the limits of the power it has been given in its enabling statute, its actions will be immune from review by the courts. This may include such matters as rudeness, stupidity, loss of documents or inefficiency. It should be noted that although judicial review might not be available here, a complaint to the ombudsman might be appropriate (see Chapter 22).

The only exception to the rule that intra vires actions are not reviewable concerns 'errors of law on the face of the record' – see Chapters 12 and 21 – when an error of law made by an administrative body may be quashed by the High Court.

Obtaining a remedy

Any individual with 'sufficient interest' can apply to the Divisional Court of the High Court for judicial review of an administrative (or 'inferior') body – see Chapter 11.

The remedies available include the private law remedies of injunction, damages and declaration, and the public law remedies, in the form of prerogative orders:

1. certiorari – which quashes an ultra vires action;
2. mandamus – an order to perform a duty;
3. prohibition – an order to refrain from certain action.

It should be remembered that these last three remedies are those granted by the Crown against an administrative body, hence the citation of many administrative law cases:

'*R (the Crown)* v *Local Authority, ex parte (on behalf of) Mr Smith*'.

The purpose of judicial review

The aim of judicial review is to ensure that public bodies act within the law. It is not aimed at compensating the individual for what he has lost because of the ultra vires decision being challenged: see *Dunlop* v *Woollahra Municipal Council* [1982] AC 158.

Consequently the courts are only concerned with the legality of a decision, not with its merits. The court is not there to substitute its own value judgments for those of the inferior body. Judicial review is to be contrasted with a statutory right of appeal where a decision can be overruled and a new decision taken on the merits of the case; with judicial review a decision can be quashed, and remitted to the inferior body to take again – this time intra vires.

By quashing decisions on the grounds that they are ultra vires the courts hope to indicate to administrative bodies the way in which they should act in future, and through this the courts can promote fairer, and more efficient administrative practices. The extent to which they succeed in this is a matter for debate.

1.6 Devices and techniques

Devices

The use of the word 'devices' refers to the way in which parliament has chosen to put a policy into effect. What sort of administrative agency (inferior body), if any would be best suited to the task?

1. *Minister.* If the aim is political control of a scheme and consistency, at the expense of impartiality, use a secretary of state as the controlling administrative agency: for example, the role of that minister in the system of town and country planning.
2. *Tribunal.* If the aim is to have disputes about the way a policy is implemented decided quickly, cheaply and impartially use a tribunal – possibly at the expense of some legal safeguards that help to ensure a fair procedure: for example, the Lands Tribunal.
3. *Public corporation.* This is useful for providing a commodity or regulation, whilst still retaining essential political control, and has the added attraction of carrying little ministerial responsibility: for example, the Civil Aviation Authority.
4. *Quango.* The period between 1980 and 1995 has seen a rapid increase in the number of quasi-autonomous non-governmental organisations. Quangos are non-elected public bodies that operate outside the civil service, funded by the taxpayer, whose members are appointed by ministers. Examples include the Equal Opportunities Commission, NHS Trusts, Training and Enterprise Councils, the British Council and the Natural History Museum. It has been estimated that there are now over 5,000 such bodies (see '*Ego Trip: Extra-governmental Organisations in the UK*' by Weir and Hall, Charter 88), many discharging functions that were previously within the jurisdiction of elected bodies, although government figures for 1995 indicate that the total is nearer 1,500. The rationale for transferring powers from elected bodies to quangos is that the latter are more accountable to citizens as the consumers of services than former were to consumers as voters, although this is a view hotly contested by the Labour Party. What is beyond doubt is that quangos are an effective method of executing government policy, via powers of appointment, without the actions of their members having to be held up to periodic democratic scrutiny.

Whenever considering the actions of an administrative agency consider this question: why was this type of body chosen to perform the function in question?

Techniques

By techniques is meant the way in which the administrative body is empowered to carry out its functions and achieve the policy goals intended. The following are illustrative:

1. *Subjectively worded powers*, so that the body has as free a hand as possible – frequently granted to the ministers. Still subject to review by the courts, however.
2. *Licensing powers* – can be used to regulate an activity and ensure a minimum and/or consistent standard: for example, 'sex establishments.'
3. *Powers of inspection* – similar to (2).
4. *Powers of investigation* – such as those possessed by an ombudsman.

Again, when considering administrative agencies, consider why they have been empowered to act in a particular way. How is this related to the perceived policy objectives?

1.7 The future

As indicated earlier in this chapter, there have, during the twentieth century, been a number of major reports debating the state of various aspects of administrative law. The 1930s saw the Donoughmore-Scott Committee on Ministers' Powers. The 1950s produced the Franks Report on Tribunals and Inquiries. In the mid-1970s the Law Commission produced its *Report on Remedies in Administrative Law*.

Many feel that the time is ripe for a complete overview of the subject, given the extent to which the importance of administrative law has grown since 1945, and the rate at which the law has developed through judicial intervention.

Perhaps the most significant attempt to assess the current state of administrative law was the joint venture by 'Justice' and All Souls entitled *Administrative Justice – Some Necessary Reforms* (Clarendon Press, 1988).

The joint committee (which was not supported by public funds) determined its terms of reference as being:

> '... to examine and report on the reforms that may be considered necessary or desirable in the law and procedure whereby a person may secure effective redress of grievances suffered as a consequence of acts or omissions of the various agencies of government, including Ministers of the Crown, public corporations, and local authorities throughout the United Kingdom'.

The most significant recommendation of the committee is that an Administrative Review Commission, along the lines of the Australian Administrative Review

Council, should be created. The Commission would be charged with the task of keeping under constant review all the procedures and institutions relating to the citizen's need to challenge the administration. Clearly such a body would have to complement the tasks already discharged by institutions such as the Council on Tribunals and the Parliamentary Commissioner for Administration. The success or failure of such a Commission would depend to a large extent on the duties placed on administrators to consult it for advice, and on the powers it might be given to enforce its findings.

There is no indication to date of any willingness on the part of government to act upon the 'Justice'/All Souls' report, although the Law Commission may decide to report on the matter of remedies in its next cycle.

It is hardly in keeping with the prevailing ideology to create more publicly funded regulatory bodies, and it is not a matter close to the hearts of most voters.

2

Delegated Legislation

2.1 Primary legislation

The constitutional principle of parliamentary sovereignty means that parliament can enact or repeal legislation as it sees fit. With a constitutional monarchy, the theory is that, following convention, the monarch will always give her assent to any legislation that has successfully passed through both Houses of Parliament.

A consequence of this is that the courts cannot question the validity of primary legislation, either on its merits, or on the grounds of procedural impropriety – even when the allegation is one of fraud: see *British Railways Board* v *Pickin* [1974] AC 765. It should be noted that improper action by a government department in a legislative capacity is also beyond the investigative powers of the 'ombudsman' – see Chapter 22.

Despite the ever increasing volume of primary legislation, (sometimes referred to as the 'parent Act' or the 'enabling Act') the complexities of governing a sophisticated society necessitate the delegation of legislative functions to inferior bodies, such as ministers and local authorities. Clearly, Parliament does not have the time nor resources to enact every single piece of legislation that is needed in the form of primary legislation which can be fully debated and scrutinised by both houses. The result is delegated legislation – legislation produced by an 'inferior body' which nevertheless has the force of law.

2.2 Delegated legislation

Forms

The most common format for delegated legislation is the statutory instrument – as to which, see 2.3 below – but it must be remembered that it is a generic term, and encompasses bye-laws, ministerial orders, departmental circulars, guidelines and codes of conduct. Caution should be exercised with these last three matters, however, because it is questionable to what extent, if at all, they have any legal effect. Although they are the result of a minister exercising a power that has been delegated to him, if they lack the status of law it would, strictly speaking, be a misnomer to include them under the heading 'legislation'.

Need for

As indicated in 2.1 above, the demands placed upon modern government are such that parliamentary time is at a premium, consequently a better use of time can be achieved by drafting primary legislation in general terms, providing the relevant minister with wide powers to introduce such measures as he considers necessary in order to implement the policy goals of the enabling Act.

This has further advantages in that it allows flexibility, measures can be introduced quickly where this is seen as desirable, and the minister concerned can introduce new measures to deal with unforeseen situations. Clearly this is more efficient than having to introduce a new piece of primary legislation to deal with each emergent problem in a given area. For example, an enabling Act may give a minister general powers to prohibit membership of proscribed organisations. Acting in response to a perceived threat the minister may issue an order prohibiting membership of the Irish Republican Army.

Similarly, an enabling Act may provide a minister with the function of running the prison service, rules for the conduct of the service to be made 'from time to time' by the minister: see the Prison Act 1952 and subsequent Prison Rules 1964 (SI 1964 No 388).

Dangers of

Not surprisingly the advantages of delegated legislation outlined above, are not without their costs. In the 1920s fears developed about the volume and nature of delegated legislation being produced, which was not receiving the parliamentary scrutiny many thought necessary or desirable.

In 1929 Lord Chief Justice Hewart published *The New Despotism* in which he railed against what he saw as a dangerous and uncontrolled growth of bureaucratic power.

In 1932 the report of the Donoughmore-Scott Committee on Ministers' Powers was issued. The report, amongst other things, explained the inevitability of delegated legislation, but also suggested some safeguards. The report also recommended better scrutiny of the vesting in ministers of 'oppressive' powers.

Particular disquiet was engendered by the use of so-called 'Henry VIII' clauses, which empowered a minister to alter the provisions of the enabling Act itself, 'so far as may appear to him to be necessary for the purpose of bringing this Act into operation'. The conventional wisdom is now that such powers should not be granted except for the purpose of bringing an Act into operation, and should be subject to strict time limitations, usually one year from the passing of the Act. Note in this regard that a limited power to amend statutory provisions is conferred under the European Communities Act 1972. Sections 2(2) and 2(4) enable ministers to give effect to Community law, providing that:

'Her Majesty may by Order in Council, and any designated Minister or department may,
by regulation, make provision:
a) for the purpose of implementing any Community obligations; or
b) for the purpose of dealing with matters arising out of or related to such obligations.'

The situation seems to have been reached whereby citizens accept the scope and quality of delegated legislation as a 'necessary evil'. It should be noted, however, that disquiet still exists about the efficacy of some of the scrutiny procedures; these are outlined below.

2.3 Statutory instruments

An initial problem is one of definition. Perhaps one way to solve the problem would be to remember that statutory instruments are always delegated legislation, but that not all delegated legislation takes the form of a statutory instrument.

The correct approach would be to follow the provisions of s1(1) Statutory Instruments Act 1946 which provides:

'1(1) Where by this Act or any Act passed after the commencement of this Act power to make, confirm or approve orders, rules, regulations or other subordinate legislation is conferred on His Majesty in Council or on any Minister of the Crown then, if the power is expressed –
a) in the case of a power conferred on His Majesty, to be exercisable by Order in Council;
b) in the case of a power conferred in a Minister of the Crown, to be exercisable by statutory instrument,
any document by which that power is exercised shall be known as a "statutory instrument" and the provision of this Act shall apply thereto accordingly ...'.

The effect of this provision is that if, under an enabling Act, rules, regulations, orders, and so on, are not stated as being exercisable by statutory instrument, then the provisions of the 1946 Act as to publication and laying do not apply.

Note also that even where the 1946 Act does apply, the precise laying procedure to be followed will still be determined by the enabling Act.

2.4 Enactment

Prior consultation

As the creation of delegated legislation is a legislative function, the rules of natural justice do not apply, and failure to consult parties likely to be affected does not amount to a breach of natural justice. In *Bates* v *Lord Hailsham* [1972] 1 WLR 1373 a committee, of which the Lord Chancellor was a member, was empowered by s56 of the Solicitors Act 1957 to make orders prescribing solicitors' remuneration in respect of non-contentious business. Section 56(3) of the Act stated:

> 'Before any such order is made, the Lord Chancellor shall cause a draft to be sent to the council [of the Law Society], and the Committee shall, before making the order, consider any observations in writing submitted to them by the council within one month of the sending to them of the draft, and may then make the order ...'

A draft copy of proposals was sent to the Law Society, but not to the British Legal Association of which the plaintiff was one of 2,900 members. He unsuccessfully sought a declaration that it would be ultra vires for the committee to confirm the making of the Order without first giving the British Legal Association an opportunity to give its views. Megarry J observed:

> 'Let me accept that in the sphere of the so-called quasi-judicial the rules of natural justice run, and that in the administrative or executive field there is a general duty of fairness. Nevertheless, these considerations do not seem to me to affect the process of legislation, whether primary or delegated. Many of those affected by delegated legislation, and affected very substantially, are never consulted in the process of enacting that legislation: and yet they have no remedy. Of course, the informal consultation of representative bodies by the legislative authority is a commonplace; but although a few statutes have specifically provided for a general process of publishing draft delegated legislation and considering objections ... I do not know of any implied right to be consulted or make objections, or any principle upon which the courts may enjoin the legislative process at the suit of those who contend that insufficient time for consultation and consideration has been given.'

Where, however, consultation with certain parties is required by the enabling Act, the courts are likely to interpret this as being a mandatory requirement; failure to comply could invalidate any resulting order: see *Agricultural, Horticultural and Forestry Industry Training Board* v *Aylesbury Mushrooms Ltd* [1972] 1 WLR 190, and Chapter 13 (below).

The nature of the consultation required will depend largely on the circumstances of the case. In *R* v *Secretary of State for Health, ex parte United States Tobacco*

International Inc [1991] 3 WLR 529, the Secretary of State was under a statutory duty to consult the applicants prior to issuing a prohibition on the sale of their main product, oral snuff. The applicants were not provided with all the information upon which the Secretary of State proposed to act, and the Divisional Court held that this unfairness justified the invalidation of the delegated legislation. Particular factors leading the court to this conclusion were: the fact that the government had encouraged the applicants to set up a business in Scotland for the manufacturing of oral snuff; the fact that the applicants were the country's sole producers of the product; and the fact that the ban would have a devastating effect on the livelihood of the applicants. In short, with so much at stake, the applicants had been entitled to more by way of consultation.

'Making' of statutory instrument

A difficult question arises of when a statutory instrument is actually 'made'. There are a number of ways of approaching the problem: first, that the statutory instrument is made as soon as it is signed by the appropriate minister and becomes effective from that point onwards, notwithstanding that any publication or laying requirements have not been complied with; secondly, that the statutory instrument is made when it is signed but only comes into effect on a certain date, specified on the order itself. Thirdly, and most commonly, the statutory instrument is signed by the minister and is due to come into effect on some specified date in the future, after one of the various laying procedures has been complied with.

Laying procedures

It is possible for an enabling Act to require ministerial orders to be enacted by way of statutory instrument, but not require any laying procedure at all. This is not uncommon, but obviously raises questions about opportunity of scrutiny in Parliament. Such a possibility should be raised when the enabling Act is progressing through Parliament.

Bare laying procedures

Where an enabling Act simply requires a statutory instrument to be laid before Parliament, s4 of the 1946 Act applies. It states:

> 'Where by this Act or any Act passed after the commencement of this Act any statutory instrument is required to be laid before Parliament after being made, a copy of the instrument shall be laid before each House of Parliament and, subject as hereinafter provided, shall be so laid before the instrument comes into operation.
>
> Provided that if it is essential that any such instrument should come into operation before copies thereof can be so laid as aforesaid, the instrument may be made so as to come into operation before it has been so laid; and where any statutory instrument comes into operation before it is laid before parliament, notification shall forthwith be sent to the Lord Chancellor and to the Speaker of the House of Commons drawing attention to the

fact that copies of the instrument have yet to be laid before Parliament and explaining why such copies were not so laid before the instrument came into operation.'

No further procedure is necessary for the provision to become effective. The statutory instrument is simply drawn to the attention of members, and can come into operation once laid.

Negative resolution procedure

Where the enabling Act requires this procedure to be followed, s5 of the 1946 Act applies. This states:

> 'Where by this Act or any Act passed after the commencement of this Act, it is provided that any statutory instrument shall be subject to annulment in pursuance of resolution of either House of Parliament, the instrument shall be laid before Parliament after being made and the provisions of the last foregoing section shall apply thereto accordingly, and if either House, within the period laid before it, resolves that an Address be presented to His Majesty praying that the instrument be annulled, no further proceedings shall be taken thereunder after the date of the resolution, and His Majesty may by Order in Council revoke the instrument, so, however, that any such resolution and revocation shall be without prejudice to the validity of anything previously done under the instrument or to the making of a new statutory instrument ...'

Two points to note regarding this procedure: first, a prayer can only seek the annulment of a statutory instrument, not its amendment; secondly, the wording of s5(1) ensures that the annulment of an instrument does not invalidate retrospectively action taken under it by the relevant minister.

Positive resolution procedure

Here the enabling Act requires the instrument to be laid before Parliament, and it can only become law if it receives the affirmative approval of Parliament.

Laying of a draft statutory instrument

A draft instrument is laid before Parliament, and the instrument itself cannot be made until 40 days have passed from the date of the laying of the draft instrument. During this period, the draft instrument may be subject to the negative resolution procedure as outlined above. The procedure is governed by s6 of the 1946 Act, which states:

> 'Where by this Act or any Act passed after the commencement of this Act it is provided that a draft of any statutory instrument shall be laid before Parliament, but the Act does not prohibit the making of the instrument without the approval of Parliament, then, in the case of an Order in Council the draft shall not be submitted to His Majesty in Council, and in any other case the statutory instrument shall not be made, until after the expiration of a period of forty days beginning with the day on which a copy of the draft is laid before each House of Parliament, or, if such copies are laid on different days, with the later of the two days, and if within that period either House resolves that the draft be not submitted to His Majesty or that the statutory instrument be not made, as the case may be, no further proceedings shall be taken thereon, but without prejudice to the laying before Parliament of a new draft ...'

2.5 Publication

Common law

It is widely accepted that ignorance of the law is no excuse. Given the great volume of delegated legislation, however, that doctrine can operate so as to cause severe hardship. As was noted in 2.4 above, under ' "Making" of a statutory instrument', it has been argued that a statutory instrument would come into effect as soon as it was signed by the minister; if this was an instrument creating criminal liability, it could have serious consequences for those concerned.

The question arose in *Johnson* v *Sargant & Sons Ltd* [1918] 1 KB 101, where an order was made on one day but its effect made known on the next. Bailache J refused to hold that, at common law, an instrument would come into effect, before those affected by it had been notified. The matter remains the subject of debate, however: see Lanham (1974) 37 MLR 510.

Under the 1946 Act

Two alternative approaches may be taken: either the enabling Act may itself lay down the procedure that must be followed for publicising any instruments made thereunder, or the enabling Act may provide that the procedures of the 1946 Act are to be followed. Sections 2 and 3 provide as follows:

'2(1) Immediately after the making of any statutory instrument, it shall be sent to the King's printer of Acts of Parliament and numbered in accordance with regulations made under this Act, and except in such cases as may be provided by any Act passed after the commencement of this Act or prescribed by regulations made under this Act, copies thereof shall as soon as possible be printed and sold by the King's printer of Acts of Parliament ...

3(1) Regulations made for the purpose of this Act shall make provision for the publication by His Majesty's Stationery Office of lists showing the date upon which every statutory instrument printed and sold by the King's printer of Acts of Parliament was first issued by that office; and in any legal proceedings a copy of any list so published purporting to bear the imprint of the King's printer shall be received in evidence as a true copy, and an entry therein shall be conclusive evidence of the date on which any statutory instrument was first issued by His Majesty's Stationery Office.'

Certain instruments may be exempt in whole or part from the publication requirements of the Act. Section 8 of the 1946 Act states:

'8(1) The Treasury may, with the concurrence of the Lord Chancellor and the Speaker of the House of Commons, by statutory instrument make regulations for the purposes of this Act, and such regulations may, in particular ...

(c) provide with respect to any classes or descriptions of statutory instrument that they shall be exempt, either altogether or to such extent as may be determined by or under the regulations from the requirements of being printed and of being sold by the King's printer of Acts of Parliament, or from either of those requirements ...'.

The Statutory Instruments Regulations 1947 (SI 1948/1) exempt the following from publication:

- local acts;
- temporary instruments;
- schedules to rules that are too bulky, provided other steps have been taken to bring their contents to the attention of the public;
- where publication of an instrument before its coming into operation would be contrary to the public interest.

In the last three cases the minister concerned must certify that the necessary conditions for the operation of the execution rules have been fulfilled.

Section 3 of the 1946 Act does provide a so-called defence of non-publication, as follows:

> '(2) In any proceedings against any person for an offence consisting of a contravention of any such statutory instrument, it shall be a defence to prove that the instrument had not been issued by His Majesty's Stationery Office at the date of the alleged contravention unless it is proved that at that date reasonable steps had been taken for the purpose of bringing the purport of the instrument to the notice of the public, or of persons likely to be affected by it, or of the person charged.
>
> (3) Save as therein otherwise expressly provided, nothing in this section shall affect any enactment or rule of law relating to the time at which any statutory instrument comes into operation.'

There have been two notable decisions concerning the ambit of this provision.

In *Simmonds* v *Newell* [1953] 2 All ER 38, the defendant appealed against a conviction for selling steel at prices higher than those permitted by provisions contained in schedules to a ministerial order. The schedules had not been published on the grounds of bulk. No certificate was produced in evidence exempting them from publication, and the Divisional Court was not satisfied that the Crown had discharged the burden of proving that it had taken reasonable steps to bring the provision to the notice of persons likely to be affected by it.

Compare with the later decision in *R* v *Sheer Metalcraft Ltd* [1954] 1 QB 586 where a similar defence of non-certification was raised to a prosecution for breaching a price fixing order. The court approached the matter by holding that an instrument could be validly made, and then issued. The very fact that s3(2) created a defence to non-publication meant that an order could be valid without being published. As in the above case, the absence of any exempting certificate placed the burden of proving that reasonable steps to notify those concerned had been taken, on the Crown. In this instance the court was satisfied, on the evidence, that these steps had been taken.

Note in this regard s50 of the draft Criminal Code Bill prepared for the Law Commission (Law Com No 143) which proposes:

> '50(1) A person is not guilty of an offence consisting of a contravention of a statutory instrument if:

(a) at the time of his act the instrument has not been issued by Her Majesty's Stationery Office; and

(b) by that time reasonable steps have not been taken to bring the purport of the instrument to the notice of the public, or of persons likely to be affected by it, or of that person.

(2) The burden of proving the matter referred to in paragraph (a) of subsection (1) shall be on the defendant.

(3) "Statutory Instrument" has the meaning given by s1 of the Statutory Instruments Act 1946.'

Other measures

There appears to be no statutory requirement concerning the publication of other measures such as circulars. In *Blackpool Corporation* v *Locker* [1948] 1 KB 349, however, Scott LJ stated, obiter, that given the nature of the circular in question, which delegated powers of compulsory purchase from the minister to local authorities, it was of vital importance that those likely to be affected should be able to ascertain the provisions of the circular.

2.6 Parliamentary scrutiny

Given that there has been, in the past, widespread concern about the uncontrolled use of delegated legislation, it is necessary to consider the controls that exist over its creation. In considering parliamentary controls one must, as well as noting their existence, consider too their usefulness.

The enabling Act

The first real opportunity for Parliament to exercise some control over the creation of delegated legislation arises when the enabling Act is being debated by the House of Commons, or the House of Lords. Members can consider whether a minister needs to be given powers to issue delegated legislation; if so, the form that the delegated legislation will take, ie whether by statutory instrument or circular; if by statutory instrument, should one of the laying procedures be followed; and generally, whether a minister is being given any wide or unusual powers.

The laying procedures

Provided that the enabling Act requires the use of one of the laying procedures, this does provide a valuable opportunity for scrutiny by members. However, several problems and weaknesses exist with this method. The sheer volume of instruments makes it impossible for any one member of Parliament to check them all. The laying procedure can be circumvented simply by the enabling Act not requiring any instrument made thereunder to be laid. The affirmative resolution procedure (see 2.4

above, under 'Positive resolution procedure') clearly provides a much better safeguard against abuse of power than the negative resolution procedure, but does not appear to be employed so frequently. Under the negative resolution procedure, parliamentary time may not be available for the prayers necessary to bring about the annulment of the instrument.

The Joint Committee on Statutory Instruments

Since 1973 it has been the function of the Joint Committee to scrutinize all statutory instruments, draft instruments, schemes requiring approval by way of statutory instrument, and so on. There are particular matters regarding which the attention of the House of Commons will be drawn by the Committee, as follows:

1. Where an instrument imposes a charge on public revenues or contains provisions requiring payments to be made to any public authority in consideration of any licence, or any consent, or of any services rendered.
2. Where an instrument purports to exclude the jurisdiction of the courts.
3. Where an instrument purports to have retrospective effect.
4. Where there appears to have been an unjustifiable delay in laying or publicising the instrument.
5. Where there is doubt as to whether the instrument is intra vires its enabling Act.
6. Where the terms of the instrument require elucidation.
7. Where for any other reason the drafting of the instrument appears to be defective.

It is important to bear in mind that the Committee is concerned neither with the merits of any given instrument, nor the soundness of the policy which it seeks to implement.

If the Committee does report to the House of Commons on a statutory instrument for any of the reasons outlined above, reliance is placed on the principle of ministerial responsibility to actually achieve some explanation of justification for, or amendment of the instrument.

As Foulkes has observed:

'Within (its) limitations the Committee does useful, thankless and unobtrusive work. It keeps an eye not only on individual instruments but on general developments in delegated legislation. It has shown itself anxious to make full use of its powers and has suggested extensions to its jurisdiction – but which, however widely it may be interpreted, is confined to "technicalities".' (Administrative Law 6th ed p88)

In 1992 an experimental Select Committee on the Scrutiny of Delegated Powers was introduced to report on the provisions of any Bill which appeared to provide for an inappropriate delegation of legislative power or the subjection of the legislative power to an inappropriate degree of parliamentary scrutiny. Its first report (HL 57 (1992–93)) was considered by the House of Lords in March 1993.

Other measures

No formal parliamentary procedure exists for the scrutiny of other forms of delegated legislation, such as circulars, guidelines and codes of conduct. It should be remembered, however, that the traditional methods of control, such as questions to ministers etc, may be used to highlight apparent irregularities or excesses.

Parliamentary Commission for Administration

Although the work of the 'ombudsman' is dealt with at more length in Chapter 22, it should be noted here that, under s5 of the Parliamentary Commissioner Act 1967, his jurisdiction is limited to administrative functions. This would seem to exclude the ombudsman from considering complaints concerning delegated legislation. Two points should, however, be borne in mind. First, he can investigate complaints concerning the application of, and effects of, delegated legislation. Secondly, some measures are not strictly speaking 'legislative', such as guidelines and codes of conduct. It could be argued that ministers act administratively when issuing such documents, and that they are therefore within the scope of the ombudsman's investigations.

2.7 Scrutiny by the courts

Unlike primary legislation, delegated legislation is reviewable by the courts and can in some cases be completely invalidated.

The more detailed heads of review are set out in Chapters 16 and 17. For present purposes it is sufficient to distinguish between cases of procedural ultra vires and substantive ultra vires.

Procedural ultra vires

One of the grounds on which an individual may seek to question the validity of delegated legislation is that the procedure laid down in its enabling Act and/or the Statutory Instruments Act 1946 for making, laying and publishing the measure in question, has not been followed.

A strict approach would be to say that if the provisions of the enabling legislation have not been observed, then the measure is void. Usually a more subtle technique is employed. The courts will distinguish between procedural requirements that are mandatory – failure to meet these results in invalidity – and directory requirements – failure to meet these does not usually affect validity.

The difficulty is in assessing which procedural requirements are likely to be regarded by the courts as mandatory and which as directory.

In *Agricultural, Horticultural (Etc)* v *Aylesbury Mushrooms Ltd* [1972] 1 WLR 190 failure to comply with a statutory requirement to consult various bodies prior to the making of delegated legislation resulted in the subsequent order affecting them being declared invalid.

By contrast, in *Bailey* v *Williamson* (1873) LR 8 QB 118 a conviction under the Rules made pursuant to the Parks Regulation Act 1872 was upheld, even though at the time, the Rules had not been laid before Parliament because of the summer recess. The implication of the conviction was that the Rules did not depend upon the laying procedures for their validity, and that consequently such procedural requirements were merely directory.

In two more recent cases the courts seem to have adopted a liberal approach to the procedural requirements for the enactment of delegated legislation.

First, in *R* v *Secretary of State for the Environment, ex parte Leicester City Council* (1985) The Times 1 February, the applicant local authority applied for judicial review of a draft order under s4(5) of the Rates Act 1984, laid before the House of Commons, specifying the maximum rate to be prescribed to the council. Under s4(1) of the Act this could only be done if the Rate Support Grant Report had been laid before Parliament. In fact the Report had only been laid before the House of Commons. The applicant contended that the subsequent order was, therefore, ultra vires.

Dismissing the application, Mr Justice Woolf was satisfied that in using the word 'Parliament', the draftsmen meant 'the House of Commons'. He stated, in deciding the effect of s4(1), that it was important to bear in mind that it was dealing with something which was procedural. It was intended that a local authority, prior to being 'ratecapped', should have notice of the maximum proposed so that it could have an opportunity to accept it or reject it or agree a different one.

The purpose of s4(1) was achieved as long as the authority had a reasonable period to consider the notice. It was unlikely that Parliament had intended that s4(1) should be mandatory. As long as s4(1) was substantially complied with the notice served was not defective. Applying that interpretation, the notice was not invalidated. The report did not have to be relaid because of technical errors and the notice was not subsequently re-served on the authority.

Consider further *R* v *Secretary of State for Social Services, ex parte Camden London Borough Council* [1987] 2 All ER 560. The minister was empowered to set levels of social security payments by way of statutory instrument. Any such statutory instrument was required to be laid before Parliament and approved by the Treasury. The minister laid the statutory instrument in question before Parliament, and obtained the necessary consents, but details of the maximum amount of benefit payable were set out, not in the statutory instrument, but in a directory published by HMSO which was not laid before Parliament.

The applicant, who was a person claiming supplementary benefit, and the local authority in whose area she resided, applied for declarations that the regulations were void for failure to comply with the laying procedures. At first instance and on appeal the application for review was dismissed. The Court of Appeal found that the directory was not part of the statutory instrument and therefore did not have to be laid before Parliament. Further, it was not a document by which the Secretary of State exercised his power to set levels of social security payments. It was quite permissible for him to refer in the statutory instrument to a formula by which levels of benefit would be set, provided he identified the source of the formula with sufficient certainty. This he had done. (See further, on the distinction drawn by the courts between mandatory and directory procedural requirements, in Chapter 13.)

Substantive ultra vires

This is a much broader ground of challenge, and can be based on the submission that the measure in question goes beyond what was envisaged by Parliament in the enabling Act, is in conflict with the aims and objects of the enabling Act, is unreasonable, vague, oppressive, or otherwise objectionable.

A number of well-known examples exist in the area of taxation, where the courts have traditionally adopted a restrictive approach to the exercise of power through the means of delegated legislation. In *Attorney-General* v *Wilts United Dairies* (1922) 91 LJKB 897 regulations under a milk price fixing scheme, requiring producers to pay a levy to the Food Controller, were invalidated by the House of Lords as amounting to unlawful taxation, since there was no clear statutory authority for such measures. Similarly, in *Customs and Excise Commissioners* v *Cure and Deely Ltd* [1962] 1 QB 340 the Commissioners had made a regulation under which they could determine the amount of tax due from the tax payer in the event of a tax return being submitted late. The High Court invalidated the regulations on a number of grounds, inter alia, that the Commissioners were only empowered to collect the amount of tax due at law, not the amount they thought fit. They had, therefore, purported to give themselves power by way of delegated legislation going way beyond what was envisaged by Parliament in passing the enabling Act. In *R* v *Inland Revenue Commissioners, ex parte Woolwich Equitable Building Society* [1990] 1 WLR 1400 the Woolwich Equitable Building Society challenged the validity of the Income Tax (Building Society) Regulations (SI 1986 No 482), which had sought to levy a tax on dividends and interest paid by the Society, in respect of which the Society had already come to an 'arrangement' with the Commissioners. The purported effect of the regulations was to transgress a fundamental principle of taxation law, ie that an annual demand for income tax could not be based on income or dividend derived from a period greater than one tax year. The House of Lords held (Lord Lowry dissenting) that the regulations would have been invalid, on the ground that they were ultra vires the enabling Act, but for the enactment (after the commencement of these proceedings) of s47(1) of the Finance Act 1986, which sought, retrospectively, to validate them by providing for sums paid in previous tax years to be taken into account. (Note that no Finance Act in the previous two hundred years had purported to levy tax on such a basis.) The Inland Revenue conceded, however, that one of the regulations, reg 11(4), was still ultra vires the enabling Act and, as the House of Lords felt unable to ascertain what the effect of the regulations as a whole would have been had this invalidity been appreciated, the regulations were declared totally void. See further *Hotel and Catering Industry Training Board* v *Automobile Proprietary Ltd* [1969] 1 WLR 677.

In theory, Parliament can give a minister very wide-ranging powers in an enabling Act. Surprise was expressed by the court in *R* v *Secretary of State for Social Services, ex parte Stitt* (1990) The Times 5 July at the extent of the powers vested in the Secretary of State by the Social Security Act 1986 (as amended by the Social Security Act 1988). The legislation creating the 'Social Fund', under which claimants could apply for loans to help meet exceptional needs, indicated specific matters in relation to which funds would be available, such as maternity expenses, cold weather payments and funeral expenses, but as regards 'other needs' provided the Security Fund Officer with a discretion as to whether or not loans should be made. The Secretary of State, who was empowered under ss32 and 33 of the 1986 Act to issue directions to Security Fund Officers concerning the exercise of their discretion, instructed fund officers not to award any loans in respect of the cost of domestic assistance and respite care. Dismissing an appeal against the refusal of the Divisional Court to grant judicial review of the ministerial directions, the Court of Appeal noted that its function was to deal with an ambiguity in the parent Act. Where such ambiguity was found the court would lean in favour of an interpretation which prevented the executive from acquiring unbridled powers. The legislation in this case had left it to the discretion of the minister to determine how and when loans for 'other needs' should be granted. Whilst it might be surprising that Parliament had left such a wide power to a minister to exercise by way of delegated legislation, there was no ground for doubting that this had been what Parliament had intended. The directions in question were subject to annulment by resolution of either House. It was contended on behalf of the applicant that this resulted in very little parliamentary scrutiny of such measures, unlike the positive laying procedure, and that if Parliament had intended the minister to have such wide powers it would have made the exercise of those powers subject to the more exacting positive procedure. Against this it should be noted that the minister was required to report annually to Parliament on the operation of the fund. It is of further interest to note that in the course of his submissions, counsel for the minister was unable to point to any previous Act of Parliament granting a minister such wholesale, unregulated, and unsupervised powers to enact delegated legislation having such a profound effect on the operation of a primary Act.

Even where the scope of the minister's power is not in question, a statutory instrument may yet be quashed on the general ground that it simply goes further than is necessary to deal with a particular 'mischief'. In *McEldowney* v *Forde* [1971] AC 632, the House of Lords, by a majority, upheld the validity of a regulation made under emergency powers legislation prohibiting membership of 'republican clubs', but in the course of their speeches, their Lordships made plain their view that such a measure was at the very limits of what was acceptable.

Other cases fall under the more readily recognisable heads of abuse of power. In *Kruse* v *Johnson* [1898] 2 QB 91, the Divisional Court declined to declare a bye-law to be invalid on the ground of unreasonableness, but accepted that such a challenge was possible. The Lord Chief Justice suggested that a bye-law could be invalidated if it was found to be partial and unequal in operation; manifestly unjust; disclosed bad faith; or involved an oppressive, gratuitious interference with the rights of individuals.

Given that the making of delegated legislation involves the exercise of executive power, whether by central or local government agencies, or indeed other statutory bodies, the process can be attacked on the grounds that the decision maker has acted irrationally, taken into account irrelevant considerations, or has failed to take into account relevant considerations. Thus, in *R* v *British Airports Authority, ex parte Wheatley* (1983) 81 LGR 794, the Divisional Court held that a bye-law passed by the respondent authority prohibiting licensed hackney carriages was invalid on the grounds that it was unreasonable and oppressive. On wrong purposes and bad faith, see further *In Re Toohey, ex parte Northern Land Council* (1981) 38 ALR 439. Even if the delegated legislation is ostensibly intra vires, the courts will not uphold it if the drafting is so defective that it is not capable of sensible construction: see *Nash* v *Finlay* (1901) 85 LT 682.

Whilst the principles upon which the courts will intervene can be broadly stated, the reality is that any party seeking to raise such a challenge faces a not inconsiderable evidential burden, especially where the court is satisfied that Parliament intended the rule maker to enjoy a wide discretion. For example, in *R* v *The Lord Chancellor, ex parte The Law Society* (1993) The Times 5 May, the applicants unsuccessfully applied for judicial review of the decision of the Lord Chancellor to introduce a scheme of standard fees for lawyers appearing in magistrates' court cases. The Society had contended that the regulations formulated under the Legal Aid Act 1988 were ultra vires on the grounds (inter alia) that they failed to address the requirement that a solicitor's remuneration had to be reasonable in each individual case. The court, rejecting this contention, found that Parliament had given the Lord Chancellor a wide discretion and was not persuaded that Parliament had intended him to devise a scheme that addressed the level of remuneration to be paid in each case. Significantly, the Lord Chancellor's desire to achieve cost neutrality in devising the revised scheme was not regarded as an irrelevant consideration.

The courts have also accepted the argument that the creation of delegated legislation is a governmental function to which certain legal requirements might not apply. In *R* v *Secretary of State for Social Services, ex parte Nessa* (1994) The Times 15 November, the applicant claimed that the operation of regulation 7(1)(c) of the Social Fund Maternity and Funeral Expenses (General) Regulations (SI 1987 No 481) contravened s20 of the Race Relations Act 1976, in that it permitted a payment from the Social Fund for funeral expenses provided the funeral took place within the United Kingdom, and thus discriminated against claimants who, for religious reasons, wished to conduct a funeral overseas. Auld J held that s75 of the 1976 Act provided that the Act applied to an act done by or for the purposes of a minister of the Crown as it applied to an act done by a private person. Applying *R* v *Entry Clearance Officer, ex parte Amin* [1983] 2 AC 818, the 1976 Act, like the Sex Discrimination Act 1975, did not, therefore, apply to acts of a minister or officer of the Crown that were of a governmental nature, such as the making of regulations, on the ground that that was a function that would not be performed by a private person.

Perhaps the most significant challenge to the exercise of ministerial discretion in the creation of delegated legislation arose in *R* v *Secretary of State for the Home Department, ex parte Brind* [1991] 2 WLR 588, where the House of Lords expressly rejected the proposition that, in exercising his power to issue directives to broadcasting authorities banning the broadcasting of interviews with terrorists, the Home Secretary was required to advert to the provisions of the European Convention on Human Rights. As Lord Bridge stated (at p592):

> '... where Parliament has conferred on the executive an administrative discretion without indicating the precise limits within which it must be exercised, to presume that it must be exercised within Convention limits would be to go far beyond the resolution of an ambiguity. It would be to impute to Parliament an intention not only that the executive should exercise the discretion in conformity with the Convention, but also that the domestic courts should enforce that conformity by the importation into domestic administrative law of the text of the Convention and the jurisprudence of the European Court of Human Rights in the interpretation and application of it. If such a presumption is to apply to the statutory discretion exercised by the Secretary of State under s29(3) of the [Broadcasting Act 1981] in the instant case, it must also apply to the other statutory discretion exercised by the executive which is capable of involving an infringement of Convention rights. When Parliament has been content for so long to leave those who complain that their Convention rights have been infringed to seek their remedy in Strasbourg, it would be surprising suddenly to find that the judiciary had, without Parliament's aid, the means to incorporate the Convention into such an important area of domestic law and I cannot escape the conclusion that this would be a judicial usurpation of the legislative function.'

Whilst it is clear that a court faced with a challenge to the validity of a statutory instrument may declare it to be ultra vires and thus of no effect, can a tribunal dealing with the same issue act similarly? The matter was considered by the House of Lords in *Chief Adjudication Officer* v *Foster* [1993] 2 WLR 292. The claimant had been in receipt of income support payments as prescribed by s22 of the Social Security Act 1986. The sum payable included a severe disability premium. The Income Support (General) Regulations 1987, which governed entitlement to the premium, were amended by the Secretary of State, with the effect that the premium would no longer be payable if a claimant was residing with other non–dependent adults. An adjudicator ruled that the claimant should no longer receive the severe disability premium as she was living with her parents. The Social Security Appeal Tribunal confirmed this ruling. The claimant then appealed to the commissioner who ruled that, in its amended form, Sch 2 para 13(2)(a)(ii)(iii) of the Income Support

(General) Regulations 1987 were ultra vires the 1986 Act, and that the claimant was entitled to continue in receipt of the severe disability premium. The Court of Appeal allowed an appeal by the Secretary of State and the Chief Adjudication Officer on the grounds that the commissioner had not had jurisdiction to declare the amendment to the regulations to be ultra vires and, by a majority, that the amendment was not ultra vires the 1986 Act. The House of Lords, dismissing the appeal, held (having referred to Hansard for guidance on what Parliament had intended when creating this statutory framework) that whilst the amendment under consideration in the instant case was within the scope of the amending power vested in the Secretary of State by Parliament, a commissioner did have jurisdiction to question the validity of regulations when an arguable case was raised by a claimant. The significance of the decision lies in the House of Lords' confirmation that welfare claimants need not resort to judicial review to test the validity of delegated legislation relied upon by adjudicators to deny benefit. Adjudication officers and Social Security Appeal Tribunals could simply refuse to apply a regulation on the ground of ultra vires, or apply a regulation and pass the issue on to the next level of appeal, typically a commissioner. Lord Bridge observed that there was a positive benefit in the courts having access to the rulings of social security commissioners as to the validity or otherwise of delegated legislation, since commissioners would be experts in what was acknowledge to be a difficult and complex area of law: see further *R* v *Crown Court at Reading, ex parte Hutchinson* [1988] 1 All ER 333, considered at Chapter 11.

Partial invalidity

In some cases the courts may be willing to uphold part of a statutory instrument, or limit the scope of its application so as to render it intra vires. The *Aylesbury Mushrooms* case (above) is one example. Another is the decision of the Divisional Court in *Dunkley* v *Evans* [1981] 1 WLR 1522 where it was held that the Order in question could be restricted so as not to apply to Northern Irish waters, without affecting the validity of the rest of the Order. The basis on which the courts will normally proceed was explained by Cussen J sitting in the Supreme Court of Victoria in *Olsen* v *City of Camberwell* (1926) VLR 58, 68 where he stated:

> 'If the enactment, with the invalid portion omitted, is so radically or substantially different a law as to the subject-matter dealt with by what remains from what it would be with the omitted portions forming part of it as to warrant a belief that the legislative body intended it as a whole only, or, in other words, to warrant a belief that if all could not be carried into effect the legislative body would not have enacted the remainder independently, then the whole must fail.'

Perhaps the high water mark of judicial creativity is represented by the decision of the House of Lords in *DPP* v *Hutchinson and Others* [1990] 3 WLR 196. A number of separate cases raised a common point of law for consideration by the court. Under s14(1) of the Military Lands Act 1892, the Secretary of State was empowered to make bye-laws regulating the use of such land. The minister was specifically empowered to prohibit all intrusions on the land, provided that no bye-law took away or prejudicially affected any right of common. The minister, acting pursuant to the 1892 Act, made the RAF Greenham Common Bye-laws 1985. Bye-law 2(b) provided that no person was to remain in the designated area without the permission of an authorised person. The defendants, who were not commoners, were charged with entering the land without permission, and were duly convicted by justices. They appealed successfully to the Crown Court on the basis that the bye-laws were invalid since they prejudicially affected rights of common. The prosecutor appealed successfully to the Divisional Court by way of case stated. The House of Lords allowed the defendants' appeal holding that bye-law 2(b) was ultra vires the 1892 Act because it prejudicially affected rights in common, and thus offended against the proviso to s1(1) of the 1892 Act. As to whether those aspects of the bye-law that had been successfully impugned could be severed from those that were intra vires, thus leaving the latter to remain in effect as a valid legislative measure, a majority of their Lordships held that for severance to be possible, it had to be shown that the part of the bye-law sought to be upheld could stand on its own as something intelligible which still reflected the original legislative purpose of its author. In the present case it was felt that this was clearly not possible, as a bye-law permitting free access by commoners would be fundamentally different in its nature from that which had been enacted. See further *R* v *IRC, ex parte Woolwich Building Society* (above).

'Ouster' clauses

See Chapter 21 for a discussion of the extent to which the courts will comply with provisions which purport to exclude their jurisdiction.

2.8 Other forms of delegated legislation

Statutory orders and directions

These expressions lack any precise definition, but would cover generally, rules, regulations, orders, directions and schemes, made by ministers pursuant to statutory powers.

No set procedure exists for parliamentary scrutiny or publication beyond that required by the revelant enabling Act.

Circulars and guidance

These are issued by ministers to various interested bodies to indicate the way in which the government department would like to see various rules implemented. For example, the Department of the Environment will issue circulars to local planning authorities as to when they should issue enforcement notices for breach of planning controls.

Codes of practice

A code of practice is a useful administrative device whereby a government department can make public its aim and policy as regards a particular scheme but maintain flexibility by being able to alter the contents of the code. The longest standing and best known examples would be the Highway Code and the Codes of Practice issued under s66 of the Police and Criminal Evidence Act 1984. There seems to be little doubt that codes have no legal status as such, but can be called as evidence to support a legal argument. This approach was adopted in *De Falco* v *Crawley Borough Council* [1980] QB 460 where it was held that the defendant authority had to have regard to the Secretary of State's code regarding intentionally homeless persons, but did not have to regard itself as bound by it. A police officer acting in breach of the Codes of Practice issued under the 1984 Act may, by virtue of s67(8), be liable to disciplinary proceedings, although by virtue of s67(10) a failure on the part of an officer to comply with any provision of such a code will not of itself render him liable to any criminal or civil proceedings. The Codes of Practice are admissible in evidence in civil and criminal proceedings.

Ministerial and departmental statements

A government department may make a public announcement as to the way it is intending to act with respect to a particular matter, such as the collection of outstanding tax, or the enforcement of a new regulation. Such statements have no force in law per se, but may be relevant if the public body concerned then proposes to act contrary to the terms of the statement. The statement may be used as evidence to support an argument that the authority is acting in breach of natural justice, see *Attorney-General of Hong Kong* v *Ng Yuen Shiu* [1983] 2 AC 629; or it might be argued that a 'quasi-contractural' obligation to comply with the public undertaking has arisen: see *R* v *Liverpool Corporation, ex parte LTFOA* [1972] 2 QB 299.

2.9 Legal challenge to circulars, etc

As will have been noted above, the validity of statutory instruments can be challenged in the courts. Is the same true of matters such as circulars, codes, and guidance? The essence of the problem is that if a code or circular has no legal effect as such, there is no purpose in instituting proceedings to assess its validity since, in theory, it can be ignored with impunity. In reality the task of assessing whether or not circulars, codes, memoranda, guidance, etc, have any legal effect can be rather complex. In *Coleshill and District Investment Co Ltd* v *MHLG* [1969] 2 All ER 525 Lord Wilberforce explained that although circulars had no legal status, they could, through continued reference, acquire weight as persuasive material in the process of statutory interpretation: see further *Bristol District Council* v *Clark* [1975] 3 All ER 976. The courts will certainly not be deterred from assessing the validity of a ministerial pronouncement merely because it is labelled as a circular. They will look at the content not form. In *Jackson Stansfield & Sons* v *Butterworth Ltd* [1948] 2 All ER 558 Scott LJ held that circulars issued by the Minister of Works concerning the delegation of his licensing functions to local authorities were legislative in nature because they were 'intended to bind the public'. A similar view was taken of a ministerial circular which sub-delegated powers of compulsory purchase to a local authority in *Blackpool Corporation* v *Locker* (see above).

The courts have acknowledged that there is a distinction to be drawn between ministerial directives, and ministerial guidance, see further the judgment of Roskill LJ in *Laker Airways Ltd* v *Department of Trade* [1977] QB 643. Directions are usually mandatory in tone placing the person to whom they are issued under a legal obligation to comply with their provisions. Guidance, on the other hand, will have little or no legal effect, being merely an indication of the minister's views as to what an administrator ought to bear in mind, although the ultimate decision as to the exercise of discretion rests with the administrator. If ministerial guidance is drafted in terms that appear mandatory, the courts will normally declare it ultra vires, on the basis that it purports to limit an administrator's discretion where there is no express ministerial power to do so: see further *R* v *Secretary of State for Social Services, ex parte Stitt* (above). In this respect ministerial directives are much closer to the narrow concept of delegated legislation and are likely to be more closely scrutinised by the courts, especially where the enabling Act makes no further provision for parliamentary approval of any directions so issued, see again *R* v *Secretary of State for Social Services, ex parte Stitt*.

If the content of a circular, guidance or memorandum falls outside the scope of judicial review because it lacks any legal status, the focus of any legal challenge may have to be altered, perhaps to an examination of the minister's decision to issue the circular, code or guidance in the first place. The question arose in *Gillick* v *West Norfolk and Wisbech Area Health Authority* [1985] 3 All ER 402, where the House of Lords was asked to consider the validity of a memorandum issued by the Department of Health and Social Security, which contained advice to the effect that doctors could prescribe contraceptives for girls below the age of 16, without first obtaining the consent of a parent. Lord Fraser and Lord Scarman made obiter comments to the effect that such guidance was amenable to judicial review. Lord Scarman summarised the issue in the following terms, at p415:

'... the case against the department was ... that ... by issuing [the memorandum] it was exercising a statutory discretion in a wholly unreasonable way ...'

Lord Bridge, however, adopted a rather different analysis, questioning whether the actions of the department fell within the scope of the court's supervisory jurisdiction at all. He stated, at p426:

'I ask myself what is the nature of the action or decision taken by the DHSS in the exercise of a power conferred upon it which entitles a court of law to intervene and declare that it has stepped beyond the proper limits of its power. I frame the question in that way because

I believe that hitherto, certainly in general terms, the court's supervisory jurisdiction over the conduct of administrative authorities has been confined to ensuring that their actions or decisions were taken within the scope of the power which they purported to exercise or conversely to providing a remedy for an authority's failure to act or decide in circumstances where some appropriate statutory action or decision was called for.

Now it is true that the [minister] ... has a general responsibility for the provision of ... family planning services ... But only in a very loose sense could the issue of the memorandum be considered as part of the discharge of that responsibility. The memorandum itself has no statutory force whatsoever. It is not and does not purport to be issued in the exercise of any statutory power or in the performance of any statutory function. It is purely advisory in character and practitioners in the National Health Service are, as a matter of law, in no way bound by it ...'

His Lordship further contended that the decision to issue the memorandum could only be challenged on the grounds of *Wednesbury* unreasonableness where there was a context of specific and detailed statutory provisions in which to consider it, which was not the case here. As a general rule, he felt that the question of whether the advice tendered to administrative bodies in 'non-statutory' guidance was good, bad, or unreasonable would not normally be subject to scrutiny in the courts.

Lord Bridge was willing to recognise one possible exception to the above proposition, where it was in the public interest for the validity of advice given in a departmental circular or memorandum to be tested in the courts. He accepted that such a situation had arisen in *Royal College of Nursing of the UK* v *DHSS* [1981] 1 All ER 545, wherein the courts had been willing to rule upon the contents of a DHSS circular which had stated that it would be lawful for nurses to perform a particular type of abortion. In the light of this decision, his Lordship (at p427) concluded that:

'... if a government department ... promulgates in a public document, albeit non-statutory in form, advice which is erroneous in law, then the court ... has jurisdiction to correct the error of law by an appropriate declaration ... But the occasions of a departmental non-statutory publication raising ... a clearly defined issue of law, unclouded by political moral or social overtones, will be rare. In cases where any proposition of law implicit in a departmental advisory document is interwoven with questions of social and ethical controversy, the court should, in my opinion, exercise its jurisdiction with the utmost restraint, [and] confine itself to deciding whether the proposition of law is erroneous ...'

This restrictive approach to exercising the supervisory jurisdiction of the courts was subsequently illustrated in *R* v *Secretary of State for the Environment, ex parte Greenwich London Borough Council* (1989) The Times 17 May. The Secretary of State had authorised the distribution of a leaflet explaining the operation of the [then] proposed Community Charge, to all households in England and Wales. The applicant local authority sought an order of prohibition to prevent the distribution, on the ground that the leaflet was inaccurate as it made no reference to the joint liability of spouses or persons living together, and a declaration that the distribution of the leaflet in its present form was ultra vires. The Divisional Court (Woolf LJ and Ian Kennedy J) held, dismissing the application, that the court could only intervene where it was shown that such a leaflet contained errors of law, or was manifestly inaccurate or misleading. Alternatively, the court could intervene on the ground enunciated in the *Wednesbury* case, but this would require proof that no reasonable minister would have taken the decision to publish the leaflet in its present form, or that the leaflet was being issued in its current form to secure some ulterior objective. No such evidence was before the court. The court found that it was inevitable that the leaflets would have to contain a selection of details concerning the Community Charge. The omissions complained of did not render it inaccurate. It is interesting to note further that the applicants had complained that the distribution of the leaflet contravened constitutional conventions concerning the use of public money for the dissemination of information on matters of government policy. Woolf LJ commented that such conventions were observed, not because they had any force in law, but because of the political difficulties that might arise if they were ignored.

It should not be assumed that the existence of a specific statutory power to issue guidance will necessarily be enough of itself to persuade the courts to review the validity of any guidance issued thereunder. In *Nottinghamshire County Council* v *Secretary of State for the Environment* [1986] 1 All ER 199, the House of Lords considered a challenge to the validity of guidance on limits to expenditure issued by the minister to local authorities. Lord Scarman indicated that in the absence of evidence indicating bad faith on the part of the minister, or evidence that the guidance was so absurd that he must have taken leave of his senses, he would not intervene to quash it. It was felt that the issuing of such guidance inevitably involved the exercise of political judgment, and that such matters were for the minister and Parliament. It is perhaps significant in this case that the guidance had received parliamentary approval prior to its being challenged in the courts. Lord Scarman went so far as to state, at p204 e–f:

> 'If a minister exercises a power conferred on him by the legislation, the courts can investigate whether he has abused his power. But if, as in this case, effect cannot be given to the Secretary of State's determination without the consent of the House of Commons and the House of Commons has consented, it is not open to the courts to intervene unless the minister and the House must have misconstrued the statute or the minister has, to put it bluntly, deceived the House.'

2.10 Bye-laws

Local authorities, and some large public commercial undertakings, are the bodies most commonly to be found promulgating bye-laws. These will be rules which are local in operation, deemed necessary by the authority in question for the regulation and management of their areas or enterprises.

Local authority bye-laws must be made under the seal of the council and submitted to the Secretary of State for approval. Steps must be taken to ensure publicity in the local press, and a copy must be available for local inspection.

Many bye-laws will give rise to criminal liability if violated, and are subject to the normal judicial controls: see *Kruse* v *Johnson*, *R* v *British Airports Authority, ex parte Wheatley*, and *Nash* v *Finlay* and 2.7 above. As to the principles to be applied by a criminal court where the defendant raises the issue of vires by way of a defence to a prosecution alleging breach of a bye-law, see *Bugg* v *DPP* [1993] 2 WLR 628, considered further at 11.6.

3

Prerogative Power

3.1 The position of the Crown

3.2 Control of prerogative power

3.3 The *GCHQ* case

3.1 The position of the Crown

The theory of prerogative power

The conventional wisdom is that the Crown is the ultimate source of power within the constitution. The history of English constitutional law is, however, littered with examples of the skirmishes between the monarchy and the courts and Parliament concerning the exact scope of prerogative power. The word 'prerogative' comes from the Latin prae (before) and rogo (I demand). The royal prerogative, accordingly, is what the monarch demands and is entitled to in preference to all others. Blackstone defined it as follows :

> 'By the word prerogative we usually understand that special pre-eminence, which the King hath, over and above all other persons, and out of the ordinary course of the common law, in right of his regal dignity ... [I]t must be in its nature singular and eccentrical ... it can only be applied to those rights and capacities which the King enjoys alone, in contradistinction to others, and not those which he enjoys in common with any of his subjects ...'

According to Dicey, the prerogative appeared to be both historically and as a matter nothing other than the residue of discretionary and arbitrary authority, which at any given time was legally left in the hands of the Crown.

Historically the term prerogative has been applied to those special rights and privileges which the King had as a feudal lord, such as, for example, the privilege that he could not be sued in his own courts, and in a more general way to all the powers and authority of the King, whether exercised directly by him, or through some other agency.

The nature and the scope of the absolute prerogative were matters of bitter dispute during Tudor times, and even more Stuart times between Royalist and Parliamentary lawyers. *R* v *Hampden* (1637) 3 St Tr 825 (*The Case of Ship Money*)

pThe position of the Crown

arose out of Charles I's wish to raise money, without calling a Parliament, for a navy to defend English shipping. The judges declared that it was lawful for him to do so by writ for the defence of the realm in times of danger, and that the King was the sole judge of the danger and how it was to be avoided. John Hampden refused to pay. Proceedings against him were heard by all the common law judges in the Exchequer Chamber. For Hampden it was argued that either the King could not tax without Parliament even for the defence of the realm or, if he could, the power existed only where a real danger was proved. A majority found for the King on both points. Similarly in *Bate's Case* (1606) 2 St Tr 371 (*The Case of Impositions*), where Bate refused to pay a duty on imported currants imposed by James I, it was argued that the duty was not lawful. The Barons of the Exchequer found unanimously for the King, holding that the King had the power to impose duties where his purpose was not the raising of revenue but the regulation of foreign trade, as this was ancillary to the King's prerogative in foreign affairs.

The extent of prerogative power was further confirmed in *Darnel's Case* (1627) 3 St Tr 1 (*The Five Knights' Case*), where Darnel, and four other knights, refused to pay contributions to a forced loan and were committed to prison. To a writ of habeas corpus from the King's Bench the warden of the prison made a return stating that Darnel was detained on the authority of a Privy Council warrant according to which he had been committed by the special command of the King. For Darnel it was argued that if such a return were sufficient it would give the King an arbitrary power of imprisonment which would be contrary to Magna Carta. Hyde CJ found for the King.

The power of the King to create new law without Parliament was considered in the *Case of Proclamations* (1611) 12 Co Rep 74, where the Lord Chancellor and others of the King's ministers asked the judges whether the King could by proclamation prohibit building in and about London and the making of starch from wheat. Part of Coke's note of their answer reads as follows:

> 'Note, the King by his proclamation or other ways, cannot change any part of the common law or statute law, or the customs of the realm ... also the King cannot create any offence by his prohibition or proclamation which was not an offence before, for that was to change the law, and to make an offence which was not ... That which cannot be punished without proclamation cannot be punished with it.'

In several cases, including *Thomas* v *Sorrell* (1674) Vaughan 330 and *Godden* v *Hales* (1686) 1 St Tr 1165, it was argued that the King had a prerogative right to suspend or dispense with laws, or the execution of laws. The judges were reluctant to admit a dispensing power in the case of malum in se (an act which would have been unlawful apart from statute) but would sometimes admit the power in the case of malum prohibitum (acts unlawful only by reason of statute). In *Godden* v *Hales* (1686) 11 St Tr 1165 the defendant was a colonel who became a Roman Catholic in 1685. James II granted him dispensation from his obligations under the Test Act. The plaintiff informer brought an action for £500 to be forfeited by the defendant for breach of the Test Act. Herbert LCJ held that the dispensation was a bar to the action.

The question as to whether the King could hear disputes between subjects himself, or only through his judges was settled by the resolution of the judges in the case of *Prohibitions del Roy* (1607) 12 Co Rep 63. As Coke noted:

> '(T)he King in his own person cannot adjudge any case, either criminal ... or between party and party ... but this ought to be determined and adjudged in some Court of Justice.'

The Bill of Rights 1689

The struggle between the Stuart monarchy and Parliament in the seventeenth century culminated in the removal of James II from the throne and his replacement by the Protestant William and Mary, who accepted the new constitutional arrangements set out by Parliament in the Bill of Rights. The preamble to the Bill sets out some of the matters which the Bill was designed to put right:

> 'King James did endeavour to subvert and extirpate the Protestant religion and the laws and liberties of this Kingdom.
> 1) by assuming and exercising a power of dispensing with and suspending of laws and execution of laws without consent of Parliament ...
> 4) by levying money for and to the use of the Crown by pretence of prerogatives for other time and in other manner than the same was granted by Parliament.
> 5) by raising and keeping a standing army within this Kingdom in times of peace without consent of Parliament and quartering soldiers contrary to law ...
> 8) by prosecutions in the Court of King's Bench for matter and cause only in Parliament and by cognisable diverse other arbitrary and illegal courses ...'

These activities were to cease and the new monarchs were to accept the proposition of law in the articles set out in the Bill which declared that:

1. The pretended power of suspending of laws or the execution of laws by regal authority without consent of Parliament is illegal.
2. The pretended power of dispensing with laws or the execution of laws by regal authority as it hath been assumed and exercised of late is illegal.
3. The Commission for erecting the late Court of Commissioners for ecclesiastic causes and all other commissions and courts of a like nature are illegal and pernicious.
4. Levying money for or to the use of the Courts by pretence of prerogative without grant of Parliament for longer time or in other manner than the same is or shall be granted is illegal.
5. It is the right of the subjects to petition the King and all commitments and prosecutions for such petitioning are illegal.
6. The raising or keeping a standing army within the kingdom in time of peace unless it be with the consent of Parliament is against law.

7. Election of Members of Parliament ought to be free.
8. The freedom of speech and debates or proceedings in Parliament ought not to be impeached or questioned in any court or place out of Parliament.
9. Excessive bail ought not to be required nor excessive fines imposed, nor cruel or unusual punishments inflicted.
10. Jurors ought to be duly empanelled and returned (and jurors which pass upon men in trials for high treason ought to be forbidden).
11. All grants and promises of fines and forfeitures of particular persons before conviction are illegal and void.
12. For the redress of all grievances and for the amending and strengthening of the laws Parliament ought to be held frequently.

Some of the complaints listed in the preamble and some of the articles of the Bill specifically refer to the prerogative. The most important legal change brought about by the events of 1689 was the emergence of the general principle that prerogative powers could be limited or even abolished by statute. Since 1689 much prerogative power has been transferred to Parliament and manifests itself in the form of primary and delegated legislation. Primary legislation still requires the assent of the monarch in order to come into effect, thus showing that, again in theory, the Crown is a party to the passing of all Acts of Parliament. Some powers still exist, however, that can be exercised either by the monarch in person, or on behalf of the Crown by ministers; these are what are now generically termed prerogative powers.

The exercise of prerogative power involving the Sovereign

The following are the main situations in which the Queen has a conventional right to exercise her prerogative powers.

The appointment of a Prime Minister

When appointing a Prime Minister, the Queen must appoint that person who can command the support of the majority in the House of Commons. Now that all the main political parties elect a leader the Queen will usually appoint the leader of the party with the majority of seats in the House of Commons. However, in situations where no one party has a majority in the House, or where a coalition agreement has broken down, the Queen may still have to take the initiative and personally choose a Prime Minister to enable a new Government to be formed.

The dissolution of Parliament

Under the prerogative the Sovereign may dissolve Parliament and thereby cause a General Election to be held. Usually the Sovereign grants a dissolution at the request of the Prime Minister. In certain circumstances the Queen may have the right to dissolve Parliament against the express wish of the Prime Minister or refuse to dissolve Parliament when the Prime Minister requests it.

Refusal of the Royal Assent
Refusal of the Royal Assent by the Sovereign to a Bill is now probably unconstitutional. There may however be extreme circumstances when refusal of assent may be justified and receive popular support.

Appointments and honours
Although the majority of Crown appointments and honours are made by the Queen on the advice of the Prime Minister, some remain in her personal gift. The Queen personally appoints members of her own private household. Appointments to the Orders of the Garter and the Thistle, the Order of Merit and membership of the Royal Victorian Order are also in her discretion.

The dismissal of ministers
In certain circumstances the Queen may be justified in dismissing the Prime Minister and her ministers, as illustrated by events in Australia in 1975 when the Queen's representative, the Governor-General Sir John Kerr, dismissed the Prime Minister, Mr Gough Whitlam, and his Labour Government following their failure to get Appropriation Bills through the Senate. Mr Whitlam was not willing to hold a General Election to resolve the deadlock, with the result that the Governor-General sacked him and invited the Leader of the Opposition to form an interim Government pending a dissolution and General Election.

The exercise of prerogative power on the Sovereign's behalf by ministers

Disposition of the armed forces
Under the prerogative and statute the Sovereign is the commander-in-chief of the armed forces of the Crown. While many matters regarding the armed forces are now regulated by statute, their control, organisation and disposition are governed by the prerogative. In *Chandler* v *DPP* [1964] AC 763, Chandler and five other members of the Campaign for Nuclear Disarmament organised a demonstration at an airfield by sitting in front of aircraft to prevent them from taking off. They were charged with conspiring to commit a breach of s1 of the Official Secrets Act 1911. In their defence they claimed that, as nuclear weapons were dangerous and illegal under international law, they were merely trying to prevent the Crown from acting in a manner prejudicial to the safety and interests of the State in allowing the airfield to be used by nuclear bombers. In rejecting the admissibility of such an argument Lord Reid said:

> 'It is in my opinion clear that the disposition and armament of the armed forces are, and for centuries have been, within the exclusive discretion of the Crown and that no one can seek a legal remedy on the ground that such discretion has been wrongly exercised.'

In *R* v *Secretary of State for War* [1896] 1 QB 121, in which an officer failed in a petition of right to recover pay, Lord Usher said:

'An officer ... cannot as between him and the Crown take proceedings in the courts of law in respect of anything which has happened between him and the Crown in consequence of his being a soldier.'

The explanation for this given in *China Navigation Co* v *Attorney-General* [1932] 2 KB 197 by Scrutton LJ is that:

'The administration of the army is in the hands of the King, who unless expressly controlled by an Act of Parliament cannot be controlled by the Court.'

In the latter case it was decided that the Sovereign's duty to protect his subjects did not extend to a duty to afford unlimited military protection in foreign parts. Accordingly it was not illegal for His Majesty to seek payment for protection afforded to shipping off the coast of China.

Prerogative of mercy
The courts are Her Majesty's courts, and certain prerogative powers remain in relation to their work, for example, the Attorney-General in England may exercise the prerogative power to enter a nolle prosequi to stop a trial on indictment. On the advice of the Home Secretary, or the Secretary of State for Scotland, the Crown may exercise the prerogative power to pardon convicted offenders or remit or reduce a sentence. The Crown may, under the prerogative, grant leave for appeal from colonial courts to the Judicial Committee of the Privy Council, where the right still exists.

Legislative powers
In addition to the power to summon, prorogue and dissolve Parliament and to assent to Bills considered above, the Crown also has powers to legislate under the prerogative by Order in Council or by letter patent; note however the effect of *The Case of Proclamations* (above).

Powers relating to external affairs
Under the prerogative the Crown may declare war or make peace. In *R* v *Bottrill, ex parte Kuechenmeister* [1947] KB 41 a certificate from the Secretary of State denying that a state of war with Germany had ended was accepted as conclusive by the court in habeas corpus proceedings brought by a German national who had been detained as an enemy alien. The making of treaties is also governed by the prerogative. The general rule is that it is a matter exclusively for the Crown whether or not to enter into a treaty, though the treaty cannot give rise to new rights and duties in United Kingdom law unless they are given effect by legislation. The prerogative also includes the power of the Crown to recognise foreign governments, acquire territory, prevent aliens from entering the United Kingdom and intern enemy aliens.

Emergency powers
In time of war the Government (in modern times) acts under statutory powers, but the older prerogative powers remain. In the early seventeenth century it was

recognised that in an emergency which threatened the realm, every man might disregard property rights in, for example, creating fortifications and digging trenches to repel the enemy. These powers were apparently not thought of as prerogatives since they were shared by the King with all his subjects. In *The Case of the King's Prerogative in Saltpetre* (1607) 12 Co Rep 12 it was held that the King had the prerogative right to mine for saltpetre on private property and to carry it away, because it was necessary for the defence of the realm. The scope of the prerogative in time of war was extensively discussed by the House of Lords in *Burmah Oil Company* v *Lord Advocate* [1965] AC 75. In 1942 the British force in Rangoon destroyed the appellants' oil installations to prevent them falling into the hands of the advancing Japanese. The preliminary question for the House was whether the appellants were entitled to compensation. The House accepted that the destruction had been carried out lawfully under the prerogative. Lord Reid said:

> 'The prerogative certainly covers doing all those things in an emergency which are necessary for the conduct of war.'

He linked this to the prerogative right to control the armed forces; the reason for leaving the waging of war to the Executive, he said, was obvious. What was necessary would depend on the circumstances. Their Lordships went on to hold that, although the installation had been lawfully destroyed under the prerogative, compensation was payable. The only common law exception to the rule that damage done under the prerogative in time of war gave rise to an entitlement to compensation was that of battle-damage: damage actually caused by the use of weapons during conflict. The case was reversed by the War Damage Act 1965 which retrospectively provided that no person is entitled at common law to receive compensation in respect of damage caused by lawful acts of the Crown during, or in contemplation of the outbreak of, a war in which the Sovereign is or was engaged. The Act only applies where there is a war, and the principle of *Burmah Oil* presumably remains intact in the case of emergencies not amounting to war. As regards the maintenance of domestic law and order, *R* v *Secretary of State for the Home Department, ex parte Northumbria Police Authority* [1988] 1 WLR 356 confirms the existence of a residual prerogative power, vested in the Home Secretary, to provide such assistance as is required to police forces in order to enforce the law.

What is 'the Crown'?

This difficult question was considered at some length by the House of Lords in *Town Investments Ltd* v *Department of the Environment* [1978] AC 359. The majority view expressed by Lord Diplock was that:

> 'Where ... we are concerned with the legal nature of the exercise of executive powers of government, I believe that some of the more Athanasian like features of the debate in your Lordships' House could have been eliminated if instead of speaking of "the Crown" we were to speak of the "government" – a term appropriate to embrace both collectively and individually all of the ministers of the Crown and parliamentary secretaries under whose direction the administrative work of government is carried on by the civil servants

employed in the various government departments. It is through them that the executive powers of Her Majesty's government in the United Kingdom are exercised, sometimes in the more important administrative matters in Her Majesty's name, but most often under their own official designation. Executive acts of government that are done by any of them are acts done by "the Crown" in the fictional sense in which that expression is now used in English public law.'

Lord Morris dissented from this view:

'The contention of the department is that "the Crown" was the tenant. This contention has to be considered in the light of the law and principles concerning the position of "the Crown" and of a Minister of "the Crown".

The expression "the Crown" may sometimes be used to designate Her Majesty in a purely personal capacity. It may sometimes be used to designate Her Majesty in her capacity as Head of the Commonwealth. It may sometimes be used to designate Her Majesty in her capacity as the constitutional monarch of the United Kingdom. Thus laws are enacted by Her Majesty in Parliament. The expression may sometimes be used in a somewhat broad sense in reference to the functions of government and the public administration. It may sometimes be used in reference to the rule of law. The case for the prosecution is the case for "the Crown". The government of the day is Her Majesty's Government. A Minister of the Crown is and is constantly referred to as a servant of the Crown. But it cannot be suggested that the Minister is or becomes "the Crown". Even if the grandiloquent description of being an "emanation" of the crown is applied to him he remains separate from the crown and is not and does not become the Crown. When acting on behalf of or for the purpose of "the Crown" some of the well recognised immunities of "the Crown" may cover what he does ...'

As H W R Wade points out:

'... the case did not concern statutory powers and it should presumably not be taken to alter the rule that powers conferred upon ministers belong to them personally and not to the Crown. Otherwise the system of remedies would be gravely weakened.' (Administrative Law 6th ed p52 n2)

The reasoning behind this comment is that the Crown has historical immunities in litigation that it can choose to waive, or agree to limit by way of legislation. Coercive remedies, particularly prerogative orders, cannot lie against the Crown, in the proper sense of that phrase. Thus a minister purporting to act on behalf of the Crown would enjoy similar immunities. The essential question, therefore, is that of when ministers are acting as the Crown, and when they are acting as administrative agents. The solution may lie in distinguishing between the exercise of prerogative and statutory power. In the case of the former, the minister is acting as the agent of the Crown, the only form of 'control' being the declaratory judgment. In the latter case the minister is a 'body of limited jurisdiction' subject to the full range of controls provided by way of judicial review. It is for this reason that certain aspects of Lord Diplock's analysis, extracted above, should be approached with caution. The matter is considered further in Chapters 4 and 20 with reference to *M* v *Home Office* [1993] 3 WLR 433.

The discussion is important because the Crown (if one can use that expression in the light of the foregoing) enjoys considerable immunities and privileges at law; if these were to extend to ministers then legal challenge to the exercise of their powers would be severely curtailed. Where a minister, or other statutory body, exercises statutory powers in his, or its, own name, normal legal controls, in particular judicial review, will be available. Problems still arise, however, where persons enter into contracts with the Crown, or are injured by the negligence of Crown servants; these matters are considered in greater depth in Chapter 4.

Choice of powers

The present position can be summarised in the following diagram:

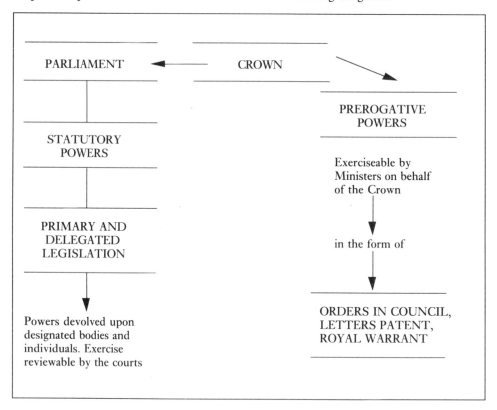

3.2 Control of prerogative power

The traditional analysis

The traditional approach to the control of any power was first to discover its source. If it was found to be statutory then, in the usual case, judicial review would be available as a means of challenge. Where the power being exercised was derived from the prerogative, the courts would traditionally decline to interfere with its exercise. On this basis two questions arose: first, if a power existed under the prerogative and under statute, which must the executive be taken to be exercising? Secondly, given the first question, what would happen to the prerogative power where the statutory power was subsequently repealed?

Three helpful decisions

Attorney-General v De Keyser's Hotel [1920] AC 508

Troops had been accommodated at the plaintiff's hotel which had been requisitioned by the Crown for this purpose. There appeared to be two different powers under which this could be carried out: the royal prerogative, which was unclear as to the property owner's right to compensation in such circumstances, and the Defence Regulations of 1803 and 1842 which provided a code for the making of compensation payments in the event of property being requisitioned. The statute under which the regulations were made made no mention of the co-extensive prerogative power, and the Crown was not expressly bound by the statute.

The House of Lords held that if an area of prerogative power is subsequently covered, or 'overlapped', by a statutory provision, the statutory provision should prevail. Compensation was, therefore, payable under the Defence Regulations. As Lord Dunedin observed:

> 'Inasmuch as the Crown is a party to every Act of Parliament it is logical enough to consider that when the Act deals with something which before the Act could be effected by the prerogative, and specially empowers the Crown to do the same thing, but subject to conditions, the Crown assents to that, and by that Act, to the prerogative being curtailed.'

Lord Atkinson added:

> '... after the statute has been passed, and while it is in force, the thing it empowers the Crown to do can thenceforth only be done by and under the statute, and subject to all the limitations, restrictions and conditions by it imposed, however unrestricted the Royal Prerogative may theretofore have been'.

R v Secretary of State for the Home Department, ex parte Northumbria Police Authority [1988] 1 All ER 556

Claiming to act either under s41 of the Police Act 1964, or under his prerogative powers, the Secretary of State issued a circular to chief constables indicating that central government would supply them with riot equipment, such as CS gas, in the event of a local police authority refusing to sanction the purchase of such equipment. The applicant authority contended that s4(4) of the 1964 Act gave police authorities the exclusive power to equip local police forces, and that this statutory power usurped any remaining prerogative power in the Secretary of State to supply such equipment. The Court of Appeal held that, notwithstanding the power granted to the Secretary of State under s41 of the 1964 Act, s4(4) of the Act had not replaced the prerogative power of the Secretary of State to maintain law and order.

Crucial to this reasoning was the finding that s4(4) did not give local police authorities a monopoly over the supply of such equipment.

Laker Airways Ltd v *Department of Trade* [1977] QB 643

The respondent airline had been designated by the government, under the Bermuda Agreement of 1946, as a recognised carrier on the transatlantic route. The Bermuda Agreement was an international treaty entered into by the Crown, and did not form any part of domestic law. Treaty making is one of the recognised aspects of prerogative power.

In 1975 the Secretary of State announced a change of policy, and Laker's designation under the treaty was revoked, the minister purporting to exercise the prerogative power to do so. Laker had invested £6,000,000 in aircraft on the strength of its designation. The Court of Appeal held that the minister had acted unlawfully.

Lord Denning approached the question of prerogative power on the basis that apart from a number of justifiable exceptions (such as declaring war, conduct of foreign affairs, and so on) prerogative power was as reviewable as any other form of discretionary power, and in this case it had been abused.

Roskill LJ adopted a more conventional approach and held that once a power had been classified as prerogative in nature it was unreviewable, unless replaced or limited by statute. In this case he held that the Civil Aviation Act 1971 impliedly limited the Secretary of State's freedom to use the prerogative power of revoking the designation. A prerogative power could not be used to detract from a statutory right.

Subsequent decisions, such as *R* v *Secretary of State for the Home Department, ex parte Fire Brigades Union and Others* (1994) The Times 10 November Court of Appeal, have confirmed that the use of prerogative power in preference to a statutory scheme (in that case the retention of compensation tariffs developed under the prerogative, despite the fact that a statutory scheme had been created) is unlawful. Sir Thomas Bingham MR and Morritt LJ expressed the view that the relevant statutory provisions would have to be repealed before the exercise of prerogative power could be permitted; see further 23.1.

3.3 The *GCHQ* case

The most significant question left largely unresolved by the decisions considered above, however, was that of whether or not the exercise of prerogative power ever be subject to judicial control on the grounds that it was ultra vires, in the sense of its being irrational or unfair etc. Lord Denning's judgment in *Laker* (above) was indicative of a growing unwillingness to accept the ritualistic reliance on prerogative power as a bar to the supervisory jurisdiction of the courts by way of judicial review. Indeed, a rejection of the 'traditional' approach had arguably already occurred in *R* v *Criminal Injuries Compensation Board, ex parte Lain* [1967] 2 QB 864. The question before the Divisional Court in that case was whether or not certiorari would lie to quash a decision of the Board for error of law on the face of the record. The Board (at that time) was not a statutory body but had been created pursuant to an act of the executive under prerogative powers, and it was contended as a consequence, that its decisions were not amenable to review by the High Court. The court, holding that the Board's decisions were reviewable because it was a public body, making decisions affecting the rights of subjects, under a duty to act judicially, and making awards to claimants from the public purse, clearly abandoned the traditional approach of looking at the source of the power in question as the determinant of reviewability, in favour of looking at the nature of the power and the effect of its use. In some senses *ex parte Lain* could have been regarded as something of an exception to the rule, possibly because it dealt with delegated prerogative power, and it was not until 1984 that the House of Lords was presented with the opportunity to assess in depth the question of the reviewability of prerogative power.

The litigation giving rise to *Council of Civil Service Unions* v *Minister for the Civil Service* [1984] 3 All ER 935 arose as a consequence of actual and threatened industrial action at the government's communications headquarters (GCHQ). The Minister for the Civil Service issued an oral instruction to the effect that civil servants employed there would be prohibited from membership of any trade union. The staff of GCHQ were not consulted prior to the taking of this decision, which was made pursuant to the Minister's powers, under Art 4 of the Civil Service Order in Council 1982, to give instructions 'for controlling the conduct of the Service, and providing for ... the conditions of service', the Order itself being made under the royal prerogative.

The House of Lords held that simply because a decision-making power was derived from a common law and not a statutory source it should not, for that reason only, be immune from judicial review. According to Lord Diplock, judicial review had developed to a stage where one could classify under three heads the grounds on which administrative action was subject to control by the courts: 'illegality', 'irrationality' and 'procedural impropriety'. As regards 'procedural impropriety', his Lordship saw no reason why it should not be a ground for judicial review of a decision made under powers of which the ultimate source was the prerogative.

Lord Roskill thought that the right of challenge could not, however, be unqualified. It must depend on the subject matter of the prerogative power that was exercised. Prerogative powers such as those relating to the making of treaties, the defence of the realm, the prerogative of mercy, the grant of honours, the dissolution of Parliament and the appointment of ministers were not, he thought, susceptible to judicial review because their nature and subject matter were such as to render them not amenable to the judicial process. It was also pointed out that prerogative decisions would usually involve the application of Government policy of which the courts were not the appropriate arbiters. According to Lord Diplock:

'... the kind of evidence that is admissible under judicial procedures and the way in which it has to be addressed tend to exclude from the attention of the court competing policy considerations which, if the executive discretion is to be wisely exercised, need to be weighed against one another – a balancing exercise which judges by their upbringing and experience are ill-qualified to perform.'

Their Lordships agreed, therefore, that executive action based on common law or the use of a prerogative power was not necessarily immune from review. This was especially so in the present case where the prerogative derived from an Order in Council, which was virtually indistinguishable from an order deriving from statute. In such cases the decision might be reviewed by the courts just as it would have been if it had rested on statutory powers. In the instant case, the decision rested upon the Minister's consideration of national security, a matter which the House of Lords thought it was for the Executive to weigh and decide. Their Lordships accepted that the overriding element of national security, in maintaining services at GCHQ, displaced any right the unions might have had to judicial review of the order.

Application of the GCHQ decision

Despite the extent to which the House of Lords' decision in *Council of Civil Service Unions* v *Minister for the Civil Service* represented a breakthrough in the extension of the ambit of judicial review, it should be borne in mind that an old limitation was largely being replaced by a modern one. Whereas previously the constitutional history of the prerogative may have made the judiciary reluctant to question the way in which it was exercised, the modern determinant of judicial intervention is the concept of justiciability. Is the exercise of the prerogative being challenged one in relation to which the judges are qualified to express a view? As a broad guide it is probably accurate to suggest that the greater the element of policy involved in the exercise of the prerogative, the less likely it is that the courts will interfere with a minister's decision. There has been no evidence that the courts would be prepared to adjudicate upon the exercise of prerogative power involved in decisions such as those to commit troops to the Gulf War, or to permit the use of British air bases for the launch of bombing raids on Libya.

Where the exercise of prerogative power involves the exercise of ministerial discretion in relation to the rights of individual citizens, and in the absence of considerations of foreign policy and national security, the courts have shown themselves willing to exercise this newfound jurisdiction, not least because they may be concerned with cases where, but for judicial review, the citizen would have no other means of challenging the decision in question. In *R* v *Secretary of State for Foreign and Commonwealth Affairs, ex parte Everett* [1989] 1 All ER 655, the Court of Appeal confirmed that the issuing of passports, although falling within the scope of prerogative power, was, following the GCHQ decision, a matter that could be the subject of review. In reversing the decision of the Divisional Court, it was held that the Foreign Office policy of not renewing the passports of individuals in respect of whom an arrest warrant had been issued was clearly sound, but that the applicant should have been informed of the grounds for the refusal, and notified that the policy might be departed from in exceptional circumstances. On the facts, however, it was felt that the applicant had sustained no injustice, since by the time the matter had reached the Divisional Court he had discovered the grounds for the refusal to renew his passport, and as there were no exceptional circumstances before that court, there were no grounds for granting the order of certiorari. Similarly the courts have shown a willingness to review the exercise of the prerogative of mercy. In *R* v *Home Secretary, ex parte Bentley* [1994] 2 WLR 101, the applicant's brother, Derek Bentley, had been convicted in 1952 of the murder of a police officer and, despite the jury's recommendation, and the advice of Home Office officials, to the effect that the death penalty should not be enforced, was subsequently executed in 1953. In 1992 the Home Secretary, whilst indicating that he had some sympathy for the view that Bentley should not have been hanged, refused to grant him a posthumous pardon, on the ground that it was not Home Office policy to do so unless the defendant concerned had been proved to have been both technically and morally innocent of any crime, and that, following a review of *Bentley's* case, he was satisfied that Bentley's innocence had not been established. The Divisional Court declined to make any order, but invited the Home Secretary to look again at the range of options that might permit some formal recognition to be given to the generally accepted view that Bentley should not have been hanged. Watkins LJ saw no reason why, in the light of the House of Lords' decision in *Council of Civil Service Unions* v *Minister for the Civil Service*, the exercise of the prerogative of mercy should not be susceptible to review. Whilst the formulation of policy relating to the granting of pardons might not be justiciable, the failure by a Home Secretary to consider the variety of ways in which that prerogative might be exercised could be reviewed. In the instant case the Home Secretary should have considered whether or not the grant of a conditional posthumous pardon was appropriate as recognition that the state had made a mistake, and that Bentley should have had his sentence commuted; see further *R* v *Secretary of State for the Home Department, ex parte Harrison* [1988] 3 All ER 86; and *R* v *Home Secretary and Criminal Injuries Compensation Board, ex parte P* [1994] NLJ 674.

As indicated above, the availability of some other form of redress is a factor that can weigh heavily with the court in its decision as to whether or not it should intervene. As May LJ observed, in *R* v *Civil Service Appeal Board, ex parte Bruce* [1989] 2 All ER 907, the mere fact that a body such as the Board derived its powers from the prerogative did not automatically mean that its decisions would be amenable to judicial review as a matter of course. The availability of other means of legal challenge, such as, in that case, the possibility of an action for breach of contract, might persuade the court not to exercise its jurisdiction. On the facts the court declined to determine the question of whether a civil servant had a contract of employment, but was satisfied that, even if the decisions of the Board were amenable to review, the application would be dismissed since the applicant could pursue any allegations of unfairness in proceedings before an industrial tribunal.

4

Crown Liability

4.1 Introduction to Crown liability

4.2 The Crown Proceedings Act 1947

4.3 Actions against the Crown in contract

4.4 Crown liability in tort

4.5 Procedure and remedies

4.1 Introduction to Crown liability

Prior to the enactment of the Crown Proceedings Act 1947, the position of the Crown as regards its legal liabilities was governed by the common law doctrine that 'the Crown can do no wrong'. The effect of this was that the monarch, in his or her personal capacity, could not be subjected to the judicial process, and that the Crown could not be liable in tort for the actions of its servants. Such legal proceedings as could be brought against the Crown, such as actions for damages in respect of debts and other property matters, could only be brought by means of a petition of right, subject to the grant of the royal fiat. In order to circumvent the restriction on proceedings against the Crown in tort a legal fiction was resorted to, whereby the plaintiff would sue a nominal Crown servant in his personal capacity, and the relevant government department would subsequently reimbursed its servant in the event of any damages being awarded. Note that the 'immunity' belonged to the Crown, not the minister or official concerned: see *Entick* v *Carrington* (1765) 19 St Tr 1030. A Crown servant could be sued in a personal capacity, for example where a minister authorised the unlawful action of a Crown servant: see *Raleigh* v *Goschen* [1898] 1 Ch 73 and *Tamaki* v *Baker* [1901] AC 561. The courts eventually rejected this resort to legal fiction, see *Royster* v *Cavey* [1947] KB 204, and it became obvious that a wholesale revision of the law was necessary. Given the increased number of important activities undertaken by State agencies, Parliament felt that the time was right to set the law on a more rational basis.

4.2 The Crown Proceedings Act 1947

The principal aim of the legislation was to place the Crown in the same situation as any other legal entity as regards proceedings in tort. Whilst the Act largely achieves this by introducing significant changes to the scope of the Crown's tortious liability, no changes are made in respect of contractual liability. The only difference for an individual proceeding against the Crown for breach of contract after 1947 as compared to before 1947, would be in respect of the procedure to be utilised. Section 1 of the Crown Proceedings Act 1947 states:

> 'Where any person has a claim against the Crown after the commencement of this Act, and if this Act had not been passed, the claim might have been enforced, subject to the grant of His Majesty's fiat, by petition of right, or might have been enforced by a proceeding provided by any statutory provision repealed by this Act, then, subject to the provisions of this Act, the claim may be enforced as of right, and without the fiat of His Majesty, by proceedings taken against the Crown for that purpose in accordance with the provisions of this Act.'

To assess Crown liability in contract, therefore, it is necessary to consider the position at common law.

4.3 Actions against the Crown in contract

It could be argued that normal contractual relationships with the Crown are impossible, given the inequality of bargaining power and the residual power of the Crown to render obligations void by means of retrospective legislation, thus undermining the principle that both sides should be equally bound by the transaction. Notwithstanding these theoretical issues, the fact remains that the Crown enters into numerous 'contracts' in the carrying out of government business, and the vast majority are discharged without any problems. From the case law it is possible, however, to identify a number of areas where a litigant may be denied a remedy should the Crown decide to terminate the agreement in question.

Where money must be provided

Government spending must be authorised by Parliament, and this is normally achieved by way of an Appropriation Act. Once the money has been allotted to departments they are free, within political and legal constraints, to spend it. In the majority of cases, therefore, no problem arises, in the sense that a government department cannot cease performance of a contract on the ground of lack of funds, when in fact these have already been provided.

An exceptional problem arose in *Churchward* v *R* (1865) LR 1 QB 173, where the plaintiff had entered into a contract with the Admiralty to provide a mail service between Dover and the continent for 11 years. An annual sum was to be provided by Parliament as consideration. After the contract had run for four years, the Admiralty terminated the agreement, and in that year the relevant Appropriation Act provided that no sum was to be made available by Parliament to provide any further payment. The plaintiff thereupon sought damages from the Crown for breach of contract in respect of the income he would have received had the agreement run its full course. The court held that the provision of funds by Parliament was a condition precedent to the enforceability of the contractual undertaking, and the court had no power to compel Parliament to vote in favour of making such funds available. As Luon J observed:

> '... I think it is in the highest degree improbable that any department of the public service would pledge the Crown to a given course of action for a series of years, in the management of any branch of the public service, especially one for which they have to go to Parliament year by year for supplies, without at all events reserving the right of putting an end to it, if the public service required it, or if Parliament disapproved of it.'

Cockburn CJ stated that the existence of sufficient funds voted by Parliament was a condition precedent to the enforceability of the contract. Where the funds have been allocated by Parliament, however, there should be no reason why, in the ordinary run of commercial contracts, the Crown should not be held to its undertakings.

In *New South Wales* v *Bardolph* (1934) 52 CLR 455 the New South Wales Government, following a change of policy, determined not to continue with a series of tourism advertisements booked in the plaintiff's publication. The plaintiff nevertheless continued to run the advertisements and at the end of the contract period claimed the sum due. Although the contract had not been expressly authorised by the State Legislature, the relevant Appropriation Acts had made sums available for 'Government advertising', and the amount available far exceeded that sought by the plaintiff. The High Court held that the plaintiff was therefore entitled to succeed in his action for damages.

Evatt J summarised the position thus:

> 'In the absence of some controlling statutory provision, contracts are enforceable against the Crown if:
> (a) the contract is entered into in the ordinary or necessary course of Government administration,
> (b) it is authorized by the responsible Ministers of the Crown, and
> (c) the payments which the contractor is seeking to recover are covered by or referable to a parliamentary grant for the class of service to which the contract relates.'

Note the distinction between the court declaring the existence of contractual rights and enforcement of those rights.

It is probably true to say that a contract can be sued on before sums have been appropriated to it, provided that there is no express provision prohibiting payment, but there may be problems in gaining anything other than declaratory relief as the courts will not be able to grant any coercive order against the Crown to enforce judgment.

Executive necessity

The effect of this doctrine is that the Crown will not be bound by a contract where there is an overriding need for it to be free to act in the national interest. In *Rederiaktiebolaget Amphitrite* v *R* [1921] 3 KB 500, the owners of the vessel *Amphitrite* were given assurances by the British Government, acting through diplomatic channels, that if the ship docked at a British port she would not be detained in the way that similar vessels were under wartime measures. Nevertheless, whilst docked at Hull, the ship was detained by the Crown, and eventually had to be sold by the owners. After the war, the owners sued the Crown for damages for breach of contract. The court held that even if there were a contract in this case (which was dubious) the petition would fail, on the ground that the Government had to remain free to take what action was necessary in the national interest, and could not be hampered by the restraints of contract in this respect. Rowlatt J expressed the view that normally commercial undertakings would be binding on the Crown, but went on to observe that:

> '... this was not a commercial contract; it was an arrangement whereby the Government purported to give an assurance as to what its executive action would be in the future in relation to a particular ship in the event of her coming to this country with a particular kind of cargo. And that is, to my mind, not a contract for the breach of which damages can be sued for in a Court of law ... it is not competent for the Government to fetter its future executive action, which must necessarily be determined by the needs of the community when the question arises. It cannot by contract hamper its freedom of action in matters which concern the welfare of the State.'

The precise extent of 'executive necessity' as a basis for releasing the Crown from its contractual liabilities has never been settled. Clearly, as the above case demonstrates, it extends to acting in the national interest during wartime. Similarly in *Crown Lands Commissioners* v *Page* [1960] 2 QB 274 the doctrine was invoked to uphold the validity of the Crown's actions in leasing land to Page, requisitioning it under wartime powers and then suing him for the rent that he had not paid during the period of requisition. The court refused to imply into the lease any right to quiet enjoyment of the property. The Crown had to be free to recover the land whenever necessary. Devlin J indicated that he would have come to the same conclusion even if a covenant to that effect had been express. He stated:

> 'When the Crown, in dealing with one of its subjects, is dealing as if it too were a private person and is granting leases or buying and selling as ordinary persons do, it is absurd to suppose that it is making any promise about the way in which it will conduct the affairs of the nation. No one can imagine, for example, that when the Crown makes a contract which could not be fulfilled in time of war, it is pledging itself not to declare war for so long as the contract lasts.'

Authorities such as *The 'Steaua Romana'* [1944] P 43, and obiter statements of Lord Denning in *Robertson* v *Ministry of Pensions* [1949] 1 KB 227, display a reluctance to extend the doctrine of 'executive necessity' to commercial contracts. The Crown could not, of course, be prevented from enacting legislation that would frustrate the performance of a commercial contract, nor does it mean that the Crown should ensure the enactment of legislation to facilitate the performance of such a contract: see *Board of Trade* v *Temperley Steam Shipping Co Ltd* (1926) 26 Ll LR 76.

Suppliers of goods to the Crown, entering into long-term contracts involving much expenditure and capital outlay on their part, may subsequently find that, following a change of government, the new administration, as a matter of policy, determines not to provide any more public funds for various contracts. As has been outlined above, there is very little that the private party to the contract can do in such situations. A government seeking to ensure that its policies are carried out even after it leaves office might consider the inclusion of a liquidated damages clause enuring to the benefit of the contractor in the event of a later administration seeking to terminate the agreement. In this regard it should be noted that the placing of government contracts is not subject to any statutory procedure and is a matter expressly excluded from the jurisdiction of the Parliamentary Commissioner for Administration.

Crown employment

Crown servants are, traditionally, 'dismissable at will'. The theory is that the Crown should not be forced to continue the employment of some individual who was no longer suitable, as this would be contrary to the public interest. In some senses, at least, the proposition can be regarded as an extension of executive necessity, although there is some doubt as to whether or not Crown servants are employed pursuant to a contract of employment. The fact that Crown servants are dismissable at will militates against there being a contractual relationship, but on the other hand, as Lord Atkin stated in *Reilly* v *R* [1934] AC 176 at 179:

'A power to determine a contract at will is not inconsistent with the existence of a contract until it is so determined.'

To some extent this view is reflected in *Dunn* v *R* [1896] 1 QB 116, where the plaintiff had been appointed as a consular official, in what was then Niger, for three years. Before the expiry of this period he was dismissed and consequently sought damages for breach of contract. The court held that no damages were payable since, as a Crown servant, he was dismissable at pleasure, but Lord Herschell's observations seem to assume the existence of a contract:

'I take it that persons employed as the petitioner was in the service of the Crown, except in cases where there is some statutory provision for a higher tenure of office, are ordinarily engaged on the understanding that they hold their employment at the pleasure of the Crown. So I think that there must be imported into the contract for the employment of the petitioner the term which is applicable to civil servants in general, namely, that the Crown may put an end to the employment at its pleasure ... The cases cited show that, such employment being for the good of the public, it is essential for the public good that it should be capable of being determined at the pleasure of the Crown, except in certain exceptional cases where it has been deemed to be more for the public good that some restriction should be imposed on the power of the Crown to dismiss its servants ...'

There is evidence to support both sides of this argument. In *Council of Civil Service Unions* v *Minister for the Civil Service* [1984] 3 All ER 935, by the time the case had reached the House of Lords both sides appeared to have agreed that the relationship was not contractual. Further support for this view is provided by *R* v *Civil Service Appeal Board, ex parte Bruce* [1988] 3 All ER 686. A civil servant employed by the Inland Revenue was given notice terminating his employment and sought judicial review of the Appeal Board's decision to uphold his dismissal. Although counsel for the Crown had contended that there could be a contract between the Crown and its servants, albeit one which was not intended to be legally binding, the court held that there was no contract. The decision was influenced by the fact that the applicant had not been appointed pursuant to any statutory power, evidence that there had never been any intention to enter into contractual obligations on the part of the Crown, and the fact that the whole matter was under review by the Government, through a Cabinet Office reappraisal of the status of Crown servants.

Against this one should consider older cases, such as *Rodwell* v *Thomas* [1944] 1 KB 596. The court proceeded on the basis that a civil servant did have a contract of employment but that the courts would never imply or incorporate into the contract any provisions/agreements which purported to limit the power of the Crown to dismiss. Similarly, in *Riordan* v *War Office* [1959] 3 All ER 552, where the plaintiff was dismissed from his post as a civil servant without being given the 14 days' notice required under Order in Council regulations, the court refused to incorporate the regulations into his contract of employment if they acted as a fetter on the Crown's discretion. Finally, in *Kodeeswaran* v *Attorney-General of Ceylon* [1970] AC 1111, the Privy Council, being asked to consider whether a civil servant had any right of action against the Crown in respect of salary due for services rendered, held that a civil servant could bring an action, under the common law of Ceylon, against the Crown to recover arrears of wages. As to the existence of a contract Lord Diplock observed:

'Their Lordships thus see nothing inconsistent with British constitutional theory in the Governor of Ceylon being empowered by the Proclamation of 1799 to enter into a contract on behalf of the Crown with a person appointed to an office in the civil administration of the colony as to the salary payable to him, provided that such contract was terminable at wil ... A right to terminate a contract of service at will coupled with a right to enter into a fresh contract of service may in effect enable the Crown to change the terms of employment in future if the true inference to be drawn from the communication of the intended change to the servant and his continuing to serve thereafter is that his existing contract has been terminated by the Crown and a fresh contract entered into on the revised terms. But this cannot affect any right to salary already earned under the terms of his existing contract before its termination.'

For the moment, the tide of judicial opinion seems to be running in favour of the view that a contract can exist but may not always do so. In *McClaren* v *Home Office*

[1990] ICR 824 the plaintiff was a prison officer who had been involved in a dispute with the Home Office over working conditions that had culminated in his suspension without pay. He sought a declaration, by way of an action in the Chancery Division, that his conditions of employment could not be altered by his employers in breach of collective agreements, and claimed compensation for loss of salary. At first instance it was held that his statement of claim would be struck out as it disclosed no claim in private law, because the plaintiff had no individual contract of employment with the Home Office that could give rise to rights in the private law of contract. *Ex parte Bruce* was cited with approval in support of this conclusion. The Court of Appeal allowed the plaintiff's appeal against this decision on the basis that his action did raise questions of private law. Dillon LJ was influenced by the fact that McClaren's appointment had been made under a statutory power, namely s3 of the Prison Act 1952. His Lordship expressed the view that in appointing prison officers the Home Office was in a position analogous to that of a nationalised industry or health authority, and as such had the power to enter into contractual relationships with staff. In his view the exercise of the statutory power of appointment was free from the restrictions inherent in an exercise of prerogative power. The question of whether or not there was a contract between McClaren and the Home Office was actually left open by the court, but it did regard the question as one which could be properly resolved by way of a private action.

A more definite opinion as to the existence of a contract was expressed by Stuart-Smith LJ in *R v Lord Chancellor's Department, ex parte Nangle* [1991] IRLR 343. The applicant had faced internal disciplinary hearings following allegations that he had sexually harassed a female colleague. The question for the Divisional Court was whether or not the applicant was employed under a contract of employment, as the existence of such a contract would militate against the existence of any public law rights to be protected by way of judicial review.

Stuart-Smith LJ held that a contract did exist in this case since all the required elements were present: offer, acceptance, consideration and, crucially, an intention to be legally bound. Interestingly, his Lordship chose to ignore paragraph 14 of the Civil Service Pay and Conditions Code which provided that no contract existed between civil servants and the Crown, regarding this as a mistaken assumption.

Allied to the question of whether or not a contract exists is that of which procedure the aggrieved Crown servant should use. A simplistic analysis suggests that if a contract does exist, he or she should proceed by way of action, and in the absence of a contract by way of an application for judicial review. Such an analysis may be flawed, since even if there is no contract there may not be a sufficient public law issue to warrant the intervention of the courts by way of judicial review: see comments of Stuart-Smith LJ in *ex parte Nangle*. See further *R v Derbyshire County Council, ex parte Noble* [1990] ICR 808.

The Employment Protection (Consolidation) Act 1978

Crown servants are permitted to take disputes relating to their employment to Industrial Tribunals. The matter is governed by s138 of the Employment Protection (Consolidation) Act 1978 Act, in which Crown employment is defined (in subs(2)) as:

> '... employment under or for the purposes of a government department or any officer or body exercising on behalf of the Crown functions conferred by an enactment'.

Subsection 138(3) expressly excludes members of the armed forces from the benefits provided by the section. Note also that the Act is silent as to the existence of a contract of employment. Under s138(4) a minister may certify that the employment of a particular Crown servant is of such a nature that he should not be permitted to take his case to an industrial tribunal as this would be prejudicial to national security.

Agency

The normal principles of agency, which apply where a Crown servant acts on behalf of the Crown, would appear to be as follows. First, the Crown is clearly bound by a servant acting with real authority. Secondly, the Crown will be bound where a servant has apparent, or ostensible, authority, provided it can be shown that the Crown represented the agent as having more authority than he in reality possessed. If no such representation by the Crown (as principal) has been made, it will not be bound. In *Attorney-General for Ceylon* v *Silva* [1953] AC 461, the Principal Collector of Customs of Ceylon obtained the permission of the Chief Secretary of Ceylon to sell, by auction, certain steel plates which were on Customs premises. The Principal Collector was unaware that the plates had already been sold by the Crown some two months earlier. Permission to auction the steel plates had been granted to the Principal Collector under the provisions of the Ceylon Customs Ordinance. The plaintiff, Silva, purchased the steel plates at the auction and claimed damages when delivery was refused because of the prior sale. The Privy Council held that the Ordinance under which the goods were sold did not bind the Crown, therefore the Principal Collector had had no actual authority to sell the steel plates at the auction because they were Crown property. The argument that he had been acting within the scope of his apparent authority, and that the Crown was therefore still bound by his actions, was also rejected on the basis that no public officer, unless he possessed some special power, could hold out on behalf of the Crown that he had the right to enter into a contract in respect of the property of the Crown when in fact no such right existed.

Finally, a Crown servant cannot be sued for breach of warranty of authority, that is be sued personally for entering into contracts he in fact had no power to make: see *Dunn* v *MacDonald* [1897] 1 QB 555.

4.4 Crown liability in tort

As stated above, the primary aim of the 1947 Act was to amend the law and place the Crown in the same position as any other individual as regard liability in tort. It has largely achieved this goal, as s2(1)(a) provides:

> 'Subject to the provisions of this Act, the Crown shall be subject to all those liabilities in tort to which, if it were a private person of full age and capacity, it would be subject ...'

Liability is extended by s2(1)(b) to any breach of those duties which a person owes to his servants or agents at common law by reason of being their employer; s2(1)(c) extends the Crown's liability to any breach of the duties attaching at common law to the ownership, occupation, possession or control of property; and s2(2) provides that:

> 'Where the Crown is bound by a statutory duty which is binding also upon persons other than the Crown and its officers, then, subject to the provisions of this Act, the Crown shall, in respect of a failure to comply with that duty, be subject to all those liabilities in tort (if any) to which it would be so subject if it were a private person of full age and capacity.'

Third party, or joint, liability is provided for by s4, which states that, in so far as liability is imposed by the 1947 Act, the law relating to indemnity and contribution shall be enforceable by or against the Crown in respect of the liability to which it is so subject as if the Crown were a private person of full age and capacity.

The Crown's liability in tort will of necessity be vicarious in nature, as it can only act through its servants and agents. For this purpose s2(6) of the 1947 Act defines a Crown servant as a person who:

> '... has been directly or indirectly appointed by the Crown and was at the material time paid in respect of his duties as an officer of the Crown wholly out of the Consolidated Fund of the United Kingdom, moneys provided by Parliament, the Road Fund, or any other Fund certified by the Treasury for the purposes of this subsection or was at the material time holding an office in respect of which the Treasury certify that the holder thereof would normally be so paid.'

The nature of this vicarious liability is adverted to by s2(3) which provides that:

> 'Where any functions are conferred or imposed upon an officer of the Crown as such either by any rule of the common law or by statute, and that officer commits a tort while performing or purporting to perform those functions, the liabilities of the Crown in respect of the tort shall be such as they would have been if those functions had been conferred or imposed solely by virtue of instructions lawfully given by the Crown.'

Clearly, the vicarious liability of the Crown depends upon the liability of the individual Crown servant; thus s2(4) provides that:

> 'Any enactment which negatives or limits the amount of the liability of any Government department or officer of the Crown in respect of any tort committed by that department or officer shall, in the case of proceedings against the Crown under this section in respect

of a tort committed by that department or officer, apply in relation to the Crown as it would have applied in relation to that department or officer if the proceedings against the Crown had been proceedings against that department or officer.'

And the proviso to s2 makes it clear that no proceedings shall lie against the Crown in respect of any act or omission of a servant or agent unless the act or omission would in any event have given rise to a cause of action in tort against the servant or agent. The effect of this latter provision is that unless the individual Crown servant or agent can be sued, the Crown will not be vicariously liable. In some cases, it may be very difficult to identify the civil servant responsible for one's loss. It also means that if, for some reason, as in *Corney* v *Minister of Labour* (1959) PL 170, no action can be taken against the individual tortfeasor, then no action is maintainable against the Crown.

The problem was adverted to in *Racz* v *Home Office* [1994] 2 WLR 23, where a prisoner sought damages for assault, battery, negligence and misfeasance in respect of his treatment whilst detained. The Home Office applied unsuccessfully to have the claim of misfeasance struck out on the ground that it could not be held vicariously liable for such actions. Lord Jauncey observed that, in order to determine whether or not a department of state could be vicariously liable for the misfeasance of an officer of the Crown, the court would distinguish between a situation on the one hand, where the officer was performing authorised acts by means of a misguided or an unauthorised means, and on the other where he was committing acts which had no connection with his duties. In the latter case there would not normally be any question of vicarious liability.

The proviso to s2 creates most difficulty where a policy is adopted by a government department and put into effect by Crown servants. If they are negligent in executing a policy then an action may lie against the Crown; but if it is the policy itself that is at fault, and the Crown servant simply follows his instructions, the Crown cannot be sued, as the servant has not been negligent.

Precisely this problem arose in *Home Office* v *Dorset Yacht Co Ltd* [1970] AC 1004. Several Borstal trainees being detained under 'open conditions' escaped from supervision and damaged property belonging to the respondents. The relaxed conditions under which the boys had been detained were the result of a policy decision by the appellants. The respondents argued that the Borstal officers owed neighbouring property owners a duty of care to ensure that none of the detainees would escape. The existence of this duty of care was tried as a preliminary matter. The House of Lords held (Viscount Dilhorne dissenting) that a duty of care was owed by the Borstal officers to neighbouring property owners, to the extent that they should use reasonable care to prevent an escape of detainees where there was a manifest risk of this. Lord Diplock made it clear, however, that in his view no duty of care was owed by the minister in exercising his rule-making powers, or in the formulation of policy; for this he was responsible to Parliament alone, as it was not the function of the courts to adjudicate upon the methods used by the executive to promote its policy. He went on to assert that Parliament could not have intended the consequences of the regime to be actionable. If it was unreasonable, the ultra vires doctrine would provide a method of control. The majority view reflects the opinion that the law should not necessarily apply the standard common law rules of negligence in an unqualified form to government departments because their functions were unlikely to have any parallel in private law: for example, the decision as to whether or not to release a felon. The majority concluded that if harm resulted because of acts or omissions of a Borstal officer (ie from something that could be identified as falling within the operational rather than policy sphere) the first inquiry should be as to whether or not he had exceeded his powers (ie acted ultra vires). If this was the case then the common law principles of negligence could be applied.

The Privy Council has been more cautious in regarding the policy/operational dichotomy as being the key to the imposition of a private law duty of care. In *Rowling* v *Takaro Properties Ltd* [1988] 1 All ER 163 it considered the circumstances in which an individual might be able to bring an action against a government minister for negligently acting ultra vires, and causing economic loss as a result. Lord Keith, delivering judgment on behalf of the Board, commented that, on the broader issue of when a private law duty of care would arise in relation to the exercise of public law powers, the distinction between policy and operational decisions was not the only relevant factor. His Lordship felt that the question of whether there was a duty of care should be approached pragmatically, with reference to the availability of judicial review in respect of the action, the likelihood of negligence actually being established, and the danger of inducing undue caution amongst administrators.'

Arguably, the only private law action that should be allowed to succeed in such circumstances is an action for malicious abuse of power. There were further difficulties in identifying those situations where a minister could be said to be under a duty to obtain legal advice as to the propriety of his proposed action.

The Privy Council's desire seems to have been to issue a clear warning against adopting an overly simplistic approach to the policy/operational dichotomy as the determinant of whether a private law action for negligence is maintainable against the Crown. Underpinning the decision is the assumption that if the exercise of discretion by a public body appears to have been invalid, the matter can be quickly rectified by way of an application for judicial review. Any losses resulting from this delay should, in theory, be minimal, given the speed with which a ruling can be obtained. As a result, there should be no need for a plaintiff to launch, in addition, an action for negligence. This 'pragmatic' approach side-steps the more difficult question of when a duty of care arises, and if it does, with what result.

Privy Council decisions are, of course, only persuasive in their authority, and the comments of Lord Keith in *Rowling* v *Takaro Properties Ltd* did not subsequently inhibit the Vice-Chancellor, Sir Nicholas Browne-Wilkinson, in *Lonrho plc* v *Tebbit and the Department of Trade and Industry* [1991] 4 All ER 973, from concluding that a minister could face an action for negligence in the exercise of ministerial powers. The plaintiff company's cause of action arose from the Secretary of State's delay in releasing it from an undertaking not to acquire shares in a particular company. By the time the release was granted a rival company had already won the take-over battle. The Vice-Chancellor took the view that the decision to release Lonrho from its undertaking could be characterised as operational, rather than one falling within the sphere of policy, and as such it would be regarded as one in respect of which a private law duty of care could be said to exist. In this respect his Lordship paid considerable attention to the issue of proximity and, given that the issue arose out of an agreement between the plaintiff and the defendants, felt that there were grounds for arguing that the economic loss suffered by the plaintiff might be reasonably foreseeable. It was clearly a case where a trial of the facts was required so that the question of proximity could be resolved, and hence the defendant's application to have the action struck out was dismissed. On appeal ([1992] 4 All ER 280) Dillon LJ, while confirming the decision at first instance, was careful to point out that the court was ruling only on the procedural issues. He noted that on the substantive issue of negligence the plaintiffs might yet face serious difficulties in persuading a court to depart from the constraints on liability indicated by Lord Keith in *Rowling* v *Takaro Properties*. Leave to appeal to the House of Lords was refused. As to the principles applicable to determining the nature of liability for economic loss see the comments of Lord Bridge in *Caparo Industries plc* v *Dickman* [1990] 1 All ER 568 at 573-4.

Judicial immunity

Section 2(5) of the 1947 Act excludes Crown liability in respect of acts of a 'judicial' nature. It provides:

> 'No proceedings shall lie against the Crown by virtue of this section in respect of anything done or omitted to be done by any person while discharging or purporting to discharge any responsibilities of a judicial nature vested in him, or any responsibilities which he has in connection with the execution of judicial process.'

The problem here is identifying 'responsibilities of a judicial nature'. Where individuals such as judges enjoy immunity in their own right, then it is clear that the Crown cannot be vicariously liable. The difficulty arises with persons such as tribunal chairmen, inquiry inspectors, and others discharging functions of a quasi-judicial nature. Statements made by tribunal members will sometimes be privileged, thus preventing any action in defamation, but there is no clear authority stating the ambit of s2(5). Cases that may be of assistance in deciding whether proceedings are 'judicial' are *Sirros* v *Moore* [1975] QB 118, *Royal Aquarium Society* v *Parkinson* [1892] 1 QB 431 and *Trapp* v *Mackie* [1979] 1 All ER 489. In *Jones* v *Department of Employment* [1988] 2 WLR 493, the Court of Appeal held that an employment benefit adjudication officer could not be described as falling within the scope of the 'judicial immunity' referred to in s2(5) of the 1947 Act as regards his giving advice to benefit claimants. The court went further, however, in rejecting the contention that a common law duty of care should be imposed on such an officer, holding that the only private law action that might be sustainable in such circumstances was an action for misfeasance. It was felt that to allow an action for negligence to proceed would run counter to the aims and objects of the relevant legislation which had established a framework of appeals from decisions of adjudication officers, appeal lying ultimately to the social security commissioner whose decision was to be regarded as 'final' on all matters other than questions of law. It has further been held that s2(5) would not provide protection from an action in negligence in respect of a solicitor employed by the Crown Prosecution Service carrying out administrative tasks prior to the presentation of a case before a magistrates' court: see further *Welsh* v *Chief Constable of the Merseyside Police* [1993] 1 All ER 692.

Provisions relating to the armed forces

Originally s10 of the 1947 Act provided that the Crown would not be liable for the death of, or personal injury occurring to, one member of the armed forces on duty caused by another member of the forces on duty. The section stated:

> 'Nothing done or omitted to be done by a member of the armed forces of the Crown while on duty as such shall subject either him or the Crown to liability in tort for causing the death of another person, or for causing personal injury to another person, in so far as the death or personal injury is due to anything suffered by that other person while he is a member of the armed forces of the Crown if –
>> at the time when that thing is suffered by that other person, he is either on duty as a member of the armed forces of the Crown or is, though not on duty as such, on any land, premises, ship, aircraft or vehicle for the time being used for the purposes of the armed forces of the Crown; and [the Secretary of State] certifies that his suffering that thing has been or will be treated as attributable to service for the purposes of entitlement to an award under the Royal Warrant Order in Council or Order of His Majesty relating to the disablement or death of members of the force of which he is a member:
>> Provided that this subsection shall not exempt a member of the said forces from liability in tort in any case in which the court is satisfied that the act or omission was not connected with the execution of his duties as a member of those forces.'

The rationale for this provision was that it was not thought appropriate for members of the armed forces to be encouraged to think in terms of bringing actions in the courts in respect of the conduct of the their colleagues; training and warfare were inherently dangerous activities making the imposition of a private law duty of care incongruous; when s10 was enacted, the medical and financial benefits available to disabled servicemen compared favourably with the award of damages that would have been obtained through litigation. Increasingly, however, the restriction on litigation imposed by s10 became subject to considerable criticism, not least because the compensation paid to injured military personnel failed to keep pace with the awards of damages being made in the courts. Bowing to the pressure for reform, Parliament enacted the Crown Proceedings (Armed Forces) Act 1987 which has the effect of removing the Crown's immunity in negligence for the actions of members of the armed forces on duty. The 1987 Act is not retrospective in operation and thus does not, for example, affect the claims made by servicemen suing in respect of injuries sustained while they were present at nuclear tests in the Pacific region during the 1950s, some of which were considered by the House of Lords in *Pearce* v *Secretary of State for Defence* [1988] 2 All ER 348. In the event, it was held that the Crown was not entitled to rely on the immunity that had been created by s10 of the 1947 Act, as the tests had actually been conducted by the United Kingdom Atomic Energy Authority, the liabilities of which had been transferred to the Crown by subsequent legislation. At the time of the tests the Authority had not been covered by the immunity created by s10; thus the Crown could not now rely on it. Note that the 1987 Act does not actually repeal s10, but provides for its reinstatement should the government of the day consider it necessary.

4.5 Procedure and remedies

As stated above, the 1947 Act replaced the petition of right by permitting a litigant to proceed by way of writ. Such writs are issued in the normal way, and documents served on solicitors for the relevant government department. By s17(3):

> 'Civil proceedings against the Crown shall be instituted against the appropriate authorised Government department, or, if none of the authorised Government departments is appropriate or the person instituting the proceedings has any reasonable doubt whether any and if so which of those departments is appropriate, against the Attorney-General.'

The 1947 Act does, however, contain certain key restrictions upon the availability of remedies, perhaps most significantly in s21 which provides:

> 'In any civil proceedings by or against the Crown the court shall, subject to the provisions of this Act, have power to make all such orders as it has power to make in proceedings between subjects, and otherwise to give such appropriate relief as the case may require:
>
> Provided that: where in any proceedings against the Crown any such relief is sought as might in proceedings between subjects be granted by way of injunction or specific performance, the court shall not grant an injunction or make an order for specific performance, but may in lieu thereof make an order declaratory of the rights of the parties; and in any proceedings against the Crown for the recovery of land or other property the court shall not make an order for the recovery of the land or the delivery of the property, but may in lieu thereof make an order declaring that the plaintiff is entitled as against the Crown to the land or property or to the possession thereof.'

Subsection (2) adds:

> 'The court shall not in any civil proceedings grant any injunction or make any order against an officer of the Crown if the effect of granting the injunction or making the order would be to give any relief against the Crown which could not have been obtained in proceedings against the Crown.'

This provision has been the cause of considerable confusion. It would appear that, prior to the enactment of the 1947 Act, injunctions, both interim and final, were available against Crown servants acting in a personal capacity: see *Ellis* v *Earl Grey*

(1833) 6 Sim 214, *Rankin* v *Huskisson* (1830) 4 Sim 13, *Tamaki* v *Baker* (above) and *Attorney-General for New South Wales* v *Trethowan* [1932] AC 526.

Injunctions were not available against the Crown, as this would have created difficulties in relation to enforcement; hence the use of the declaration in such cases. In any event there were, and still are, good policy reasons for the Crown being free to exercise prerogative power in the national interest without fear of restraint by the courts. The confusion arises as a result of s21 being read as an extension of the Crown's immunity, as regards injunctions, to Crown servants: see *Merricks* v *Heathcoat Amory* [1955] Ch 567. The argument that the 1947 Act, despite its overriding purpose of removing Crown immunities in litigation, should have succeeded in extending the immunity of ministers as regards injunctive relief was criticised in *R* v *Home Secretary, ex parte Herbage* [1987] QB 872 and *R* v *Licensing Authority, ex parte Smith Kline & French Laboratories Ltd (No 2)* [1988] 3 WLR 896. The contention that found support in these cases was that if prerogative orders could lie against a minister, why not injunctive relief? As regards the views expressed on the availability of injunctive relief, both of these decisions were overruled by the House of Lords' decision in *Factortame Ltd* v *Secretary of State for Transport* [1989] 2 All ER 692, but Their Lordships' interpretation of s21 has been the subject of trenchant academic criticism. In any event, as a result of the ruling of the European Court of Justice, considered by the House of Lords in *Factortame Ltd* v *Secretary of State for Transport* (No 2) [1991] 1 All ER 70, the House of Lords had to concede that Community law required the granting of an interim injunction against a minister where the applicant sought to protect a purported right arising as an incident of Community membership. It is respectfully submitted that the luminous analysis provided by Wade ('The Crown – old platitudes and new heresies' [1992] NLJ 1275 and 1315) should be adopted. The true purposes of s21, as the Notes on Clauses provided by the parliamentary draughtsman reveal, was to prevent the immunity of the Crown from being circumvented by the grant of injunctive relief against a minister. Thus a minister enforcing an Order in Council could not be the subject of an injunction, because he would be acting as an agent of the Crown. If, however, he was purporting to exercise his statutory power by promulgating regulations thought to be invalid, or in breach of Community law, the court would not be restrained by s21 from granting interim relief.

Wade's view has now largely been adopted by the House of Lords in *M* v *Home Office* [1993] 3 WLR 433, where it was held that an injunction could be granted to prevent a minister from flouting a court order preventing the deportation of someone who claimed to be a political refugee.

Lord Woolf recognised that s21 of the Crown Proceedings Act 1947 had not been intended to affect the right of an individual to seek injunctive relief against an individual Crown servant, acting in his official capacity, to prevent the commission of a tort. He explained further that, as prerogative orders have never been available against the Crown, when s31(2) of the Supreme Court Act 1981 extended the prerogative jurisdiction to include the granting of injunctions, including interim injunctions, by way of judicial review proceedings, it was not creating a conflict with s21 of the 1947 Act (that is, it did not create the possibility of injunctions being granted against the Crown as such). The provision merely created a procedure by which an injunction could be obtained against a minister exercising statutory power in his official capacity. It was obvious that prior to 1947 prerogative orders had been available in respect of a minister of the Crown acting in an official capacity. Hence the effect of s31(2) was to make injunctive relief available in such cases, although, in Lord Woolf's view, the power to do so should be exercised sparingly.

Although no finding of contempt could be made against the Crown if a minister flouted a coercive order, contempt proceedings could be maintained against the minister in his official capacity, and against his department. It followed that, although the sanctions for such contempt could not be personal or punitive, the court's finding of contempt would be an indication that the minister had acted improperly, an appropriate order as to costs could be made, and there would in all likelihood be repercussions for the minister in terms of parliamentary scrutiny.

Similarly, s25(4) of the 1947 Act, which provides that no execution or attachment shall issue from any court for enforcing payment by the Crown of any damages or costs awarded, should be read as preventing proceedings for enforcement from being brought against ministers and civil servants in order to recover such sums in circumstances where enforcement would not be possible against the Crown. It should not be interpreted as extending the Crown's immunities from enforcement to ministers exercising statutory powers.

5

Public Interest Immunity

5.1 The purpose of discovery

The purpose of discovery is for each party to litigation to receive relevant documents from the other. This helps to avoid trial by ambush, in which one side produces at the trial a devastating piece of evidence which destroys the case of the other; it is also intended to promote an early settlement of the dispute by both sides being better informed as to the strength of the other side's case. For information on the detailed procedure to be followed see O.24 Rules of the Supreme Court; the following is a brief account.

Automatic discovery

In a High Court action, the parties to litigation will, in theory, within 14 days of the close of pleadings, exchange a list of documents that relate to the dispute, provided that they are, or have been, in the possession or custody of the parties. In this listing each party indicates the documents which he is willing to disclose and those for which he claims privilege.

Note that in *Barrett* v *Ministry of Defence* (1990) The Times 24 January the court appeared willing to accept the notion that discovery might be granted in order to assist the plaintiff to draft her statement of claim properly. In considering the issue of public interest immunity the court felt that, regardless of whether discovery was being sought before or after the exchange of pleadings, there should be no difference in the way in which the rules were applied.

All relevant documents must be disclosed, ie their existence admitted, but those for which privilege is claimed may be protected from inspection. The criteria for disclosure are generally set out in *Compagnie Financière et Commerciale du Pacifique* v *Peruvian Guano Co* (1882) 11 QBD 55. The documents must contain information which may enable one's opponent to advance his own case or damage one's own case or which may fairly lead him to a train of inquiry which may have either of these two consequences.

Who makes the claim?

Generally, a claim of public interest immunity will be made by a minister providing a certificate that explains why certain documents should not be revealed. In some cases a claim arises from an affidavit sworn by a senior official of a local authority or police force. In *Rodgers* v *Home Secretary* [1973] AC 388, the House of Lords held that a letter written by an assistant chief constable to the Gaming Board should not be subject to disclosure, as this might adversely affect the position of police informers relied upon to provide information about underworld activities. As to the issue of who might raise an objection to discovery Lord Reid observed:

> 'The ground put forward has been said to be Crown privilege. I think that that expression is wrong and may be misleading. There is no question of any privilege in the ordinary sense of the word. The real question is whether the public interest requires that the letter shall not be produced and whether that public interest is so strong as to override the ordinary right and interest of a litigant that he shall be able to lay before a court of justice all relevant evidence. A Minister of the Crown is always an appropriate and often the most appropriate person to assert this public interest, and the evidence or advice which he gives to the court is always valuable and may sometimes be indispensable. But, in my view, it must always be open to any person interested to raise the question and there may be cases where the trial judge should himself raise the question if no one else has done so. In the present case the question of public interest was raised by both the Attorney-General and the Gaming Board. In my judgment both were entitled to raise the matter. Indeed I think that in the circumstances it was the duty of the board to do as they have done.'

5.2 The key decisions

Duncan v *Cammell Laird & Co Ltd* [1942] AC 624 involved an action brought by the widow of a sailor who had drowned when the submarine *Thetis* sank during trials in Liverpool Bay. She alleged that the defendants had been negligent in their design of the submarine, and in an effort to establish this sought discovery of the blueprints for the craft. The First Lord of the Admiralty swore an affidavit to the effect that disclosure of these plans would be against the national interest which, considering the date of the litigation, was difficult to refute, and the House of Lords accordingly accepted that the affidavit could not be questioned. Discovery of the documents was refused. While few people sought to question the correctness or otherwise of their Lordships' decision, bearing in mind that the country was at war, the decision did set the tone for future cases in the post-war period. The courts were criticised for adopting too much of an 'administration minded' approach, leaning in favour of allowing ministerial claims of privilege in perhaps questionable cases. For example, in *Ellis* v *Home Office* [1953] 2 QB 135 the plaintiff, a prison inmate, was unable to succeed with an action in negligence against the government department because discovery of documents revealing inadequate supervision of a fellow prisoner, known to the authorities to be violent, was refused on the ground that their production would be injurious to the smooth functioning of this branch of a public service.

The decision that marked a reassertion of authority by the judiciary, and is thus widely regarded as being the basis for the modern (ie post-war) law on public interest immunity is the House of Lords' decision in *Conway* v *Rimmer* [1968] AC 910. The appellant, a probationary constable who had successfully defended a charge of theft, subsequently sought evidence in order to succeed with an action for malicious prosecution against the respondent. The Crown claimed immunity for five documents in this case, four on the ground that they belonged to a class of document that ought to remain confidential because they were reports on probationary constables for senior officers and the fifth on the basis that it concerned a report for senior officers on the conduct of an inquiry into the commission of a crime. The House of Lords held unanimously that the documents in question should be produced, notwithstanding the fact that the Home Secretary had certified that their production could be injurious to the public interest. The decision is significant for a number of reasons. First, as a constitutional issue the House of Lords made it clear that the courts should not always allow a ministerial certificate to be conclusive. As Lord Reid stated:

> 'I would ... propose that the House ought now to decide that courts have, and are entitled to exercise, a power and a duty to hold a balance between public interest, as expressed by a Minister, to withhold certain documents and other evidence, and the public interest in ensuring the proper administration of justice.'

Secondly, the decision clarifies the procedure to be followed in cases where privilege is claimed, as the diagram opposite illustrates.

Thirdly, as Lord Reid indicated, there were certain matters of which a minister would be a better judge than the courts, such as whether documents should be suppressed on grounds of national security, and in any event great weight would always be given to any ministerial view. Documents such as Cabinet papers, he felt, should not be disclosed until they were of historical interest only. On other matters, such as the effect of disclosure of documents on the smooth running of a public service, the courts were in just as good a position as the minister to decide what should and should not be produced. The significance of ministerial reliance on national security is seldom lost on the courts. For example, in *Balfour* v *Foreign and Commonwealth Office* [1994] 1 WLR 681, the applicant, who had been dismissed by his employers, the Foreign and Commonwealth Office, took his case to an industrial tribunal, and in support of his claim sought various documents, production of which was resisted by both the Foreign Secretary and the Home Secretary on the ground that the documents related to national security. The tribunal chairman's refusal to order disclosure was upheld on appeal by the Court of Appeal, where it was held that once a minister had demonstrated the potential harm to national security that might be caused by disclosure, a court should not exercise its right to inspect. Having referred to dicta in *Conway* v *Rimmer* [1968] AC 910, and *Council of Civil Service Unions* v *Minister for the Civil Service* [1985] AC 374 highlighting the importance of the courts showing due deference to ministerial claims to be acting to protect national security, Russell LJ. observed:

> '[Counsel for the appellant] boldly invites this court to depart from these powerful dicta, contending that they were obiter and that in the society in which we now live the time is right for what he described as a more open approach when issues of national security are raised by the appropriate ministers. Even if not constrained by authority we firmly decline to accept that invitation, for it seems to us to be contrary to principle and to good sense. In this case the court has not abdicated its responsibility, but it has recognised the constraints placed upon it by the terms of the certificates issued by the executive. There must always be vigilance by the courts to ensure that public interest immunity of whatever kind is raised only in appropriate circumstances and with appropriate particularity, but once there is an actual or potential risk to national security demonstrated by an appropriate certificate the court should not exercise its right to inspect.'

The House of Lords' decision in *Air Canada* v *Secretary of State for Trade* [1983] 1 All ER 910, serves to indicate the issues in respect of which the party seeking disclosure must persuade the court. The plaintiffs were a group of major international airlines wishing to contest the validity of increases in landing charges at Heathrow Airport. Their case was that the Minister had acted ultra vires in authorising the increases, in that charges were being increased in pursuit of a central government policy of reducing public expenditure, and not because charges in reality had to be increased. In order to substantiate this claim the airlines sought discovery of documents containing details of communications between ministers, and memoranda produced for the use of ministers at meetings – all documents related to the development of government policy. The Secretary of State tendered the necessary certificates claiming that the documents should not be produced, but the trial judge chose to inspect them.

A majority of their Lordships took the view that, given the nature of the adversarial system, the task of the court was to decide a case fairly between the parties on the evidence available, and not to ascertain some independent truth by seeking out evidence of its own accord. Thus a party was free, if he so wished, to withhold information that would help his opponent's case. It followed that a party seeking to compel the other party or an independent person to disclose information was required to show that the information was likely to help his own case or damage his adversary's case, in the sense that there was a reasonable probability and not just a mere speculative belief that it would do so. Furthermore, that principle applied both at the stage of a private inspection of documents by the judge and at the later stage of ordering production of the documents to the other party, since the purpose of a private inspection was to determine whether production should be ordered. As any information contained in the ministerial documents would almost certainly tend merely to repeat published information already known to, and relied upon, by the plaintiffs and would be unlikely to assist the plaintiffs further, it was felt that the case for inspection of the documents had not been made out. Note that Lord Fraser went so far as to suggest that, in some situations, even cabinet papers would not be immune from disclosure: see further *R* v *Secretary of State for Foreign Affairs, ex parte World Development Movement Ltd* (1994) The Times 27 December.

Lords Scarman and Templeman expressed the view that, although the court should order inspection of documents when it considered that their disclosure might materially assist either of the parties or the court in determining the issues, and not merely when the party seeking production established that the documents were likely to assist his own case, it was nevertheless for the party seeking production to establish that the documents were likely to be necessary for fairly disposing of the issues. On the facts, the plaintiffs had failed to do that in respect of the ministerial documents.

In some respects the decision can be seen as evidence of a hardening of attitude as regards in applications for disclosure. A number of practical considerations arise. Should a trial judge inspect evidence (documents) in the absence of one party, decline to order disclosure and then proceed with the case? Is there any possibility that this might amount to a breach of natural justice? A plaintiff may need discovery of a document before he can make out his case. He will not be granted discovery unless he can explain to the court the way in which the document in question will help his case or damage his opponent's. A plaintiff may, therefore, be caught in a 'Catch 22' situation – until he reads a document he will not know whether it will help him, but unless he can explain how its contents will help him, discovery will not be ordered. In *HIV Haemophiliac Litigation* [1990] NLJ 1349, where the plaintiffs sought discovery of documents relating to the formulation of the Department of Health's policy of self-sufficiency in blood products, Ralph Gibson LJ, for the court, expressed the view that establishing a cause of action was not of itself sufficient to justify disclosure. He adopted the test propounded by Lord Fraser in *Air Canada* v *Secretary of State for Trade* to the effect that the party seeking disclosure should demonstrate that:

> '... the documents are very likely to contain material which would give substantial support to his contention on an issue which arises in the case and that, without them, he might be deprived of the means of "proper presentation of his case".'

It is interesting to speculate how much that which Ralph Gibson LJ referred to as the 'great public interest and concern' aroused by the case led the court to boldly brush aside the Department's protestations regarding the damage that would be done to the operation of the National Health Service by the production of these documents.

Summary

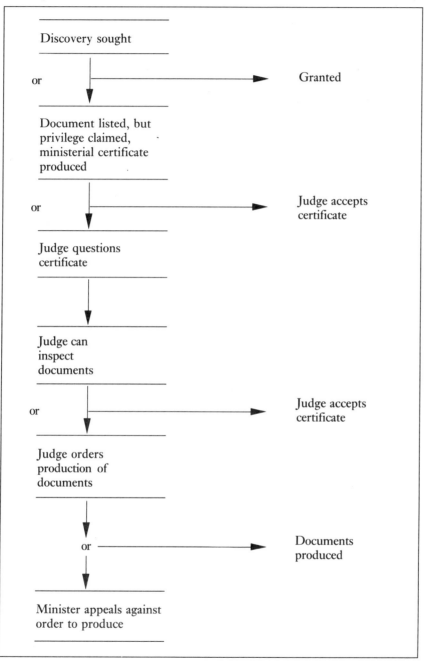

5.3 Grounds for resisting disclosure

It is traditional to identify two grounds for non-disclosure of documents: either because they belong to a class of document that ought to be protected, eg Cabinet papers, or because of their contents, eg the design drawings for a piece of military hardware. Given the current trends revealed in the case law it is useful to divide the authorities into the following three groups, although they are by no means mutually exclusive.

Undermining the administration of government

These are cases where production of documents has been resisted on the basis that it would be injurious to the efficient running of government. For example, collective responsibility is generally regarded as being an essential constitutional convention; thus in *Attorney-General* v *Jonathan Cape Ltd* [1976] QB 752, Lord Widgery CJ stated that:

> '... no court will compel production of Cabinet papers in the course of discovery in an action'.

And Lord Reid in *Conway* v *Rimmer* (see 5.2 above) observed:

> 'Virtually everyone agrees that Cabinet minutes and the like ought not to be disclosed until such time as they are only of historical interest. But I do not think that many people would give as the reason that premature disclosure would prevent candour in the Cabinet. To my mind the most important reason is that such disclosure would create or fan ill-informed or captious public or political criticism. The business of government is difficult enough as it is, and no government could contemplate with equanimity the inner workings of the government machine being exposed to the gaze of those ready to criticise without adequate knowledge of the background and perhaps with some axe to grind. And that must, in my view, also apply to all documents concerned with policy making within departments including, it may be, minutes and the like by quite junior officials and correspondence with outside bodies. Further, it may be that deliberations about a particular case require protection as much as deliberations about policy.'

This protective approach towards the administration is reflected in decisions such as *Evans* v *Chief Constable of Surrey* (1988) The Times 21 January, where the applicant was seeking to bring an action for damages for wrongful imprisonment against the police, following his detention in connection with a murder case, and the court refused to grant the applicant access to papers that had been sent by the Chief Constable to the Director of Public Prosecutions about the case, feeling that it was of paramount importance that the police should be able to communicate with, and seek advice from, the DPP without fear of these communications subsequently being used in court as evidence. This remained the case even where a prosecution was successfully completed. See further *R* v *DPP, ex parte Hallas* (1987) The Times 11 December, wherein the court acted to prevent the disclosure of evidence collated by the Crown Prosecution Service, which was sought for the purpose of bringing a private prosecution for causing death by reckless driving.

In *Burmah Oil* v *Bank of England* [1980] AC 1090, the House of Lords had to consider claims of privilege relating to documents concerned with the formation of government policy, and documents containing information given in confidence by businessmen to the Bank of England. Lord Wilberforce felt that, given the obvious importance of the documents as regards policy formulation, there was no question of their being produced. The majority expressed a variety of views, all of which were in favour of inspection, but in the event the documents were found not to have anything recorded in them that needed to be disclosed for fairly disposing of the case. Lords Scarman and Keith both doubted the excessive weight given in past cases to the need to secure secrecy for those giving information in confidence, or for civil servants who needed to feel free to state their opinions, and Lord Scarman felt that the 'candour' argument was only really appropriate where a civil servant was advising a minister on a matter of national security. This more 'open' approach was reflected in *Williams* v *Home Office (No 2)* [1981] 1 All ER 1151. The plaintiff was a prisoner who wished to challenge the legality of his transfer to a special 'control unit'. The Home Office, on an application for discovery, resisted production of 23 documents containing details of communications between ministers, and records of meetings between ministers and officials, on the ground that their production would inhibit full and frank discussions between the parties concerned. In the event disclosure of six of the documents was allowed, McNeill J ruling that the danger of injustice to the plaintiff overrode the Home Office's objections.

Formal complaints procedures

Although the courts have not extended the protection of public interest immunity to formal statements of complaint (for example, complaints made pursuant to s49 of the Police Act 1964: *Conerney* v *Jacklin* (1985) The Times 2 February) they have in the past, perhaps understandably, been reluctant to permit the disclosure of statements made during the course of statutory complaints procedures (such as that now provided for under the Police and Criminal Evidence Act 1984), on the basis that the subsequent use of any such evidence in later civil proceedings might have the effect of inhibiting individuals from co-operating with the inquiry or investigation. This reluctance manifested itself in decisions such as *Neilson* v *Laugharne* [1981] QB 736, and *Makanjuola* v *Commissioner of Police of the Metropolis and Another* [1992] 3 All ER 617. In the former case Lord Denning MR referred to statements made in the course of an investigation of a complaint against the police as being privileged from production in a manner that was analogous to legal professional privilege. In the latter case discovery was refused even though the plaintiff was seeking disclosure of a statement she herself had made, on the ground that it would be unwise to create a situation where the makers of such statements, made in the course of complaints investigation procedures, might be at risk of being pressurised into consenting to disclosure.

Whilst there is an acknowledged need to balance the public's interest in the proper functioning of administrative devices such as complaints procedures, with the individual's right to justice, it was arguable that the effect of these decisions was to go much further than was necessary to protect the administrative process, a view reflected in a number of decisions that suggested a reluctance on the part of some members of the judiciary to give full effect to restrictive consequences of *Neilson*. First, in *Peach* v *Commissioner of Police of the Metropolis* [1986] 2 WLR 1080, the Court of Appeal upheld the Divisional Court's decision to order the production of documents containing answers to questionnaires obtained by the police during the investigation into the death of Blair Peach during a demonstration in Southall. The Court of Appeal rejected the contention that the documents concerned belonged to a 'class' that should not, in the public interest, be disclosed. *Neilson* was distinguished on the basis that it had concerned a private inquiry, where the applicant for discovery had been 'fishing', whereas in the present case there was a public interest in the documents being disclosed for use in a public inquiry, and the applicant was not 'fishing' as it was well known that answers in the questionnaires contained information which would enable the applicant to further her case in some way.

Secondly, the need to ensure justice for the individual clearly outweighed the public interest in confidentiality in *ex parte Coventry Newspapers Ltd* [1992] 3 WLR 936. The applicants were the proprietors of a newspaper that had carried an article concerning the activities of members of the West Midlands Serious Crimes Squad. The officers concerned had been involved in a case that resulted in B being convicted of unlawful wounding. B complained to the West Midlands Police about malpractice by officers in relation to his evidence. Thereafter, officers who had been involved in his case were allowed unsupervised access to the Crown Court file on B's case, and certain key interview notes went missing. The officers concerned were suspended from duty, but subsequently reinstated, following the Chief Constable's ruling that the investigation had produced no proof that the officers had tampered with B's file. The article in question cast doubt on the significance of these reinstatements, and the officers concerned commenced proceedings for libel. Meanwhile B's case was referred to the Court of Appeal by the Home Secretary, and in order for it to be prepared, B was granted access to the evidence collected by the Police Complaints Authority in the course of its investigation of the officers. Access had been allowed on the undertaking that B would only use the evidence in support of the reference. The Court of Appeal quashed B's conviction, a result directly related to the evidence revealed by the Authority's investigations, and granted the newspaper a variation of that order in order so as to allow access to the evidence for preparation of the libel defence. Lord Taylor CJ expressed the view that those who had given statements to the Authority during its investigation would not be aggrieved at seeing those statements being made available to defend a potentially corrupt claim for damages by the officers concerned. In his Lordship's view justice required that the libel allegations should be tested in the courts, and that the newspaper should be supplied with the necessary evidence to defend the matter. He observed:

'If, as the wider public now have every reason to suspect, these documents appear to point clearly towards corruption on the part of the named officers, it is surely not to be tolerated that those same officers should continue to mulct the press in damages whilst the courts disable their adversaries from an effective defence by withholding the documents from them.'

Whilst Lord Taylor CJ did not seek to distinguish the *Coventry* case from *Neilson*, the fact that he felt compelled to support disclosure in the interests of justice clearly called into question the rationale of *Neilson* and the subsequent decisions that sought to apply it.

It fell to the House of Lords in *R v Chief Constable of West Midlands, ex parte Wiley, R v Chief Constable of Nottinghamshire Police, ex parte Sunderland* [1994] 3 WLR 433, to go some considerable way towards resolving the issue. In two separate trials the applicants were acquitted following the decision of the prosecution to offer no evidence. Both applicants instituted complaints to the Police Complaints Authority and civil actions for damages. Given the state of the law at the time, neither applicant was allowed access to the complaints file in order to prepare for the civil action, hence solicitors for the applicants had sought undertakings from the respondents to the effect that they would not rely on, or make use of, any information, provided by the applicants in the course of their complaints to the authority. The undertakings were refused, and the applicants sought judicial review of these refusals; the second applicant also sought an injunction to prevent the Chief Constable from using the material in question. At first instance Popplewell J granted the relief sought and the Chief Constables' appeals to the Court of Appeal were dismissed. On appeal to the House of Lords it was argued by both sides that public interest immunity did not attach to the documents collated in the course of an investigation into complaints against the police under Part IX of the Police and Criminal Evidence Act 1984. Allowing the appeals, and in the process overruling *Neilson, Hehir v Commissioner of Police of the Metropolis* [1982] 1 WLR 715, *Makanjuola v Commissioner of Police of the Metropolis* (above) and *Halford v Sharples* [1992] 1 WLR 736, the House of Lords held that there was no compelling case for the creation of a new category of class based public interest immunity in respect of statements made during police complaints investigations, as had been suggested in the earlier cases. The House of Lords did not, however, rule out the possibility of statements made during complaints investigations attracting immunity on a contents basis, as may be the position with, for example, statements made by police informers. Lord Browne-Wilkinson, expressly rejecting the contentions in *Neilson* to the effect that immunity was required to prevent police officers and other witnesses from being inhibited by the fear that their statements might subsequently be used in civil proceedings, and that the need to check statements individually to see if they should be the subject of a 'contents' claim placed too heavy a burden on the police, observed that the Police Complaints Authority itself no longer supported the automatic 'class' immunity that followed from the *Neilson* decision. In agreement Lord Woolf added that despite Lord Hailsham's comments in *D v National Society for the Prevention of Cruelty to Children* [1978] AC 171, to the effect that the categories of public interest were not closed and must alter from time to time as social changes required, no sufficient case had been made out to justify the class of public interest immunity erroneously created by the Court of Appeal in *Neilson*.

Information given in confidence

This subdivision of privilege claims is to some extent artificial, as a number of cases fall into several categories, as both *Burmah Oil* v *Bank of England* and *Neilson* v *Laugharne* illustrate. The cases detailed below, however, do turn more on the point that the information sought was given in confidence rather than on the fact that documents contained records of meetings between certain persons, or ministerial communications on policy formation. In *Rodgers* v *Home Secretary* (above), documents containing information given by police informers to the Gaming Board were held to be privileged, on the grounds that anonymity had been promised to the informers and that the Board would be unable to function properly if its supply of information were to 'dry up'. Similarly, in *Alfred Crompton Amusement Machines Ltd* v *Customs and Excise Commissioners (No 2)* [1974] AC 405 information given in confidence to the Inland Revenue was held to be privileged. Again, the fear that such information might become difficult to obtain if sources were disclosed was a paramount consideration. See also *D* v *NSPCC* [1978] AC 171, where the identity of an informant supplying evidence of alleged child abuse was held to be privileged, again to protect the continued supply of information.

The principle has been reaffirmed in *Bookbinder* v *Tebbit* [1992] 1 WLR 217, where the court refused to order disclosure of statements and other documents from Audit Commission employees who had been investigating a local authority's finances. The plaintiff, the leader of the local authority concerned, sought to use the documents in support of a libel action. Drake J expressed the view that public interest immunity should extend to evidence obtained by the Audit Commission during its investigations, particularly that which might disclose the identity of informants, since the Commission performed a public duty of inquiring into the legality of public expenditure, and the performance of that duty might be hampered if informants felt less at ease about coming forward.

6

Introduction to Tribunals and Inquiries

6.1 Introduction

6.2 The Report of the Committee on Administrative Tribunals and Inquiries

6.3 The Council on Tribunals

6.1 Introduction

Tribunals were conceived principally as an alternative form of dispute resolution. Parliament enacts legislation giving effect to particular policy aims, perhaps the setting up of a welfare scheme, licensing, or rent regulation. The legislation provides for the setting up of tribunals for the resolution of disputes arising from the operation of the scheme. Such disputes could obviously be left to be resolved by the courts, but in many cases Parliament views it as inappropriate for such problems to be dealt with by means of fullscale litigation, with all its attendant drawbacks. Since 1945 there has been a proliferation of administrative tribunals dealing with many aspects of public life, largely mirroring the changing role of the state in modern society. The operation of tribunals and the extent of judicial control exercised over them is considered further in Chapter 7.

Inquiries take a number of forms, but their chief purpose is usually the conduct of an investigation of some sort, whether into planning proposals, natural disasters or political scandals. Unlike tribunals, where the body concerned will be a decision-making one, inquiries usually produce reports, written by inquiry inspectors, with the subsequent decision being taken by a different administrative body such as a minister, although provisions exist for decisions to be taken by the inquiry inspector himself. The operation of inquiries is considered in more depth in Chapter 8.

The principal concern of this chapter is to consider the Report of the Committee on Administrative Tribunals and Inquiries, which provided the basis of the modern system of tribunals and inquiries, and the role of the Council on Tribunals.

6.2 The Report of the Committee on Administrative Tribunals and Inquiries

Background

Since the early part of the twentieth century, concern had been growing about the scope and power of the administration; the Report on Ministers' Powers (1932) (see Chapter 2) evidenced this. Little came of that report, however, and it was not until the post-war period that any thorough going review of administrative processes was initiated. Particular concern existed regarding the independence of many tribunals, and also the extent to which their decisions were beyond the control of the courts. Similarly, with inquiries, there was widespread dissatisfaction with procedures adopted and ministerial responses to inspectors' reports. The response of the Government was the setting up of a committee under Sir Oliver Franks to review the operation of such bodies (hereinafter referred to as the 'Franks Committee'). Its report was published in 1957 (Cmnd 218, hereinafter referred to as the 'Franks Report').

Terms of reference

The Franks Committee explained its own scope of reference as follows:

> 'Our terms of reference involve the consideration of an important part of the relationship between the individual and authority. At different times in the history of this country it has been necessary to adjust this relationship and to seek a new balance between private rights and public advantage, between fair play for the individual and efficiency of administration. The balance found has varied with different governmental systems and different social patterns. Since the war the British electorate has chosen Governments which accepted general responsibilities for the provision of extended social services and for the broad management of the economy. It has consequently become desirable to consider afresh the procedures by which the rights of individual citizens can be harmonised with wider public interests.' (Part 1; chapter 2, para 5)

The Franks Committee was subsequently criticised for confining its investigation to procedures which were basically sound anyway. As the Committee stated in its own report (Chapter 2, para 9), it was concerned only with decisions subject to some statutory procedure – not decisions where no formal procedure was prescribed. Such an approach is criticised because many of the most important administrative decisions affecting the individual's rights and liberties were taken without any formal statutory procedure having to be followed; by adopting these narrow terms of reference the Franks Committee inevitably shut its eyes to those aspects of administrative decision-making most in need of scrutiny.

As the Committee itself observed:

> 'It follows therefore that the celebrated case of Crichel Down, which is widely regarded as a principal reason for our appointment, itself in fact falls outside the subjects with which

we have been asked to deal. It is true that an enquiry was held in this case, but it was an ad hoc enquiry for which there was no statutory requirement. It resulted from the exercise of those informal methods of raising objections to which we have referred, and was therefore unlike the enquiries with which we are concerned.'

Committee's findings regarding tribunals

The Committee affirmed its view that, in laying down procedures for tribunals, Parliament was assumed to be seeking to promote good administration and public confidence in the decisions of tribunals. Its Report states:

'Administration must not only be efficient in the sense that the objectives of policy are securely attained without delay. It must also satisfy the general body of citizens that it is proceeding with reasonable regard to the balance between the public interest which it promotes and the private interest which it disturb … adjudications must be acceptable as having been properly made. It is natural that Parliament should have taken this view of what constitutes good administration. In this country government rests fundamentally upon the consent of the governed. The general acceptability of these adjudications is one of the vital elements in sustaining that consent.'

Openness, fairness and impartiality were identified by the Committee as essential characteristics of tribunal procedures. As the Report states:

'Take openness. If these procedures were wholly secret, the basis of confidence and acceptability would be lacking. Next take fairness. If the objector were not allowed to state his case, there would be nothing to stop oppression. Thirdly, there is impartiality. How can the citizen be satisfied unless he feels that those who decide his case come to their decision with open minds?

Difference in the nature of the issue for adjudication may give good reason for difference in the degree to which the three general characteristics should be developed and applied. Again, the method by which a Minister arrives at a decision after a hearing or enquiry cannot be the same as that by which a tribunal arrives at a decision. This difference is brought out later in the Report. For the moment it is sufficient to point out that when Parliament sets up a tribunal to decide cases, the adjudication is placed outside the Department concerned. The members of the tribunal are neutral and impartial in relation to the policy of the Minister, except in so far as that policy is contained in the rules which the tribunal has been set up to apply. But the Minister, deciding in the cases under the second part of our terms of reference, is committed to a policy which he has been charged by Parliament to carry out. In this sense he is not, and cannot be, impartial.'

The Committee concluded that tribunals were not to be viewed as courts of law, but neither were they to be regarded as appendages of Government departments. It seems clear from the tenor of its Report, however, that the Committee saw tribunals as being closer to courts than to the machinery of administration. There was no evidence found of partiality among tribunal members, and the Committee was satisfied with the degree of independence from central government, but it did recommend that the appointment of chairmen should be the responsibility of the Lord Chancellor, and that chairmen should ordinarily be legally qualified. On this issue the Report provides:

'We appreciate the force of the contention that all appointments to tribunals should be made by the Lord Chancellor so as to demonstrate clearly the intention that tribunals should be wholly independent of departmental influence. But we feel that the best practical course would be for the responsibility of the Lord Chancellor for such appointments not to be extended beyond the chairman, though we consider that he should retain his present responsibility for appointing members of certain tribunals and that there may be scope for extending this responsibility to a few other tribunals.

Although we are unable to recommend that all members of tribunals should be appointed by the Lord Chancellor we are satisfied that their appointment should not rest with the Ministers concerned with the subject-matter of the adjudications. In order to enhance the independence of tribunals, both in appearance and in fact, we consider that the Council on Tribunals should make these appointments. We see no need for the Council to review any existing appointments.'

The Committee rejected the proposal that clerks to tribunals should be drawn from a newly created corps of clerks under the Lord Chancellor's Department, the reasoning being that a career structure might be difficult to create for such persons. Given that the role of the clerk can be very influential, and that they are frequently seconded from relevant government departments, thus giving rise to doubts as to their impartiality, this reasoning of the Committee has always seemed difficult to support. The Report provides:

'The practice whereby the majority of clerks of tribunals are provided by the Government Departments concerned from their local and regional staffs seems partly to be responsible for the feeling in the minds of some people that tribunals are dependent upon and influenced by those Departments. Not only for this reason but also because there would appear to be advantages in improving the general quality of tribunal clerks we have considered the possibility of establishing under the Lord Chancellor's Department a central corps of clerks from which a service could be provided for all tribunals.

Though this idea has many attractions we have, after careful consideration, rejected it. It would have the advantage of further enhancing the independence of tribunals, and it would be more appropriate for independent clerks to advise and help applicants than for departmental clerks to do so. The main objection is that it is difficult to see how any reasonable prospect of a career could be held out to the members of such a general service. It would also be difficult to arrange sittings for the various tribunals in one area in such a way that the clerks were fully occupied and the tribunals could meet when most convenient to the members. Finally, it would no longer be possible for the social service departments to give some members of their staff a period of service as clerks of tribunals which is doubtless valuable in developing the outlook appropriate to the administration of a social service.

We therefore consider that the present arrangements for providing clerks of tribunals should continue. In order, however, to ensure that departmental clerks cannot exercise a departmental influence upon tribunals, we regard it as essential that their duties and conduct should be regulated on the advice of the Council on Tribunals. The general principles to be followed are that the duties of a clerk should be confined to secretarial work, the taking of such notes of evidence as may be required and the tendering of advice, when requested, on points connected with the tribunal's functions. Like a magistrates' clerk he should be debarred from retiring with the tribunal when they consider their decision, unless he is sent for to advise on a specific point.'

The Report made no effective recommendations as to standardisation of procedures at tribunals, which is possibly one of its major failings. On the need for a more informal atmosphere at tribunal hearings it stated:

'Informality without rules of procedure may be positively inimical to right adjudication, since the proceedings may well assume an unordered character which makes it difficult, if not impossible, for the tribunal properly to sift the facts and weigh the evidence. It should here be remembered that by their very nature tribunals may well be less skilled in adjudication than courts of law. None of our witnesses would seek to make tribunals in all respects like courts of law, but there is a wide measure of agreement that in many instances their procedure could be made more orderly without impairing the desired informality of atmosphere. The object to be aimed at in most tribunals is the combination of a formal procedure with an informal atmosphere. We see no reason why this cannot be achieved. On the one hand it means a manifestly sympathetic attitude on the part of the tribunal and the absence of the trappings of a court, but on the other hand such prescription of procedure as makes the proceedings clear and orderly.'

The Committee was of the view that proceedings should be in public wherever possible, with in camera sessions only being necessary in cases involving national security, financial details personal to the individual involved or the professional reputation of the individual involved. Where possible the Committee felt that reasons should be given for a tribunal's decision, preferably in writing. The Committee generally favoured the proposition that each tribunal should have an appellate body to deal with appeals on fact, law or merits, save where the tribunal of first instance was exceptionally well qualified, and was firmly of the opinion that appeal on a point of law should lie from all tribunal decisions to the High Court.

The Committee's findings regarding inquiries

Most of the evidence before the Franks Committee concerned the workings of inquiries dealing with land use. The Committee saw inquiries as having a two-fold purpose, to provide an opportunity for public participation in decision-making and to enable a minister to arrive at a better informed decision. As to the question of whether inquiries were administrative or judicial in nature, the Committee commented:

'Our general conclusion is that these procedures cannot be classified as purely administrative or purely judicial. They are not purely administrative because of the provision for a special procedure preliminary to the decision – a feature not to be found in the ordinary course of administration – and because this procedure, as we have shown, involves the testing of an issue, often partly in public. They are not on the other hand purely judicial, because the final decision cannot be reached by the application of rules and must allow the exercise of a wide discretion in the balancing of public and private interest. Neither view at its extreme is tenable, nor should either be emphasised at the expense of the other.

If the administrative view is dominant the public enquiry cannot play its full part in the total process, and there is a danger that the rights and interests of the individual citizens affected will not be sufficiently protected. In these cases it is idle to argue that Parliament can be relied upon to protect the citizen, save exceptionally. We agree with the following views expressed in the pamphlet entitled *Rule of Law*: "Whatever the theoretical validity of this argument, those of us who are Members of Parliament have no hesitation in saying that it bears little relation to reality. Parliament has neither the time nor the knowledge to supervise the Minister and call him to account for his administrative decisions."

If the judicial view is dominant there is a danger that people will regard the person before whom they state their case as a kind of judge provisionally deciding the matter, subject to an appeal to the Minister. This view overlooks the true nature of the proceeding, the form of which is necessitated by the fact that the Minister himself, who is responsible to Parliament for the ultimate decision, cannot conduct the enquiry in person.

Most of the evidence which we have received, other than the evidence from Government Departments, has placed greater emphasis on judicial aspects of the procedure. The view is that present procedure, either in regard to actual law or to practice, does not sufficiently reflect the essentially adjudicative nature of the process. From the point of view of the citizen, what begins in many ways like an action at law, with two or more parties appearing before a judge-like inspector and stating their case to him, usually in public, is thereafter suddenly removed from public gaze until the ministerial decision is made. Often the main factors at the enquiry seem to have counted for little in the final decision. New factors – they may have been considerations of broad policy – have come in so that the final decision does not seem to flow from the proceedings at the enquiry.

... we shall ... address ourselves to the task of finding a reasonable balance between the conflicting interests. On the one hand there are Ministers and other administrative authorities enjoined by legislation to carry out certain duties. On the other hand there are the rights and feelings of individual citizens who find their possessions or plans interfered with by the administration. There is also the public interest, which requires both that Ministers and other administrative authorities should not be frustrated in carrying out their duties and also that their decisions should be subject to effective checks or controls, and these, as we have pointed out, can no longer be applied by Parliament in the general run of cases.'

The Committee further recommended that the case against which objections were being raised at an inquiry should be clearly made out, and the objections themselves developed with sufficient detail to permit proper consideration. As regards the position of inquiry inspectors, and the respective merits and demerits of both departmental and independent inspectors, the Committee recommended that inspectors be brought under the control of the Lord Chancellor's Department, thereby stressing their unquestioned independence and impartiality. It was nevertheless accepted that inspectors would have to be kept informed of central government policy, where appropriate. Many of these recommendations now form part of the Town and Country Planning (Inquiries Procedure) Rules 1992 (SI 1992/2038).

Reaction to the Franks Report

The achievements of the Franks Committee should not be underestimated. Most, if not all, of its recommendations were implemented, albeit in a substantially modified form in some cases, and the details of these reforms are given, where appropriate, in the two following chapters. In addition to addressing the constitutional and procedural aspects of the work of tribunals and inquiries, however, the Franks Committee is largely responsible for the creation of the Council on Tribunals, a body having a potentially important supervisory role.

6.3 The Council on Tribunals

Creation

In paragraph 43 of the Franks Report, the Committee recommended the setting up of standing councils in England and Scotland:

> '... to keep the constitution and working of tribunals under continuous review ...'

It further recommended that the councils should be consulted whenever it was proposed to establish a new type of tribunal; they should have the power to appoint tribunal members, formulate procedural rules for tribunals and advise on associated matters. The Council on Tribunals was eventually brought to life by the Tribunals and Inquiries Act 1958 – now 1992. As will be seen, the Council was not blessed with quite the range of powers envisaged by the Franks Committee.

Powers and functions of the Council

The primary function of the Council is to keep under review the constitution and working of the tribunals specified in Schedule 1 to the Tribunals and Inquiries Act 1992. It is also required to consider and report on particular matters referred to the Council by the Lord Chancellor and the Lord Advocate with respect to any tribunal other than an ordinary court of law, whether or not specified in Schedule 1 to the 1992 Act; and to consider and report on such matters as may be so referred, or which the Council may consider to be of special importance, with respect to administrative procedures which may involve the holding by or on behalf of a minister of a statutory inquiry. The Council has to be consulted by the appropriate rule-making authority before the procedural rules are made for any tribunal specified in Schedule 1 to the 1992 Act, and similarly for procedural rules made by the Lord Chancellor in connection with statutory inquiries. It must also be consulted before any tribunal is exempted from the requirement of giving reasons for its decision under s12 of the Tribunals and Inquiries Act 1992. The Council can make recommendations to relevant ministers on tribunal membership, and is required to make an annual report to the Lord Chancellor on the workings of the tribunal and inquiry system.

Staffing and operation of the Council

There are between ten and 15 part-time members, a number of whom are lawyers, generally appointed for terms of three years. The Parliamentary Commissioner for

Administration is an ex officio member. The Council meets 11 times a year. Some members visit tribunals and inquiries to see them in operation, and members have frequent meetings with representatives of government departments. The Council possesses a small secretariat and has to deal with a considerable volume of communications from the general public.

The contribution of the Council on Tribunals

In 1980 the report entitled *The Functions of the Council on Tribunals*, Cmnd 7805, stated:

> 'Our most important contribution over the years has, we believe, been our constant effort to translate the general ideals of the Franks Committee into workable codes of principles and practice, accepted and followed by all those who are responsible for setting up administrative tribunals, devising their manner of operation and, indeed, serving upon them as chairmen and members.'

The Council has succeeded in promoting the standardisation of procedures at statutory inquiries and in ensuring an effective implementation of the Franks Committee's goals of fairness, openness and impartiality. It has been influential as regards the content of draft legislation and in developing a convention of prior consultation by government departments. Furthermore, the Council has promoted the 'presidential' system of organising tribunals, whereby a particular class of tribunal has a national president or chairman – thus providing for better communications between tribunals of the same class. In addition, the Council has published guidelines for tribunal members and helped organise training conferences and meetings of chairmen.

On the debit side, the Council, while under a duty to review the workings of specified tribunals, has no corresponding duty as regards statutory inquiries. Its power to consider and report on the workings of certain tribunals is limited, while no such limit exists on its power to report on the workings of inquiries. By its own admission the council is understaffed and underfinanced. To be more effective it requires full-time members meeting on a more regular basis. Its powers are consultative and advisory, not executive. In short the Council can achieve nothing of its own volition. It cannot appoint tribunal members, nor make binding procedural rules independently of the Lord Chancellor. There is no requirement that the Council be consulted during the drafting of primary legislation, and it lacks any statutory jurisdiction to deal with complaints from members of the public. In *The Functions of the Council on Tribunals* the Council itself proposed:

> '... that we should be given specific responsibility for complaints in relation to our field of works, it is important that the extent of our jurisdiction be clearly defined. The power could be on the following lines:
>
> A member of the public alleging a procedural irregularity in a hearing before a tribunal or statutory inquiry would be entitled to make a formal complaint to us;
>
> We would then have to consider whether the complaint prima facie raised a substantial point of principle relating to procedure;

If we came to that conclusion, we would be empowered to obtain papers and other information from the relevant tribunal or inquiry and from the Government department concerned, to question the complainant and any other person involved, and to submit a report to the complainant, the department and, at our discretion, to anyone else ...

If we decided that the complaint did not prima facie raise a substantial point of principle we would refer the matter without comment to the department concerned, who would be required to report to us the outcome of their own enquiries.

In addition to this action on complaints from members of the public, we would be empowered at our discretion to conduct an investigation into an alleged procedural irregularity referred to us by the department concerned. We would not, however, at any time investigate a complaint relating to the merits of a decision or recommendation; or concerning the conduct of chairmen or members; or which fell within the competence of the Parliamentary Commissioners; or which could reasonably form the basis for an appeal or some other proceeding in a court of law ...

This solution would not remove the slight overlap of functions between the Parliamentary Commissioner and ourselves, which already exists. The Parliamentary Commissioner would retain his jurisdiction to investigate complaints of maladministration against Government departments in relation to procedures which included public inquiries, and in relation to the pre-hearing and post-decision administrative handling by departments of matters referred to tribunals. Our jurisdiction would be limited to the form and operation of procedures, but within that limitation it would extend to events which took place within the doors of the tribunal or inquiry.'

At present the Council lacks the resources for carrying out any detailed research into the workings of the tribunal and inquiry system. There are no formal channels through which it can carry out such monitoring. Finally, it is generally accepted that the Council has failed to stop the proliferation in the number of tribunals, and has further failed to introduce anything approaching a standardised procedure for such bodies.

Conclusion

It should be evident from the above that the hopes of the Franks Committee as regards the Council on Tribunals were only partly realised. The Council itself is strongly of the view that it needs much wider powers and a much expanded administrative support if it is to function properly. It has been entrusted with an increasingly important yet complex task, and in failing to discharge its duties properly it can fairly point the finger of blame at successive governments which have failed to take the action necessary to rectify the situation. For the present it seems as though the Council will continue its good work as best it can, providing administrative lawyers with an invaluable insight into how the administrative machine operates, by means of its annual reports. As the 1980 report *The Functions of the Council on Tribunals* concludes:

'The case for a statutory advisory body with ... (a) ... general oversight appears to us to be even stronger now than at the time of the Franks Committee. Since then the tendency for issues arising out of legislative schemes to be referred to tribunals has continued unabated, in a largely piecemeal manner. Not only has there been considerable growth in the number of tribunals, they are operating increasingly in difficult and sensitive areas – for example, immigration, compulsory detention under mental health legislation, misuse of drugs, equal pay, redundancy, unfair dismissal from employment, and supplementary benefits.

Moreover, the changed situation since 1957 is not confined to tribunals. Statutory inquiries have assumed an increasingly controversial role. Planning, redevelopment, land usage, highway policy, siting of major airports, development of natural resources and exploitation of new sources of energy are raising issues of a greater order of magnitude than those current at the time of the Franks Committee. Our position as an independent statutory advisory body with the broadest range of knowledge in this field is being recognised by Ministers, Government departments and other organisations.

Since we were set up, significant changes have also taken place in the general constitutional and administrative climate. There is, for example, a movement towards greater formalism in procedures for settling disputes. The process started with reforms following the Franks Report which, in general, made tribunals more like courts. It had to be demonstrated that tribunals were not adjuncts of Government departments and that in their decision-making they followed a judicial process. Since then the trend towards judicialisation has gathered momentum with the result that tribunals are becoming more formal, expensive and procedurally complex. Consequently they tend to become more difficult for an ordinary citizen to comprehend and cope with on his own. There is, we believe, an urgent need to keep the whole of this movement under the closest scrutiny. We believe that we are in a position to play a key role in the achievement of a right balance.

There is also a constant need, as was emphasised in discussion with our Committee, for an independent body able to offer advice to Government on what kinds of dispute are appropriate or inappropriate for adjudication by tribunals. We believe that we can exercise this function, and can develop criteria indicating the kinds of decision which, if disputed, should be subject to review by processes external to the departments concerned; the most appropriate form of review; the degree of formality required, according to the type of decision; and whether a proposed tribunal should come under our supervision.

Finally, we draw attention to particular problems running across the whole field which need co-ordinated rather than piecemeal approach: for example, a much wider system for recruitment of tribunal members, including more women; arrangements for training of both chairmen and members; the presidential system; conferences and seminars; the publication of explanatory leaflets; and the clarification and simplification of official forms.

... At present, we are perhaps in a better position than any other official body to appreciate the wider implications of the particular matters referred to us, and to consider the important issues relating to the system as a statutory power of the Council to act as a general advisory body in the field of administrative adjudication be placed beyond doubt.'

7

Tribunals

7.1 Why tribunals ?

7.2 Constitution and membership

7.3 Tribunal procedure

7.4 Challenge in the courts and diagrammatic summary

7.1 Why tribunals?

The tasks performed by tribunals can, to a large extent be divided into two categories: the resolution of disputes between the individual and the state, and the resolution of disputes between private individuals. Examples of the former include Mental Health Review Tribunals, entrusted with the task of reviewing the continued detention of persons suffering from mental disorders, where they have been made the subjects of compulsory hospital attendance orders; various National Health Service Tribunals dealing with such diverse matters as complaints against general practitioners, and other matters relating to services provided by National Health Service personnel; and Income Tax Commissioners, dealing with disputed assessments of liability to pay taxation. The best example of the second is the Industrial Tribunal, the jurisdiction of which extends to matters such as unfair dismissal, sex discrimination in employment, redundancy payments, and health and safety at work issues.

In entrusting decision-making to a tribunal, Parliament will have made a conscious choice between various other methods of dispute resolution. Where the problem is one of resolving disputes between individuals and government departments, the task could be carried out by a minister (or more realistically a civil servant acting on his behalf) exercising his discretion, but only by sacrificing impartiality. The individual concerned would, quite legitimately, feel that the minister was bound to suffer from 'pro-departmental bias'. As an alternative, such disputes could be left to be resolved by the courts, but for a number of reasons tribunals are likely to be more suitable. Many disputes before tribunals require swift resolution, and the delays attendant upon litigation are well known. A claimant seeking a welfare benefit clearly cannot wait months to have the validity of his claim determined. The tribunal procedure should involve far less expense than going to court. Savings result partly from the speed and brevity of proceedings, partly from the reduced role played by lawyers, and partly from the fact that the schemes will be financed by central government. By promoting an atmosphere less formal than that to be found in courts of law, tribunals hope to encourage individuals to represent themselves. The extent to which this has been achieved, or is indeed desirable, is debatable. In normal court proceedings a considerable amount of time is taken up presenting expert evidence, simply to explain to the trial judge the complex issues involved. Tribunals have an advantage in that members can be appointed who have an expert knowledge of the subject matter raised in disputes brought before them, for example, persons with knowledge of the social services, local property values or industrial relations. Although not courts of law, tribunals are, in theory, independent of government departments which may be parties to disputes before the tribunals. Regardless of the reality of the situation, an important factor is the impression made upon the individual bringing his case before the tribunal; it must at least appear to be separate from the government.

Workload

The following statistics, derived from the Judicial Statistics for 1993, provide a 'snapshot' of the workload of certain key tribunals for which the Lord Chancellor has administrative responsibility.

1. *Employment Appeal Tribunal*: cases received totalled 1,088; cases disposed of totalled 954, an increase of 259 over the previous year; of those cases disposed of 463 were dismissed.
2. *Lands Tribunal*: disposed of 346 cases of the 1,095 received, compared with 474 cases disposed of in 1992. There remains a significant backlog of 3,140 cases pending.
3. *Pensions Appeals Tribunals*: received 3,740 cases, an increase of 42 per cent on the previous year, and disposed of 3,293 cases, an increase of 184 on the previous year.
4. *Special Commissioners of Income Tax*: disposed of 222 cases of the 238 received. The number of cases pending increased to 259.
5. *The Social Security Commissioners*: applications for leave to appeal fell by 11 per cent to 2,124 compared with 1992. The number of appeals received rose by 77 per cent to 1,993. The total number of applications and appeals received was 4,117 (3,517 in 1992) while the number disposed of was 4,229 (4,802 in 1992). The number of cases pending at the end of 1993 was 2,824 an increase of 212 on the figure for 1992.
6. *Value Added Tax Tribunals*: received 5,114 appeals (5,362 in 1992) and disposed of 2,329 (2,208 in 1992), leaving 3,844 cases pending (4,316 in 1992) a reduction of 11 per cent.

7. *Immigration Adjudicators*: received 25,244 cases (26,226 in 1992) disposed of 27,576 (32,260 in 1992), leaving 18,709 cases pending (21,041 in 1992).
8. *Immigration Appeal Tribunal*: applications for leave to appeal received 5,662 (4,961 in 1992); disposal of appeals decreased by 37 per cent from 1,560 to 985. There were 696 cases pending at the end of 1993.

7.2 Constitution and membership

Appointment of members

As regards those tribunals listed in Schedule 1 to the Tribunal and Inquiries Act 1992, the procedure for the appointment of tribunal chairman is set out in the 1992 Act itself. Section 5(1) provides that the Council on Tribunals may make to the appropriate minister general recommendations as to the making of appointments to membership of any tribunal. The minister is required to have regard to the recommendations. By virtue of s6(1) the chairman will be selected from a panel of persons appointed by the Lord Chancellor.

Under s7(1) the power of a minister, other than the Lord Chancellor, to terminate a person's membership of any tribunal can only be exercised with the consent of the Lord Chancellor. Terms and conditions of service vary with the enabling Act.

Note in this regard the recommendations of the Franks Report (see Chapter 6 above):

'There has been substantial agreement among witnesses that at any rate the majority of chairmen of tribunals should have legal qualifications. We attach great importance to the quality of chairmanship. Objectivity in the treatment of cases and the proper sifting of facts are most often best secured by having a legally qualified chairman, though we recognise that suitable chairmen can be drawn from fields other than the law. We therefore recommend that chairmen of tribunals should ordinarily have legal qualifications but that the appointment of persons without legal qualifications should not be ruled out when they are particularly suitable.

It is impossible, we think, to lay down any such general desideratum in the case of members because of the wide variety of experience which has to be drawn on for the different tribunals. Such evidence as we have received indicates that the quality of members is on the whole satisfactory, and we have ourselves no general proposals to make with regard to their qualifications. The new arrangements which we have recommended for the appointment of members will maintain and may well improve their quality.'

Constitution of tribunals

There is no fixed format as to the number of persons sitting on a tribunal. Unless statute provides otherwise, a tribunal may determine a question by a majority decision. Frequently a panel of potential members is drawn up and they serve in rotation. Depending on the nature of the tribunal, sittings may be local, regional or national.

Administrative staff

The clerks to tribunals and other administrative staff connected with a tribunal will usually be civil servants, frequently members of the government department that is a party to the disputes before the tribunal; this is a matter that has raised questions as to apparent impartiality.

7.3 Tribunal procedure

Public hearings

The Franks Committee regarded openness as one of the three essential features of the satisfactory working of tribunals. It was therefore of the view that tribunal proceedings should normally be held in public. The Franks Report stated:

> 'We are in no doubt that if adjudicating bodies, whether courts or tribunals, are to inspire that confidence in the administration of justice which is a condition of civil liberty they should, in general, sit in public. But just as on occasion the courts are prepared to try certain types of case wholly or partly in camera so, in the wide field covered by tribunals, there are occasions on which we think that justice may be better done, and the interests of the citizen better served, by privacy.
>
> The first type of case is where considerations of public security are involved. Such cases are not often likely to arise before tribunals, but provision should be included in the codes of procedure for enabling a tribunal to sit in private on this type of case.
>
> The more frequent type of case in which privacy is desirable is that in which intimate personal or financial circumstances have to be disclosed. Few people would doubt the wisdom of the practice whereby hearings before the General and Special Commissioners of Income Tax are held in private in order that details of taxpayers' affairs shall not become public knowledge ... Another case in which the privacy of proceedings is justified is the hearing at which a medical examination of the applicant may take place.
>
> A third type of case in which privacy is on balance desirable is that involving professional capacity and reputation where the machinery includes provision for a preliminary and largely informal hearing before any decision is made to institute formal proceedings which may involve penalties ... Accordingly we recommend that where a tribunal is of a class which has to deal almost exclusively with any of these three types of case the hearing should continue to be in private. In the case of all other classes of tribunal, however, the hearing should be in public, subject to a discretionary power in the chairman to exclude the public should he think that a particular case involves any of these considerations.'

The power to sit in camera will be addressed in the procedural rules as devised for each tribunal. Prior to September 1994 hearings of the Special Commissioners of Income Tax were held in private because of the desire to maintain confidentiality concerning tax payers' wealth. Revised procedural rules now ensure that the hearings are open to the public.

Natural justice

The common law rules of natural justice apply to tribunals, just as they do to any other administrative body exercising 'quasi-judicial' powers. The extent and content of these rules is detailed in Chapters 14 and 15. Broadly, the common law would require adherence to a number of the following basic principles, to a lesser or greater extent depending on the context of the case. To the extent that these matters are dealt with in the procedural rules laid down for any particular tribunal they can be assumed to have displaced the common law.

A person appearing before a tribunal should be given proper notice of the scheduling of the hearing, and where appropriate adequate notice of the case against him. As the Franks Report notes:

> 'The second most important requirement before the hearing is that citizens should know in good time the case which they will have to meet, whether the issue to be heard by the tribunal is one between citizen and administration or between citizen and citizen. This constituent of fairness is one to which much of the evidence we have received has rightly drawn attention ... We do not suggest that the procedure should be formalised to the extent of requiring documents in the nature of legal pleadings. What is needed is that the citizen should receive in good time beforehand a document setting out the main points of the opposing case. It should not be necessary, and indeed in view of the type of persons frequently appearing before tribunals it would in many cases be positively undesirable, to require the parties to adhere rigidly to the case previously set out, provided always that the interests of another party are not prejudiced by such flexibility.'

A tribunal should permit legal representation when requested, unless there are compelling policy reasons for excluding it. In reality legal representation is permitted at all tribunals except those hearing complaints against NHS practitioners, largely because doctors will almost always be able to afford representation, whilst those appearing against them will not. Frequently individuals are represented by friends, family, trade union officials, and so on. Legal aid to pay for legal representation before tribunals is normally only available in the case of the Lands Tribunal, Employment Appeal Tribunal, or Commons Commissioners, although some limited assistance is available in respect of proceedings before Mental Health Review Tribunals. Legal advice may be available under the 'Green Form' scheme to help an individual prepare his case for presentation before a tribunal.

Each party should be permitted to put its case, calling and cross-examining witnesses as appropriate. Tribunals are generally not bound by the strict rules of evidence. In *R* v *Deputy Industrial Injuries Commissioner, ex parte Moore* [1965] 1 QB 456 Diplock LJ observed:

> '... "evidence" is not restricted to evidence which would be admissible in a court of law. For historical reasons, based on the fear that juries who might be illiterate would be incapable of differentiating between the probative values of different methods of proof, the practice of the common law courts has been to admit only what the judges then regarded as the best evidence of any disputed fact, and thereby to exclude much material which, as a matter of common sense, would assist a fact-finding tribunal to reach a correct conclusion ... These technical rules of evidence, however, form no part of the rules of

natural justice. The requirement that a person exercising quasi-judicial functions must base his decision on evidence means no more than it must be based upon material which tends logically to show the existence or non-existence of facts relevant to the issue to be determined, or to show the likelihood or unlikelihood of the occurrence of some future event the occurrence of which would be relevant. It means that he must not spin a coin or consult an astrologer, but he may take into account any material which, as a matter of reason, has some probative value in the sense mentioned above. If it is capable of having any probative value, the weight to be attached to it is a matter for the person to whom Parliament has entrusted the responsibility of deciding the issue. The supervisory jurisdiction of the High Court does not entitle it to usurp this responsibility and to substitute its own view for his.'

See further *Mahon* v *Air New Zealand Ltd* [1984] 3 All ER 201 (PC). Tribunal members are, of course, frequently appointed on the basis of their expertise, and they can rely on their own knowledge to determine an issue, even though the parties themselves have not referred to this information. The vital point is that if a tribunal chairman wishes to rely on evidence not adduced by the parties, he must inform them of this and invite their representations upon it. In *Kavanagh* v *Chief Constable of Devon and Cornwall* [1974] 1 QB 624, the Court of Appeal held that when a Crown Court was considering Kavanagh's appeal against the Chief Constable's refusal of a firearms certificate under the Firearms Act 1968, it was acting in an administrative capacity, and as such the normally strict rules of evidence could be relaxed, permitting the Chief Constable to put forward hearsay evidence to support his decision. As Lord Denning MR observed:

'It seems to me that the Crown Court is in the same position as the court of quarter sessions ... justices never held themselves bound by the strict rules of evidence. They acted on any material that appeared to be useful in coming to a decision, including their own knowledge. No doubt they admitted hearsay, though there is nothing to be found in the books about it. To bring the procedure up to modern requirements, I think they should act on the same lines as any administrative body which is charged with an inquiry. They may receive any material which is logically probative even though it is not evidence in a court of law. Hearsay can be permitted where it can fairly be regarded as reliable.'

See further *T A Miller Ltd* v *Minister of Housing and Local Government* [1968] 1 WLR 992, and *Dugdale* v *Kraft Foods Ltd* [1977] ICR 48. At present only a limited number of tribunals have the power to administer the oath and receive sworn evidence. The Law Commission has recommended that all tribunals should have a discretion to accept sworn evidence where appropriate. It should be noted that this may be at the expense of informality.

Precedent

A system of precedent can only operate if decisions are reported. At present there is only a limited system of reporting tribunal decisions at first instance. Various appeal tribunals have their decisions more widely published in specialist reports. Selected decisions of the Social Security Commissioners, and of the Lands Tribunal are available, but even then are only persuasive, not binding, on future cases. Tribunals clearly have to follow previous decisions of courts of law. The Council on Tribunals has shown itself to be in favour of the more important tribunal decisions being reported, as this would be a major aid in promoting consistency in decision-making.

Privilege and contempt

Proceedings in a court of law are protected by absolute privilege, so that no proceedings may be brought for defamation in respect of anything said during a trial. It is questionable whether the same protection extends to tribunals. Much depends on the tribunal's constitution and the subject matter covered. That absolute privilege can apply is not in doubt: see *Trapp* v *Mackie* [1979] 1 All ER 489. There is no one factor which will decide conclusively that proceedings are privileged, but generally the courts will consider the extent to which the procedure of the tribunal in question has become 'judicialised'. The Council on Tribunals has suggested that protecting proceedings by way of privilege may create dangers of groundless allegations and rumours being put in evidence during a hearing.

In *Attorney-General* v *BBC* [1981] AC 303, the House of Lords held that a Valuation Court was not a 'court of law' within the terms of the Contempt of Court Act 1981 and hence its proceedings were not protected by the provisions of that Act. It would appear that the fact that a body may have the word 'court' as part of its nomenclature was not to be regarded as decisive of the matter. The history and pedigree of the body in question was also significant. The decision was followed in *Attorney-General* v *Associated Newspaper Group plc* [1989] 1 All ER 604, where the Divisional Court held that a Mental Health Review Tribunal was not a 'court' for the purposes of the 1981 Act on the basis that, while the tribunal had to act judicially in considering applications for release, its decisions did not affect personal liberty in a manner that was analogous to a court of law. The court also found it persuasive that the tribunal's decisions were not final, as an unsuccessful applicant could renew his application before the tribunal after a period of 12 months.

The decision should, however, be assessed in the light of the House of Lords' decision in *Pickering* v *Liverpool Daily Post and Echo Newspapers plc and Others* [1991] 2 WLR 513. The plaintiff, whose previous application for early release from prison had given rise to the proceedings in *Attorney-General* v *Associated Newspaper Group plc* sought to minimise press coverage of his latest application for a discharge by applying for an injunction to prevent a number of newspapers from publishing any information about his application. The injunction was granted, ex parte, by Mr Justice Simon Brown, but Roch J had refused to allow the injunction to continue, and the plaintiff appealed to the Court of Appeal. In allowing the appeal (Glidewell LJ dissenting in part), the court held that *Attorney-General* v *Associated Newspaper Group plc*, to the extent that it had held that a Mental Health Review Tribunal was not a court of law for the purposes of s19 of the Contempt of Court Act 1981, was wrongly decided. In the view of Lord Donaldson MR, such a tribunal was undoubtedly a court, given such factors as its power to subpoena witnesses, and to make decisions affecting the liberty of individuals. In particular his Lordship thought it significant that the European Convention on Human Rights required the lawfulness of an individual's detention to be determined by a court, and so if the tribunal was not to be regarded as a court, article 5(4) of the European Convention was not being complied with. On the substantive issue, the court held that there were no grounds for granting an injunction to prevent a contempt of court as there was no evidence that the defendants intended to publish material that would impede or prejudice the course of justice. The House of Lords, while happy to endorse the views of the Master of the Rolls, expressed the view that the same conclusions would be reached by an examination of s12(1)(b) of the Administration of Justice Act 1960, which expressly sought to protect proceedings in private before a Mental Health Review Tribunal by means of applying the law of contempt.

The giving of reasons

Unless special reasons exist, one is entitled to cast doubt on the merits of a decision for which reasons will not be provided. At common law, failure to give reasons may amount to a breach of natural justice and be remediable by way of judicial review. The view of the Franks Committee as evidenced in its report was expressed thus:

> 'We are convinced that if tribunal proceedings are to be fair to the citizen reasons should be given to the fullest practicable extent. A decision is apt to be better if the reasons for it have to be set out in writing because the reasons are then more likely to have been properly thought out. Further, a reasoned decision is essential in order that where there is a right of appeal, the applicant can assess whether he has good grounds of appeal and know the case he will have to meet if he decides to appeal.'

If a tribunal is listed in Schedule 1 of the Tribunals and Inquiries Act 1992 it is, by virtue of s10 of that Act under a duty to give reasons for its decisions if requested to do so. Reasons may by refused, or the specification of the reasons restricted, on grounds of national security, and a tribunal may refuse to furnish reasons to a person not primarily concerned with the decision, or if of the opinion that to furnish it would be contrary to the interests of any person primarily concerned. Any reasons that are provided become, by virtue of s10(6), part of the decision and accordingly are regarded as having been incorporated in the record.

The reasons given must be sufficient and adequate in the context of the decision: see *Mountview Court Properties Ltd* v *Devlin* (1970) 21 P & Cr 689. In *Elliot* v *Southwark London Borough Council* [1976] 2 All ER 781, James LJ stated obiter that:

> 'The duty to give reasons pursuant to statute [was] a responsible one and [could not] be discharged by the use of vague general words ...'

Generally, the reasons given should: indicate the important points in the decision; show that the mind of the decision-maker has been directed to these points, and what view he has taken on these points; be clear and intelligible. If the duty to give reasons is not complied with, the courts may order the tribunal to produce them by way of mandamus.

7.4 Challenge in the courts and diagrammatic summary

Appeals

In many cases where a tribunal has been created by statute, provision will also have been made for an appellate tribunal, to consider appeals. Appeals can either deal with a mixture of fact and law or only be available on a point of law. Where appeal is available against findings of fact and law there is in effect a complete rehearing of the case, and the appellate tribunal can uphold the decision at first instance or quash it and substitute its own. Clearly appeal on a point of law is more limited. A problem arises where no provision is made for appeals to be heard, as there is no common law right to appeal against a tribunal's decision; it is only possible where statute so provides. A situation may arise, therefore, where an individual is dissatisfied with a tribunal's determination on a point of fact, but in the absence of any right to appeal, or perhaps only being able to appeal on a point of law, the tribunal's decision is unchallengeable – subject to what is said about judicial review, below. The Franks Report recommended that there should always be a right of appeal, but this has not been implemented. Where an enabling Act does provide for an appeal, however, this should be an individual's first resort.

Appeal on a point of law to the High Court

If a tribunal is listed in Schedule 1 to the Tribunals and Inquiries Act 1992, s11 provides that an appeal will lie to the High Court on a point of law. A Schedule 1 listing is therefore obviously a useful safeguard where no appellate body is provided. Section 11 provides (inter alia):

> '... if any party to proceedings before any tribunal specified [in] Schedule 1 is dissatisfied in point of law with a decision of the tribunal he may, according as rules of court may provide, either appeal from the tribunal to the High Court or require the tribunal to state and sign a case for the opinion of the High Court.'

While this provides an important avenue of challenge to a tribunal decision, there remains a problem of identifying a 'point of law'. It is not possible to provide a categorical definition, but it would appear that the courts are willing to take a liberal view, where there is a desire to intervene. As H W R Wade has commented:

> 'The courts ought ... to guard against any artificial narrowing of the right of appeal on a point of law, which is clearly intended to be a wide and beneficial remedy. Very difficult questions of law have to be determined by many tribunals and for the sake of consistency and fairness it is important that the guidance of the courts should be available.' (Administrative Law 6th ed p943)

Examples include *Woodhouse* v *Peter Brotherhood Ltd* [1972] 2 QB 520 (whether there had been a transfer of business for the purposes of the Redundancy Payments Act); *O'Brien* v *Associated Fire Alarms Ltd* [1969] 1 All ER 93 (the construction of a contract of employment held to constitute a point of law); *Lord Advocate* v *Reliant Tool Co Ltd* [1968] 1 All ER 162 (statutory interpretation held to involve a point of law); *Tandon* v *Trustees of Spurgeon's Homes* [1982] 2 WLR 735 (the question of whether a building constituted a 'house' for the purposes of the Housing Acts was one of law); see further the discussion of this problem in *Edwards* v *Bairstow* [1956] AC 14.

Error of law on the face of the record

When a tribunal arrives at a decision there will usually be some 'record' of it; as indicated above, if reasons are given they become part of the record. If the record reveals that the body has made an error of law, then, notwithstanding that the tribunal's decision is still intra vires, the individual wishing to challenge the decision can apply to the Divisional Court for certiorari to quash the decision. Note that while the reviewing court can quash a decision vitiated by an error of law, it cannot substitute a new decision of its own for that of the tribunal. This method of challenge is not limited to the tribunals listed in Schedule 1 of the 1992 Act; and it is a common law remedy, given the large number of tribunals covered by the 1992 Act, instances of applications for review for error of law on the face of the record are fairly rare. This subject is dealt with in more detail in Chapter 12.

Judicial review generally

As well as cases of error of law, judicial review is available generally as a way of challenging tribunal decisions on the basis that they are ultra vires possibly on the grounds of unreasonableness or breach of natural justice. Review must be contrasted with appeal. Review is a common law remedy; appeal is only available where statute so provides. An appeal can look into the merits of a decision to determine whether it was 'good' or 'bad'; review is concerned solely with legality – was the decision ultra vires? Finally, as noted earlier, an appeal can result in a first instance decision being quashed, and the appellate body substituting its own decision; review can only quash or remit the decision to be taken again where appropriate. Judicial review is discretionary, as are the remedies thereunder. Review may be refused where Parliament has provided a more suitable channel of challenge to a tribunal's decision, for example, a right of appeal to an appellate tribunal or minister, or appeal on a point of law under s11 of the 1992 Act. Parliament may expressly wish, by including an 'ouster' clause in the enabling Act, to exclude any recourse to the courts; for example, see *Anisminic* v *Foreign Compensation Commission* [1969] 2 AC 147. Such clauses have proved largely unsuccessful in preventing intervention by the courts;

the only type to have been in any way effective is the 'partial ouster' clause that allows a decision to be challenged within a short period of time. In this respect note s12 of the 1992 Act, which provides:

'... as respects England and Wales –
(a) any provision in an Act passed before 1 August 1958 that any order or determination shall not be called into question in any court, or
(b) any provision in such an Act which by similar words excludes any of the powers of the High Court,
shall not have effect so as to prevent the removal of the proceedings into the High Court by order of certiorari or to prejudice the powers of the High Court to make orders of mandamus.
[ss(2) deals with Scotland.]
(3) Nothing in this section shall apply –
(a) to any order or determination of a court of law, or
(b) where an Act makes special provision for application to the High Court or the Court of Session within a time limited by the Act.'

Conclusion and diagrammatic summary

A number of significant criticisms can still be aimed at the tribunal system. There is no standardised procedure before tribunals, despite the efforts of the Council on Tribunals. Not all tribunals have an appellate body that can provide for a rehearing. The non-availability of legal aid must undoubtedly prejudice the less able litigant. Training for, and co-ordination of, tribunal members could undoubtedly be improved. In the case of some tribunals there have been criticisms of 'creeping judicialisation' – partly due to the presence of lawyers, resulting in an intimidating atmosphere in which some individuals find it difficult to express their views. Such research as has been conducted indicates that some chairmen fail to prevent purely prejudicial evidence from being submitted, and in some tribunals there is an inability among tribunal members to differentiate properly between government policy, for example non-statutory guidance, and the law that has to be applied. Finally, concern inevitably persists over the extent to which some tribunals can truly be said to be independent of government departments, when they sometimes hold their sittings in the same building as that occupied by the department, and are staffed by civil servants. Ministers still exercise considerable control over tribunals by appointing members, and deciding not to re-appoint members when their periods of service expire.

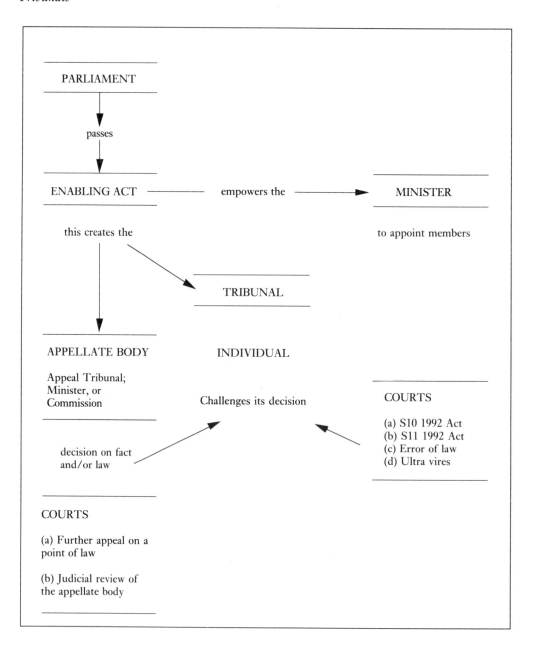

8

Inquiries

8.1 The use of inquiries

8.2 Inquiry procedures

8.3 The role of the minister

8.4 Problems arising from the use of inquiries

8.1 The use of inquiries

Whereas tribunals will normally be called upon to resolve a dispute between two parties by arriving at a determination, the public inquiry has, traditionally, been seen as an administrative device through which evidence can be gathered and views canvassed, prior to a decision being made, typically by a minister. It is in the sphere of planning control that public inquiries play their most significant role. Under s320 of the Town and Country Planning Act 1990 (consolidating the previous Act of 1971) the Secretary of State may cause a local inquiry to be held for the purposes of the exercise of any of his functions under any of the provisions of the Act. In effect this means that inquiries might be held into matters such as the compulsory purchase of property, the refusal of planning permission, alterations to listed buildings, the placing of advertising hoardings etc. Some inquiries deal with issues of very localised concern, for example, road widening schemes; others will raise issues of national significance, such as inquiries into major developments such as airports or power stations. Inevitably questions are raised as to the extent to which the public inquiry is an appropriate means of dealing with such a wide range of problems. Under s101 of the 1990 Act the Secretary of State can appoint a Planning Inquiry Commission to consider planning appeals that have wide implications beyond the locality of the site in question, or involve very complex technicalities. The Commission, if appointed, should consist of a chairman and not less than two or more than four other members appointed by the Secretary of State.

The rationale for these provisions is that issues of this nature are not suitable for consideration by a local public inquiry. Planning Inquiry Commissions are allowed to consider the broader implications of the planning appeal, such as possible alternative sites for the development. To date no use has been made of this special inquiry procedure, despite the recommendation of the House of Common's Select

Committee in 1986 that the possibilities offered by the Commission should be exploited, and despite the suitability of some planning applications such as those relating to the building of a nuclear fuel reprocessing plant (now known as 'Sellafield') at Windscale, in Cumbria, or the National Coal Board's application to mine coal in the Vale of Belvoir.

Under the Tribunals of Inquiry (Evidence) Act 1921, a tribunal can be appointed to inquire into 'a definite matter of urgent public importance'. Despite the misleading title the procedure more closely resembles that of an inquiry than a tribunal. The tribunal, chaired by a lawyer who sits with two other persons, conducts its business in an inquisitorial fashion. It can compel the attendance of witnesses and production of documents; witnesses are privileged in giving their evidence and can be legally represented. The tribunal does not make any decisions or hand down punishments, but produces a report on its findings which is forwarded to the appropriate minister. Examples of those matters referred to the tribunal in the past include: disclosure of budget secrets; the causes of the 1966 Aberfan disaster; the events in Londonderry in January 1972; the failure of the Vehicle and General Insurance Company. Many of the matters investigated also fall within the ambit of the Parliamentary Commissioner for Administration, but are dealt with under the 1921 Act because of the scale of the maladministration involved and the need for a public investigation.

In addition to the above cases, many 'ad hoc' inquiries are established, under the prerogative, on a 'one-off' basis to enquire into a specific event or issue. Examples include the inquiry under Lord Scarman into the Brixton riots of April 1981, the inquiry into events leading up to the Falklands War and the inquiry into the fire at Bradford City Football Club in May 1985. The most significant recent example is the Scott Inquiry into the so-called 'Iraqi Supergun' affair, and it is interesting to note that Scott LJ was promised that he would be given powers similar to those enjoyed by Tribunals of Inquiry under the 1921 Act if he requested them.

8.2 Inquiry procedures

As with tribunals, there is no universal procedure adopted by all inquiries. The Council on Tribunals has, however, been successful in introducing a measure of consistency as regards the procedure adopted by inquiries dealing with land use. Section 9 of the Tribunals and Inquiries Act 1992 provides:

> '9(1) The Lord Chancellor, after consultation with the Council, may make rules regulating the procedure to be followed in connection with statutory inquiries held by or on behalf of Ministers; and different provision may be made by any such rules in relation to different classes of such inquiries.
> (2) Any rules made by the Lord Chancellor under this section shall have effect, in relation to any statutory inquiry, subject to the provisions of the enactment under which the inquiry is held, and of any rules or regulations made under that enactment.

(3) Subject to subsection (2), rules made under this section may regulate procedure in connection with matters preparatory to such statutory inquiries as are mentioned in subsection (1), and in connection with matters subsequent to such inquiries, as well as in connection with the conduct of proceedings at such inquiries.'

For these purposes, s16(1) defines a statutory inquiry as:

'(a) an inquiry or hearing held or to be held in pursuance or a duty imposed by any statutory provision, or
(b) an inquiry or hearing, or an inquiry or hearing of a class, designated for the purposes of this section by an order under subsection (2) ...'

Section 16(2) further provides:

'(2) The Lord Chancellor and the Lord Advocate may by order designate for the purposes of this section any inquiry or hearing held or to be held in pursuance of a power conferred by any statutory provision specified or described in the order, or any class of such inquiries or hearings.'

To date over one hundred have been so designated.

The standard procedural rules for land use inquiries are now to be found in the Town and Country Planning (Inquiries Procedure) Rules 1992 (SI 1992/2038) (replacing the 1988 Rules). The revised inquiry procedure Rules, which came into effect on 30 September 1992, apply to any local inquiry caused by the Secretary of State to be held in England or Wales before he determines; to an application in relation to planning permission referred to him under s78 of the Town and Country Planning Act 1990; to an application for consent referred to him under a tree preservation order or an appeal to him under such an order; and to an application in relation to listed building consent, or an appeal to him under s20 of the Planning (Listed Buildings and Conservation Areas) Act 1990.

Subject to certain exceptions, s321 of the 1990 Act provides that all oral evidence at local inquiries must be given in public and the documentary evidence must be available to the public for inspection. The aim of the Rules is to ensure fairness and openness, so far as is compatible with the purpose of the inquiry.

Rule 4 details the preliminary information to be supplied by a local planning authority; Rule 5 provides the procedure to be followed where the Secretary of State causes a pre-inquiry meeting to be held to address those matters that need to be resolved in order to ensure that the inquiry itself is conducted effectively and efficiently; and Rule 6 deals with the statements that have to be served by the various interested parties prior to the inquiry. Rule 11 details those entitled to appear at the inquiry the list includes the applicant (ie the appellant), the local planning authority, other statutory bodies such as local authorities and National Parks Committees, and any other person permitted to appear at the discretion of the inquiry inspector.

A representative of the relevant government department may attend if the applicant so requests, but note that under Rule 12(4) the representative is not required to answer any question which in the opinion of the inspector is directed to the merits of government policy. Under Rule 11(3), any person entitled or permitted to appear may be represented by counsel, solicitor or some other person. Under Rule 14 the inspector will invite the applicant to commence the proceedings and will permit him the right of final reply. Others entitled or permitted to appear are heard in such order as the inspector may determine. A person entitled to appear at an inquiry is entitled to call evidence and the applicant, the local planning authority, and a statutory party will be entitled to cross-examine any person giving evidence. In all other cases the calling of evidence and the cross-examination of persons giving evidence is at the inspector's discretion. The inspector may refuse to permit the giving or production of evidence, the cross-examination of persons giving evidence, or the presentation of any other matter, which he considers to be irrelevant or repetitious. Any person refused permission to present oral evidence may put evidence in writing before the close of the inquiry. The inspector has powers to maintain order at the inquiry. Under Rule 14(7) he may require any person appearing or present at an inquiry who, in his opinion, is behaving in a disruptive manner to leave and may refuse to permit that person to return, or may permit him to return only on such conditions as he may specify. The rules place on a legislative basis decisions such as *Lovelock* v *Secretary of State for Transport* (1979) P & CR 468, in which it was held that an inspector ordering the exclusion of a disruptive member of the public or participant would not be acting in breach of natural justice.

Where he considers it necessary to do so, the inspector may visit the site relevant to the inquiry. Under Rule 15 he may make an unaccompanied inspection of the land before or during an inquiry without giving notice of his intention to the persons entitled to appear at the inquiry, or may, during an inquiry or after its close, inspect the land in the company of the applicant, the local planning authority and any statutory party. In addition he is required to make such an inspection if requested to do so by the applicant or the local planning authority before or during an inquiry.

Natural justice

While it is trite law to state that the rules of natural justice apply to the public inquiry process, as Kerr J stated in *Lake District Special Planning Board* v *Secretary of State for the Environment* (1975) JPL 220:

> '[The litigant] faces a heavy burden in seeking to establish a breach of the rules of natural justice when the allegation in question relates to something which is comprised within the scope of a statutory procedure ... which is itself designed to lay down the requirements which must be complied with to ensure that justice is done, but when no breach of this procedure has been established.'

There are, however, some notable instances of the rules of natural justice being applied to the actual inquiry procedure. In *Fairmount Investments Ltd* v *Secretary of State for the Environment* [1976] 2 All ER 865 a compulsory purchase order was quashed when an inspector attached great weight in his report to a matter not directly raised during the inquiry; on this point see also *H Sabey and Co v Secretary of State for the Environment* [1978] 1 All ER 586. In *R v Secretary of State for the Environment, ex parte Fiedler Estates (Canvey) Ltd and Another* (1988) The Times 10 June, the applicants for review had applied unsuccessfully for planning permission to build houses in the vicinity of Canvey Island, and had appealed to the Secretary of State who had instituted a public inquiry which was expected to last for three days. One interested group, the Canvey Ratepayers' Association, sought to give evidence, through its chairman, on the second day of the inquiry. By the end of the first day of the inquiry all those present who had wanted to give evidence had done so, and the inspector declared the inquiry closed. The Association's chairman arrived to give evidence the following day only to find that the inquiry had closed. On receiving a complaint from the Association, the Secretary of State decided to hold a new inquiry at which the Association gave evidence, but he failed to notify any of the other interested parties of this decision. The Divisional Court held that the conduct of the Secretary of State, in failing to notify the other parties of his decision to hold a fresh inquiry, was so unreasonable that it verged on the absurd and amounted to a failure to comply with procedural fairness. He had acted ultra vires in hearing one side in the absence of the other. Roch J expressed the view that the minister could quite properly have dealt with the matter by receiving written evidence from the Association after the inquiry and asking the applicants to comment upon it.

The decision of the House of Lords in *Bushell v Secretary of State for the Environment* [1981] AC 75 involved a valuable discussion by their Lordships of the extent to which natural justice applied to inquiry proceedings where no statutory rules were in force. Lord Diplock was at pains to point out that it was wrong to equate a public inquiry with a court of law. In the absence of any particular procedural rules which may require certain steps to be taken, his Lordship felt that all that natural justice required of public inquiries was fairness to 'all those who have an interest in the decision that will follow'. He held that natural justice was satisfied by objectors to a proposed motorway scheme being allowed to put their objections before the inspector; it did not necessitate their being allowed to cross-examine departmental representatives on the veracity of their evidence. In *R v Secretary of State for Transport, ex parte Gwent County Council* [1987] 2 WLR 961, the Court of Appeal endorsed the views of Lord Diplock expounded in *Bushell*, where the court stressed that the inquiry process should be looked at as a whole. Some degree of procedural impropriety by the inspector could be remedied by the minister when considering the inspector's report.

Inquiry inspectors

Although the format of inquiries can vary widely, the majority of those concerned with issues of land use will be held by inquiry inspectors. The Franks Committee recommended that inspectors should be appointed by the Lord Chancellor. In practice, where the inquiry inspector is adjudicating between a local authority and a citizen, he will be from the Department of the Environment Inspectorate. Where a government department is promoting a scheme, an independent inspector will be appointed, eg a QC (Sizewell) or a High Court judge (Windscale). There are approximately 400 inspectors, a quarter of whom are freelance and the rest civil servants. Under the Town and Country Planning Appeals (Determination by Inspectors) (Inquiries Procedure) Rules 1992 (SI 1992/2039) (replacing the 1988 Rules), the minister may appoint an inspector to act on his behalf and decide upon the outcome of the inquiry process. Recent statistics indicate that a great many inquiries are now determined by inspectors. When determining the outcome of an inquiry on behalf of the minister, inspectors are subject to supervision by the courts to ensure that they act lawfully. For example, in *Surrey Heath Borough Council* v *Secretary of State for the Environment* (1986) The Times 3 November an inquiry inspector's decision was quashed on the basis that he had paid too much regard to the minister's circular suggesting that development that would bring employment should be encouraged, whilst failing to pay sufficient regard to the local structure plan which discouraged speculative development.

8.3 The role of the minister

Unless the inquiry is one in respect of which the inspector has been empowered to determine the matter on behalf of the minister, he will normally make a report in writing, following the close of the inquiry, setting out his recommendations for consideration by the minister. The minister's discretion to disagree with the inspector's findings is rather narrow. Under Rule 16(4), if, after receiving the inspector's report, the minister is minded to differ on any material factual point, or take into consideration new evidence on any matter of fact, with the result that he is disposed to disagree with the inspector's recommendations, he must first notify those who were entitled to appear at the inquiry and inform them of his reasons for so doing. He must further allow at least 21 days for those who were entitled to attend the inquiry to make representations, or re-open the inquiry.

The result is that the minister is not bound by the inspector's findings, but cannot disagree with him on a question of fact without reopening the issue. Note that he is clearly free to reject the inspector's findings on policy grounds: see *Lord Luke of Pavenham* v *MHLG* [1967] 1 QB 172 and *Nelsovil Ltd* v *MHLG* [1963] 1 All ER 423.

By virtue of Rule 17(1), the minister is obliged to give reasons for his decision. Where reasons are required by statute, the basic principles, established in *Re Poyser and Mills Arbitration* [1964] 2 QB 467, are that the reasons given should be proper, intelligible and adequate. The first two criteria are unlikely to give rise to difficulties in the context of Rule 17, but the latter issue of adequacy has been considered by the House of Lords in *Save Britain's Heritage* v *Number 1 Poultry Ltd* [1991] 1 WLR 153. Lord Bridge, whilst accepting that on the facts of the case before him the

Secretary of State's reasons lacked clarity and precision, rejected the notion that courts were required to set a standard of draughtsmanship that decision letters had to achieve. In his view the essential issue was that the reasons given for a decision should enable a person entitled to contest it to make a proper assessment as to the validity of the decision. He stated (at 167):

> 'Whatever may be the position in any other legislative context, under the planning legislation, when it comes to deciding in any particular case whether the reasons given are deficient, the question is not to be answered in vacuo. The alleged deficiency will only afford a ground for quashing the decision if the court is satisfied that the interests of the applicant have been substantially prejudiced by it. This reinforces the view I have already expressed that the adequacy of reasons is not to be judged by reference to some abstract standard. There are in truth not two separate questions: (1) were the reasons adequate? (2) if not, were the interests of the applicant substantially prejudiced thereby? The single indivisible question, in my opinion, which the court must ask itself whenever a planning decision is challenged on the ground of a failure to give reasons is whether the interests of the applicant have been substantially prejudiced by the deficiency of the reasons given.'

8.4 Problems arising from the use of inquiries

There are conflicting views of the purpose that local planning inquiries are supposed to serve. On the one hand they are seen as providing a forum for public participation in decision-making; on the other they provide a means by which the person entrusted with decision-making powers (inspector or minister) can arrive at a better informed decision.

The House of Lords in *Bushell* v *Secretary of State for the Environment* (above) adhered very much to the latter approach, holding that inquiries were not like courts of law because there was 'nothing at stake'. Nobody was going to 'win' anything. As a consequence natural justice did not require the procedure adopted at an inquiry to mirror that found in a court of law, reflecting an 'administrative' as compared to 'judicial' approach to inquiries. As Lord Diplock stated:

> 'The purpose of the inquiry is to provide the minister with as much information about those objections as will ensure that in reaching his decision he will have weighed the harm to local interests and private persons who may be adversely affected by the scheme against the public benefit which the scheme is likely to achieve and will not have failed to take into consideration any matters which he ought to have taken into consideration.'

Cynics might argue that inquiries, those into large-scale projects at least, are really an exercise in public relations by the promoting authority or department, with the aim of making the public feel as though they have participated in some way in the decision-making process, or at least of allowing them to 'let off steam'.

Where the inquiry is a relatively small-scale one, for example, into development being proposed by a private individual, then the views of individual members of the public might actually influence the outcome. Where the development is of regional or national significance, it is likely to be departmental policy that the development is going to go ahead, therefore individual objections are going to count for very little. The problem arises when members of the public become frustrated through their inability to challenge the latter style of proposal effectively and manifests itself either as a long-lingering suspicion of the processes of government or in scenes of public disorder at the inquiry itself. Perhaps the fact that central government policy cannot be questioned or changed at inquiries should be made clearer. Those objecting to proposed development are often handicapped at inquiries, either by their lack of resources which prevents them from presenting a better researched case, or because, as is sometimes the case with highway inquiries, the inquiry into the development is split into sections, each concerned only with a small stretch of the proposed route, and the overall plan for the motorway cannot be challenged.

As the holding of an inquiry is frequently a procedural prerequisite before development can take place, the easiest way to prevent development is to disrupt the inquiry.

The inquiry process, in its current form, causes delays and is very expensive; this is due in part to the adversarial approach adopted by some parties, but isdue to the time taken in preparing and deciding upon the inspector's report. It is not surprising that there has been a tendency in recent years for the government to seek specific statutory approval for large-scale development projects, thus side-stepping the framework of the planning legislation.

9

Statutory Corporations

9.1 Introduction

9.2 Organisation of local government

9.3 Constitution of local government

9.4 Control by central government

9.5 Powers and duties of local authorities

9.6 Controls over other public corporations

9.1 Introduction

Public corporations are statutory bodies created by Parliament to carry out specific executive functions. The most important examples of such bodies are the local authorities, all of which, with the exception of the Corporation of the City of London, owe their existence to statute. Other functions given to public corporations include the provision of goods and services on a commercial basis (British Rail, the Post Office), the regulation of a particular industry (Independent Television Commission, The Radio Authority, Health and Safety at Work Executive, Civil Aviation Authority) or the furtherance of some other policy goal (Commission for Racial Equality, Equal Opportunities Commission). Commercial activities may be conducted by public corporations for a number of reasons. It may be the case that the products could not be made at a profit by private enterprise, but are seen as essential to the economy, such as steel, coal, or railway services. On the other hand it may be more practical for one large undertaker to supply a service, such as gas, or electricity. On a more ideological level there may be a view that certain goods and services are so important their supply should not be left in private hands; further, any profit made should be returned to the nation, or the business not run at a profit at all, thus reducing costs to the consumer. In addition public corporations have been created in the past to provide public welfare services, such as area health authorities.

Public corporations are not normally emanations of the Crown, despite the close involvement of government departments. In *Tamlin* v *Hannaford* [1950] 1 KB 18, the Court of Appeal held that public corporations (in this case the British Transport Commission) were their own masters – enjoying none of the immunities or privileges of the Crown, with the consequences that their employees were not civil servants, and their property was not Crown property: see further *BBC* v *Johns* [1965] Ch 32. Many statutes creating public corporations now make this point explicit. The National Health Service, by contrast, is regarded as providing a service on behalf of the Crown, and thus is able to avail itself of the Crown's immunities (see *Pfizer Corporation* v *Ministry of Health* [1965] AC 512), although the area health authorities, by virtue of para 15, Sch 5, National Health Service Act 1977, are regarded as being in the same position as regards legal liability as any other legal person.

9.2 Organisation of local government

London

Originally, under the London Government Act 1963, Greater London was given two tiers of local government. The 'upper tier' authority was to be known as the Greater London Council (GLC) (replacing the old London County Council), and the 'lower tier' authorities were to be called London borough councils. There were 32 London borough councils in all, 12 of them forming a sub-group of 'inner London' councils. The Corporation of the City of London remained unaffected by these changes. Inner and Middle Temple also retained their ancient status as local authorities. The GLC was abolished by the Local Government Act 1985, leaving London without any overall local government body since 1986.

England and Wales

The current organisation of local government in England and Wales is based upon the provisions of the Local Government Act 1972. Originally, areas were divided into 39 counties and six metropolitan counties, which in turn were sub-divided into 296 district councils and 36 metropolitan districts. In 1986 the six metropolitan county councils were abolished and their functions transferred to either residuary bodies or joint authorities made up of members of district councils. Within district council areas there are local parish councils or, in Wales, 'communities'.

9.3 Constitution of local government

Elections

Prior to 1992, local government constituency boundaries were established by the Local Government Boundary Commissions for England and Wales. Under the Local

Government Act 1992, the Local Government Commission replaces the Local Government Boundary Commission. The Local Government Commission will make recommendations to the Secretary of State as to structural, electoral or boundary changes. Following the recommendations of the Commission the Secretary of State may make orders concerning the areas of authorities, the establishment of new authorities, and the abolition of existing authorities.

County council elections take place every four years and all the councillors retire together. Metropolitan district council elections take place in each year in which there is no county council election and councillors retire one-third at a time.

In other district councils there is an option between all the councillors retiring simultaneously for an election every four years, or the system of one-third retiring at a time in years where there is no county council election. Parish and community council elections take place every four years and all the councillors retire together. London borough council elections take place every four years and all the councillors retire together.

A register of electors must be prepared each year and is effective for elections occurring in the 12 months commencing 16 February. The register serves both parliamentary and local government elections. The Representation of the People Act 1983 provides that a person is eligible to vote at a local government election if: at the qualifying date he has a qualification based on residence or *alternatively* has a service qualification or a qualification as a merchant seaman or a qualification as a voluntary mental patient; and on the qualifying date and the date of the poll is a Commonwealth citizen or a citizen of the Republic of Ireland, and not suffering from any legal incapacity to vote; and on the date of the poll is of voting age, ie 18 years or over, provided that he is registered as an elector. The qualifying date is defined as 10 October for elections falling within the period of 12 months beginning on 16 February in the following year. Unless disqualified, a person is qualified to be elected and to be a member of a local authority if he is a British subject or a citizen of the Republic of Ireland and on the 'relevant day' he is: 21 years of age and; on that day he is and thereafter continues to be a local government elector for the area of the authority; or he has during the whole of the 12 months preceding that day occupied as owner or tenant any land or other premises in that area; or his principal or only place of work during that 12 months has been in that area; or he has during the whole of those 12 months resided in that area; or in the case of a member of a parish or community council he has during the whole of those 12 months resided either in the parish or community or within three miles of it. The 'relevant day' is the day of nomination and the day of the poll if there is one.

A person is disqualified from being elected or being a member of a local authority if: he holds any paid office or employment (other than that of chairman, vice-chairman or deputy chairman), appointment to which is made or confirmed by the local authority or a committee or sub-committee of the authority, or by a joint board, joint authority or joint committee on which the authority is represented, or by any person who is himself in the employment of the authority; or is a person who has been adjudged bankrupt, or made a composition or arrangement with his creditors; or has within five years before the day of election or since his election been convicted of any offence and has had passed on him any sentence of imprisonment (whether suspended or not) for a period of not less than three months without the option of a fine; or is disqualified from being elected or being a member of that authority under Part III of the Representation of the People Act 1983 (which relates to corrupt or illegal practices); or is disqualified from membership for a specified period by order of the court because of his involvement in expenditure contrary to law; or is disqualified from membership for five years following an auditor's certificate that a loss or deficiency has been caused by his wilful misconduct while a member of a local authority; or holds a politically restricted post under the local authority or any other local authority in Great Britain. The Representation of the People Act 1989 increased fourfold the permitted level of expenses for candidates for local government elections, without altering the limits for parliamentary elections.

Council meetings

Council meetings are held according to the requirements of the standing orders that each authority produces for this purpose. Council meetings must be held at least once a year, and a quorum is 25 per cent of all members. Notice of a meeting must be given at least three clear days ahead, and the agenda and any reports to be considered must be available for inspection at least three days before the meeting. Decisions are normally made on the basis of a majority vote at council meetings. The duties of councillors exercising their voting powers was considered by the Court of Appeal in *R* v *Waltham Forest London Borough Council, ex parte Waltham Forest Ratepayers' Action Group* [1987] 2 WLR 257. The local authority, which was controlled by the Labour Party, had voted to increase rates by over 60 per cent. A number of Labour councillors had privately expressed their disquiet at the proposed increase, but had voted in favour of the resolution rather than resign the party whip. The challenge to the validity of the council's resolution, which had been brought on the basis that the councillors who had voted in favour had either taken into account an irrelevant consideration, the party whip system, or that the party whip system had had the effect of causing them to abdicate the exercise of their discretion, failed on the ground that there was insufficient evidence that those councillors who had supported the rates increase had blindly followed party policy in the way in which they had cast their votes. Lord Donaldson MR observed that the voting by the councillors could not be impugned simply because there was a party whip system in operation. The whip might have been a relevant factor in determining how votes might be cast, but it was only one of several. To impugn the whip system would be to call into question the way in which Parliament itself operated. His Lordship felt that such a system would only become objectionable if a councillor were to be forced to resign not only from his party but also from the council itself if he decided to defy the relevant party whip.

Where the votes cast at a council meeting produce a tied result the Chairman or Mayor can use his casting vote to resolve the matter. The question of whether such a power should or should not be exercised with reference to party political loyalties was considered in *R v Bradford City Council, ex parte Wilson* [1989] 3 All ER 140, the Divisional Court holding that it was clearly the Mayor's (or Chairman's) duty to act impartially to ensure that council meetings proceeded efficiently and effectively, with a full and fair debate involving various viewpoints. It did not necessarily follow, however, that when such a person came to consider the exercise of his own vote he had to remain above party politics. In particular there was no authority for the proposition that a casting vote should be used in a manner that would ensure that debate on a particular topic could be continued. Bingham LJ expressly rejected any analogy between the role of a Lord Mayor in chairing council meetings and that of the Speaker in the House of Commons. This decision was followed in *R v Bradford Metropolitan County Council, ex parte Corris* [1989] 3 All ER 156. Note that the Local Government Finance Act 1992 provides that councillors who fail to pay the Council Tax can be disqualified from voting at council meetings as a consequence.

Public access

The public has a general right to attend meetings of local authorities, under the Public Bodies (Admission to Meetings) Act 1960. Section 100 of the Local Government Act 1972 extends the scope of this right of attendance to meetings of committees and sub-committees. Section 100 has in turn been amended by the Local Government (Access to Information) Act 1985, which increases public access to local authority meetings, reports and documents. Members of the public and press now have a right to attend meetings of principal councils (previously local authorities had a discretion to exclude the public and the press from access to such meetings and materials), but this can be displaced by the authorities' duty to exclude the public where evidence the disclosure of which would constitute a breach of confidence is to be considered. Confidential information comprises information which government departments provide on terms forbidding disclosure, and information disclosure of which is otherwise forbidden by law. Where 'exempt information' may be disclosed at a meeting the local authority may pass a resolution excluding the public. Exempt information is defined in Schedule 1 of the Act and includes any information relating to particular individuals any information relating to prevention, investigation or prosecution of crime, any information connected with legal proceedings, and the identity of a protected informant. Local authorities whose meetings are governed by s100A of the 1972 Act retain a residual power to exclude members of the public who have been admitted to a meeting if such action is considered necessary in order to maintain order.

Bodies such as parish or community councils, and meetings of regional or district health authorities, continue to be governed by the Public Bodies (Admission to Meetings) Act 1960. The Act provides a power to exclude the public where confidential information is to be considered, and where there are 'special reasons' for exclusion, for example where the meeting is considering a report from one of its officers. Thus in *R* v *Liverpool City Council, ex parte LTFOA* [1975] 1 All ER 379, a local authority committee, meeting to consider the issuing of taxi cab licences, passed a resolution under the 1960 Act excluding the public from the meeting because of the small number of seats available (most were occupied by members and officers of the local authority), and because it believed that its business could not be properly conducted in the presence of those competing to be granted licences. The Divisional Court upheld the validity of the resolution on the basis that the two reasons relied upon were entirely justified, and the failure to state these reasons in the resolution was a breach of a directory, not a mandatory, provision. Furthermore, the applicants were unable to show any significant injury in consequences of the irregularity. Similarly, in *R* v *Brent Health Authority, ex parte Francis* [1985] 1 All ER 74, where the applicant, a member of the public, applied unsuccessfully for an order of certiorari to quash the respondent authority's decision to exclude the public from its meetings where spending cuts were being considered – three previous meetings on the same topic having resulted in disorderly conduct on the part of members of the public attending – Mr Justice Forbes held that a public body had a common law right to exclude the public from its meetings, notwithstanding the Public Bodies (Admissions to Meetings) Act 1960, if it feared on reasonable grounds that members of the public planned to disrupt the meeting. On the facts the court was satisfied that the power had been exercised bona fide.

Council committees

Much decision-making is actually delegated to committees. Section 101 of the 1972 Act allows local authorities to arrange for the discharge of their functions by committees, sub-committees, officers or other local authorities, although this does not prevent the full council from exercising the functions as well. Certain committees have to be established in order to ensure compliance with statutory requirements; these include education committees, social services committees and (in non-metropolitan county councils) police committees. A local authority is empowered, under s111 Local Government Act 1972, to discharge its functions by establishing a working party where this is appropriate, and there is no common law requirement that a councillor should be allowed to attend: see *R* v *Eden District Council, ex parte Moffat* (1988) The Times 24 November.

Prior to the introduction of the Local Government and Housing Act 1989, it appeared that the courts would not necessarily intervene where the majority group on a local authority voted to exclude opposition members from committees; see *R* v *Rushmore Borough Council, ex parte Crawford* (1981) 27 November (unreported).

Under the 1989 Act, appointments to relevant committees and sub-committees are required to achieve a political balance. The appointment committee of a local authority is required to review the political balance of the authority and to ensure that this is reflected in the composition of its committees. In particular an authority should ensure that not all seats on a committee are allocated to one political group, and the committee reflects the fact that there is a controlling group on the council as a whole if this is the case.

Subject to the requirements of the 1989 Act, however, it remains open to an authority to prevent a councillor from sitting on a particular committee. The question of a councillor's right to sit on a committee and to see documents before it was considered in *R v Hackney London Borough Council, ex parte Gamper* [1985] 3 All ER 275 where a Liberal councillor, who was a member of the respondent authority, applied successfully for judicial review of its decision to deny him access to meetings and the documents of the direct labour organisation sub-committees. Mr Justice Lloyd held that the authority should have asked itself whether the applicant had a need to know such information in order to perform his duties as a councillor properly, even though he was not a member of the sub-committee in question. His Lordship was satisfied that on the facts the decision to exclude the respondent was one that no reasonable authority could have made. Similarly in *R v Sheffield City Council, ex parte Chadwick* (1985) The Times 17 December a Liberal councillor successfully applied for judicial review of a decision of the council to deny him admission to meetings of its budget sub-committee and to refuse him copies of its reports. The applicant was a member of the council's policy committee, but not of the budget sub-committee, which consisted entirely of Labour councillors, the Labour Party having control of the council as a whole. The applicant's exclusion was held to be unlawful since he would not be properly informed when, as a member of the policy committee, he was called upon to endorse or reject the recommendations of the budget sub-committee. Following *R v Hackney London Borough Council, ex parte Gamper*, the applicant had a need to know what the deliberations of the budget sub-committee had been in order to perform his duties properly. Furthermore, in coming to its conclusion to exclude the applicant, the committee had taken into account considerations that were irrelevant, for example, the desire to maintain the secrecy of what were in reality party policy discussions taking place in sub-committee meetings.

The 1989 Act would also not prevent an authority from resolving to remove a councillor from one of its committees, although regard would have to be had to any standing orders applying to such procedures. The courts will not intervene to assist council members excluded from committees unless such exclusion is unreasonable. In *R v Greenwich London Borough Council, ex parte Lovelace* (1990) The Times 17 December, the respondent Labour-controlled local authority was pursuing a policy of increasing council house rents, the policy being implemented by the authority's housing committee of which the applicants, who were both Labour party councillors, were members. The applicants were opposed to the policy and voted against it at meetings of the committee, action that prompted the controlling Labour group, exercising its discretion under the authority's standing orders, to remove the applicants from the housing committee. The Court of Appeal, dismissing the applicants' appeals against the Divisional Court's refusal to allow an application for judicial review of the authority's actions, held that since the local authority clearly had the power under its standing orders to dissolve any committee or alter its membership at any time, the crucial questions became, what was the reason for removing the applicants from the housing committee, and was the reason legitimate? The court accepted that local authorities invariably operated on party political lines, and recognised that the modern reality was that a political party would seek cohesion amongst its members so as to promote party policy. The applicants had been removed because their membership of the committee prevented it from giving effect to party policy which was to present a balanced budget. The reason for the removal of the applicants was, therefore, legitimate. The line that had to be drawn was between steps taken to impose party discipline, which were prima facie lawful, and steps taken primarily to punish an individual councillor, which would be unlawful. Deciding on which side of that line a particular action fell could be problematic, but it was a function that the courts were well equipped to perform: see further *R* v *Waltham Forest London Borough Council, ex parte Waltham Forest Ratepayers' Action Group* (above).

Council officers

The appointment of staff is within the discretion of the authority; see s112 of the 1972 Act. Certain officers, such as chief education officers and inspectors of weights and measures, must be appointed.

Corruption

In addition to the Prevention of Corruption Act 1906, and the Public Bodies Corrupt Practices Act 1889, special provisions exist to prevent corruption in local authorities. The Local Government Act 1972, s117 (officers) and ss94–98 (members), provides that it is an offence, punishable on summary conviction, if a member of a local authority has any pecuniary interest, direct or indirect, in any contract, proposed contract or other matter, and is present at a meeting of the local authority at which the contract or other matter is the subject of consideration. Members are expected to disclose any interest as soon as is reasonably possible and take no further part in the proceedings.

The prohibition is against participation of any kind, including voting against the matter and thereby against one's own interest: see *Brown* v *DPP* [1956] 2 QB 369. A pecuniary interest includes an interest of a spouse, or a partner, or being a member of a company which has an interest. The words 'contract or other matter' have been given a wide interpretation by the courts. In *Rands* v *Oldroyd* [1959] 1 QB 204 it was held that a councillor had an interest by being a local building contractor, and participating in a vote on the council's direct labour workforce. Prosecutions for these offences can only be instituted on behalf of the Director of Public Prosecutions. By analogy with the position of private companies entering into ultra vires contracts, any contract entered into by a local authority following the illegal involvement of a councillor is likely to be voidable at the instance of the authority: see *Hely-Hutchinson Ltd* v *Brayhead Ltd* [1967] 1 QB 549.

9.4 Control by central government

The whole purpose of local government is that there should be some control over local matters by locally elected local persons, independent of central government. The extent to which the foregoing is met by reality is open to question. The following examples of central government control indicate all too clearly where the real power lies. Many problems seem to arise from the fact that central government is organised along party political lines, as is local government; when the two are of different political beliefs, conflict is inevitable.

Abolition

As local authorities are creatures of statute, the ultimate sanction rests with Parliament of repealing an enabling Act and destroying a local authority by removing its legal personality. As mentioned above, this was the fate which overtook the GLC and the six metropolitan counties in 1986.

Finance

Local authorities cannot act without resources. Central government clearly has the power to determine how those resources are to be provided, and in particular what method of local taxation is to be employed in order to raise revenue for local authority functions. The current system is governed by the Local Government Finance Act 1992, which provides for the introduction of the Council Tax as the replacement for the Community Charge. The Council Tax represents a move back towards a property-based tax, like the old rating system, with relief available to those who are sole occupants. The proportion of local authority income provided by the Council Tax will be between 25 per cent and 33 per cent, the remainder being contributed by central government.

The raising of loans by local authorities will have to be sanctioned by the Secretary of State, whose decision may rest upon the government's view as to the desirability of the proposals for which finance is sought.

Allocation of functions

A local authority is an example of an administrative device by means of which executive functions can be discharged. In allocating functions to local authorities, central government may be motivated by the belief that certain matters should be under the control of locally elected representatives, as this ensures that the views of local people are reflected in decision-making. Alternatively, and more cynically, it may be that central government does not want to have responsibility for certain functions. The main provision governing the distribution of functions between the different tiers of local government is the Local Government Act 1972.

County councils have responsibility for education, town and country planning (some functions shared with district and borough councils), social services, major highways, libraries and recreation facilities, fire and police services and public transport. District or borough councils are responsible for housing, including slum clearance, public health and sanitary services, refuse collection, minor roads and local licensing matters. Parish councils (communities in Wales) deal with footpaths, allotments, bus shelters, burial grounds, village greens, and parking places for motor cycles and bicycles.

Directives, orders, guidance and codes

Ministers can exercise control and influence over the actions of local authorities by statutory and non-statutory means. For example, wide powers by which ministers can issue statutory orders concerning local authority functions exist under the 1972 Act. Many other statutes have within them provisions empowering the relevant minister to take such action as he deems necessary: for example, by issuing a directive, to make a local authority conform with a particular policy: see *Secretary of State for Education* v *Tameside Metropolitan Borough Council* [1977] AC 1014, and its aftermath, the Education Act 1976. In *De Falco* v *Crawley Borough Council* [1980] QB 460, where the Secretary of State had issued a code to local authorities on how the Housing (Homeless Persons) Act 1977 Act should be implemented, the Court of Appeal held that, although the code did not have the force of statute, the local authority had to have regard to it in deciding whether a person was 'intentionally homeless'.

In *R* v *Secretary of State for the Environment, ex parte Hackney London Borough Council* (1984) The Times 21 March, the local authority applied for a judicial review of the expenditure guidance for 1984–85 issued to it by the Secretary of State, on the ground that such guidance was ultra vires s59 of the Local Government Planning and Land Act 1980. The local authority contended that such guidance was only lawful if it was possible for the recipient authority to comply with it without precluding the reasonable discharge of its statutory duties, and that it could not, in fact, comply with the guidance and fulfil all its statutory duties. Dismissing the application, the court held that it was open to the Secretary of State to issue spending guidelines which he knew could not be achieved by the local authority, and thus force an increase in rates if he believed that was necessary, in order to reduce the level of local authority expenditure. The court felt that the guidance was certainly not unreasonable in the *Wednesbury* sense, as it was clearly the Secretary of State's view that pressure from the ratepayers to reduce council spending was likely to be more effective than pressure from central government. The court felt that it was not equipped to adjudicate on the merits of policies on local government spending.

In other fields, such as town and country planning, it is common practice for the minister to issue circulars to local authorities indicating the view of central government as to how a scheme should be administered, or certain cases be dealt with.

Default powers

Although the 1972 Act itself contains no overall default power allowing for the Secretary of State to take over the functions of a local authority, many of the statutes imposing duties on the authorities provide for default powers which allow the minister to take over specific functions if this appears necessary. Instances of such default powers being exercised are rare, but see for example the litigation resulting in *Asher* v *Lacey* [1973] 3 All ER 1008 and *Asher* v *Secretary of State for the Environment* [1974] Ch 208, arising out of the refusal of Clay Cross Urban District Council to implement the Housing Finance Act 1972 and increase council house rents. The Secretary of State under ss95–99 of the Act appointed a 'housing commissioner' to take over the authority's functions, and issued a 'default' order against it.

9.5 Powers and duties of local authorities

Local authorities, as public bodies, are subject to the constraints imposed by the ultra vires principle. Many of the most significant and historic cases in administrative law have concerned the legality of the exercise of discretion by local authorities, whether in respect of the exercise of licensing functions, raising revenue, or expenditure. Decisions such as *Associated Provincial Picture Houses* v *Wednesbury Corporation* [1948] 1 KB 223, *Roberts* v *Hopwood* [1925] AC 578, *Prescott* v *Birmingham Corporation* [1955] Ch 210 and *Bromley London Borough Council* v *Greater London Council* [1983] 1 AC 768 provide key examples.

Provided that a statutory duty is drawn in sufficiently clear terms, the courts may be willing to grant an order of mandamus directing the local authority to comply with the terms of the statute. Impecuniosity is not viewed by the courts as a valid excuse for non-performance – see *R* v *Poplar Borough Council, ex parte London County Council (No 2)* [1922] 1 KB 95 – although this may be relaxed in the case of provision of social services: see *R* v *Bristol Corporation, ex parte Hendy* [1974] 1 All ER 1047.

Section 101 of the 1972 Act relaxes the normal prohibition on delegation of power, to enable local authorities to discharge their functions through committees, sub-committees and, where appropriate, other authorities. Section 111 relaxes the strict application of the ultra vires principle as regards the actions of local authorities, by empowering them to do anything:

> '... which is calculated to facilitate or is conducive to or incidental to the discharge of any of their functions'.

For discussion of an identical provision under s111 of the Housing Act 1957 see *Attorney-General* v *Crayford Urban District Council* [1962] Ch 575. Useful as this provision is, the courts will be alive to excessive reliance upon it by local authorities. In *McCarthy & Stone Developments Ltd* v *Richmond London Borough Council* [1991] 3 WLR 941 the council had adopted a policy of charging property developers in respect of the cost of handling inquiries relating to speculative development or redevelopment proposals, relying on s111 as authority. The House of Lords held that, in the absence of an express statutory provision, there was no power to levy the charges in question. The requirement of express statutory authority for the raising of revenue is well established (see *Attorney-General* v *Wilts United Dairies* (1921) 37 TLR 884) but, as Lord Lowry observed, s111 could not provide such authority. The House of Lords expressed the view that the mainstream function of the council, as a planning authority, was the consideration and determining of planning applications. The provision of a planning inquiry and consultation service could be authorised by s111 as ancillary to that function, but to suggest that it provided a power to charge for such a service was to claim that it provided the power to engage in activities which were ancillary to an activity which was in itself ancillary to its statutory planning functions. Similarly, in *Hazell* v *Hammersmith and Fulham London Borough Council* [1991] 2 WLR 372 the House of Lords held that, while borrowing was a function of the local authority that could be facilitated by reliance upon s111, so-called interest rate swap agreements were ultra vires the authority's borrowing powers and could not, therefore, be legitimised by reliance upon s111.

Section 137 of the 1972 Act empowers local authorities to spend up to the product of a 2p rate on purposes for which they have no statutory power, and which they consider to be in the interests of their area. Section 142 empowers a local authority to take steps to inform inhabitants of its area of important developments regarding its activities. In *R* v *ILEA, ex parte Westminster City Council* (1984) The Times 31 December, the Divisional Court held that this did not empower ILEA to finance an advertising campaign persuading the public to oppose central government policy on education spending.

Other forms of control

The Local Commissioners Act 1974 provides for local government 'ombudsmen' in England and Wales, who are empowered to investigate complaints of maladministration by local authorities and can produce reports on their findings. In England and Wales such reports carry no compulsory effect and are often ignored by local authorities; see further Chapter 22.

The Local Government Finance Act 1982 created the Audit Commission, absorbing much of the District Audit Service, which has as its main aims the scrutiny of local government spending to ensure that instances of unlawful or wasteful expenditure are brought to light, and the introduction of commercial accounting methods into local government finance to encourage greater cost-effectiveness.

9.6 Controls over other public corporations

Creation

A number of different procedures have been followed in the creation of public corporations. Where the body has a welfare or regulatory role it will be created by the relevant enabling Act, and be given a budget by the usual means. Where a corporation is created by Parliament to carry out a commercial activity the assets of others engaged in the industry may be compulsorily acquired and transferred to the new corporation, as was the case with the National Coal Board, subsequently British Coal, under the Coal Industry Nationalisation Act 1946. Alternatively, the government may decide to purchase the shares in an industry compulsorily, thereby gaining control under the normal principles of company law. The shares are then vested in a newly created public corporation. An example of this procedure being followed is provided by the creation of the British Steel Corporation. Finally, functions may be transferred from a government department to a public corporation, a technique used in 1969 when the Post Office was created under the Post Office Act 1969.

Ministerial power

The enabling Act will invariably provide for appointments to be made by the relevant minister, thus underlining the political control he can exercise. These appointments are usually for a period of three to five years. The minister has the power to remove a member from office, if that member is absent from board meetings for three consecutive months, has become bankrupt, becomes physically or mentally incapacitated or otherwise unfit. The minister will seek to appoint a chairman with whom he can establish a good working relationship but also, one who understands the policy goals that the minister has created for the industry in question.

The enabling Act will usually give the minister the power to issue directives to the board of a public corporation, indicating the way in which the industry should proceed. This does not relate to the day-to-day running of the industry but to more general long-term strategy. Matters covered may range from pricing policy to buying from British suppliers of goods where possible.

Apart from the revenue that their own activities may, where appropriate, generate, public corporations will be largely dependent on central government to make up any short-fall in their accounts. For long-term projects the public corporation may depend on central government for subsidies, or on the minister for the sanctioning of loan agreements. Given this financial dependence, ministers are able to use the granting or withholding of money as a bargaining tool in persuading the board of a corporation to implement government policy.

Given that the boards of public corporations are, by statute, responsible for the day-to-day running of their industries, the minister will not be answerable to Parliament for such matters. The minister is given a statutory power to issue directives to the boards of corporations, and consequently is answerable to Parliament for these publicly articulated statements of policy.

The problem with accountability concerns the 'behind the scenes' activities of ministers and corporation chairmen. They may meet and agree informally on a policy and its implementation, yet when it is carried out the minister can refuse to answer questions in Parliament about the matter on the ground that it is not his responsibility. Events during the 1984–5 miners' strike illustrates this. At various points in the dispute the management of the National Coal Board, led by its chairman, adopted a 'hard line' attitude to the strike and refused to negotiate with the union members. Allegations were made at the time that the board was responding to instructions from ministers to adopt this line. When questioned in the House of Commons, however, the Prime Minister and Energy Secretary both declined to comment on the Coal Board's management of the strike negotiations, claiming that it was not the Government's responsibility.

The period since 1979 has seen the implementation of a government policy to return public corporations responsible for commercial undertakings to private ownership, most spectacularly as regards telecommunications, gas, electricity and water. On 1 April 1994 the process of denationalising the railways commenced, with Railtrack taking over some responsibilities from British Rail. The privatisation of the coal industry is still very much on the political agenda. The coal industry and the railways may follow suit in due course. The process of 'privatisation' has usually been marked by the vesting of certain controls over pricing in the relevant government minister, and by the creation of an independent consumer watchdog group to report on the conduct of the industry concerned. The result is that the functions left to public corporations, other than local authorities, tend now to be welfare based. As regards regulatory functions, the policy since 1979 has been to leave industries to regulate themselves (eg financial services, advertising, the City), rather than create new regulatory bodies. It is significant that when the system of

House of Commons Select Committees was reorganised in 1979, the Select Committee on Nationalised Industries was abolished and has not since been replaced.

Judicial control

In theory, the ultra vires principle applies to public corporations as it does to other public law bodies, but the control may prove more illusory than real. This point is illustrated by the comments of the Master of the Rolls in *R* v *Independent Broadcasting Authority, ex parte Whitehouse* (1985) The Times 4 April. The applicant alleged that the Director General of the IBA had acted in breach of s4(1) of the Broadcasting Act 1981 in deciding not to refer his decision, to screen the film *Scum*, to other members of the IBA. At first instance declarations were granted that the Director General of the IBA had committed a grave error in not consulting other members of the institution, and that the IBA itself had failed to inform the Director General fully on the procedures relating to referral of controversial films. The Court of Appeal, allowing the appeal, declined to interfere with the Director General's decision.

As Sir John Donaldson MR observed:

'The relevant duty of the IBA was set out in section 4(1), namely, "to satisfy themselves that, so far as possible, the programmes broadcast by the Authority comply with" certain requirements. Those requirements were none of them precise. All required value judgments. The parliamentary intention seemed to have been to create a statutory body, the IBA, consisting of a number of responsible persons as members who would occupy a position analogous to that of the Governors of the BBC. The role of the IBA was to control independent broadcasting and the role of the members to act as policy makers and supervisors. In using the phrase "it shall be the duty of the Authority to satisfy themselves" Parliament was creating what might be described qualitatively as a "best endeavours" obligation and was leaving it to the members to adopt methods of working, or a system, which, in their opinion, was best adapted to securing the requirements set out in section 4(1). [T]he IBA's duty was to devise and operate a system designed to ensure that the statutory requirements were met. The court's right and duty to interfere only arose if the system so devised was not operated or if it was such as no reasonable person could have adopted in compliance with the IBA's statutory duty. Their Lordships were quite unpersuaded that the system fell into that category.'

Note that Mrs Whitehouse was held to have locus standi in this case by virtue of being a television licence holder. Although her challenge was unsuccessful, it does illustrate that in theory, judicial review can be used against public corporations.

Again, in theory, mandamus might be available to order a public corporation to perform its statutory duty. In reality these duties tend to be drawn in such general and vague terms that mandamus would not be a suitable means of ensuring their performance.

10

Liabilities of Local Authorities

10.1 Contract

10.2 Tort

10.3 Liability in negligence

10.4 Individual council officers

10.5 Damages for ultra vires action

10.1 Contract

Generally, local authorities are in the same position as any other corporate body as regards entering into contractual obligations. Section 111 of the Local Government Act 1972 empowers an authority to do anything which is reasonably incidental to the discharge of its functions, and this extends to incurring contractual obligations. Being statutory bodies, local authorities must act within the limits of their power and will not be bound by any ultra vires agreements. Section 9 of the European Communities Act 1972 does not apply to local authorities. For more on this point see Chapter 19.

When entering into contracts, especially for goods and services, local authorities will have to observe standing orders relating to tenders, price paid, and selection of contractor; see s135 Local Government Act 1972. The fiduciary duty owed to ratepayers must be borne in mind, and refusing to accept tenders, for example, from firms having non-unionised work forces, may be of dubious legality.

10.2 Tort

Introduction

As with contractual liability, one starts with the proposition that local authorities are in the same position as regards tortious liability, as any other body with legal personality. Highlighted below are those situations where special considerations apply that might make an action in tort more difficult to pursue against a local authority.

Nuisance – the defence of statutory authority

In an action against a local authority (or any other body) for nuisance, a defence that may be raised is that the nuisance complained of is an inevitable consequence of carrying out what the statute required; the so-called defence of statutory authority.

In *Dormer* v *Newcastle upon Tyne Corporation* [1940] 2 KB 204 the defendants, purporting to exercise their powers under s22 of the Newcastle upon Tyne Improvement Act 1865, placed guard rails in front of Grainger House in the highway between the pavement and the road for a distance of about 138 feet, in order to protect pedestrians. The defendants relied on a plea of 'inevitable nuisance', citing the provisions of s22 as empowering it to place barriers for the prevention of accidents and to make the crossing less dangerous to passengers. The court held that the action failed because the nuisance complained of was a result of steps expressly authorised by statute; see further *Goldberg & Sons Ltd* v *Liverpool Corporation* (1900) 82 LT 362, and *Allen* v *Gulf Oil Refining Ltd* [1981] 2 WLR 141, where the appellants' claim that the nuisance arising out of the operation of an oil refinery, the provision of which had been authorised by a private Act of Parliament (the Gulf Oil Refining Act 1965), was an inevitable consequence of the construction or operation of the refinery was accepted by the House of Lords.

Where a local authority has a number of options as to how and where it will exercise its powers, and it is clear that the amount of nuisance caused will vary with the choice made, it is required to select the option likely to create the least nuisance, so far as that is reasonably possible, if it wishes to be able to rely on the defence of statutory authority. *Metropolitan Asylum District* v *Hill* (1881) 6 App Cas 193 raised the question of whether the appellants could rely on the defence of statutory authority in respect of nuisance found to have been caused by the building of a hospital for sufferers from contagious diseases. The appellants had built the hospital pursuant to their powers under the Metropolitan Poor Act 1867. Dismissing the appeal, the court accepted that the provision of the hospital would necessarily cause some nuisance, but the powers in the relevant Act were permissive not imperative. The appellants had failed to show that they had no choice but to build on the site chosen. As Lord Watson observed:

'... the Respondents did not dispute that if the Appellants or the Local Government Board had been, by the Metropolitan Poor Act, 1867, expressly empowered to build the identical hospital which they have erected at Hampstead, upon the very site which it now occupies, and that with a view to its being used for the treatment of patients suffering from small-pox, the Respondents would not be entitled to the judgment which they have obtained ... I am disposed to hold that if the Legislature, without specifying either plan or site, were to prescribe by statute that a public body shall, within certain defined limits, provide hospital accommodation for a class or classes of persons labouring under infectious disease, no injunction could issue against the use of an hospital established in pursuance of the Act, provided that it were either apparent or proved to the satisfaction of the Court that the directions of the Act could not be complied with at all, without creating a nuisance. In that case, the necessary result of that which they have directed to be done must presumably have been in the view of the Legislature at the time when the Act was passed ... On the other hand, I do not think that the Legislature can be held to have sanctioned that which is a nuisance at common law, except in the case where it has authorized a certain use of a specific building in a specified position, which cannot be used without occasioning nuisance, or in the case where the particular plan or locality not being prescribed, it has imperatively directed that a building shall be provided within a certain area and so used, it being an obvious or established fact that nuisance must be the result. In the latter case the onus of proving that the creation of a nuisance will be the inevitable result of carrying out the directions of the Legislature, lies upon the persons seeking to justify the nuisance. Their justification depends upon their making good these two propositions - in the first place, that such are the imperative orders of the Legislature; and in the second place, that they cannot possibly obey those orders without infringing private rights. If the order of the Legislature can be implemented without nuisance, they cannot, in my opinion, plead the protection of the statute; and, on the other hand, it is insufficient for their protection that what is contemplated by the statute cannot be done without nuisance, unless they are also able to show that the Legislature has directed it to be done. Where the terms of the statute are not imperative, but permissive, when it is left to the discretion of the persons empowered to determine whether the general powers committed to them shall be put into execution or not, I think the fair inference is that the Legislature intended that discretion to be exercised in strict conformity with private rights, and did not intend to confer licence to commit nuisance in any place which might be selected for the purpose.'

See also *Manchester Corporation* v *Farnworth* [1930] AC 171, where the local authority could not rely on statutory authority as a defence to an action in nuisance caused by pollution from an electricity generating station, having failed to exercise all due diligence to prevent the pollution, and *Tate & Lyle Ltd* v *Greater London Council* [1983] 1 All ER 1159, where the defendant authority was not permitted to rely on statutory authority as a defence to an action in nuisance arising out of siltation of the River Thames, which rendered stretches of it unnavigable, because it had not shown that they had taken all reasonable care to prevent the siltation or had sufficient regard for the interests of members of the public likely to be affected.

Trespass

Local authorities can be liable to trespass, as *Cooper* v *Wandsworth Board of Works* (1863) 14 CBNS 180, where the plaintiff's property was demolished without adequate notice being given, illustrates. (See Chapter 14.) Again, a statute may authorise trespass, thus removing any right of action.

Breach of statutory duty

Legislation places a large number of duties upon local authorities, and a major problem is in determining whether any recourse to the courts is possible in the event of a duty not being complied with, or inadequately performed. Two courses of action are open.

First, an individual may seek a remedy in public law, by applying for a judicial review of the local authority's inaction and requesting an order of mandamus, directing the local authority to perform its duty. This is dealt with in more depth in

Chapter 20, but some problems are noted here. Judicial review is discretionary, as are the remedies, and the court may decide that it is not an appropriate case for the granting of mandamus, either because some other more suitable remedy exists, or because the duty is worded in such broad, vague terms, supervision of its (non-) performance would be impossible. The applicant for mandamus will have to establish that he has locus standi to apply, and if he wishes to add a request for damages to his application, it will only be granted if he can show that such a remedy would have been available in an action started by writ.

The second course of action is to proceed by way of writ and sue for the tort of breach of statutory duty. If the plaintiff is successful the result will be an award of damages; there are, however, a number of 'hurdles' the plaintiff will have to clear before this can be achieved.

1. An action in tort by a private individual may be expressly excluded by the statute creating the duty as, for example, is the case with s18 of the Civic Amenities Act 1967 which provides that no action for damages shall lie against a local authority arising from its failure to provide refuse tips.

2. On the basis of the principles set out by Lord Bridge in *Hague* v *Deputy Governor of Parkhurst Prison* [1991] 3 All ER 733, in assessing whether or not the existence of an actionable breach of statutory duty would create a right to sue for damages, the questions to consider are: (1) Was the duty created by the Act owed to a particular class including the plaintiff?; (2) If the answer is 'Yes', had Parliament intended to give such persons an enforceable right of action under the legislation? See further *Cutler* v *Wandsworth Stadium Ltd* [1949] AC 398, and *West Wiltshire District Council* v *Garland & Others* [1994] NLJ 1733 detailed at 23.2.

   Examination of a group of cases concerning alleged breaches of statutory duties owed by local authorities to children illustrates the difficulties in successfully establishing a claim for damages. In *T* v *Surrey County Council* [1994] 4 All ER 577, T, the infant plaintiff was injured whilst in the care of W, a child-minder registered with the defendant local authority, under the Nurseries and Child-Minders Regulation Act 1948. T's mother had sought the advice of the defendant authority before placing T in the care of W, but the authority had failed to advise T's mother of the unresolved inquiry into how a previous child, placed in the care of W, had suffered injuries similar to those inflicted on T. The court based its rejection of T's claim on the ground that the 1948 Act did not give rise to a private right to damages. As Scott Baker J observed:

   'It by no means follows that because the local authority failed to meet its obligations under the Act, an action lies against it for breach of statutory duty. It is a question of the true construction of the Act, whether an action lies with a private individual for a breach of its provisions ... I have read the helpful analysis by Turner J in *X* v *Bedfordshire County Council* (1993) NLJ 1783 ... In that case he considered a similar question in relation to the child care legislation. He held that it was not the intention of Parliament to confer a private law right of action on a child injured as a result of the failure by a local authority to comply with the duties imposed on it by virtue of any of the Child Care Acts. I respectfully agree with his reasoning ... [t]he Act was passed for the benefit of the public as a whole and only, in the very broadest sense, for the benefit of children under the age of five ... [t]he fact that the Act itself provides no remedy for any breach by the local authority does not of itself give an individual a right to damages.'

His Lordship went on, however, to hold that an action for negligent misstatement could be maintained on the basis of the advice given by the defendant's officer: see *Hedley Byrne & Co Ltd* v *Heller & Partners Ltd* [1963] 2 All ER 575.

The first instance decision of Turner J in *X* v *Bedfordshire County Council*, referred to above by Scott Baker J, was subsequently upheld on appeal in *M* v *Newham London Borough Council and Others; X and Others* v *Bedfordshire County Council* [1994] 2 WLR 554. In the first appeal, the child plaintiff M had been made a ward of court following interviews in which she had named her mother's boyfriend as the person responsible for sexually abusing her. When M's mother eventually saw the transcript of her daughter's evidence she was able to point out that the person her daughter had identified as the perpetrator of the abuse was in fact a cousin, who had lived with M and her mother some time previously. The local authority took steps to rehabilitate M with her mother. M, her mother, and the mother's boyfriend, sought damages in respect of the distress caused by these events, alleging that the local authority, the health authority, and the psychiatrist employed by the health authority, had failed to take reasonable care to investigate the allegations of sexual abuse properly. In the second appeal the local authority delayed for over two years before seeking care orders in respect of the infant plaintiffs, despite evidence from the NSPCC, schools, the police, and neighbours that the children were living in dreadful conditions, were malnourished, and at risk of sexual abuse. In both cases the actions brought against the local authority were struck out and the plaintiffs appealed unsuccessfully on the issue of breach of statutory duty. As Sir Thomas Bingham MR observed:

'... I can detect nothing in any of the legislation which persuades me that Parliament intended to confer a right of action on any person who could show, without more, a breach of any of these statutory duties injurious to him. It seems to me fatal to the plaintiff's contentions (1) that the duties imposed on local authorities were framed in terms too general and unparticular to lend themselves at all readily to direct enforcement by individuals; and (2) that the local authorities were accorded so large an area for the exercise of their subjective judgment as to suggest that direct enforcement by individuals was not contemplated.'

Staughton LJ approached the issue from the perspective of the public law private law dichotomy, and regarded a private law action in such circumstances to be inappropriate:

'... the statutory duties relied upon in these two appeals are in the nature of public law functions ... [t]hey involve ... an exercise by the local authority of its own judgment or discretion, with a view to invoking the assistance of the courts (or not doing so). For

... these reasons I conclude that the statutory provisions in question here do not give rise to a private law remedy in damages.'

Note that Staughton J went on to hold that no action could lie at the suit of the plaintiff M in respect of the psychiatrist's negligence as he owed a duty of care to the health authority that had employed him. See further 23.2.

In *E v Dorset County Council* [1994] 4 All ER 640 the plaintiff was one of a number of school pupils seeking damages from their respective educations authorities arising out of alleged failures by the authorities to diagnose, and provide for, the special educational needs of the plaintiffs. Although their appeals were partly successful, in that the actions alleging negligence at common law were allowed to proceed (*M v Newham London Borough Council* distinguished), the claims based on damages for breach of statutory duty were struck out on the basis that there was no evidence that Parliament had intended that an action for damages should be the appropriate procedure for obtaining relief. On the contrary, the court was persuaded by the fact that the Education (Special Education Needs) Regulations 1983 provided administrative procedures to deal with allegations that an education authority was not fulfilling its obligations under the Education Act 1981, and that parents were provided with a right of appeal to an appeal committee and further to the Secretary of State if necessary. If these procedures were not conducted satisfactorily the possibility of judicial review existed, but the purpose of such proceedings would not be to obtain financial redress.

3. What will often be a deciding factor is the provision in the Act of some other means of enforcing the performance of the duty, the reasoning usually adopted being that Parliament cannot have intended the breach of duty to be actionable at the suit of an individual where it has expressly created the procedure for imposing criminal liability for non-performance, or has vested default powers in another public body such as a minister, or provided some other procedure for challenge. Hence in *Southwark London Borough Council v Williams* [1971] Ch 734 the court held that the only way of enforcing a local authority's duty towards its homeless population was through default powers provided in the relevant Act, and not by way of personal action. As Lord Denning observed:

'Seeing that [the default power] is the remedy given by the statute, I do not think there is any other remedy available. The case falls within the principle that: "Where an Act creates an obligation, and enforces the obligation in a specified manner, we take it to be a general rule that performance cannot be enforced in any other manner"; see *Doe d. Rochester (Bp) v Bridges* (1831) 1 B & Ad 847, 859. A good instance of that principle is *Pasmore v Oswaldtwistle Urban District Council* [1898] AC 387, where a local authority was put by statute under an obligation to make sewers for draining their district. It was held by the House of Lords that the only remedy was the specific remedy given by the statute, namely, a complaint to the Local Government Board. Policy and convenience dictated that decision in the case of sewers. Likewise here in the case of temporary accommodation for those in need. It cannot have been intended by Parliament that every person who was in need of temporary accommodation should be able to sue the local authority for it: or to take the law into his own hands for the purpose.'

Similarly, in *R* v *ILEA, ex parte Ali* (1990) The Times 21 February the applicant unsuccessfully sought damages in respect of ILEA's failure to provide an adequate number of primary school places in Tower Hamlets, despite the fact that the minister had refused to invoke his default powers provided under the Education Act 1944. The court took the view that ILEA's statutory duty was not absolute. It had to do its best to discharges its duty, but might not be able to do so because of unforeseen circumstances. The court concluded that Parliament had not intended to provide a member of the public with a private law right to compensation: see further *Wyatt* v *Hillingdon London Borough Council* (1978) 76 LGR 727.

Despite the above, the courts will not regard themselves as powerless to act simply because a default power exists, especially where there is evidence of an ultra vires refusal to exercise such default powers. In *Meade* v *Haringey London Borough* Council [1979] 1 WLR 637, the local authority had closed its schools due to a caretakers' strike, and a number of parents brought an action claiming that the authority was in breach of its duty under s8 of the Education Act 1944 to provide sufficient schools in its area. Section 99 of the 1944 Act provided the Secretary of State for Education with powers to compel performance of this duty which he declined to exercise after concluding that the authority was not in breach of its duty. Although the Court of Appeal dismissed the parents' action, Lord Denning expressed the view that:

> '... although that section does give a remedy – by complaint to a Minister – it does not exclude any other remedy. To my mind it leaves open all the established remedies which the law provides in cases where a public authority fails to perform its statutory duty either by an act of commission or omission ... I am clearly of opinion that if the borough council of Haringey, of their own free will, deliberately closed one school in their borough for one week – without just cause or excuse – it would be ultra vires: and each of the parents whose child suffered thereby would have an action for damages. All the more so if they closed it for five weeks or more. Or for all schools. No one can suppose that Parliament authorised the borough council to renounce their duties to such an extent as deliberately to close the schools without just cause or excuse. To use Lord Reid's words, it was their duty "not to act so as to frustrate the policy and objects of the Act".'

4. The provision of a criminal sanction may well dissuade a court from recognising a right to bring proceedings for breach of statutory duty, see *Keating* v *Elvan Reinforced Concrete Co Ltd* [1968] 2 All ER 139 and *Cutler* v *Wandsworth Stadium Ltd* (above) and the provision of a statutory right of appeal may do the same. In *R* v *Knowsley Borough Council, ex parte Maguire and Others* [1992] NLJ 1375, where the decision of the local authority not to grant taxi cab licences was challenged by the applicants, the court refused to recognise a right to damages

for breach of duty in respect of the respondent authority's exercise of its powers under the Town Police Clauses Act 1847, on the basis that the Act had not been intended by Parliament to provide such a remedy, since, if a licence was refused, there was a right of appeal to the Crown Court or, if a condition attached to the grant of a licence was challenged, to the magistrates' court.

10.3 Liability in negligence

As creatures of statute, local authorities will of necessity be exercising statutory powers when discharging their functions. While, as explained above, an authority might be able to rely on a statute as providing authority for causing an 'inevitable' nuisance, the law does not recognise negligence as inevitable and hence the defence of statutory authority will not be available. For example, in *Geddis* v *Proprietors of Bann Reservoir*, where the plaintiff successfully sued for damages consequent to the flooding of his land following the failure of the defendants to cleanse a channel leading from a reservoir that they had constructed pursuant to statutory authority, Lord Blackburn observed:

> '... an action does lie for doing that which the legislature has authorised, if it be done negligently. And I think that if by a reasonable exercise of the powers, either given by statute ... or ... at common law ... the damage could have been prevented, it is, within this rule, "negligence" not to make such reasonable exercise of their powers.'

More recently, in *Targett* v *Torfaen Borough Council* [1992] 3 All ER 27, the plaintiff, a tenant of the defendant local authority, was injured as a result of falling down the steps to his house. He had, in the past, complained to the council of the danger presented by the steps in that they were unlit and had no handrail. At first instance the trial judge found for the plaintiff, subject to his being 25 per cent responsible for the injuries on the ground of contributory negligence. The council appealed, contending that since the plaintiff had known of the danger he was under a duty to take greater care. Following *Rimmer* v *Liverpool City Council* [1984] 1 All ER 930, the appeal was dismissed on the basis that the plaintiff's knowledge of the danger did not negative the council's duty of care, or break the chain of causation. Although it had been practicable for the plaintiff to take greater care, it had not been practicable for him to avoid the danger altogether.

In short, local authorities are subject to the same liability in negligence as other legal persons, save that the courts may, on public policy grounds, recognise particular principles concerning the scope and imposition of a duty of care, in the light of the fact that a local authority may be called upon to discharge functions that have no parallel in private law. Three key problems need to be addressed by the plaintiff; the existence of a duty of care; causation; and the scope of any such duty of care.

Policy and operational spheres of action

A line of authorities originating in *Home Office* v *Dorset Yacht Co* [1970] AC 1004, and developed via *Dutton* v *Bognor Regis Urban District Council* [1972] 1 QB 373 and *Anns* v *Merton London Borough Council* [1978] AC 728, has resulted in recognition that there may be some instances of public bodies exercising discretion that may not be amenable to the imposition of the common law duty of care essential for the imposition of liability in negligence.

In *Home Office* v *Dorset Yacht Co* Borstal trainees escaped from custody and damaged the plaintiff company's property. The escape was partly due to a more relaxed system of control over inmates which was designed to teach them self discipline. The new regime had been adopted as a matter of Home Office policy. It was held that no action would lie in negligence at the suit of a litigant claiming to have suffered damaged as a result of the adoption of the policy. The legality or otherwise of policies could only be challenged by way of judicial review on public law grounds. The actual supervision of the Borstal trainees was more clearly operational, but the officers did possess a certain amount of discretion and, before an action in negligence could succeed, it would have to be shown that the officers concerned had been acting outside the scope of the powers delegated to them. Consequently, if the officers had simply been following their instructions, no action in negligence would have been possible because no ultra vires act could have been established on their part.

This policy/operational dichotomy was further developed, as regards the non-exercise of statutory discretion, by the House of Lords in *Anns* v *Merton London Borough Council*. Under the Public Health Act 1936 the local authority had powers to inspect and approve foundations for buildings being erected in its area. Actions were brought against the authority by the occupants of flats who had purchased long leases. Cracks had developed in the walls of their dwellings, and it became obvious that the whole block had inadequate foundations. It was never established whether any inspection of the foundations had actually been made by the local authority; consequently the plaintiffs' actions were based on allegations that the authority's inspection had been negligent or that they had negligently failed to inspect. Lord Wilberforce observed that if the local authority had been under a duty to inspect, no real problem would have arisen. In the case of a power, it was widely accepted that liability could arise in negligence if it was wrongly exercised. It had been argued that no liability could arise where an authority declined to exercise a power, but Lord Wilberforce rejected this, stating that although non-exercise of powers might attract a high degree of immunity, it was not absolutely immune. The House held that a local authority could be in breach of its duty of care if it could be shown that it had not properly exercised its discretion as to the making of inspections, and had failed to exercise reasonable care to secure that the bye-laws applicable to the specifications for foundations had been complied with. The duty of care extended to protecting owners or occupiers of buildings from losses caused by developers as a result of defective building work. More particularly, liability could arise where an inspector employed by the authority, acting otherwise than in the bona fide exercise of his delegated discretion, failed to exercise reasonable care to ensure that the foundations were in conformity with the legal requirements. These comments are subject to a significant qualification, however. As Lord Wilberforce went on to observe:

> 'Most, indeed probably all, statutes relating to public authorities or public bodies, contain in them a large area of policy. The courts call this "discretion" meaning that the decision is one for the authority or body to make, and not for the courts. Many statutes also prescribe or at least presuppose the practical execution of policy decisions: a convenient description of this is to say that in addition to the area of policy or discretion, there is an operational area. Although this distinction between the policy area and the operational area is convenient, and illuminating, it is probably a distinction of degree; many "operational" powers or duties have in them some element of "discretion". It can safely be said that the more "operational" a power or duty may be, the easier it is to superimpose upon it a common law duty of care ... I do not think that it is right to limit this to a duty to avoid causing extra or additional damage beyond what must be expected to arise from the exercise of the power or duty. That may be correct when the act done under the statute inherently must adversely affect the interest of individuals. But many other acts can be done without causing any harm to anyone – indeed may be directed to preventing harm from occurring. In these cases the duty is the normal one of taking care to avoid harm to those likely to be affected.'

The policy/operational dichotomy has subsequently been used as the basis for a number of decisions.

In *Fellowes* v *Rother District Council* [1983] 1 All ER 513, the plaintiff alleged that the defendant authority, in exercising statutory powers to carry out coastal protection work, had negligently lowered the height of a groyne on the seashore with the result that some of the plaintiff's land had been washed away. The court held that, to succeed in negligence, the plaintiff would have to prove that the actions were in the operational, and not the policy, sphere; that they had been carried out by a council employee or agent in excess of the discretion delegated to him; and that the normal principles of negligence could be established. In *West* v *Buckinghamshire County Council* (1984) The Times 13 November, it was held that a local authority's decision not to place double white lines on a road, pursuant to its statutory powers, was a policy decision not giving rise to any duty of care in private law: see also *Rigby* v *Chief Constable of Northamptonshire* [1985] 1 WLR 1242.

On the basis of *Anns*, were the facts in *Sheppard* v *Glossop Corporation* (below) to recur, it might be contended that the decision whether or not to provide lighting in a particular street was one based on policy, the result of the local authority balancing the needs of its area with available resources. The actual siting of the lamp post, although within the discretion of the local authority, would arguably be much more in the operational sphere; ie the execution of a policy decision. Lord Wilberforce's warning in *Anns*, to the effect that liability in negligence could be based on an authority's failure act as much as its positive acts, has been borne out in a number of subsequent cases, notably *Stovin* v *Wise; Norfolk County Council (third party)* [1994] 1 WLR 1124. The plaintiff motorcyclist was injured in a collision with a car being driven by the defendant. The plaintiff's visibility at the junction where the collision occurred had been obscured by a raised bank of earth to his left. The local highway authority were aware of the dangerous nature of the junction, and the fact that a number of accidents had occurred there in the recent past. Efforts had been made to secure the agreement of the landowner to the levelling of the ground to improve visibility at the junction, but by the time of the plaintiff's accident no response had been received. The plaintiff's action against the defendant was settled, but the defendant joined the highway authority as a third party alleging that it was to blame for not having taken more steps to improve safety at the junction. The decision at first instance to the effect that the highway authority had breached its common law duty of care and was 30 per cent to blame for the collision was upheld on appeal. The court holding that the authority, having become aware of the danger at the junction, and having decided to allocate resources to deal with the problem, came under a common law duty to act with reasonable expedition to resolve the matter. The failure to improve the safety of road users at the junction was a breach of that duty; see further 23.2.

Causation

The plaintiff must show that the local authority's exercise of power has actually caused damage that would not otherwise have occurred. In *Sheppard* v *Glossop Corporation* [1921] 3 KB 132, the respondent alleged that the appellant, the Glossop Corporation, was liable to him in damages for personal injuries sustained by him through its failure to keep a lamp alight at a dangerous spot within its area. The appellant had decided that the lights would be extinguished after 9 o'clock at night in the interests of economy. The court held that s161 of the Public Health Act 1875 gave local authorities a power to light streets; it did not impose a duty upon them to do so. Having decided to light the street until 9 o'clock in the evening the authority was free to extinguish the lights thereafter. By resolving to extinguish the street lights at this time, the authority was not making the street any more dangerous than it would have been. Banks LJ observed:

> 'If in lighting the district they act negligently, if for instance they should erect a lamp post and leave it unprotected in the middle of a highway or so close by the highway as to be a danger to persons passing along unless it was properly protected, or allow their gas to escape into some one's house, those would be negligent acts in the course of doing that which the Legislature has authorized ... This is not a case of a statutory power, like a power to make a reservoir and maintain a sufficient supply of water therein, negligently exercised; the appellants have merely exercised the discretion vested in them by the Legislature. They were under no obligation to place a lamp post at this particular spot; and if they kept it there they were not bound to supply it with gas, and are not to be made liable for merely extinguishing the light at any particular hour.'

For further authority on this point, see *East Suffolk Rivers Catchment Board* v *Kent* [1941] AC 74.

The scope of any duty of care arising

Provided that, notwithstanding the policy/operation, a local authority is held to owe a duty of care in the discharge of a particular function, the question arises as to the scope of the duty. In an *Anns* situation is the duty owed to the developers, the initial occupiers, or the subsequent owners or occupiers? What type of losses are recoverable? In *Investors in Industry Commercial Properties v South Bedfordshire District Council & Others* [1986] 1 All ER 787, the plaintiffs were owners of a number of warehouses built on the site of a former rubbish tip that had rapidly disintegrated due to the inadequacy of the foundations. The plans for the warehouses had been approved by the defendant local authority, and the foundations inspected and approved. The plaintiffs argued, inter alia, that the local authority had been negligent, but the court, relying on *Anns v Merton London Borough Council* and *Governors of the Peabody Donation Fund v Sir Lindsay Parkinson & Co Ltd* [1985] AC 210 (in which the court had held that the plaintiffs could not recover in negligence, because the statutory power of inspection had been conferred on the local authority to safeguard the occupiers of houses and not to protect developers from economic losses), held that the local authority owed no duty of care to the plaintiffs. In the course of his judgment Slade LJ stated three propositions that now applied to this situation. First, the supervisory powers given to local authorities in relation to building plans and inspection of foundations were for the benefit of members of the public and the occupants of such buildings, not to safeguard the developer, or anyone else, from purely economic loss. Secondly, it was possible that a local authority could be regarded as owing a duty of care to a subsequent occupier other than the original building owner: to take reasonable care to ensure that a building was erected in accordance with the building regulations so as not to endanger life or health. Thirdly, in the majority of situations, the original owner of a property (ie the developer) would not normally be able to recover damages from a local authority if plans and foundations were negligently approved, as it was incumbent on the original owner to ensure that the building complied with the building regulations, a fortiori where the owner had had the benefit of the advice of architects, engineers and contractors: see further *Curran v Northern Ireland Co-Ownership Housing Association Ltd* [1987] 2 All ER 13.

The limited scope of a local authority's duty of care as regards economic loss is now clear following the House of Lords' decision in *Murphy v Brentwood District Council* [1990] 3 WLR 414, where it was held that the principle in *Donoghue v Stevenson* [1932] AC 562 should not be extended to impose liability for pure economic loss on local authorities supervising plans to ensure compliance with building regulations. It is submitted that *Anns* is still the relevant authority as regards liability for physical harm or economic loss consequent upon such harm. In *Stovin v Wise; Norfolk County Council (third party)* (above) Kennedy LJ regarded the House of Lords' decision in *Anns v Merton London Borough Council* [1978] AC

728 as providing more guidance as to the resolution of the problem of liability than *Murphy*, observing that:

> '... in the context of the present case, it is, as it seems to me, important to recognise two things: first, that the decision in *Murphy's* case is confined to economic loss, more than one of their Lordships indicating that the position might be different if foreseeable personal injury were sustained ... [S]econd, the decision was concerned with the wide-ranging common law duty to which local authorities had been held to be subject as a result of their limited involvement in the erection of buildings which later turned out to be defective. On any view there was not the close link between the alleged breach of duty and the damage which there is when a road accident is found to be due in part to an obstruction to visibility which a highway authority charged with the duty of maintaining the highway had decided ought to be removed, and had been in a position to carry that decision to effect before the relevant accident occurred ... it seems to me to be entirely in line ... with the *Anns* approach ... to say that in this case once the highway authority decided to seek the co-operation of British Rail [the landowner] it owed a duty of care to road users to press forward with its proposals with reasonable expedition. [The highway authority] was in breach of that duty, and as a result it contributed to the injury which the plaintiff sustained.'

See further comments of Sir Donald Nicholls V-C broadly supportive of this approach in *Targett* v *Torfaen Borough Council* (above).

10.4 Individual council officers

In some situations it may be the individual council officer who is to be held liable in tort and not the employing authority. In *Stanbury* v *Exeter Corporation* [1905] 2 KB 838, an inspector appointed by the defendant authority, but acting under a duty imposed by central government, ordered the destruction of the plaintiff's sheep. The plaintiff claimed that the local authority was vicariously liable for the inspector's negligence in ordering the destruction of the animals. The court held that the defendant was not vicariously liable as the inspector was not acting in pursuance of duties imposed by it.

In *Ministry of Housing and Local Government* v *Sharp* [1970] 2 QB 223, a landowner applied unsuccessfully for planning permission and was paid compensation by the Ministry. A compensation notice was placed on the register of local land charges, so that if planning permission was later granted the Ministry could be reimbursed. Planning permission was later granted to the owner, who sold the land. The purchaser had requested a search of the local land register, and this was conducted negligently by a local authority clerk, with the result that the purchaser bought the land with no notice of the charge. The purchaser was thus entitled to refuse to reimburse the Ministry. The Ministry then sought damages from the Registrar, Mr Sharp, for breach of statutory duty; and against the local authority on the basis that it was vicariously liable for its clerk's negligence. At first instance Fisher J held that the registrar was in breach of his statutory duty; that the clerk who made the search knew or ought to have known that if he did not use proper care any incumbrancer against whom the certificate was conclusive would be damaged; that accordingly the clerk owed a duty of care to the minister and was in breach of it; and that the local authority was vicariously liable for the negligence of the clerk. The Court of Appeal (Lord Denning MR dissenting) held that the Registrar was not under an absolute statutory duty to issue accurate certificates, and as he himself had not been negligent no action would lie against him. The clerk, on the other hand, had been negligent and the local authority was vicariously liable for his actions.

Salmon LJ observed:

'The real question is whether Parliament intended that in the event of a search being inaccurate and the certificate failing to set out the relevant entries in the register, the registrar should be personally liable to the incumbrancer for the financial loss which this failure may have caused him ... There have been numerous attempts in the books to lay down guidelines as to when a civil action may be brought claiming damages for breach of an absolute statutory obligation against the person upon whom such an obligation is imposed ... If the Legislature had intended to make the registrar absolutely liable for any damage caused (through no fault of his or anyone else) by an inaccurate certificate, I am convinced that it would have imposed that liability in very much clearer language than that used in s17 ... I can see no reason why the Legislature should impose such a liability upon a registrar, however tender it may be to purchasers and incumbrancers. It does not seem to me to be any answer to say that the Crown would probably stand behind the registrar. No doubt it would, but only as a matter of grace ... I hope that nothing I have said can be taken to mean that I consider that anyone in this country is allowed to shelter behind any kind of droit administratif. Indeed I consider that one of the most important functions of our courts is vigilantly to protect the rights of the individual against unlawful encroachment by public officers and by the administration. The courts' powers to this end might well, in my view, be enlarged. Certainly such powers as we possess should be vigorously exercised. I do not suggest that the registrar escapes liability because he is a public officer. The question is not: Can the registrar escape from some absolute obligation which the statute imposes upon him? but: What obligation (if any) does the statute impose upon him? ... '

An individual council employee may also incur liability for malicious abuse of power, or acting in bad faith: see comments in *Smith* v *East Elloe Rural District Council* [1956] AC 736 and *Davies* v *Bromley Corporation* [1908] 1 KB 170.

10.5 Damages for ultra vires action

At present, no damages are recoverable in English law simply because a public body has negligently acted ultra vires and an individual has suffered loss.

In *Dunlop* v *Woollahra MC* [1982] AC 158, where the plaintiff suffered considerable financial loss following the imposition of ultra vires building restrictions on his property, damages were sought on the basis that the defendant authority had not taken reasonable care to ensure that they were not proposing to act in an ultra vires way. His action failed, Lord Diplock doubting whether any duty of care was owed by the local authority in imposing the building restrictions. In this respect, see *Rowling* v *Takaro Properties Ltd* [1988] 1 All ER 163 and *Lonrho* v *Tebbit* [1991] 4 All ER 973.

That damages may be recoverable where a public body acts in bad faith, that is it deliberately acts ultra vires, knowing that such action will adversely affect the interests of another, is confirmed by the decision of the House of Lords in *Jones* v *Swansea City Council* [1990] 1 WLR 1453. The plaintiff leased commercial premises from the local authority under a 99-year lease which restricted the use of the premises to shops/offices. In January 1979 she applied to the local authority for a variation in the terms of the lease so that the premises could be used as a club. In April 1979 this application was granted. During the debate on the application, the leader of the Labour grouping on the council, a Mr Lewis, stated that if he was returned to power he would ensure that the decision to allow the change of use would be reversed. In May 1979 the local elections resulted in the Labour group being returned to power on the council, and in June 1979 the majority Labour group on the council voted that the change of use decision should be rescinded. The plaintiff brought an action claiming damages for malicious abuse of power against the council and its leader, alleging that the Labour group had acted out of spite because of its opposition to the Ratepayers' Party, led by the plaintiff's husband, that had taken control of the council in 1978. At first instance the trial judge held that there was insufficient evidence of actual malice on the part of the council. In particular he was influenced by the evidence that the Labour councillors had not voted in this matter upon obedience to the party whip. On appeal to the Court of Appeal it was held that the appeal would be allowed and a retrial ordered. The appeal court felt that, on the facts, the trial judge's determination that there was no malice could not be sustained. As the Court of Appeal was not in a position to try the issue itself, a retrial was appropriate. The court added, however, that the fact that the council, in rescinding the permission to use the premises as a club, had been exercising a power arising from a private agreement, did not preclude the plaintiff from bringing an action for malicious abuse of power, or misfeasance. All powers possessed by a public authority, whatever their source or nature, were to be exercised for the public good. In allowing the council's appeal against this decision, the House of Lords held that although an action for misfeasance in public office would lie against the council where the plaintiff was able to show that the majority of councillors voting had done so with the intention of damaging the plaintiff's interests, the trial judge had been entitled to find that there was insufficient evidence that Mr Lewis had been motivated by malice. Their Lordships went on to hold that even if malice on the part of Mr Lewis had been found by the trial judge, there were insufficient grounds for contending that his malice had been known to the other Labour councillors and had infected their thinking at the time they had cast their votes.

11

Introduction to Judicial Review

11.1 Control of power

The main concern of administrative law, as will have been seen from Chapter 1, is the control of power. Attention is now to be focused on judicial review, the mechanism of control. The step-by-step detail of its workings are laid out in the following chapters. The purpose of this chapter is to present an overview of judicial review so that the reader can grasp the nature of review and its shortcomings.

The source of power

The essence of judicial review is that an 'inferior body' (other expressions employed include subordinate body; administrative body, or administrative agency) has acted outside the scope of its power. The expressions used are:

- intra vires – within its powers;
- ultra vires – beyond its powers.

Because the powers (or jurisdiction) of these bodies are limited by the terms of the statutes, royal charters, or prerogative orders, from which they are created, they can be referred to as 'bodies of limited jurisdiction'. Logic dictates that if a body has unlimited powers it cannot act ultra vires, see Lord Diplock's explanation of this in *Re Racal Communications Ltd* [1981] AC 374. Unless the decision-making body under consideration is one of 'limited jurisdiction', therefore, the ultra vires doctrine cannot apply.

Summary

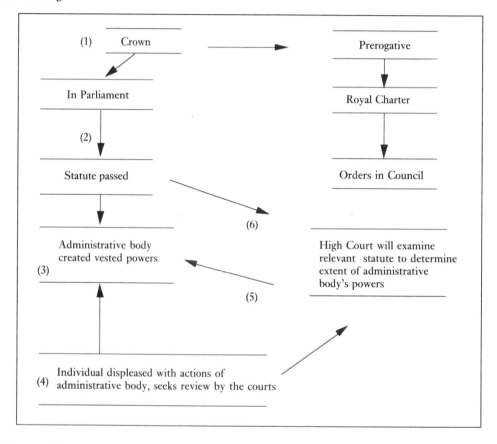

Key to diagram
1. Body created by statute or under the prerogative.
2. Statute passed, where this method of creation chosen.
3. Administrative body created, and given various powers.
4. Administrative body takes a decision that an individual seeks to challenge.
5. Individual applies for judicial review.
6. Reviewing court examines the provisions of the enabling Act, and will decide on whether the body has acted intra vires or ultra vires.

The diagram illustrates the traditional analysis.

Following the Court of Appeal's decision in *R v Panel on Take-overs and Mergers, ex parte Datafin plc* [1987] 2 WLR 699, it is arguable that the scope of judicial review has been extended to any 'entity' having de facto power to take decisions that affect the public. This matter is considered below at 11.4.

11.2 Procedural problems

An initial concern for any litigant in the field of administrative law is the issue of the procedure to be used in order to challenge the decision in question. If the respondent body is classified as existing and operating within the sphere of private law, then a litigant may be able to proceed by way of writ. Where, however, the respondent is a public law body, the further question arises as to whether the issue of law arising is one of public law or private law. If the former, judicial review has to be used. The way in which this problem has arisen can be summarised as follows:

Pre-1977

Traditionally there were two ways in which the actions of administrative agencies could be challenged.

Private law An action started by writ or originating summons, in the plaintiff's own name. The advantages were: flexible time limits, availability of discovery, no requirement to obtain the leave of the court to proceed. Remedies available were damages, declaration, and injunction.

Public law An application had to be made for a prerogative order. The problems were the short time limits for bringing an application, locus standi requirements, unavailability of discovery, interrogation or cross-examination of deponents, and inflexibility regarding remedies.

Processes compared

Note the essential difference between the action by writ and the application for judicial review. In the former the plaintiff is bringing the action in his own name. Hence the citation of such cases, eg *Ridge* v *Baldwin*; *Anisminic Ltd* v *FCC*.

In the latter case the applicant seeking judicial review is requesting one of the prerogative orders: certiorari, mandamus or prohibition. These orders are issued by the Crown on behalf of the applicant against the public body alleged to have acted illegally. Hence the citation of such cases, eg *R* v *Home Secretary, ex parte Santillo*.

Reforms

The former procedure for applying for the prerogative orders was entirely replaced in 1977 with a reformed procedure for applying for judicial review, introduced by way of statutory instrument RSC (Amendment No 3) 1977 (SI 1977/1955). These changes were largely the result of recommendations made by the Law Commission in its *Report on Remedies in Administrative Law* (Law Com No 73, Cmnd 6407, 1976).

The effect of the changes was substantially to reduce the procedural handicaps imposed upon applicants for judicial review, and they were later given the status of changes in substantive law by being enshrined in s31 of the Supreme Court Act 1981.

Effect of the changes

Initially it was thought that the new O.53 had simply made the procedure for obtaining judicial review less burdensome, and if a plaintiff nevertheless still preferred to proceed by way of writ and seek damages, a declaration or an injunction against a public body, he was free to do so.

In a number of decisions, however, the courts began to question whether or not plaintiffs proceeding by way of action, when judicial review would have been available, were abusing the processes of the court. This growing concern was reflected in two decisions: *Barrs* v *Bethell* [1981] 3 WLR 874 and *Re Tillmire Common, Heslington* [1982] 2 All ER 615. In both cases actions were struck out on the ground that, given the nature of the challenges involved (in both cases to the public law actions of a public law body), proceeding by way of O.53 would have been more appropriate. Despite this, however, the law was still unclear as to when and if each procedure could be used.

11.3 *O'Reilly* v *Mackman*

The decision of the House of Lords in *O'Reilly* v *Mackman* [1983] 2 AC 237, principally the speech of Lord Diplock, forms the basis of the modern law (and much of its uncertainty) as to when O.53 should be used.

The decision

The appellants in the case were prisoners serving long sentences of imprisonment, who issued writs and originating summonses against members of the Board of Visitors of Hull Prison, seeking declarations that the disciplinary awards of forfeiture of remission made by the Board were null and void on the ground of breach of natural justice.

The House of Lords held that the appellants had no private law rights as regards the Board, only a public law right to be given a fair hearing.

Further, the Board was a public law body, deriving its status and powers from statute. As a result, it would be an abuse of the court's processes to proceed by way of action to challenge its determinations.

The appellants had to proceed by way of O.53 to challenge the decision of a body affecting their public law right. By now, of course, the time limit for applying for review had expired.

The reasoning

Lord Diplock considered the problems associated with judicial review prior to 1977 and the changes instituted as a result of the Law Commission's Report, and concluded that many of the procedural handicaps that would previously have led a complainant to avoid having to apply for a prerogative order if at all possible had since been removed. Specific improvements were:

1. Discovery was now available.
2. Interrogatories could now be administered.
3. Deponents could now be cross-examined on affidavits.
4. A claim for damages could be added to the application.
5. A declaration or an injunction could now be included in an application for review.

The result was that there were no longer any compelling reasons for permitting a plaintiff to proceed by way of action in a public law matter. Further, there were sound policy reasons for insisting that O.53 be used where the respondent was a public body, because of the procedural provided safeguards.

Applications for review had to be made without delay, usually within three months of the action complained of; compare this with the six-year time limit on some actions by writ. It was important that a public body should know quickly of any significant challenge to the legality of its actions in public law so that third party interests were not adversely affected.

The requirement that those seeking review should have to possess 'sufficient interest' in the matter to which their application relates and should have to obtain leave to apply for review, provided an important 'filter' of cases against public bodies. By the very nature of their activities such bodies were likely to attract the attention of 'cranks and busybodies'. If such persons were allowed to proceed by way of writ the defendant body would be put to the expense of instructing lawyers to put in a defence, no matter how worthless the allegation. The requirement of leave ensured that no participation from the respondent body was required until a prima facie case for review had been made out by the applicant.

The exceptions

From the foregoing it would appear that every case involving a public law body and a public law issue now had to be brought by way of O.53. In his speech, however,

Lord Diplock did contemplate exceptional situations where an action by writ would be allowed:

> 'My Lords, I have described this as a general rule; for, though it may normally be appropriate to apply it by the summary process of striking out the action, there may be exceptions, particularly where the invalidity of the decision arises as a collateral issue in a claim for infringement of a right of the plaintiff arising under private law, or where none of the parties objects to the adoption of the procedure by writ or originating summons. Whether there should be other exceptions should, in my view, at this stage in the development of procedural public law, be left to be decided on a case to case basis.'

11.4 What is a public law body?

It is evident from Lord Diplock's speech in *O'Reilly* v *Mackman* that his Lordship favoured the resolution of public law issues (subject to exceptions considered below) by way of judicial review. Given that judicial review has always been associated with public law bodies, the question of how one identifies a public body as such arises. It is submitted that the Court of Appeal decision in *R* v *Panel on Take-overs and Mergers, ex parte Datafin plc* (above) now provides the key. In that case the body subject to review exercised no statutory or prerogative powers, and was not even based on a private contract or constitution. As the Master of the Rolls observed, it possessed no visible means of legal support. The court held that its functions were amenable to review, however, on the basis of the Panel's enormous de facto power to take decisions affecting the public and, crucially, the fact that there was no other means by which those affected by the decisions of the Panel could have challenged them in the courts.

Thus it is submitted that the classification of a body as 'public', and so amenable to judicial review, has just as much to do with the functions it performs, and the inadequacy of legal controls over its actions, as it has to do with the source of its power. This approach has at least the advantage of avoiding the continued agonising over the public/private dichotomy so beloved of some English administrative lawyers, when such a distinction is almost impossible to maintain in English law. Two questions remain, however.

First, if a body has no visible means of legal support, how does one apply the ultra vires doctrine to its actions, assuming that this is still the basis for judicial review? The question was addressed, albeit obliquely, by the Court of Appeal when it considered the second application for judicial review of a decision of the Take-over Panel in *R* v *Panel on Take-overs and Mergers, ex parte Guinness* [1989] 2 WLR 863. Lord Donaldson MR observed that there were difficulties attendant upon reviewing the decisions of a body such as the Panel on the established grounds of irrationality, illegality, and procedural impropriety: as regards illegality, because the Panel acted as both legislator and interpreter of its rules; as regards irrationality, because it was itself charged with determining what were and were not relevant considerations; as regards procedural unfairness, because what was fair would depend upon underlying value judgments made by the Panel as to what was appropriate in a given case. Since the constitution, functions, and powers of the Panel were, to a large extent, sui generis, his Lordship felt that it was better to adopt a broad view of its actions, without resorting to formal classifications of illegality.

The second, admittedly more academic, question is that of how a body such as the Panel, having no legal personality, can be a party to legal proceedings.

Since the landmark decision in *Datafin*, the courts seem to have taken two paces forward and one pace back in developing the scope of judicial review. Illustrative of the bold expansionist approach is the decision in *R v Ethical Committee of St Mary's Hospital, ex parte Harriot* (1987) The Times 27 October, where the court held, apparently without any detailed consideration of the point, that an ad hoc committee comprised of professionals working at the hospital in question could be made subject to judicial review, where it was determining whether a patient should be permitted to undergo in vitro fertilisation treatment.

Given that *Datafin* marked the extension of review to bodies lacking any legal basis for their existence, the courts displayed little reluctance in extending review to regulatory bodies incorporated as companies under the Companies Acts. The lead here was perhaps provided by the Scottish courts in *Bank of Scotland (Petitioner)* (1988) The Times 21 November, where it was held that the Investment Management Regulatory Organisation (IMRO), a self regulatory body established in the wake of the Financial Services Act 1986 as a company limited by guarantee, with offices registered in London, was nevertheless a body amenable to judicial review. The court confirmed that the determining factor when assessing the reviewability of such a body should be the public nature of its functions, rather than its legal character or constitution; this was true even where the action complained of allegedly took the form of a breach of contractual obligations.

This decision has subsequently been followed by the Divisional Court in *R v Advertising Standards Authority Ltd, ex parte The Insurance Service plc* (1989) The Times 14 July. The Advertising Standards Authority Ltd (the ASA) had investigated and upheld a complaint that the applicant insurance company's advertising leaflets were misleading, amounting to a breach of advertising standards. In granting the company's application for judicial review, Glidewell LJ indicated that the ASA exhibited many similarities to the Panel on Take-overs and Mergers. Like the Panel, it had no statutory or common law powers, although unlike the Panel it did have legal identity derived from its status as a company under the Companies Acts. Looking at the functions of the ASA, his Lordship had no doubt that they fell within the sphere of 'public law'. The following factors were found by the court to be significant. First, if the ASA had not discharged the function of regulating the advertising industry, the task would almost certainly have been discharged by the Director General of Fair Trading. Secondly, there was no provision in the memorandum or articles of association of the ASA for any appeal against its rulings. Thirdly, a ruling by the ASA that an advertisement was in breach of the code of advertising resulted in it being almost impossible for a company to continue with its campaign. Fourthly, the regulation of advertising was now supported by legislation in the form of 'The Control of Misleading Advertisements Regulations' (SI 1988/915), implementing European Council Directive 84/450/EEC.

Compare this with *R v Football Association, ex parte Football League* [1993] 2 All ER 833, where the Football League sought to challenge by way of judicial review the decision of the Football Association to form a Premier League and introduce consequent changes to its regulations. The Football League had a contractual agreement with the Football Association whereby it was permitted each year to operate the leagues. The Football League contended that the Football Association was amenable to review because it exercised monopoly control over the game and controlled the rules governing it. Dismissing the application, the court held that the Football Association was not discharging functions of a governmental nature and there was no evidence that its functions would be exercised by an governmental body if it did not exist.

It may yet be unwise, however, to assume that the functionalist approach will be the touchstone for review. The Court of Appeal's ruling in *R v Jockey Club, ex parte Aga Khan* [1993] 1 WLR 909 indicates a considerable degree of confusion on the point. The applicant was the owner of the filly 'Aliysa', the winner of the Epsom Oaks in 1989. Following a routine test after the race, the horse's urine was found to contain traces of a banned substance. The Jockey Club fined the trainer £200, and disqualified the horse. There was no allegation of wrongdoing on the part of the applicant, but he alleged that his reputation had been injured, and the value of the horse adversely affected. On a trial of a preliminary issue, the susceptibility of the Jockey Club to judicial review, the Divisional Court ruled in favour of the applicant, but this decision was reversed on appeal. Sir Thomas Bingham MR accepted that the Jockey Club enjoyed a virtual monopoly over the regulation of a significant national activity, exercised powers that affected the public, recognised that if the Jockey Club did not carry out its functions the government would probably have created a public body for the purpose, and admitted that those submitting to the Club's jurisdiction did so voluntarily. Yet despite all of this his Lordship was unable to accept that the Club met the requirements of a public body for the purposes of review, because:

> '... [it] has not been woven into any system of governmental control of horse-racing ... while the ... Club's powers may be described as, in many ways, public, they are in no sense governmental ...'

Similar views were expressed by Hoffman LJ. Farquharson LJ felt that the Club fell outside the scope of public law because its members agreed to be bound by its rules and was thus a '... domestic body acting by consent.'

In short the decision marks a narrowing of the approach in *Datafin*, in that it qualifies the functions test by requiring them to be not only public in nature but also governmental; the meaning of this term, however, is not made particularly clear.

Farquharson LJ's observations are particularly curious in that they appear to mark a return towards a 'source of power' approach in determining reviewability.

As regards the question of whether or not the Jockey Club would ever be regarded as a public body for the purposes of review, the Master of the Rolls observed;

> 'Cases where the applicant ... has no contract on which to rely may raise different considerations and the existence or non-existence of alternative remedies may then be material.'

This suggests that the status of the Jockey Club, for the purposes of review, can alter depending upon the relationship that the applicant has with it; in other words the jurisdiction of the court depends on the existence or non-existence of a contract. This may reflect a laudable desire on the part of the courts to provide a residual form of control, but it does not provide any clear guidance for potential litigants. Arguably it would be better for the courts to claim jurisdiction on the basis of the functionalist approach, but to decline to exercise it when an alternative remedy, such as the right to sue for breach of contract, is available.

In a sense this was the approach adopted by the Privy Council in *Mercury Energy Ltd* v *Electricity Corporation of New Zealand Ltd* [1994] 1 WLR 521. The defendant organisation was held to be a public body amenable to judicial review on the basis that it was a designated state enterprise under the New Zealand State Owned Enterprises Act 1986, its shares were held by ministers, it carried on business in the interests of the public, and could make decisions adversely affecting the rights and liabilities of private individuals without affording them any redress. On the facts, however, its decision to terminate an electricity supply contract with the plaintiff was not reviewable, given that there was no evidence of illegality, and that the express statutory duty and principle objective of the defendant body was the operation of a successful and efficient business enterprise. The Privy Council took the view that it was for the defendant to determine if those objectives could be achieved by terminating the contract with the plaintiff. On the basis that the courts should only intervene if the decision could be shown to be wrong in law, it was doubtful whether such a decision would ever be the subject of a successful application for judicial review unless the applicant could show fraud, corruption or bad faith. As Lord Templeman observed:

> 'Industrial disputes over prices and other elated matters can only be solved by industry or by government interference and not by judicial interference in the absence of a breach of law.'

The retreat from *Datafin* does, alas, appear to be continuing apace. The office of the Insurance Ombudsman was created in 1981 as part of the self-regulatory framework of the insurance industry. Insurance companies agreed by contract to submit to his jurisdiction. When the Financial Services Act 1986 came into effect the self-regulatory body LAUTRO recognised the Insurance Ombudsman as carrying out a complaints investigation activity under the Act similar to that which had been exercised on the basis of contract. In *R* v *Insurance Ombudsman Bureau and the Insurance Ombudsman, ex parte Aegon Life* (1993) unreported, the applicants unsuccessfully sought review of the Insurance Ombudsman's award that had been made against them in respect of a number of policies. **Rose LJ declined to exercise the court's reviewing jurisdiction in respect of the Insurance Ombudsman on the basis that, even though such a person might be exercising governmental functions, the source of jurisdiction was nevertheless the consensus of others to be bound by his findings.** He observed:

> '... when Sir Thomas Bingham MR [in the *Aga Khan* case] spoke of the Jockey Club not being "woven into any system of governmental control" I do not accept that he was thereby indicating that such interweaving was in itself determinative ... the [Insurance Ombudsman Bureau's] power over its members is [despite the Financial Services Act 1986] solely derived from contract and it simply cannot be said that it exercises government functions. In a nutshell, even if it can be said that that it has now been woven into a governmental system, the source of its power is still contractual.'

11.5   What is a public law issue?

Although the identification of a public law body and a public law issue are taken separately here, reflecting Lord Diplock's approach in *O'Reilly* v *Mackman*, it will be appreciated that in reality the two are closely intertwined, particulary where the courts are invited to review the decisions of domestic regulatory bodies. On the assumption that English law can no more provide a clear answer to the question 'What is a public law issue?' than it can to the question of 'What constitutes a public law body?', it is submitted that the **courts again proceed on the basis of expediency.** Two factors seem to be of paramount significance; first, **has the litigant chosen to proceed by way of writ to circumvent the procedural requirements of O.53?** Secondly, **is proceeding by way of judicial review the only means by which the litigant can obtain a remedy at law?** Evidence of the relevance of this latter factor is supplied by *R* v *Birmingham City Council, ex parte Dredger* (1993) The Times 28 January, where the Divisional Court rejected the local authority's contention that its decision to increase the rent to be paid by market traders was a private law matter based on commercial considerations. **Significantly the court noted that the local authority had monopoly control over the letting of stalls, and that in the absence of judicial review there was no basis for any challenge by the applicant;** see also *R* v *Lord Chancellor, ex parte Hibbit and Saunders* (1993) The Times 12 March.

Decision-making and executive powers of public bodies

Immediately following *O'Reilly* v *Mackman*, the House of Lords gave judgment in *Cocks* v *Thanet District Council* [1982] 3 All ER 1135. This case was clearly meant to provide an illustration of how the **public/private dichotomy was to work in practice.** The respondent had issued a writ claiming a declaration that the appellant authority was in breach of its statutory duty to house him, pursuant to the Housing (Homeless

Persons) Act 1977. The House of Lords held, for the reasons outlined below, that the actions of the authority could only be challenged by way of an application for review. The authority was clearly a public body in the traditional sense of that term. Lord Bridge characterised the duty of the housing authority to inquire into the applicant's status to determine whether or not there was a duty to house him, as a decision-making function falling within the sphere of public law, challengeable only by way of judicial review. Once the authority accepted that there was a duty to house, however, it would be exercising its executive powers in relation to the discharge of that duty. As Lord Bridge expressed it:

> 'Once a decision has been reached ... which gives rise to the temporary, the limited or the full housing duty, rights and obligations are immediately created in the field of private law.'

The distinction between decision-making and executive powers is not one easily drawn, any error having possibly calamitous consequences for the litigant. The effect must surely be to induce applicants to use O.53 for fear of their cases being struck out on the ground that they have wrongly concluded that what they are attacking is the discharge of an executive function challengeable by way of action.

Fears that *Cocks* v *Thanet* indicated a restrictive approach by the courts as to the procedures used by the homeless to challenge the decisions of housing authorities have been vindicated by later decisions such as *Ali* v *Tower Hamlets London Borough Council* [1992] 3 WLR 208. The respondent refused to accept accommodation offered by the appellant authority on the grounds that it was unsuitable. He believed that, because of his disabilities and those of his wife, only a ground floor dwelling would be suitable. The authority accepted that the respondent was not intentionally homeless, and that he was a priority need case, but took the view that the sixth floor flat he had been offered was suitable. The respondent commenced proceedings against the authority in the County Court, claiming breach of statutory duty (ss65 and 69 Housing Act 1985), and a mandatory injunction compelling the authority to provide suitable accommodation. On the preliminary issue of jurisdiction the Court of Appeal held that the respondent should have proceeded by way of judicial review. The court adopted the view that until the authority completed the process of deciding on suitable accommodation for a homeless person, it was still discharging a public law function, the suitability of any given accommodation being a matter to be determined by the authority using its own discretion and subjective judgment.

Mindful of the comments of Lord Bridge in *Cocks* v *Thanet District Council* [1982] 3 All ER 1135, to the effect that once the full housing duty was shown to exist a homeless person had private law rights that could be asserted vis-à-vis a housing authority, Nolan LJ sought to distinguish this case as one where the authority was still discharging its decision-making, as opposed to executive, functions. In his Lordship's view, the authority had to arrive at a decision as to the suitability of accommodation before it could perform 'the executive act of securing the ... accommodation'.

Is public sector employment a public law issue?

An alleged breach of a contract of employment by an employer is generally regarded as falling within the sphere of private law, albeit a specialised area based on a body of legislative measures with adjudicatory functions being allocated to tribunals. Determining whether or not an employee of a public body can apply for review of the employer's decision to terminate his employment is not a straightforward task. It is perhaps safest to proceed on the basis of a rebuttable assumption to the effect that review would be inappropriate, unless the applicant can show that there is some particular statutory basis for his employment that justifies categorising the decision to dismiss as one of public law, that the dismissal raises wider constitutional issues going beyond the applicant's rights, or possibly that in the absence of judicial review he would have no other means of challenging the decision.

R v *East Berkshire Health Authority, ex parte Walsh* [1984] 3 WLR 818 illustrates the conventional approach to this issue, where the Court of Appeal held that it would be inappropriate for a senior nursing officer, employed under the National Health Service, to challenge his dismissal by way of judicial review. As the Master of the Rolls explained, employment by a public authority per se did not inject an element of public law, neither did the interest of the public, although where a senior officer was involved more weight might be given to those factors. The applicant would have been able to seek a public law remedy if his conditions of service had differed from those laid down by the Whitely Council's regulations for the Health Service, as approved by the Secretary of State. As these had been incorporated into his contract of employment, any breach would be a matter of private law, falling outside the scope of judicial review. In the view of the court, only if the authority refused to incorporate the Whitely Council regulations would a public law issue arise. Two subsequent decisions bear out this analysis. In *R* v *Derbyshire County Council, ex parte Noble* [1990] ICR 808, a police surgeon sought unsuccessfully to challenge his dismissal on the basis that it was unfair and unreasonable, the court holding that the matter was not reviewable as it arose out of a private contract for services with no statutory underpinning. Similarly, in *McClaren* v *Home Office* [1990] ICR 824, a prison officer was allowed to proceed with an action seeking a declaration by way of writ regarding the legality of a revised shift system that he had been asked to work. See also *Doyle* v *Northumbria Probation Committee*, considered at 11.6. In *R* v *Crown Prosecution Service, ex parte Hogg* (1994) The Times 14 April, where the Court of Appeal confirmed that the dismissal of a Crown prosecutor was a not amenable to review, Sir Thomas Bingham MR stated that the absence of any other means of challenging the dismissal, and the designation of the applicant as a public servant, were not, in themselves, conclusive factors in determining that the matter was one suitable for judicial review. It is submitted, however, that his observation that the test to be applied was to ask whether or not the subject matter of the issue was a public law matter, leaves itself open to criticism on grounds of circularity of reasoning. Although the matter did not arise directly for consideration, his Lordship indicated that if Crown prosecutors were granted rights of audience, questions might emerge as to the extent to which their independence might be undermined by threats of dismissal. If a case should come before the courts where there was evidence of such a threat, the courts might be minded to permit judicial review as this would involve a matter of high constitutional principle, and therefore of public law, presumably on the basis that the existence of a private law right of challenge would be merely collateral.

By contrast, in *R v Secretary of State for the Home Department, ex parte Benwell* [1985] QB 554, the court seems to have been persuaded that the presumption referred to above had been rebutted on the facts. The applicant was a prison officer who sought to challenge the validity of his dismissal from the Prison Service by way of judicial review. The court ruled that this would not be an inappropriate procedure. The distinguishing factors were that the applicant was subject to a statutory code of discipline which denied him any private law right to challenge the validity of his dismissal. In short judicial review was the only means by which the Secretary of State's decision to uphold his dismissal could be challenged.

Anyone seeking to determine a deeper logic in the categorisation of these public employment cases could be forgiven for asking why the absence of any other remedy should make the dismissal of a prison officer any more a matter of public law that the dismissal of an NHS nurse. An explanation for the apparent inconsistency in the approach of the courts may lie in the fact that there is continuing uncertainty regarding whether or not civil servants, such as prison officers, have contracts of employment. If they do, it is easier to contend that disputes concerning terms and conditions of employment fall within the sphere of private law. See further *R v Lord Chancellor's Department, ex parte Nangle* [1991] ILR 343 (considered at 4.3).

Can other contractual rights raise public law issues?

The authorities reveal a reluctance on the part of the courts to extend judicial review to domestic or statutory bodies where an applicant claims that his contractual rights have been infringed.

Where the respondent is a statutory body, the matter may not be reviewable because it does not raise any issues of public law: see *Mercury Energy Ltd v Electricity Corporation of New Zealand Ltd* (above) defendant's decision to terminate a contract consistent with its express statutory duty and principle objective of operating a successful and efficient business enterprise not reviewable.

Where the body is a domestic tribunal or self-regulatory agency, the existence of a power relationship derived from contract can be cited by the court as justification for its declining jurisdiction either because the body in question is not amenable to review, or because the issue in question can be resolved under private law.

This state of affairs is bound to promote confusion, however, since if a court wants to review the actions of a domestic body it will have to hold that it comes within the term 'public law body' because of what it does, rather than from the source of its power.

In *Law* v *National Greyhound Racing Club Ltd* [1983] 3 All ER 300, it was held not to be an abuse of the court process for greyhound trainers who had been suspended by the Club to seek declarations by way of writ that their treatment had been in breach of an implied term in their contracts with the Club to the effect that they would be dealt with fairly. The fact that the Club dealt with an important activity for the benefit of the public, and was incorporated under the Companies Act 1948, did not bring it exclusively within the ambit of O.53. The Court of Appeal placed great weight upon the fact that the stewards' authority arose from a contract, with the consequence that there was no public law element in their jurisdiction.

Similarly, in *R* v *Disciplinary Committee of the Jockey Club, ex parte Massingberd-Mundy* (1990) The Times 3 January, the Divisional Court had to consider an application for review brought by the former chairman of the Doncaster December meeting who had been dismissed by the disciplinary committee of the Jockey Club. Again, one of the issues before the court was that of whether the Club's decisions were amenable to judicial review. The court held, inter alia, that the fact that the Jockey Club derived its legal identity from Royal Charter, and thus the prerogative, was not to be regarded as decisive of the question of whether all of its decisions were amenable to judicial review. A more important factor was whether the decision complained of had a sufficient 'public law element'. The court, citing with approval the Court of Appeal's decision in *Law* v *National Greyhound Racing Club Ltd* felt that on the facts the applicant's relationship with the Club was based upon contract, and as such was primarily a private law matter.

Subsequently, in *R* v *Jockey Club, ex parte Ram Racecourses Ltd* (1990) The Times 6 April, the Divisional Court considered an application for judicial review of the Jockey Club's decision not to allocate 15 fixtures to its Telford course for the 1991 season. The applicants claimed that they had had a legitimate expectation, based upon previous dealings with the Club, that the fixtures would be so allocated. Although the application was dismissed on a finding that there was no evidence to support any such legitimate expectation, the significance of the case lies in the court's comments as to its jurisdiction. Stuart-Smith LJ expressed the view that, but for the *Massingberd-Mundy* decision, he would have held that the Club's decisions in the case before him were amenable to review. Mr Justice Simon Brown, on the other hand, disagreed to the extent that he regarded the Club's decisions as open to challenge by way of review where, as on the facts before him, it was exercising a quasi-licensing power; see further *R* v *Jockey Club, ex parte Aga Khan* (considered in 11.4 above).

11.6 Exceptions to *O'Reilly* v *Mackman*

As noted above at 11.3 Lord Diplock envisaged that there would be exceptions to the rule that public law issues would have to be pursued by way of judicial review.

Where none of the parties objects to the adoption of the procedure by writ or originating summons

Lord Diplock's statement to the effect that a matter could be pursued by way of action if the parties so wished seemed to be at odds with the essential aspect of the decision in *O'Reilly* v *Mackman*, namely that it was for the courts to determine what procedure would be appropriate in any given case. If it would be an abuse of process to proceed by way of writ or originating summons, how could the consent of the parties rectify this? The comments of Dillon LJ in *Kent* v *University College London* (1992) The Times 18 February, clearly indicate that if a case involved substantive public law issues it would be inappropriate to proceed by way of action even if this was with the agreement of the parties, since the role of the court in private law proceedings would clearly be different from its role in public law proceedings, where its jurisdiction was limited to supervising the legality of action taken. Similarly, where parties to litigation agree between themselves that public law issues are involved and the matter should proceed as an application for judicial review, the court seized of the matter can still choose to transfer the case to proceed as if commenced by way of writ. Such is likely to happen if the issues are primarily ones arising under a contract where the remedy claimed is damages: see *R* v *Durham City Council, ex parte Robinson* (1992) The Times 31 January.

Cases where the public law issue arises as a collateral matter

This exception was considered by the House of Lords in *Davy* v *Spelthorne Borough Council* [1984] AC 262. In September 1977 the plaintiff, the owner of premises used to produce concrete, applied to the council for permission to continue using his site for this purpose for another ten years. The application was rejected, but as a result of further negotiations with council officers an agreement was reached in November 1979 under which the council would issue an enforcement notice directing him to cease the use of the land, but the operation of this notice would be suspended for three years. In exchange the plaintiff promised not to exercise his statutory right of appeal against the notice, which had to be exercised within 35 days of its being issued. In October 1980 the notice was issued in accordance with the agreement.

In August 1982 the plaintiff issued a writ against the council seeking an injunction to stop the notice taking effect, damages for negligent advice, and the setting aside of the notice. The Court of Appeal struck out the claim for an injunction and the application to have the notice set aside on the basis that such public law activities of the local authority were only challengeable by way of O.53, but allowed the claim for damages to survive. The council's appeal to the House of Lords was unsuccessful. In view of Lord Wilberforce the action for damages was not a public law question because the plaintiff was no longer contesting the validity of the enforcement notice, but the nature of the advice that led to his failing to challenge it. If the case still had a public law element it was no more than collateral to the main action and this came within the exceptions envisaged by Lord Diplock in *O'Reilly* v *Mackman*. Furthermore, the court had no power to transfer the action to proceed as if it had been commenced under O.53, with the result that if the writ was struck out, the plaintiff would have to start afresh with an application under O.53. This might prejudice the plaintiff as he would be out of time; at the very least such a course of action would be uncertain.

Subsequent decisions reveal a discernable trend away from the rigid procedural dichotomy advocated in *O'Reilly* v *Mackman* where the plaintiff can show that he has a substantive private law right that he is seeking to vindicate. The courts appear to be increasingly willing to accept that to force the litigant to use O.53 may actually result in a denial of justice. Two more recent decisions in particular are worthy of note on this point. In *Doyle* v *Northumbria Probation Committee* [1991] 1 WLR 1340, the plaintiff probation officers proceeded by way of action claiming damages for breach of contract and a declaration as to their contractual rights. Since 1975 they had been paid a mileage allowance that compensated them for the cost of travel between work and home. In 1983, however, these payments were abolished, the defendant committee claiming that it had never had the power to make such payments under the Probation (Consolidation of Service) Rules 1975. The committee's application to have the proceedings struck out as an abuse of process, on the ground that the plaintiffs were essentially seeking to contest an issue of public law, ie the legality of the payments made under statutory authority, was dismissed. In rejecting the assertion that the plaintiffs should have sought review of the decision to phase out payments in 1983, Henry J observed:

> '... it is not incumbent on employees of a public authority faced with a prima facie breach of contract to investigate or prove that the public body which employed them had power to contract with them on the terms agreed'.

It could be argued that this case does not fall entirely within the scope of the exceptions to *O'Reilly* v *Mackman*, as there was no substantive public law issue, other than that raised by the defendants. As Henry J observed:

> '... the rule as set out [in *O'Reilly* v *Mackman*] does not cover this case and that is common ground. The reason for that is that the plaintiffs here do not seek to establish that they had any public law entitlement to the disputed allowance: their claim to it is purely contractual. Therefore they do not claim any remedy for infringement of their public law rights. Public law only comes into the action as a result of the committee's assertion by way of defence or anticipated assertion by way of defence that they had no power to pay the disputed allowance.'

It is submitted, however, that the decision evinces a more relaxed or liberal approach to the question of appropriate procedure, an approach that was subsequently endorsed by the House of Lords itself in *Roy* v *Kensington and Chelsea and Westminster Family Practitioner Committee* [1992] 1 All ER 705. The plaintiff, a general practitioner, sought payment from the defendant committee of part of his basic practice allowance which the committee had decided to withhold, having concluded that the plaintiff had failed to devote a substantial amount of his time to general practice. The committee, which derived its jurisdiction in this matter from the National Health Service (General Medical and Pharmaceutical) Regulations 1974, and the Statement of Fees and Allowances published thereunder, applied unsuccessfully to have the plaintiff's claim struck out as an abuse of process on the basis that he was seeking to challenge a public law decision. Lord Lowry, emphasising the extent to which an over-rigid adherence to the public law – private law dichotomy could prejudice the plaintiff's case, observed:

> 'An important point is that the court clearly has jurisdiction to entertain the doctor's action. Furthermore, even if one accepts the full rigour of *O'Reilly* v *Mackman*, there is ample room to hold that this case comes within the exceptions allowed for by Lord Diplock. It is concerned with a private law right, it involves a question which could in some circumstances give rise to a dispute of fact and one object of the plaintiff is to obtain an order for the payment (not by way of damages) of an ascertained or ascertainable sum of money. If it is wrong to allow such a claim to be litigated by action, what is to be said of other disputed claims for remuneration? I think it is right to consider the whole spectrum of claims which a doctor might make against the committee. The existence of any dispute as to entitlement means that he will be alleging a breach of his private law rights through a failure by the committee to perform their public duty. If the committee's argument prevails, the doctor must in all these cases go by judicial review, even when the facts are not clear. I scarcely think that this can be the right answer ...'

See further *Lonrho* v *Tebbit* [1992] 4 All ER 280 (considered in Chapter 4).

Where the public law issue arises by way of a defence

This matter was not expressly referred to by Lord Diplock in *O'Reilly* v *Mackman*, but has subsequently emerged as a significant exception to the rule that such issues must be resolved by way of judicial review.

In *Wandsworth London Borough Council* v *Winder* [1984] 3 All ER 976 the appellant, Mr Winder, was a tenant of the respondent local authority, living in a flat on a weekly tenancy. Acting under the Housing Act 1957 the council resolved to increase the rent. The appellant refused to pay the increased rent, arguing that the increase was ultra vires and void. A notice seeking possession of the property was served on the appellant for non-payment of rent. The appellant relied on the defence that the increase was ultra vires. The council applied to strike out the defence on the ground that it was an abuse of the court process to challenge a public law decision in a private law action.

The defence was struck out at first instance in the County Court, but the Court of Appeal allowed Winder's defence to stand. The local authority appealed unsuccessfully to the House of Lords, where it was held that the respondent was entitled to raise a defence based on allegations of ultra vires action in an action started by writ. There was no evidence that the defendant was attempting to abuse the process of the court, indeed he had not instigated the proceedings at all. Further, there was nothing in *O'Reilly* v *Mackman* to suggest that the House of

Lords had intended to remove the right of a defendant to raise a public law issue by way of defence to a private law action.

A distinction may be made by the courts, however, where the defendant, seeking to raise a public law issue by way of a defence to civil proceedings for possession of property, is in law a trespasser on that property. In *Avon County Council v Buscott* [1988] 2 WLR 788 the appellants had been living as gypsies in a property owned by the respondent council. The council sought an eviction order against the appellants. The order was granted at first instance. In the course of the hearing the appellants had requested an adjournment in order to prepare a defence based on the assertion that, because the council was in breach of its statutory duty in providing sites for gypsies, its decision to evict the appellants must be unreasonable. The request was refused. The matter for the Court of Appeal to consider was whether the trial judge had rightly refused to allow the appellants to raise such a defence. The court dismissed the appeal, stating that the reasonableness of the council's decision could only be tested by way of an application for judicial review. The Master of the Rolls expressed his view that to have allowed the defence to be raised would have involved an abuse of the process of the court. The situation was to be distinguished from that in *Wandsworth London Borough Council v Winder*, where the defendant had a 'true defence' in the sense that he was in lawful occupation of the land. Here the appellants readily conceded that they had no right to occupy the land in question.

Wandsworth London Borough Council v Winder was followed by the Court of Appeal in *Thrasyvoulou v Secretary of State for the Environment* [1988] 3 WLR 1, wherein it was held that, as regards the defending of enforcement notice proceedings, the House of Lords' decision in *O'Reilly v Mackman* did not exclude the right of a defendant to raise the invalidity of an enforcement notice, on the grounds of issue estoppel.

In *Plymouth City Council v Quietlynn Ltd* [1987] 2 All ER 1040 it was held that when magistrates' courts and Crown Courts were considering prosecutions the effectiveness of which depended upon the validity of the action taken by an administrative body, they were entitled to assume that the administrative body's action was valid, unless it could be shown that the decision had previously been quashed by way of judicial review. The court's attempt to create a distinction between civil actions such as *Wandsworth London Borough Council v Winder* and criminal litigation was, however, severely criticised in *R v Crown Court at Reading, ex parte Hutchinson* [1988] 1 All ER 333.

The applicants, arrested for allegedly breaching bye-laws relating to trespass on the air base at Greenham Common, were convicted before the magistrates' court and appealed to the Crown Court. At the appeal they contended, by way of defence, that the bye-laws under which the prosecution had been brought were invalid. The Crown Court, regarding itself as bound by the *Quietlynn* decision in this matter, adjourned the proceedings pending resolution of this matter by the Divisional Court on an application for judicial review. The applicants objected to this course of action and applied successfully for an order of mandamus to compel the Crown Court to consider the validity of the bye-law and conclude the hearing of the appeal. Lloyd LJ held that the Crown Court had jurisdiction to inquire into the validity of bye-laws upon which the validity of a conviction rested. In his view neither the revisions to RSC O.53 nor the enactment of s31 Supreme Court Act 1981 had removed a defendant's right to raise such matters by way of defence to a criminal prosecution. The applicants in the present case could not be described as 'abusing the process of the court' as that phrase was understood by Lord Diplock in *O'Reilly* v *Mackman*; they were in the position of defendants, not plaintiffs or prosecutors. Note that the fine imposed in this case was £25. The Court of Appeal recognised that it was unrealistic to contend that the applicants should be put to the expense and inconvenience of applying for judicial review simply to determine the validity of the bye-law. The legal fees would easily outstrip the cost of the fine, resulting in an obvious disincentive to challenging the bye-law. Such a state of affairs would be convenient for the Crown Prosecution Service, but that did not justify the Crown Court's decision.

The *Hutchinson* approach has subsequently been approved by the Divisional Court in *R* v *Oxford Crown Court, ex parte Smith* (1989) The Times 27 December. The applicant, a scrap metal merchant, had been ordered by his local authority, under s65 Town and Country Planning Act 1971, to clear his yard on the basis that it constituted an eyesore in an area of outstanding natural beauty. He had unsuccessfully appealed to the magistrates' court against the notice, and from there to the Crown Court at Oxford. The Crown Court had refused to consider the vires challenge that the applicant had sought to raise in opposition to the notice, on the ground that it lacked jurisdiction to do so, as proceedings for judicial review of the order were pending. Although the subsequent proceedings for judicial review of the local authority's decision to issue the notice were unsuccessful, Mr Justice Simon Brown pointed out that, on the basis of *R* v *Crown Court at Reading, ex parte Hutchinson*, the Crown Court had been wrong to regard itself as powerless to deal with the vires argument. Presumably it would always have been open to the applicant, once he had lost his appeal in the Crown Court, to refuse to comply with the order and await prosecution for non-compliance, during which proceedings he could have renewed his vires argument by way of defence. While the tactic of raising the vires issue by way of defence has thus been accepted by the courts, it would appear that a distinction may still be drawn between different types of alleged illegality. In *Bugg* v *DPP*; *DPP* v *Percy* [1993] 2 WLR 628 (both cases involving challenge to the vires of bye-laws in criminal proceedings) the Divisional Court held that, while a bye-law could be challenged on the grounds of substantive invalidity or procedural impropriety where substantial prejudice had resulted, an allegation of procedural impropriety could only be determined by a civil court, pending which determination the bye-law should be treated as valid. Further, where a defendant alleges that a bye-law is invalid because of mala fides on the part of the maker, the criminal court should continue to hear the case unless the defendant can prove his allegations on the balance of probabilities.

11.7 Procedure in applications for judicial review

The basic procedural requirements are to be found in **Rules of the Supreme Court O.53**, re-enacted in s31 **Supreme Court Act 1981**. References are to O.53 unless indicated.

Cases appropriate for application for judicial review

Order 53 r.1 provides:

'1. (1) An application for
(a) an order of mandamus, prohibition or certiorari, or
(b) an injunction under s9 of the Administration of Justice (Miscellaneous Provisions) Act 1938 restraining a person from acting in any office in which he is not entitled to act, shall be made by way of an application for judicial review in accordance with the provisions of this Order.
2. An application for a declaration or an injunction may be made by way of an application for judicial review, and on such an application the Court may grant the declaration or injunction claimed if it considers that, having regard to
(a) the nature of the matters in respect of which relief may be granted by way of an order of mandamus, prohibition or certiorari,
(b) the nature of the persons and bodies against whom relief may be granted by way of such an order, and
(c) all the circumstances of the case, it would be just and convenient for the declaration or injunction to be granted on an application for judicial review.'

Note that the prerogative orders are only available by way of O.53, whereas the declaration or injunction may be applied for under O.53. In practice, if a declaration or injunction is sought against a statutory body and in relation to a public law matter, then O.53 would have to be used: see *O'Reilly* v *Mackman* (above).

Placing these changes on a statutory basis, the Supreme Court Act 1981 provides:

31 (1) An application to the High Court for one or more of the following forms of relief, namely -
(a) an order of mandamus, prohibition or certiorari;
(b) a declaration or injunction under subsection (2) ...
shall be made in accordance with rules of court by a procedure to be known as an application for judicial review.
(2) A declaration may be made or an injunction granted under this sub-section in any case where an application for judicial review, seeking that relief, has been made and the High Court considers that, having regard to –
(a) the nature of the matters in respect of which relief may be granted by orders of mandamus, prohibition or certiorari;
(b) the nature of the persons and bodies against whom relief may be granted by such orders; and
(c) all the circumstances of the case,
it would be just and convenient for the declaration to be made or the injunction to be granted, as the case may be.
(3) No application for judicial review shall be made unless the leave of the High Court has

been obtained in accordance with rules of court; and the court shall not grant leave to make such an application unless it considers that the applicant has a sufficient interest in the matter to which the application relates.

(4) On an application for judicial review the High Court may award damages to the applicant if –

(a) he has joined with his application a claim for damages arising from any matter to which the application relates; and

(b) the court is satisfied that, if the claim had been made in an action begun by the applicant at the time of making his application, he would have been awarded damages.

(5) If, on an application for judicial review seeking an order of certiorari, the High Court quashes the decision to which the application relates, the High Court may remit the matter to the court, tribunal or authority concerned, with a direction to reconsider it and reach a decision in accordance with the findings of the High Court.'

Obtaining leave to apply for judicial review

One of the protections offered to public bodies by applicants having to obtain leave to apply for judicial review is that unmeritorious cases can be 'filtered out' at this stage, saving the respondent body the cost of having to enter an appearance of any kind. Order 53 r.3 stipulates that:

'No application for judicial review shall be made unless the leave of the Court has been obtained in accordance with this rule.'

The application is made ex parte to a judge who may determine the application without a hearing, unless a hearing is requested in the notice of application, and he need not sit in open court. Where leave is refused the applicant may appeal to a single judge sitting in open court, or to a Divisional Court of the Queen's Bench Division.

In *R* v *Secretary of State for the Home Department, ex parte Angur Begum* (1989) The Times 3 April, Lord Donaldson MR indicated that leave to apply for judicial review should be granted if it was felt that the matter disclosed a point suitable for further debate on an inter partes basis. Where it was clear that no arguable case was disclosed, the application should be dismissed. In intermediate cases, where a judge was unsure, the correct course of action might be to invite the putative respondent to attend the application hearing in order to make representations on the matter. The purpose of such a hearing should not be to trespass upon the full hearing, but to give the judge a 'bird's eye view' of the matter. Following the *Practice Direction: Crown Office List* (1991) The Times 21 March applications for leave to apply for judicial review have been listed on the footing that the application will take no more than 20 minutes, with an additional ten minutes for a reply by the respondent if appropriate. Special arrangements have been made in advance for those cases where counsel expects the hearing to be of greater length. For an excellent analysis of the operation of the application for leave procedure, see Sunkin and Le Sueur [1992] PL 102.

Locus standi

The right to challenge the decisions of public bodies by way of judicial review is restricted to those who have some connection with the decision being impugned. O.53 r.3(7) states that:

'The Court shall not grant leave unless it considers that the applicant has a sufficient interest in the matter to which the application relates.'

The 'sufficient interest' criterion, replacing the somewhat narrower 'person aggrieved' formulation used prior to the reforms of 1977, has presented the courts with an inevitable problem of interpretation. How is the balance to be struck between ensuring that vexatious litigants are denied access whilst bona fide pressure groups are permitted to assert the interests of those they represent?

The starting point for consideration of locus standi is now the decision of the House of Lords in *Inland Revenue Commissioners* v *National Federation of Self-Employed and Small Businesses* [1982] AC 617. In an effort to prevent large-scale tax evasion by casual workers in Fleet Street, the Revenue came to an understanding with the relevant trade unions, whereby it would agree to an amnesty as regards the investigation of unpaid tax in previous years, in return for the casual workers now providing accurate information when they registered for work so that tax could be collected. The Federation, which felt that its members were often unfairly harassed by the Revenue with regard to the collection of tax, sought a declaration that the amnesty was ultra vires the Revenue, and an order of mandamus to compel it to recover the tax due. In concluding that the Federation did not have locus standi to challenge the tax amnesty Lord Wilberforce sought to outline how the matter should be addressed. He explained that the issue of sufficient interest was to be regarded as a mixed decision of fact and law for the courts to decide on legal principles, ie it was not simply a matter of judicial discretion. Further, that it should not be assumed that because one generic phrase was used as the test for standing it would necessarily be applied in the same way regardless of the remedy sought. As regards mandamus, for example, he agreed with the views expressed by the Lord Advocate to the effect that the courts should be guided by the definition of the duty, and should inquire whether expressly, or by implication, the definition indicates that the complaining applicant is within the scope or ambit of the duty.

His Lordship was at pains to emphasise that standing should not be viewed as a preliminary or threshold issue. As he observed:

'There may be simple cases in which it can be seen at the earliest stage that the person applying for judicial review has no interest at all, or no sufficient interest to support the application: then it would be quite correct at the threshold to refuse him leave to apply. The right to do so is an important safeguard against the courts being flooded and public bodies harassed by irresponsible applications. But in other cases this will not be so. In these it will be necessary to consider the powers or the duties in law of those against whom the relief is asked, the position of the applicant in relation to those powers or duties, and to the breach of those said to have been committed. In other words, the question of sufficient interest cannot, in such case, be considered in the abstract, or as an isolated point: it must be taken together with the legal and factual context.'

What was seen as fatal to the success of the Federation's application was not only its failure to establish any illegality on the part of the Revenue, but also the confidential nature of the relationship between the Revenue and any individual taxpayer. As Lord Wilberforce observed:

'As a matter of general principle I would hold that one taxpayer has no sufficient interest in asking the court to investigate the tax affairs of another taxpayer or to complain that the latter has been under-assessed or over-assessed: indeed, there is a strong public interest that he should not. And this principle applies equally to groups of taxpayers: an aggregate of individuals each of whom has no interest cannot of itself have an interest ...'

Lord Diplock sought to explain the rationale for the two-stage approach to the application for judicial review, and the way in which the assessment of standing might alter from one stage to another. He regarded the application for leave stage as involving the court in determining whether or not the case disclosed 'what might on further consideration turn out to be an arguable case in favour of granting to the applicant the relief claimed'. This was to be contrasted with the consideration of standing when the application for review was considered, with all the evidence in, and full argument delivered. Hence it would be perfectly possible for an applicant to be regarded as having standing for the purposes of the application for leave, but not for the full application for review.

The *Federation* case was hailed by many as indicative of a liberalisation of the rules on standing, a view borne out by a number of subsequent decisions. For example, in *R v IBA, ex parte Whitehouse* (1984) The Times 14 April, it was held that the applicant had locus standi to challenge the decision of the IBA to broadcast the film '*Scum*', simply on the basis of her being a television licence holder (as opposed to her being chair of the National Viewers and Listeners Association). Similarly, in *R v HM Treasury, ex parte Smedley* [1985] 1 All ER 589, the Court of Appeal held that the applicant had locus standi to challenge the legality of a draft Order in Council authorising payments to the EEC, on the basis that he was a British taxpayer. The Divisional Court in *R v Felixstowe Justices, ex parte Leigh* [1987] 2 WLR 380 held that the applicant, a journalist, had locus standi to apply for a declaration that a justices' policy of maintaining anonymity was contrary to law, on the basis that the case raised issues of constitutional significance.

It is tempting to identify common factors that might explain the willingness of the courts to grant standing in some cases rather than others. The *Leigh* and *Smedley* cases suggest that identification of a constitutional issue of general importance will be persuasive. Can the same be said of a financial interest in the decision? *R v Legal Aid Board, ex parte Bateman* [1992] 1 WLR 711 suggests that whilst the existence of a financial interest in the outcome of an application is not a precondition of sufficient interest, its absence may persuade the court to find that locus standi is not established. In that case the applicant had received legal aid in respect of proceedings initiated to establish that she possessed a beneficial interest in certain property, the litigation being settled before coming to trial. Her solicitors, despite having agreed to limit their costs to such sums as were recovered under the consent order drawn up following the settlement, expressed their dissatisfaction with the taxation of their costs, and sought authority from the Legal Aid Board to apply to a judge for a further review of the costs order. This application was refused, whereupon the applicant applied for judicial review of the Board's refusal. Dismissing the application, the court noted that the applicant could not claim any financial interest in the decision, since if the Board ultimately ruled in favour of her solicitors on the issue of costs, the benefit would enure to them, not her. As Nolan LJ stated (at p718 a c):

> 'I accept that sufficient interest need not be a financial interest ... I fully accept the desirability of the courts recognising in appropriate cases the right of responsible citizens to enter the lists for the benefit of the public, or a section of the public, of which they themselves are members ... I cannot accept that the feelings of gratitude and sympathy which [the applicant] entertains for Makins [the applicant's solicitors] afford any sufficient justification for her, either in her own interest or in the public interest, to enter the lists on their behalf. It would be inaccurate as well as discourteous to describe her as a busybody, but her attempt to intervene is at best quixotic ...'

Jowitt J, arriving at the same conclusion, commented (p721c d):

> '... though the problem of definition is elusive, common sense should enable one to identify a sufficient interest when it presents itself, like the horse which is difficult to define but not difficult to recognise when one sees it. Nor do I regard the absence of any financial or legal interest as irrelevant to the issue of sufficient interest even though their absence cannot standing alone be fatal ... [N]othing of this amounts in my judgment to a sufficient interest. I have no doubt [that the applicant] will be disappointed if Mr Makin obtains no increase in his taxed costs, but her concern for him does not affect any personal interest of hers or her way of life or her environment. It does not relate to something which affects the public in general or any section of the public but only to Mr Makin who was perfectly well able to make his own application for leave and, if he is entitled to it, obtain the redress she wishes for him.'

Curiously no clear or convincing answer was given to the question of why the applicant was bringing these proceedings and not Makins. It may have been connected with the fact that she was granted legal aid to bring the application for judicial review, whereas, it is assumed, Makins would not have been so assisted.

As the *Federation* case itself shows, the interpretation of the phrase 'sufficient interest' is of especial significance to campaigning pressure groups who, by their very nature, may not be directly affected by the decision being challenged, but will represent those who have a concern about the issues involved. It is perhaps not unfair to describe the development of the law on this issue as a case of 'two steps forwards, one step back'. Decisions such as that in *R v Secretary of State for Social Services, ex parte Child Poverty Action Group, Same, ex parte Greater London Council* (1985) The Times 8 August, displayed a broadly rational approach, suggested that if there is a sufficient nexus between the pressure group and those affected by the decision, the courts will normally find the locus standi requirement satisfied. Against this, there was what can only be described as the somewhat aberrant decision of Schiemann J in *R* v *Secretary of State for the Environment, ex parte Rose Theatre Trust Company* [1990] 1 All ER 754, where he refused to accept that a pressure group, which had formed itself into a company solely for the purpose of challenging the minister's failure to grant the site of the Rose Theatre protected status, had locus standi to challenge the minister's decision. It was his view that merely because an applicant asserted that he or she had an interest did not of itself create such an interest; that a company would not necessarily have sufficient interest simply because it was formed by persons sharing a common view, even if the company's memorandum empowered it to campaign on a particular issue; that the company could have no greater claim to standing than that possessed by individual members of the campaign prior to its incorporation; that the minister's decision was not one in respect of which the ordinary citizen had sufficient interest so as to entitle him to apply for judicial review. In his Lordship's view, the law was not there for every individual who wished to challenge the legality of an administrative decision, and on the facts 'no individual [had] the standing to apply for judicial review'.

Regardless of the view one might take as to the narrow question of whether or not the applicants had sufficient interest, the assertion that there are some executive decisions that no one has sufficient interest to challenge cannot be correct. It subverts the notion of the rule of law to contend that a manifestly ultra vires decision should go unchecked for the want of an applicant with sufficient standing.

Lord Diplock in the *Federation* case was willing to accept that if the Federation had been able to make out its claim of ultra vires action by the Revenue he would have held that this was a matter in which the Federation had a sufficient interest in obtaining an appropriate order. As he stated:

> 'It would, in my view, be a grave lacuna in our system of public law if a pressure group, like the Federation, or even a single public-spirited taxpayer, were prevented by outdated technical rules of locus standi from bringing the matter to the attention of the court to vindicate the rule of law and get the unlawful conduct stopped.'

Significantly, the Divisional Court refused to follow the decision of Schiemann J in *R* v *Inspectorate of Pollution and Another, ex parte Greenpeace Ltd (No 2)* [1994] 4 All ER 329. British Nuclear Fuels (BNFL), which was authorised to discharge radioactive waste resulting from its undertakings by virtue of permission granted by the Inspectorate of Pollution and the Ministry of Agriculture, acting pursuant to the Radioactive Substances Act 1960 sought, in 1992, further authorisation to discharge waste resulting from the operation of its thermal oxide reprocessing plant. Prior to the granting of these new authorisations BNFL sought variations to its existing authorisations in order to test its new plant before it came into operation. The applicants applied for judicial review, seeking an order of certiorari to quash the respondents' decision to grant the variation, and an injunction to prevent the new authorisations from taking effect. Leave to apply for review was granted but the court refused to grant a stay on the implementation of the authorisations. On the hearing of the application for review the respondents unsuccessfully contended that the applicants lacked locus standi to challenge the variations. Otton J explained his ruling on standing in favour of the applicants on the grounds that the court would take into account the nature of the applicant body, the extent of its interest, the remedies sought, the extent to which the applicant was a responsible body, its consultative status if any, the extent of its membership and support and whether the applicant body would have any other viable means of challenging the matter in question. He explained further that he was also mindful of the fact that if the objections to the authorisations had not been consolidated and organised by a pressure group such as Greenpeace the proceedings could have been far lengthier and more expensive. Although this was a decision of the High Court Otton J felt at liberty not to follow the decision of the Court of Appeal in *ex parte Rose Theatre Trust Co* on the ground that in that case:

> '... the circumstances were different, the interest group had been formed for the exclusive purpose of saving the Rose Theatre site and no individual member could show any personal interest in the outcome.'

Note that this ruling on standing was arrived at despite the fact that the substantive application failed on its merits. The public interest trend has been maintained by the Divisional Court in decisions such as *R v Secretary of State for Foreign Affairs, ex parte World Development Movement Ltd* (1994) The Times 27 December, wherein it was held that the applicants had sufficient interest to challenge the provision of grants to the Malaysian government for the building of the Pergau Dam. Rose LJ recognised that, whilst the dominant factor was the merit of the application itself, other significant matters included the need to uphold the rule of law, the fact that no other organisation was likely to launch such a challenge, and the key role played by the applicants in giving advice, guidance and assistance regarding aid. In particular it was felt that if the applicant in *ex parte Rees-Mogg* [1994] 2 WLR 115 was properly regarded as having had locus standi on the basis of his 'sincere concerns for constitutional issues', then a fotiori the applicants in the present case should have standing, given their track record in promoting aid for under-developed nations.

The House of Lords has itself added to the weight of authority recognising the legitimacy of bona fide interested organisations, albeit without citing either the *Rose Theatre* or *Greenpeace* cases, by way of its ruling in *R v Secretary of State for Employment, ex parte Equal Opportunities Commission and Another* [1994] 2 WLR 409; see further 23.3. The Equal Opportunities Commission [EOC] made representations to the Secretary of State to the effect that existing domestic law relating to redundancy and unfair dismissal was contrary to EC law as it indirectly discriminated against female employees by offering reduced protection to part-time workers. The Secretary of State rejected these assertions, whereupon the EOC applied for judicial review (seeking a declaration and an order of mandamus) of the Secretary of State's decision not to act in this matter, with a view to challenging the differential in the qualifying dates for redundancy compensation, and his failure to amend the law to take into account an earlier period of full-time employment in calculating the amount of redundancy payment due. The House of Lords held (inter alia) (Lord Jauncy dissenting) that the EOC did have locus standi, as the litigation concerned the extent to which the legislation ensured equality of treatment of employees. As Lord Keith observed:

> '... it would be a very retrograde step now to hold that the EOC has no locus standi to agitate in judicial review proceedings questions related to sex discrimination which are of public importance and affect a large section of the population. The determination of this issue turns essentially upon a consideration of the statutory duties and public law role of the EOC as regards which no helpful guidance is to be gathered from decided cases ...'

The significance of the decision may the extent to which it encourages statutory bodies to adopt a dynamic role in applying for declarations concerning the compatibility of domestic and EC law, rather than waiting for a suitable case to arise as a vehicle for such a challenge. The extent to which the Court of Appeal is willing to endorse the Divisional Court's approach to the *ex parte Greenpeace* case, and take its cue from the majority of their Lordships in the EOC case remains to be seen.

Delay in applying for relief

Broadly stated, the time limit for applying for judicial review is three months. The rationale for such a short time limit for challenging executive decisions in public law was partly explained by Lord Diplock in *O'Reilly* v *Mackman* (above) where he stated:

> 'The public interest in good administration requires that public authorities and third parties should not be kept in suspense as to the legal validity of a decision the authority has reached in purported exercise of decision-making powers for any longer period than is absolutely necessary in fairness to the person affected by the decision ... the public policy that underlies the grant of those protections [is] ... the need, in the interests of good administration and of third parties who may be indirectly affected by the decision, for speedy certainty as to whether [a] ... decision ... is valid in public law. An action for a declaration or injunction need not be commenced until the very end of the limitation period ... unless such an action can be struck out summarily at the outset as an abuse of the process of the court the whole purpose of the public policy to which the change in Order 53 was directed would be defeated.'

The application of the time limit for applications for review is not an entirely straightforward matter, as it is governed by two provisions. O.53 r.4 states:

> 'An application for judicial review shall be made promptly and in any event within three months from the date when grounds for the application first arose unless the Court considers that there is good reason for extending the period within which the application shall be made.'

This provision is said to be without prejudice to any statutory provision which has the effect of limiting the time within which an application for judicial review may be made, and has to be considered in conjunction with s31(6) of the Supreme Court Act 1981 which provides:

> 'Where the High Court considers that there has been undue delay in making an application for judicial review, the court may refuse to grant (a) leave for the making of the application; or (b) any relief sought on the application, if it considers that the granting of the relief sought would be likely to cause substantial hardship to, or substantially prejudice the rights of, any person or would be detrimental to good administration.'

These provisions have been interpreted by the courts to mean that even if an application is brought within the three month time limit, it can still be refused, or the relief sought denied, if the court is nevertheless of the opinion that there has been undue delay: see *R* v *Swale Borough Council, ex parte The Royal Society for the Protection of Birds* (1990) 2 Admin LR 790. In particular the court held in that case that the issue of 'promptness' could be reviewed at the inter partes hearing of the substantive application even if it had been concluded in the applicant's favour at the application for leave. It was the view of the court that when an application for leave was made within the three month limit it was invariably determined either on the basis of documents or at most on the basis of an ex parte hearing. Either way, the question of promptness would not have been dealt with either objectively, or in depth: see further *R* v *Independent Television Commission, ex parte TVNI Ltd* (1991) The Times 30 December.

What constitutes 'good reason' for delay under O.53 r.4 will clearly depend upon the facts of each case. For example, in *R* v *Stratford-upon-Avon District Council, ex parte Jackson* [1985] 1 WLR 1319, the Court of Appeal allowed the appellant to apply for judicial review outside the usual time limits where the delay in applying arose from difficulties in being granted legal aid. In *R* v *Secretary of State for Foreign Affairs, ex parte World Development Movement Ltd* (above), despite the fact that the application for review related in part to a decision taken in July 1991, and was hence technically out of time, the court accepted that the applicants could not have been aware of the material matters until early 1994. Given the importance of the matters raised the court was persuaded that there had been good reasons for the delay in applying .

It should not be assumed, however, that establishing evidence of good reasons for delay will be decisive of the matter. The court will still have regard to the further issues referred to in s31(6) of the Supreme Court Act 1981, in particular the possibility of causing substantial hardship to a third party, causing substantial prejudice to the rights of, any person, or that permitting an application would be detrimental to good administration.

Permitting an application to be brought outside the three month limit can, for example, adversely affect third party rights where the decision challenged concerns the allocation of a finite resource. In *R* v *Dairy Produce Quota Tribunal, ex parte Caswell* [1990] 2 WLR 1320. In 1985, the applicants were granted a quota by the Dairy Produce Quota Tribunal (the DPQT) under which they were permitted to produce milk from a herd of 70 cows. They had intended to increase the size of the milking herd to 150 in due course and believed they would obtain the necessary increase in their quota when this occurred. In 1987 the applicants, who had by this time increased the size of their herd to 150, were charged a super levy for overproduction of milk. The applicants discovered that the quota they had been granted in 1985 could not be increased to take account of the increase in the size of their herd. Before both the Divisional Court and the Court of Appeal, the applicants were refused judicial review on the grounds of delay in making the application. These refusals were upheld on appeal to the House of Lords, where it was held that, where the words 'an application for judicial review' appeared in s31(6) and (7) of the 1981 Act and RSC O.53 r.4, they were to be interpreted as referring to the application for leave to apply for judicial review. Under these provisions an application for review was to be made promptly, or at least within three months. The combined effect of RSC O.53 r.4, and s31 was that if an application was not made within the three month time limit, or was not made promptly, any delay was to be regarded as undue delay within the meaning given to that phrase in s31(6). Leave might still be refused, or where leave had been granted relief might be refused, even if the court accepted that there were good reasons for the undue delay, if nevertheless, the court was of the opinion that the granting of either leave or of relief was likely to have a detrimental effect on good administration, or would cause hardship or prejudice within the terms of s31(6). The House of Lords appears to have concluded that to allow the Caswells to contest the DPQT's determinations would have encouraged others to act similarly, with consequent problems for the administration of the quota system, concerned as it was with the allocation of a limited resource. Is this a good reason for denying the citizen relief in respect of a dubious exercise of power by a public body? Taken to its logical conclusion the reasoning suggests that if only a small number of persons are affected by an impugned decision, a late application for review might be permitted if there are good reasons for the delay. Where, however, the decision affects a large number of persons the daunting prospect of resolving the ensuing chaos justifies a denial of relief. A similarly restrictive approach can be discerned in *R* v *Secretary of State for Health, ex parte Furneaux* [1994] 2 All ER 652; see further 23.3.

Other procedural matters

Order 53 r.8 allows for discovery of documents, administering of interrogatories, and cross-examination of deponents on affidavits.

Order 53 r.7 allows an applicant to claim damages if the court is satisfied that damages would have been available in action started by writ.

Order 53 r.9(1) provides that:

> 'On the hearing of any motion or summons under r.5, any person who desires to be heard in opposition to the motion or summons, and appears to the Court to be a proper person to be heard, shall be heard, notwithstanding that he has not been served with notice of the motion or the summons.'

Compare this with the 'sufficient interest' that has to be shown by the applicant himself.

In the case of an applicant who has applied for judicial review only to find that he has chosen the wrong procedure, O.53 r.9(5) provides:

'Where the relief sought is a declaration, an injunction or damages and the Court considers that it should not be granted on an application for judicial review but might have been granted if it had been sought in an action begun by writ by the applicant at the time of making his application, the Court may, instead of refusing the application, order the proceedings to continue as if they had been begun by writ; and O.28 r.8 shall apply as if, in the case of an application made by motion, it had been made by summons.'

This provision was considered in *R v Secretary of State for the Home Dept, ex parte Dew* [1987] 2 All ER 1049. The applicant, a prisoner who had suffered a gunshot wound while he was being arrested, was diagnosed in June 1984 as needing a bone graft. By September 1985 the proper treatment had still not been provided, and he applied for an order of mandamus to compel the prison authorities to perform the operation, as required under the Prison Rules 1964, and pay damages for the unnecessary pain and suffering caused. In December 1985 proper treatment was given to the applicant. As a result he then sought to pursue his claim for damages as if it had been started by way of writ, and sought to have the court exercise its discretion to transfer the proceedings accordingly under RSC O.53 r.9(5). McNeill J held that the court could only exercise its discretion in this matter if the original claim was in itself one based on public law. In this case it was at best doubtful whether the applicant had ever had an arguable case based on a breach of public law rights, with the result that the application for judicial review had been an abuse of the court process, and the court did not have the discretion to transfer the proceedings as if they had started by way of writ. Note that *Dew* would still have been well within the limitation period for commencing a fresh action for damages by way of writ, despite this decision.

By contrast, a litigant who commences an action by way of writ, only to have it struck out as an abuse of process for the reasons indicated in *O'Reilly v Mackman*, may find that he is out of time if he wishes to pursue the matter by way of an application for judicial review. The unfairness that may result from this was considered by Lord Donaldson MR in *Calveley v Chief Constable of Merseyside* [1988] 3 All ER 385 at 391, where he observed:

'That the Rules of the Supreme Court should make provision to ensure that a claimant is not unduly disadvantaged if he, acting reasonably, begins proceedings by the judicial review route which he should have begun by writ is only right and reasonable. What is more surprising is that there is no similar provision made for the situation which arises if the claimant reasonably, but mistakenly, begins an action when his true remedy is by way of judicial review. This is something which the Supreme Court Procedure Committee may wish to consider. It would not be difficult to provide that in an action begun by writ either party could apply to have the action treated, or the court could of its own motion consider treating it, as an application for judicial review. In either event the court would, of course, take account of the various matters of which account is taken on an application for leave to apply for judicial review.'

Following changes to the Rules of the Supreme Court (SI 93/2133 (L20)), where a party to an application for judicial review seeks to appeal against a decision of the Divisional Court, leave will have to be obtained, unless the case involves an immigration or asylum issue. Given that a significant number of applicants will be legally aided (and will thus have had to satisfy a merits test before commencing review proceedings), and given that an application for review can only proceed if leave to apply is granted by the High Court itself (and if it is refused, this decision it self may be appealed), it is not entirely clear why this additional hurdle has been introduced before the matter can be taken on appeal.

11.8 Grounds for review   *"abuse of power"*

Considered below, in outline, are the grounds upon which an application for judicial review may be brought. Generally one would describe them as 'abuse of power', but a more precise itemisation is necessary.

Procedural ultra vires

The administrative body may have failed to follow some procedural step laid down by its enabling Act. Such a failure does not automatically render a decision ultra vires. The courts distinguish between mandatory requirements, which must be observed, and directory requirements, which are more flexible. See Chapter 13 for more detail.

Jurisdictional error

This arises where a body makes an error as to the extent of its powers. An enabling Act may provide that a tribunal has jurisdiction to determine the fair rent for dwellings within a certain area. The tribunal may decide to assess the rent to be paid for a dwelling that is in fact outside its area of control; in so doing it would have committed an error as to the scope of its jurisdiction – hence a jurisdictional error. These are always reviewable by the courts. See Chapter 12.

Error of law

Inferior bodies are entitled to make mistakes, both as to fact and law, and in so doing do not necessarily act ultra vires. The supervisory jurisdiction of the High Court, however, extends to correcting errors of law made by inferior bodies, even though they are intra vires, provided these errors are apparent on the 'record' of its proceedings; hence review for 'error of law on the face of the record'. This is the only type of intra vires act that is reviewable by the courts. See Chapter 12.

Breach of implied limitations

The implied limitations on power are those imposed by the courts. The judges 'read in' certain limitations that it is assumed Parliament intended. These can be listed briefly as: unreasonableness; failing to take into account relevant considerations; taking into account irrelevant considerations; using power for an ulterior purpose; acting on no evidence; bias; denial of a fair hearing; bad faith; unlawful delegation of power; fettering power by adoption of over-rigid policies; and fettering discretion by contract.

11.9 Nature of review

The primary purpose of review is to ensure that public bodies act within the law, and this can be achieved by: quashing a decision so that it has to be taken again, properly; ordering the performance of a duty; or prohibiting a proposed course of conduct which would be unlawful. It is to be contrasted with an appeal which can not only overturn an earlier decision but also result in the substitution of the appellate body's decision for the original. On review the court cannot replace the original decision with its own.

An appeal can therefore consider the merits of a decision; review is only concerned with legality. Further, review is a common law right; appeal is only available where statute so provides.

Review is not concerned with compensating the individual for any loss he may have suffered. Damages are not available for loss resulting from acts that are ultra vires per se: see *Dunlop v Woollahra MC* [1982] AC 158. A claim for damages can be added to an application for judicial review, but will only be awarded if they would have been available in an action started by way of writ.

The High Court should only be required to exercise its supervisory jurisdiction in relation to a decision that affects the legal rights and duties of an individual or organisation. A purely administrative decision that does not have either of these consequences is an inappropriate target for judicial review because, if it has no legal effect there is nothing for judicial review to deal with. Thus, in *R v Secretary of State for Employment, ex parte Equal Opportunities Commission and Another* (above) the House of Lords held (inter alia) that the case was not one where the court would have been empowered to grant a prerogative order, as there was no 'decision' of the Secretary of State to quash, although it should be noted that this does not mean that declaratory relief will necessarily be denied. See further the comments of Lord Bridge in *Gillick v West Norfolk and Wisbech Area Health Authority* detailed at 2.9.

11.10 Problems of judicial review

The traditional view of judicial review is that it is the cornerstone of administrative law, representing the importance of independent judicial control over the executive, and providing an important safeguard for the rights of the individual dealing with the state. This view seems to ignore the following shortcomings:

Sporadic nature of review

Like any branch of the common law, judicial review can only respond to those cases coming before it. The development of administrative law, which is tied to judicial review, will necessarily be sporadic. A new concept or new approach must wait for the right conflict to come before the courts before it can be introduced into the law. Further, there may be many 'illegal' administrative practices that are not challenged by way of judicial review because those affected are ignorant, impecunious, cannot be bothered, or simply accept the actions of administrators unquestioningly.

Limits of the ultra vires doctrine

With the exception of error of law, review is only possible where an allegation of ultra vires action is made out. The problem here is that there are many forms of intra vires action that are objectionable, or questionable, that cannot be corrected by means of judicial review, such as delay, rudeness, stupidity, or loss of documents. In many ways this failing was recognised by the creation in 1967 of the Parliamentary Commissioner for Administration in 1967. See Chapter 22.

Futility of review

Even when a court has declared a particular decision to have been unlawful, the results may prove the whole process to have been futile.

The decision may simply be ignored by the administrative body in question, on the assumption that no one will bother to challenge its action in future, thus emphasising the point that a reviewing court is merely deciding one case, and ruling the decision or procedure adopted in that case to have been ultra vires. There is no guarantee that the administrative body will not continue to make such decisions, or follow such procedures.

The decision declared to have been ultra vires may be retaken by the administrative body and the same conclusion reached, for example, that the individual concerned should not be granted a licence. As the decision has now been taken properly it is immune from review, yet the individual has still not achieved what he really wanted, the grant of a licence.

A court decision on a matter such as entitlement to benefit, or the scope of a minister's powers, may prove so inconvenient to the administrative process that the government of the day responds with amending legislation to nullify the effect of the court's decision. For example, consider *Secretary of State for Education* v *Tameside Metropolitan Borough Council* [1977] AC 1014 and the consequent Education Act 1976.

Delay

From time to time the courts will justify their insistence on judicial review being used as the means for challenging the legality of the actions of a public body on the ground that it provides a means by which the matter can be resolved speedily; see comments of Lord Diplock in *O'Reilly* v *Mackman* [1983] AC 237 or in *Dunlop* v *Woollahra Municipal Council* [1982] AC 158. Given the fourfold increase in the number of applications for judicial review since 1980, however, delays have developed in the hearing of cases to the point where a gap of 18 months between the application for leave and the substantive hearing is not unheard of. Such a delay inevitably considerably undermines the usefulness of the procedure and calls into question the faith placed in the review procedure by some members of the judiciary. Urgent applications can be expedited, but this simply 'shuffles the pack'; it does not reduce the overall load. The current situation lends support to those who argue that the time has come for the establishment of a permanent Administrative Division of the High Court staffed by judges with the appropriate expertise.

The contribution of the judiciary

Judicial review is discretionary; consequently immense trust is placed in the judiciary to ensure its proper functioning.

Problems arise where review is sought on grounds of unreasonableness, or unfairness, because here, although in theory the courts are only concerned with legality, they will be involved in making value judgments as to what is 'reasonable' and what is 'fair'. These value judgments may not accord with the views of the general public. Further, remedies are at the discretion of the courts, and once again value judgments may deny an individual a remedy, despite the fact that unfairness may have been established: see *Ward* v *Bradford Corporation* (1972) 70 LGR 27.

Where the courts decline to intervene the individual may be left without an effective remedy. Witness the options open to the homeless in the wake of the House of Lords' decision in *Puhlhofer* v *Hillingdon London Borough Council* [1986] 1 All ER 467.

Non-justiciable issues

Even though the court may possess a supervisory jurisdiction over the exercise of ministerial power, there are situations where judicial intervention is unlikely given the non-justiciable nature of the issue involved. These tend to be situations where the correctness of a decision is more a question of political judgment than of legality. The speeches in *Council of Civil Service Unions* v *Minister for the Civil Service* [1984] 3 All ER 935 identify those matters traditionally considered to fall outside the scope of justiciability, including the conduct of foreign affairs, disposition of troops, appointment of ministers and so forth. Courts are particularly reluctant to intervene where a minister claims to have acted to protect national security. This is the basis for the decision in *Council of Civil Service Unions* v *Minister for the Civil Service*, and continues to influence the role played by the judges. In *R* v *Secretary of State for the Home Department, ex parte Cheblak* (1991) The Times 7 February, the applicant had been made the subject of a deportation order, on the ground that such deportation was conducive to the public good. The minister had indicated to the court that he had evidence to suggest that the applicant might engage in terrorist activities if he was allowed to remain in the United Kingdom during the Gulf war. The applicant, who had appealed unsuccessfully to the non-statutory panel established by the minister to consider appeals before deportation decisions, was not permitted to challenge the deportation by way of review. The Court of Appeal was satisfied that the statutory requirement that reasons be given for detention under the relevant regulations was satisfied by the statement that the applicant had been detained in the interests of national security. Lord Donaldson MR went out of his way to deny strenuously suggestions that since (at that time) hostilities in the Gulf were imminent the courts would start to become 'executive minded'. He added, however, that the courts would be unlikely to intervene where a decision was being made in the interests of national security, as this was, in his view, a par excellence example of a non-justiciable issue. He regarded the constitutional safeguard in such cases as being supplied by ministerial responsibility to Parliament.

Judicial interference undesirable or inappropriate

Judicial reluctance to intervene by way of judicial review may stem from a belief that, although such power exists, and the matter concerned is justiciable, it would nevertheless be undesirable for such a power to be exercised. In cases such as *Puhlhofer* it may be the prospect of increased use of judicial review that is seen as undesirable, in others it is because the courts do not want to be drawn into what are perceived to be primarily domestic disputes. Some indication as to how the court should approach the question of reviewability was provided by Mr Justice Simon Brown in *R* v *Chief Rabbi, ex parte Wachman* [1992] 1 WLR 1036, where, in a case involving a challenge to disciplinary proceedings, he expressed the view that, while the review jurisdiction of the High Court clearly had been extended to non-statutory bodies, this had only occurred where such bodies performed a governmental or at least quasi-governmental function. The key was to ask if the body performed a regulatory function which in the absence of such a body would have been performed by an executive authority. In the light of this he held that there was no question of the State ever regulating religious activities; hence the Chief Rabbi did not come within the scope of 'public law body' as that term was now understood in administrative law. In any event there would be the further problem of the courts ruling upon the fairness of the procedures followed by the rabbinical authorities. Where these were in accordance with Jewish law, but possibly in breach of the principles of natural justice, as those principles were now understood, the court would be placed in the invidious position of having to rule upon the validity of the Jewish laws. He felt such a situation should be avoided if at all possible. See further *R* v *Imam of Bury Park Jame Masjid, Luton, ex parte Sulaiman Ali* (1991) The Independent 13 September.

11.11 Reform

October 1994 saw the publication of the Law Commission's long awaited proposals for the reform of judicial review, in the shape of *Administrative Law: Judicial Review and Statutory Appeals* (Law Com No 226). The report proposes a number of key changes, but equally recommends the maintenance of the status quo in some areas.

The Commission recommends that the leave to apply for judicial review stage be replaced with a 'preliminary consideration' stage, conducted largely on paper. Cases would be permitted to proceed if the court was satisfied that there was a serious issue that ought to be determined. Perhaps surprisingly the report stops short of recommending any change in the time limit for applying for judicial review.

Under the proposals the test for standing would become whether or not the court was satisfied that the applicant has been, or would be, adversely affected by the decision in question, or alternatively whether or not the court considered that it was in the public interest for the application to proceed. This would appear to be an acceptance of the importance of pressure groups and, if enacted, could lead to a significant increase in the level of public interest litigation.

Litigants commencing their cases by way of action, only to find that they should have proceeded by way of an application for review would be able to take advantage of a proposed provision permitting such cases to be to be converted into judicial review proceedings.

One aspect of the current procedure for applying for judicial review that has attracted particular criticism is the procedural exclusivity rule based on Lord Diplock's speech in *O'Reilly* v *Mackman*. In *Doyle* v *Northumbria Probation Committee* (above) Henry J observed that:

'The principles that Lord Diplock expected would emerge from the decisions of *O'Reilly* v *Mackman* have clearly not yet fully been worked out, and the reason for this seems to me to be clear, namely that the circumstances in which there may be such a mixture of private and public law claims are infinitely various and can arise in very disparate situations. But the wealth of authority on this point and the potential for expensive appeals on it leads one to conclude that, until the principles are worked out, there is potentially a formidable extra hurdle for plaintiffs in litigation where public law and private law mix. It seems to me that this is at present an area of the law where the forms of action abolished by the

Common Law Procedure Act 1854 (17 & 18 Vic c 125) in the nineteenth century appear to be in danger of returning to rule us from their graves.'

He went on to re-emphasise the point made in both *Wandsworth* v *Winder* (above) and *Davy* v *Spelthorne* (above) to the effect that it had not been the intention of those responsible for the reforms of O.53, as consolidated in s31 of the Supreme Court Act 1981, to deprive litigants of access to the courts by prohibiting them from raising public law issues by way of defence to private actions.

Lord Lowry, in the course of his speech in *Roy* v *Kensington etc* (above) drew a comparison between what he described as the broad and narrow approaches to the application of O'Reilly thus:

'The broad approach was that the rule in *O'Reilly* v *Mackman* did not apply generally against bringing actions to vindicate private rights in all circumstances in which those actions involved a challenge to a public law act or decision, but that it merely required the aggrieved person to proceed by judicial review only when private law rights were not at stake. The narrow approach assumed that the rule applied generally to all proceedings in which public law acts or decisions were challenged, subject to some exceptions when private law rights were involved. There was no need in *O'Reilly* v *Mackman* to choose between these approaches, but it seems clear that Lord Diplock considered himself to be stating a general rule with exceptions. For my part, I much prefer the broad approach, which is both traditionally orthodox and consistent with the *Pyx Granite* principle ... as applied in *Davy* v *Spelthorne Borough Council* ... *Wandsworth London Borough Council* v *Winder* [1985] AC 461, 510. It would also, if adopted, have the practical merit of getting rid of a procedural minefield.'

The Law Commission's report, reflecting the views of Lord Lowry, recommends that an applicant should only be required to use the judicial review procedure where the case involved matters falling solely within the sphere of public law.

A major change recommended as regards remedies is the introduction of a judicial discretion to grant interim and advisory declarations. The latter would be granted if the case involved a point of general public importance. Disappointingly, no change is proposed regarding the rules relating to discovery in judicial review proceedings. In addition to the procedural changes outlined above, the report recommends that the traditional latin terminology used to describe the prerogative orders of certiorari, mandamus, should be replaced by more 'user-friendly' terms, such as restraining, quashing or mandatory orders.

12

Error of Law:
Jurisdictional Error

12.1 Introduction to jurisdiction

12.2 Mistakes of fact

12.3 Error of law on the face of the record

12.1 Introduction to jurisdiction

In administrative law, the term jurisdiction can most readily be equated with power. Inferior bodies, created by statute, are bodies of 'limited' jurisdiction because they can only do what they are empowered to do by the terms of their enabling Acts. The terminology used by the courts is to describe acts of inferior bodies as 'intra vires' if they are within the limits of power provided by the enabling Act, and ultra vires if outside the limits of the enabling Act.

It is essential to remember that, with the exception of error of law on the face of the record, discussed later in this chapter, the High Court can only exercise its right to review the actions of inferior bodies if they have acted ultra vires.

The central problem with judicial review, therefore, is in trying to determine whether or not a body has acted ultra vires, and this can only be discovered when the limits of its powers have been assessed.

In dealing with any problem involving consideration of ultra vires, the first matter to be considered is the actual wording of the enabling Act. More than with any other subject, the process of statutory interpretation is of central significance to judicial review, and consequently administrative law. A reading of the enabling Act will provide the reviewing court with information on two possible limits on power.

First, express limits; these are clearly stated in the statute and may be in the form of procedural requirements which must be observed before power can be exercised, or in the form of geographical/financial limits on power, for example, stating that a tribunal can only deal with cases arising within a particular area, or may only award compensation up to a certain limit. In many ways these latter limits are special instances of procedural ultra vires, but it is convenient to deal with them separately.

Secondly, the courts will look for the implied limits on power: limits that have not been expressed in the enabling Act but, to the mind of the reviewing court, must have been in the contemplation of Parliament at the time of enactment – for example, the oft-cited proposition that Parliament cannot possibly have delegated power to a particular inferior body with the intention that it should be used unreasonably. The enabling Act will not state that the power is not to be used unreasonably, but this is only because it is such an obvious point that it 'went without saying'; hence the expression 'implied limits on power'.

12.2 Mistakes of fact

Clearly when an inferior body such as a tribunal is given jurisdiction by statute to perform a particular task, Parliament envisages the possibility that the inferior body may make a mistake in the course of its deliberations. Simply because a mistake has been made does not mean that judicial review is available. In other words, a mistake made by an inferior body does not necessarily render its decision ultra vires.

An inferior body will have to make decisions on factual questions. These can arise in two ways. First, there are facts which must exist objectively before a body can act. Secondly, there are the facts that it is specifically empowered to determine. An example will illustrate the point.

Suppose there to be a tribunal given jurisdiction to assess the level of rent payable for private domestic dwellings, on the basis of the quality of the accommodation provided. The question of whether a building was used for 'private domestic dwelling' purposes would be a question of fact that would have been determined objectively before the tribunal had jurisdiction to go on and consider the actual question of fact it was empowered to deal with, the quality of the accommodation.

Normally decisions of inferior bodies on questions of fact are not reviewable because, whether they get the answer 'right' or 'wrong', they are merely deciding something that they have power to determine, that is, they are acting intra vires. Such decisions will be unchallengeable, therefore, unless Parliament has provided for some appellate body to consider the question afresh.

Despite this, the decisions of tribunals on certain questions of fact must be open to the courts to challenge. These are questions of fact that must be judged objectively (that is, by a court). The term given to such questions is to describe them as disputes on points of 'jurisdictional fact'. In short, a fact which must objectively be proved to exist before a body has jurisdiction. In the example given, the jurisdictional fact that must be established before the tribunal can act is that the building for which it is planning to set the correct level of rent is one used for 'private domestic dwelling' purposes. If it is not, then the tribunal has no jurisdiction to set the level of rent payable.

Notwithstanding that decisions on fact are not normally reviewable, the courts must be able to review an inferior body's decision on a question of jurisdictional fact, otherwise the body would be able to exercise power over any situation it chose, simply by stating that it was satisfied that certain jurisdictional facts existed.

To return to the example cited above, if the tribunal decided that a building which was in fact a church was a private domestic dwelling, it would be able to assess the appropriate rent to be paid for it, unless, in the absence of a statutory right of appeal, those affected by its decision were able to apply for judicial review to have its decision quashed. In short, determinations of inferior bodies on points of jurisdictional fact must be open to challenge in the courts by way of review, to prevent an inferior body from assuming jurisdiction it does not possess.

Before considering the case law, it should be borne in mind that there are two very real difficulties in this area. The first is in trying to distinguish between so-called jurisdictional facts, and the facts that an inferior body has actually been empowered to determine. Secondly, there is the daunting problem of trying to distinguish between questions of fact and questions of law.

Case law on jurisdictional fact

In *R v Fulham, Hammersmith and Kensington Rent Tribunal, ex parte Zerek* [1951] 2 KB 1, a rent tribunal was empowered to assess the correct level of rent payable for unfurnished lettings, and proceeded to reduce the rent payable to a landlord, who contested its decision on the basis that it had no jurisdiction to set a rent because the letting was in fact furnished. The Divisional Court refused his application for certiorari to quash the tribunal's determination, but in the course of so doing Lord Goddard CJ stated:

> '... if a certain state of facts has to exist before an inferior tribunal have jurisdiction, they can inquire into the facts in order to decide whether or not they have jurisdiction, but cannot give themselves jurisdiction by a wrong decision upon them; and this court may, by means of proceedings for ceriorari, inquire into the correctness of the decision.'

If the problem of jurisdictional fact arises just as a tribunal proposes to consider a case, what should it do? Proceed, or adjourn? The answer would seem to lie in the nature of the jurisdictional fact problem. If it feels competent to decide the point it should proceed, and its ultimate decision can be challenged because of this wrong determination on jurisdiction. Where the problem can only be resolved by consideration of matters beyond its competence, such as whether a document is a forgery or not, then the wise course would be for the tribunal to adjourn for the matter to be decided by the High Court. As Darlia J observed in *ex parte Zerek*:

> 'When, at the inception of an inquiry by a tribunal of limited jurisdiction, a challenge is made to their jurisdiction, the tribunal have to make up their minds whether they will act or not, and for that purpose to arrive at some decision on whether they have jurisdiction or not. If their jurisdiction depends upon the existence of a state of facts, they must inform themselves about them, and if the facts are in dispute reach some conclusion on

the merits of the dispute. If they reach a wrong conclusion, the rights of the parties against each other are not affected. For, if the tribunal wrongly assume jurisdiction, the party who apparently obtains an order from it in reality takes nothing. The whole proceeding is, in the phrase used in the old reports, coram non judice.'

See further *R* v *Camden London Borough Council, ex parte Ebiri* [1981] 1 WLR 881.

Again, in *White and Collins* v *Minister of Health* [1939] 2 KB 838, the court of Appeal considered the power of a local authority to exercise compulsory purchase powers over land not forming 'part of any park, garden, or pleasure ground'. The court concluded that the question of whether an area of land did, or did not, compromise part of a park or pleasure ground was one of jurisdictional fact. The local authority's decision on such a matter must always be open to challenge in the courts, otherwise they would be able to exercise their powers of compulsory purchase over any land they chose, simply by determining that it did not, in their view, comprise any part of a park etc.

Whilst proof of a jurisdictional fact is normally seen as a precondition to the exercise of power, it can equally be the determinant of whether or not a duty has arisen. In *R* v *South Hams District Council, ex parte Gibbs* (1994) The Times 8 June, the Court of Appeal held that before a duty to provide sites for gypsies under the Caravan Sites Act 1968 could arise the question of status (ie was the individual seeking to be provided with a site a gypsy or not) had to be resolved. Provided a local authority applied the correct test in law, the court would not interfere with the authority's conclusions unless the decision could be shown to be vitiated by irrationality, as Parliament must have intended that the detailed inquires necessitated by having to determine whether an individual was or was not a gypsy, were to be undertaken by the relevant local authority.

Summary

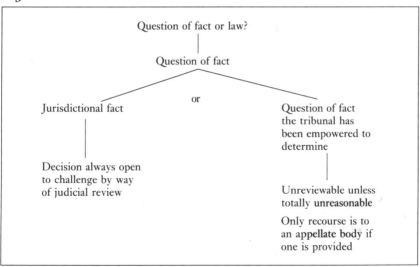

12.3 Error of law on the face of the record

Introduction

As stated above, an administrative body does not act ultra vires simply by making a mistake of fact. The same applies when it makes a mistake of law. The courts are concerned that inferior bodies, which generally have no particular legal expertise, should apply the law correctly. Were the courts not to exercise their inherent common law right to supervise such decisions, the rule of law would in fact be flouted, because the law would not be being followed by inferior bodies as it should be.

Review for error of law on the face of the record is the ancient remedy invoked to deal with such errors, but until comparatively recent times its existence seemed to be in doubt.

Re-birth of the remedy

When an applicant applies to the High Court for review of an error of law, he is in fact applying for the prerogative order of certiorari to quash the decision which he claims to be vitiated by the error of law. Despite its history of being used to call up and quash the decisions of inferior bodies such as Justices of the Peace during the eighteenth and nineteenth centuries, certiorari seemed to be a forgotten means of controlling errors of law in the first half of the twentieth century. In *Racecourse Betting Control Board* v *Secretary for Air* [1944] Ch 114, the Court of Appeal went so far as to deny that it would be available to quash a mistake of law made in an award of a statutory tribunal.

Fortunately, review for error of law received the judicial 'kiss of life' from a differently constituted Court of Appeal in *R* v *Northumberland Compensation Appeal Tribunal, ex parte Shaw* [1952] 1 KB 338. The tribunal in question was appealing against the grant of certiorari by the Divisional Court to quash its decision for error of law. The Court of Appeal dismissed the appeal. In explaining the availability of certiorari as a remedy for dealing with errors of law made by statutory bodies, Lord Denning (then Denning LJ) stated:

> '... the court of King's Bench has an inherent jurisdiction to control all inferior tribunals, not in an appellate capacity, but in a supervisory capacity. This control extends not only to seeing that the inferior tribunals keep within their jurisdiction but also to seeing that they observe the law. The control is exercised by means of a power to quash any determination by the tribunal which on the face of it offends against the law. The King's Bench does not substitute its own views for those of the tribunal, as a court of appeal would do. It leaves it to the tribunal to hear the case again, and in a proper case may command it to do so. *When the King's Bench exercises its control over tribunals in this way, it is not usurping a jurisdiction which does not belong to it. It is only exercising a jurisdiction it has always had.*'

There must be an error of law

The problem of deciding whether an error is one of law or fact is exceedingly complex. It can safely be assumed that the interpretation to be given to a word in a statute is a question of law, but cases coming before the courts are rarely as simple as that. Instead one has to develop a sense of what the courts are likely to regard as an error of law by looking at decided cases. To arrive at a conclusion unsupported by the facts could constitute an error of law: see *R v Medical Appeal Tribunal, ex parte Gilmore* [1957] 1 QB 574. In a sense this is a variant on the 'no evidence' ground of review. Failing to apply the correct legal test to the facts will constitute an error of law. For example, see *R v Minister of Housing and Local Government, ex parte Chichester Rural District Council* [1960] 2 All ER 407, where the Minister's decision was quashed for error of law after he applied the wrong test to determine whether or not land was 'capable of reasonably beneficial use'. Procedural irregularities, such as wrongly refusing to grant an adjournment so that an applicant can prepare his case properly, has been held to amount to an error of law, for example in *R v Medical Appeal Tribunal, ex parte Carrarini* [1966] 1 WLR 883. Generally, the courts seem to give a wide meaning to the expression 'error of law' so as to maintain the usefulness of the remedy. Consider further the meaning given to the expression 'appeal on a point of law' in the context of an appeal under s11 of the Tribunals and Inquiries Act 1992.

What constitutes the 'record'?

As with the interpretation of error of law, the meaning of the phrase 'face of the record' has been liberally interpreted by the courts. As Griffiths LJ observed in *R v Knightsbridge Crown Court, ex parte International Sporting Club Ltd* [1982] QB 304:

> 'Although the old authorities do show a stricter approach to what constituted the "record", the modern authorities show that the judges have relaxed the strictness of that rule and taken a broader view of the "record" in order that certiorari may give relief to those against whom a decision has been given which is based upon a manifest error of law.'

In *ex parte Shaw* (above) Denning LJ stated that the record would comprise at least the documents initiating the proceedings, the pleadings if any, and the adjudication. In *R v Greater Birmingham Supplementary Benefit Appeal Tribunal, ex parte Khan* [1979] 3 All ER 759 the concept of 'record' was extended to include a letter containing the reasons for the tribunal's decision sent by the tribunal to the applicant. In *R v Knightsbridge Crown Court, ex parte International Sporting Club Ltd*, the record was held to include the judgment, the reasons for the judgment, and the affidavit evidence upon which it was based. Two points in particular should be noted. First, that no remedy will be available even if there has been an error of law if it does not appear on the face of the record. Secondly, the requirement placed upon certain specified tribunals, by s10 of the Tribunals and Inquiries Act 1992, to provide reasons for their decisions if requested to do so may expand the scope of review for error of law, as any reasons given will become part of the record.

Review for error of law inappropriate

It should not be assumed that review for error of law will lie in respect of any tribunal making decisions within the sphere of public law. The reviewing court will have regard to the status and expertise of the decision-making body, and consider the wider implications of any decision to review. In *R* v *Lord President of the Privy Council, ex parte Page* [1992] 3 WLR 1112, the House of Lords held that the Lord President of the Privy Council, acting on behalf of a university Visitor, upholding the decision of a university to terminate a lecturer's employment on the ground of redundancy, was not amenable to judicial review in respect of any ruling in fact or law that he might make in the course of exercising that jurisdiction. Lord Browne-Wilkinson relied upon two lines of reasoning to justify non-intervention on the grounds of error of law. The first related to the peculiar type of law applied by the Visitor:

> 'Although the general rule is that decisions affected by errors of law made by industrial tribunals or inferior courts can be quashed, in my judgment there are two reasons why that rule does not apply in the case of visitors. First, as I have sought to explain, the constitutional basis of the courts' power to quash is that the decision of the inferior tribunal is unlawful on the grounds that it is ultra vires. In the ordinary case, the law applicable to a decision made by such a body is the general law of the land. Therefore, a tribunal or inferior court acts ultra vires if it reaches its conclusion on a basis erroneous under the general law. But the position of decisions made by a visitor is different. As the authorities which I have cited demonstrate, the visitor is applying not the general law of the land but a peculiar, domestic law of which he is the sole arbiter and of which the courts have no cognisance. If the visitor has power under the regulating documents to enter into the adjudication of the dispute (ie is acting within his jurisdiction in the narrow sense) he cannot err in law in reaching this decision since the general law is not the applicable law. Therefore he cannot be acting ultra vires and unlawfully by applying his view of the domestic law in reaching his decision. The court has no jurisdiction either to say that he erred in his application of the general law (since the general law is not applicable to the decision) or to reach a contrary view as to the effect of the domestic law (since the visitor is the sole judge of such domestic law).'

The second line of reasoning related to Lord Diplock's speech in *Re Racal Communications* [1981] AC 374, at 384B–D and 390F–391D, where the distinction between administrative and judicial bodies was drawn with reference to the greater readiness of the courts to intervene and quash decisions on the grounds of error of law where the decision-making body was classified as administrative as opposed to judicial. Lord Browne-Wilkinson viewed the Visitor to a university as coming within the 'judicial' class of decision-maker. Thus if a statutory ouster clause had been enacted to protect the decisions of the Visitor, the courts would be slow to disregard it. The reality under the common law was that the courts had for 300 years treated decisions of university Visitors as being final and conclusive and thus unchallengeable in the courts. His Lordship saw no reason for departing from that line of authority on this occasion. For a consideration of ultra vires errors of law and ouster clauses, see Chapter 21.

Ex parte Page was followed by the Court of Appeal in *R v Visitors to Lincoln's Inn, ex parte Calder; Same, ex parte Persuad* [1993] 3 WLR 287, where the applicants, practising barristers who had been found guilty of professional misconduct by the disciplinary tribunal of the Council of the Inns of Court and subsequently disbarred, sought to challenge the decisions of High Court judges, sitting as Visitors, to uphold the tribunal's decisions. The Divisional Court held that judges performing the visitorial function were still acting judicially to maintain the proper administration of justice in the courts, and as such their functions were not amenable to review. The Court of Appeal allowed the appeals on the basis that, prior to the enactment of the Supreme Court of Judicature Act 1873, judges exercising a visitorial function in respect of the Inns of Court had done so as members of a domestic tribunal, in the sense that they had not sat as 'judges', and the effect of s12 of the 1873 Act had been to transfer this visitorial function to all judges of the High Court; thus the decisions of judges sitting as visitors to the Inns were reviewable if they exceeded their jurisdiction, acted in breach of natural justice or abused their powers. In relation to the 'narrow' issue of intervention on grounds of error of law, however, Sir Donald Nicholls V-C observed that:

'... the principle enunciated [in *Page*] regarding the finality of the visitorial jurisdiction is applicable to visitors to the Inns of Court'.

His Lordship was led to this conclusion by the fact that the Visitors to the Inns would not be applying the ordinary law of the land but the Bar's Code of Conduct.

13

Procedural Ultra Vires

13.1 Procedural ultra vires

13.2 Case law on procedural requirements

13.1 Procedural ultra vires

Introduction

When a statute creates a body to perform some task on behalf of the executive, such as the granting of licences, or payment of benefit, it is likely to also lay down a procedure that the body should follow in performing its functions. Where a body is left largely to decide upon its own procedure, the courts will apply the common law rules of natural justice to ensure that basic fairness is complied with. What follows is concerned, however, with statutory requirements.

Purpose

Why do enabling Acts lay down a particular procedure? The question can be answered by considering the aims Parliament is trying to achieve by the use of the procedure required. Time limits are often prescribed to reduce delays. Matters are required to be recorded in writing to aid certainty. Notice of decisions being taken and of rights of appeal are provided to promote fairness. The requirement of prior consultation may also be to promote fairness and a better informed decision.

Failure to observe

What is the consequence of an inferior body failing to comply with a procedural requirement laid down in its enabling Act? One's response might logically be that if an inferior body fails to act in a way prescribed by statute it must result in its decision being ultra vires. In reality this is not the case. Procedural requirements can be allocated to one of two broad categories. Either the requirement is mandatory, failure to observe such a requirement normally rendering any subsequent action void, or the requirement is directory failure to observe such a requirement will not normally be fatal to the validity of the ensuing determination.

Making a distinction

How does one tell if a procedural requirement is mandatory or directory? There is no one simple test. Everything depends on context. In *Howard* v *Boddington* (1877) 2 PD 203 Lord Penzance expressed the problem thus:

'You cannot safely go further than that in each case you must look to the subject matter; consider the importance of the provision that has been disregarded and the relation of that provision to the general object intended to be secured by the Act.'

Inevitably the courts will want to avoid an over-rigid approach and retain for themselves a degree of discretion to be exercised on a case by case basis. As Lord Hailsham LC observed in *London and Clydeside Estates Ltd* v *Aberdeen District Council* [1980] 1 WLR 182:

'When Parliament lays down a statutory requirement for the exercise of legal authority it expects its authority to be obeyed down to the minutest detail. But what the courts have to decide in a particular case is the legal consequence of non-compliance on the rights of the subject viewed in the light of a concrete state of facts and a continuing chain of events. It may be that what the courts are faced with is not so much a stark choice of alternatives but a spectrum of possibilities in which one compartment or description fades gradually into another. At one end of this spectrum there may be cases in which a fundamental obligation may have been so outrageously and flagrantly ignored or defied that the subject may safely ignore what has been done and treat it as having no legal consequences upon himself. In such a case if the defaulting authority seeks to rely on its action it may be that the subject is entitled to use the defect in procedure simply as a shield or defence without having taken any positive action of his own. At the other end of the spectrum the defect in procedure may be so nugatory or trivial that the authority can safely proceed without remedial action, confident that, if the subject is so misguided as to rely on the fault, the courts will decline to listen to his complaint. But in a very great number of cases, it may be in a majority of them, it may be necessary for a subject, in order to safeguard himself, to go to the court for declaration of his rights, the grant of which may well be discretionary, and by the like token it may be wise for an authority (as it certainly would have been here) to do everything in its power to remedy the fault in its procedure so as not to deprive the subject of his due or themselves of their power to act. In such cases, though language like "mandatory", "directory", "void", "voidable", "nullity" and so forth may be helpful in argument, it may be misleading in effect if relied on to show that the courts, in deciding the consequences of a defect in the exercise of power, are necessarily bound to fit the facts of a particular case and a developing chain of events into rigid legal categories or to stretch or cramp them on a bed of Procrustes invented by lawyers for the purposes of convenient exposition ... I do not wish to be understood in the field of administrative law and in the domain where the courts apply a supervisory jurisdiction over the acts of subordinate authority purporting to exercise statutory powers, to encourage the use of rigid legal classifications. The jurisdiction is inherently discretionary and the court is frequently in the presence of differences of degree which merge almost imperceptibly into differences of kind.'

Even when the distinction appears to have been made, and one has decided that a requirement must be mandatory because of its significance, one still has to bear in mind the doctrine of 'substantial compliance'. This operates with the effect that, even though a requirement is generally mandatory, an inferior body's actions will not be invalidated because it has failed to comply with it in some minor way: see *Coney* v *Choice* [1975] 1 All ER 979, discussed further in 13.2 below.

A further complication is that the classification of a requirement as mandatory or directory may depend to some extent on the extent to which it has been breached. An example of this problem is provided by the decision in *Cullimore* v *Lyme Regis Corporation* [1962] 1 QB 718. (When considering this decision, bear in mind the point that time limits are generally regarded as being directory.) The local authority was empowered to carry out coastal protection works and levy charges on landowners for the work done. Charges had to be levied within six months of the work being carried out. The local authority delayed for nearly two years before submitting its charges. The court held the charges to be void as a result of being out of time. Note that this means the time limit must have been regarded as mandatory. The court went on to point out that if the charges had been levied only a few days late they would have been valid. This is either an application of the substantial compliance doctrine, or implicit recognition that the time limit would normally have been regarded as directory.

In the light of the general observations above, as regards making the distinction between whether a procedural requirement is mandatory or directory, perhaps the most useful approach is one that assesses the case law by reference to how specific requirements have been dealt with by the courts.

13.2 Case law on procedural requirements

Consultation

A statutory requirement that a body should consult prior to using its powers is almost invariably regarded as mandatory by the courts.

In *Agricultural (Etc) Training Board* v *Aylesbury Mushrooms Ltd* [1972] 1 All ER 280, the Minister had failed to consult a small group of workers in the mushroom growers' industry, as he was expressly required to do by the relevant statute, as a precondition of establishing a training board scheme to which those affeced would have to contribute a levy. The court held that the scheme was invalid, as against the mushroom growers, as they had not been consulted. They did not, therefore, have to make a contribution. Note, however, that the court did not invalidate the whole scheme.

Similarly, in *Grunwick Processing Laboratories* v *ACAS* [1978] AC 655 the House of Lords held that a failure by ACAS to consult the whole of the workforce at the appellant's factory rendered the subsequent report produced by ACAS invalid, because the express statutory requirement of consultation had not been satisfied. Lord Diplock refused to imply the words 'so far as is practicable' into the statutory duty to consult. See further *R* v *Tunbridge Wells Health Authority, ex parte Goodridge* (1988) The Times 21 May.

Giving of notice

The requirement that prior notice of a decision be given is generally regarded as mandatory. In *R* v *Swansea City Council, ex parte Quietlynn* (1983) The Times 19 October a local authority proposed to introduce a statutory scheme for licensing 'sex establishments' under which it became a criminal offence to run such an enterprise without first obtaining a licence from the local authority. Twenty-eight days' clear notice of the scheme's introduction had to be given by the authority. The local authority conceded that this time limit had not been observed, and certiorari was granted to quash the refusal of the application. The importance of the notice provision relates not only to the natural justice issue of giving a person affected adequate time to prepare a case but also to the seriousness of the consequences – the possibility of criminal lability being imposed. Where, however, there has been a genuine attempt to comply with the requirement of giving notice, and the failure to secure complete compliance does not cause any quantifiable prejudice, the courts will exercise their discretion to uphold the validity of the consequent administrative action. In *Coney* v *Choice* (above), the Education Act 1944 required a local education authority to place notices outside all schools in its area that were due to be made the subject of a comprehensivisation scheme. Templeman J (as he then was) observed:

> '... here is an Act, which is concerned with the administration of education in which ... the ramifications can be considerable as regards different areas and as regards a host of children. It would in my judgment be lamentable if the carrying out of the purposes of the Education Act 1944 (as amended) were hampered by a strict insistence on the letter of the regulations being carried out subject to the dire penalty of the whole thing being invalid. In my judgment, this is a case where the regulations must be treated as directory. Both the object and the terms of the regulations themselves seem to me to support that, and the consequences of the contrary also seem to me to require it. I accept there must be substantial compliance with the regulations, and in my judgment there has been. Asking myself whether any substantial prejudice has been suffered by those for whose benefit the requirements were introduced, I am quite satisfied the answer is "No". The plaintiffs, having lost the battle on the merits, are now fighting a battle purely on the technicalities. I make no criticism. If the Education Act 1944 is so full of technicalities that the proposals can be tripped up, well, the plaintiffs are entitled to do just that. But in my judgment this is not an Act where Parliament intended that the technicalities should rule rather than the spirit of the law.'

Presumably a woeful failure on the part of the local education authority to provide the required notices would have invalidated the scheme, but would this have been because the requirement was mandatory, or because of the failure to comply with what Templeman J described as a directory requirement? Again, it suggests that a normally mandatory requirement becomes directory in cases of substantial compliance so as to justify upholding the validity of the following administrative action. It would perhaps aid certainty to adopt the view that such requirements are in fact mandatory, but where there has been substantial compliance the courts will not intervene to provide relief.

Where notice is required it should be given in the correct form. In *R* v

Lambeth London Borough Council, ex parte Sharp (1984) The Times 28 December, Lambeth London Borough Council granted itself deemed planning permission in respect of the construction of an athletics track within a conservation area. The relevant regulations required that the authority should publish in a local newspaper, and display on or near the land, notices describing the development, and in each case such notice was required to state that any objection to the proposal should be made to the authority in writing within a specified period. The notice which the council had published in a newspaper had referred to 'representations' rather than 'objections' and had not specified the period within which objections were to be made; neither notice had indicated that objections should be in writing. The appellant successfully contended that these irregularities invalidated the deemed grant of planning permission, the court holding that the requirements as to the giving of notice were mandatory.

Matters put in writing

Where statute requires certain to be put in writing, the requirement is generally regarded as being mandatory.

In *Epping Forest District Council* v *Essex Rendering Ltd* [1983] 1 WLR 158, the House of Lords held that the requirement that the consent of a local authority under s107 of the Public Health Act 1936, to the establishment of an offensive trade was to be in writing, in accordance with s283(1) of that Act, was mandatory and not directory, because the object of s107 was to protect the public by making the establishment of an offensive trade without written consent a criminal offence. It was, therefore, important that the grant of consent should not be accidental, vague or informal. Since the appellants had not obtained the written consent of the authority they had been rightly convicted of an offence. Similarly, in *Howard* v *Secretary of State for the Environment* [1975] QB 235 the requirement that an appeal against an enforcement notice be put in writing was regarded as mandatory, in the interests of certainty. The administration had to have a permanent record of whether an appeal had been made or not.

Notice of the right to appeal

This procedural requirement is almost always regarded as mandatory. In *London and Clydeside Estates Ltd* v *Aberdeen District Council* [1979] 3 All ER 876, the House of Lords held a certificate issued in connection with a compulsory purchase order to be invalid for failing to inform the plaintiff of his right of appeal, such a requirement being mandatory. Similarly, in *Agricultural (Etc) Training Board* v *Kent* [1970] 2 QB 19 it was held that not only was the requirement of giving notice of the right to appeal mandatory but also failure to give adequate details of how to appeal could result in invalidity.

Time limits

Generally time limits will be regarded as directory, especially where no substantial hardship can be made out, but note the observations in *Cullimore* v *Lyme Regis Corporation* (above). Furthermore, time limits may be regarded as directory on grounds of administrative convenience. See *Simpson* v *Attorney-General* [1955] NZLR 271 where the court refused to invalidate a general election result on the ground that the writ for it had been issued out of time.

Measures imposing financial burden

Where a measure seeks to impose some financial burden, the courts apply any procedural requirements strictly. In *Sheffield City Council* v *Graingers Wines Ltd* [1978] 2 All ER 70, the court held invalid a rating resolution that failed to state the day on which it was to come into effect.

14

Introduction to Natural Justice

14.1 Introduction

14.2 Development of natural justice

14.3 When does natural justice apply?

14.4 Legitimate expectation cases

14.5 Consequences of a breach of natural justice

14.1 Introduction

The purpose of both this and the following chapter is to outline the nature of natural justice and consider the situations in which it needs to be observed and the consequences of its non-observance.

What is natural justice?

The term itself is misleading; as has been said many times there is **nothing natural about justice, and very little justice in nature**. A useful approach to natural justice, it is submitted, is to remember that most of its requirements are **procedural**. The real **purpose of the rules of natural justice is to ensure that a fair procedure has been followed by the decision-making body.** The following two points should be noted here:

1. The precise requirements of natural justice will vary with the circumstances of each case, such as the nature of the decisions being taken, the status of the applicant, and so on. It is very difficult to do more than extract general principles from the case law.
2. Many of the cases considered arise out of disputes between private parties, and may seem 'out of place' in administrative law. It should be remembered that the concept of natural justice is not exclusive to public law. A plaintiff may bring an action in his own name against a private body alleging that his expulsion or suspension therefrom is in breach of an implied term in his contract, to the effect that disciplinary proceedings were to be conducted fairly. The principles of natural justice developed in such cases can be applied (sometimes with necessary modifications) to the actions of public bodies.

The rules

The traditional view of natural justice is that it comprises two procedural rules:

1. Audi alteram partem – the rule that no man is to be condemned without a hearing.
2. Nemo judex in causa sua – no man should sit as a judge in his own case.

Since 1967 a third 'limb' of natural justice has appeared, the so-called duty to act fairly. In many ways this duty encompasses both of the traditional rules but, as will be seen, it can possibly be applied to a wider range of decisions.

14.2 Development of natural justice

Introduction

The concept of natural justice is of respectable vintage. Evidence of its antiquity is provided, inter alia, by the remarkable facts of *Bagg's Case* (1615) 11 Co Rep 936 where the disfranchisement of a freeman of Plymouth was declared void because he was not first given a hearing.

A more contemporary example of the principles being applied is afforded by *Cooper* v *Wandsworth Board of Works* (1863) 14 CBNS 180. The plaintiff successfully sued the Board in trespass after its workmen had pulled down his house without providing him with any notice of their actions. The Board tried to justify its action by reference to its statutory powers to demolish buildings whose foundations it had not been given an opportunity to inspect during construction. Although the statute in question did not provide for property owners to be heard before their buildings were demolished, Byles J stated that there was a long line of authority to the effect that a man was not to be deprived of his property without first being heard, and in any event the common law would supply the omission of the legislature and provide that a hearing should be granted.

The 'simple' approach

Much later confusion and hardship would have been avoided if the dictum of Lord Loreburn LC in *Board of Education* v *Rice* [1911] AC 179 had been applied to subsequent cases. The House of Lords in this case was considering a decision by the Board of Education concerning conditions of service for teachers. The decisions did not actually involve a breach of natural justice, but in the course of his speech the Lord Chancellor stated:

'In the present instance ... what comes for determination ... (by the Board) is a matter of administrative kind ... In such cases the Board of Education will have to ascertain the law and also to ascertain the facts. I need not add that in doing either they must act in good faith and listen fairly to both sides, for that is the duty laying upon every one who decides anything.'

Note that the observance of natural justice here does not depend upon the classification of functions, or the status of those affected by the decision, but simply argues that **decision-making must be 'fair'**. As will be seen, the ensuing 50-year period saw this simple approach lost in a maze of conflicting decisions.

The retreat from natural justice

During the period from 1911 to 1964 the courts proved themselves unable to adapt and develop administrative law to deal adequately with the demands of a rapidly developing state. One particular casualty of this judicial failure was natural justice. The courts seemed unable, or unwilling, to apply well known principles to the actions of inferior bodies. The judiciary remained firmly committed to the view that natural justice only applied to judicial functions; as most inferior bodies such as ministers and tribunals exercised administrative functions, their actions were immune from attack on grounds of failing to apply the rules of natural justice.

The following four decisions illustrate what is often described as the retreat from natural justice:

1. In *Local Government Board* v *Arlidge* [1915] AC 120 the House of Lords held that the standards of fairness required of a court of law could not be demanded of a government department, with the result that it was not a violation of natural justice for the Board to refuse to disclose the contents of a report to Arlidge which contained the evidence upon which it had upheld a decision to demolish his property. As H W R Wade comments:

   'The *Arlidge* case was ... a turning point, in which the law failed to keep abreast of the standard of fairness which public opinion demanded ... in the procedure of government departments.' (Administrative Law 6th ed p 509)

2. In *Franklin* v *Minister of Town and Country Planning* [1948] AC 87 the House of Lords held that the Minister's statutory duties, including the making of a draft order designating Stevenage as a 'new town', were 'purely administrative', with the result that allegations that he had acted in breach of natural justice were irrelevant, even where the challenge was on the ground of bias.

3. In *R* v *Metropolitan Police Commissioner, ex parte Parker* [1953] 2 All ER 353, the Divisional Court refused to quash the revocation of Parker's licence to operate as a cab-driver despite the fact that he had not been granted a hearing before this was done. The court held that the Commissioner's powers of revocation were 'administrative' and therefore certiorari was not available to quash decision made as a result.

4. Finally, in *Nakkuda Ali* v *Jayaratne* [1951] AC 66, the Privy Council had to consider the validity of the action of the Controller of Textiles of Ceylon who had cancelled the appellant's textile licence, because he had 'reasonable ground to believe' that the appellant was unfit to continue in business. The appellant argued that the hearing he had been given before revocation of his licence had been

inadequate, and therefore the revocation had been in breach of natural justice. The Privy Council held that the Controller in cancelling licences was exercising powers that were administrative in nature; consequently there was no obligation upon him to grant the appellant any hearing, let alone an adequate one.

Natural justice restored

It will be apparent from the foregoing that the courts seemed most reluctant to impose the rules of natural justice on the proceedings of inferior bodies because their activities were seen as 'administrative' not 'judicial'. This restrictive view threatened to make natural justice redundant as a means of ensuring fairness in the administrative process.

The decline was halted, however, by the House of Lords' decision in *Ridge* v *Baldwin* [1964] AC 40. Charles Ridge had been dismissed from his position as Chief Constable of the County Borough of Brighton by the local watch committee. He contended before the House of Lords that the principles of natural justice applied to the exercise of powers to dismiss him, and that these had been breached by not allowing him to know the full case against him, and by not allowing him to put his case properly. The House of Lords allowed his appeal, holding that natural justice did apply and had not been observed. The main speech was that of Lord Reid, who made the following points:

1. The application of the rules of natural justice varied, depending upon the nature of the dispute in question.
2. Where what was challenged was a dismissal from a position, there were three different kinds of case: first, that of master and servant, where natural justice did not really have any relevance. A master was free to dispense with a servant's services as he wished, without granting the latter any hearing. The servant's remedy lay in an action for breach of contract. Secondly, there were cases where individuals held office 'at pleasure', such as Crown servants. Such persons had no right to be heard before being dismissed. Thirdly, there were cases such as the present where an individual was being stripped of some office or status. Lord Reid stated that there was an 'unbroken line of authority' to the effect that a man could not be denied an office without first being told what it was that was being alleged against him and being given an opportunity of putting his defence or providing an explanation.
3. Of the judicial/administrative dichotomy, Lord Reid explained that previous cases might have been wrongly decided by courts assuming that certiorari was only available to quash a decision in breach of natural justice where a body was acting 'judicially'.

Atkin LJ's celebrated dictum from *R* v *Electricity Commissioners, ex parte London Electricity Joint Committee Co* [1924] 1 KB 171, which explained the availability of certiorari, stated that it was only available in respect of bodies having a duty to act judicially. This had been taken too literally in subsequent cases, with the result that the remedy had not been extended to administrative bodies making decisions affecting the rights of individuals. Lord Reid suggested that the 'judicial' element should be deduced from the nature of the power being exercised. In short, the applicability of the rules of natural justice should not depend so much on a sterile academic classification of powers as administrative or judicial, but on the importance of what was at stake for the individual whose rights were affected by the decision. It should be noted that Ridge was principally concerned with succeeding with this action so as to protect his pension rights.

Since the decision in *Ridge* v *Baldwin*, the scope of the rights protected by the rules of natural justice, and the range of decision-makers whose functions are now reviewable on the ground of breach of natural justice, has been expanded considerably. In *Leech* v *Deputy Governor of Parkhurst Prison* [1988] 1 All ER 485 the applicants sought judicial review of the decisions of a prison governor in relation to his imposition of punishments for breach of prison rules, alleging that he had acted in breach of natural justice. The House of Lords (rejecting the approach in *R* v *Deputy Governor of Camphill Prison* [1984] 3 All ER 897) held that the actions of a prison governor in exercising his statutory powers to discipline prisoners were amenable to judicial review, because he was exercising a power which affected the legitimate expectations or rights of citizens, and such a power had to be exercised in accordance with the rules of natural justice. In the course of his speech, Lord Bridge stressed the significance of the rights affected as the key to the application of natural justice:

> 'Can it then be right for the court to refuse jurisdiction to afford what seems prima facie to be both the appropriate and the necessary remedy on the ground of "public policy"? My Lords ... It may be virtual certainty that a number of trouble makers will take every opportunity to exploit and abuse the jurisdiction. But that is only one side of the coin. On the other side it can hardly be doubted that governors and deputy governors dealing with the offences against discipline may occasionally fall short of the standards of fairness which are called for in the performance of any judicial function. Nothing, I believe, is so likely to generate unrest among ordinary prisoners as a sense that they have been treated unfairly and have no effective means of redress. If a prisoner has a genuine grievance arising from disciplinary proceedings unfairly conducted, his right to petition a faceless authority in Whitehall for a remedy will not be of much comfort to him. Thus, I believe, it is at least possible that any damage to prison discipline that may result from frivolous and vexatious applications for judicial review may be substantially offset by the advantages which access to the court will provide for the proper ventilation of genuine grievances and perhaps also that the availability of the court's supervisory role may have the effect on the conduct of judicial proceedings by governors which it appears to have had in the case of boards of visitors of enhancing the standards of fairness observed ... I am firmly of the opinion that, if the social consequences of the availability of judicial review to supervise governors' disciplinary awards are ... detrimental to the proper functioning of the prison system ... it lies in the province of the legislature, not of the judiciary, to exclude the court's jurisdiction.'

Further, in *R* v *Board of Governors of London Oratory School, ex parte R* (1988) The Times 17 February the mother of a pupil at the school applied for judicial review of the Governors' decision to expel him. Although the court rejected the application for review on its facts, in that the expulsion had not been preceded by an unfair process, McCullough J observed that there was no reason why the rules of natural justice should not apply to such a procedure. The consequences of expulsion for the pupil were at least as serious as those resulting from an undergraduate being 'sent down'. The pupil about to be expelled was entitled to know the case against him, and should be granted a hearing before an unbiased tribunal.

McInnes *v* Onslow-Fane *[1978] 1 WLR 1520*

This decision provides a useful basis for consideration of the modern approach to the application of natural justice.

Between 1972 and 1975 the plaintiff made five unsuccessful applications to the British Boxing Board of Control for a boxing manager's licence. On 28 May 1976 he applied to the Board through an area council for a manager's licence and asked for an oral hearing and prior notification of anything that might prevent the council making a favourable recommendation to the Board. On 16 July the Board replied saying that it had considered the application and had decided not to grant it. The plaintiff sought a declaration that the Board had acted in breach of natural justice and/or unfairly in failing to comply with his request to be informed of the case against him or to grant him an oral hearing.

Having reviewed the authorities, Megarry V-C went on to consider the situations in which natural justice might apply. First there were what he called the 'forfeiture' cases where what was being taken away was some existing right. In such cases there was a right to an unbiased tribunal, notice of the charges, and the right to be heard. Secondly there were the 'mere applicant' cases, where the individual was seeking a right or privilege, not defending one. In such cases there was rarely any right to be heard, because no charges were being made. The third intermediate category comprised cases such as that of the licence holder, who had held a licence for many years which had now expired, and who now sought to renew that licence. Such cases were closer to forfeiture cases than application cases, in that the individual concerned had a legitimate expectation of being granted a hearing.

The present case was clearly an 'application' case, and in dealing with it the Board was under a duty to act fairly. This did not necessitate granting McInnes an oral hearing, or of informing him of the case against him. Indeed, in such cases there may be no case against the applicant, merely an absence of sufficient reasons to grant him a licence. In many cases all that the duty to act fairly required was that the body making the decision did so honestly, without bias and caprice. More may be required where the refusal of a licence put a slur on an individual's character, but that was not the case here. The fact that a decision-making body exercises monopoly control over the means by which an individual may pursue his livelihood may also be instrumental in requiring more in the way of fairness, but again that consideration did not invalidate the determination of the board under consideration.

The duty to act fairly

The approach of the courts now seems to be that even if the 'full' rules of natural justice do not apply, the duty to act fairly will. Whilst not incorrect, this is a very crude and simplistic analysis, notable for its clarity more than its accuracy. It represents the duty to act fairly as an alternative to natural justice, not an extension of it. Despite the dictum of Lord Loreburn LC in *Board of Education* v *Rice* (above) the modern genesis of the duty to act fairly is seen as being *Re HK (an infant)* [1967] 2 QB 617, in which Lord Parker CJ held that even though an immigration officer, in determining K's entitlement to enter the country, was acting administratively, he was still under a duty to act fairly, which in this case involved giving the applicant an opportunity of proving that he was under 16 years of age and thus had a right to enter the country. The Divisional Court was satisfied that the officer had acted fairly. While *Re HK* served to weaken further the stranglehold of the administrative/judicial dichotomy on the growth of natural justice, the question remained as to the extent to which the newly liberated concepts of natural justice/ duty to act fairly actually applied to various situations.

Reasonableness

A procedure which violates the principles of natural justice may also be attacked on the basis that it was unreasonable to adopt such a procedure. In *R* v *Secretary of State for the Home Department, ex parte Tarrant* [1984] 1 All ER 799 the decision of the board of visitors not to allow a prisoner legal representation was regarded as both unfair and unreasonable by the court on the ground that no reasonable tribunal would have refused the prisoner representation given the gravity of the charges and the possible loss of remission.

In *R* v *Norfolk County Council, ex parte M* [1989] 2 All ER 359, the applicant, who had been employed as a plumber, was alleged to have behaved indecently towards a 13-year-old girl while he had been working at her parents' house. He had strenuously denied these allegations. Without giving any notice to the applicant, the social services department of the local authority convened a case conference at which the decision was taken to place his name on the authority's register of child abusers. When the applicant was made aware of this decision he complained formally to the local authority, through his solicitors. He was given an opportunity to appear with a solicitor before a re-convened case conference in order to make representations, but the applicant declined this invitation in the light of the course that the proceedings had already taken. The Divisional Court granted his application for an order of certiorari to quash the registration. The court held that the consequences of registering a person as a child abuser were sufficiently serious to require the local authority to act fairly towards that person. Natural justice had not been observed in the present case, in that the applicant had not been given advance warning of the decision, had not been consulted, and had not been made aware of all the circumstances surrounding the decision. The court felt that the actions of the authority were so much at odds with the requirements of fairness that they could properly be described as unreasonable in the 'Wednesbury' sense. It is perhaps interesting to note that counsel for the authority had submitted that the decision to register the applicant as an abuser was not one amenable to judicial review, being of a clerical or administrative nature. This submission was rejected by the court in the light of the effect that such a decision could have upon an individual. It might also be sugested that the court was motivated to intervene in this case because of the absence of any other viable remedy open to the applicant. See further *R* v *Harrow London Borough Council, ex parte D* [1989] 3 WLR 1239.

14.3 When does natural justice apply?

Before considering the case law, it would be useful to bear in mind two of the approaches to the application of natural justice so far encountered, because the cases themselves sometimes seem to involve a mixture of all three theories.

Judicial/administrative dichotomy

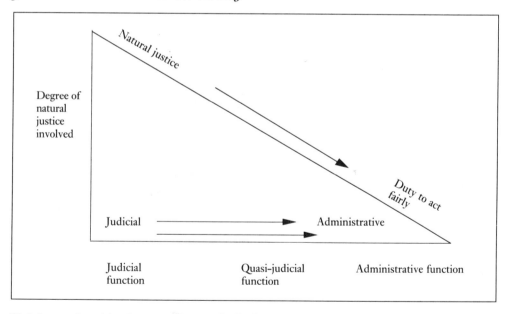

Plainly, under this theory, the more administrative a function becomes the more the requirements of natural justice are relaxed. The logical conclusion is reached in the case of 'purely administrative' functions that no duty to act fairly applies.

Reference to the rights affected – the McInnes v Onslow-Fane *method*

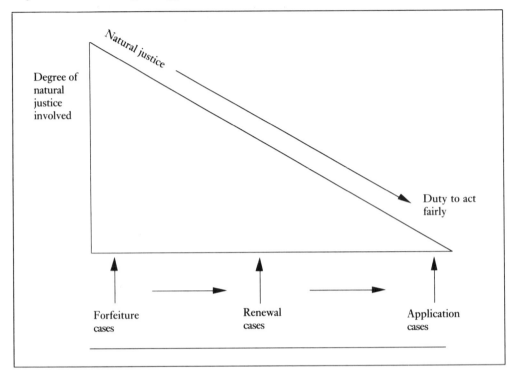

Again under this theory, the more one moves from forfeiture to application cases, the more the rules of natural justice are relaxed.

Legislative process

Bates v *Lord Hailsham* [1972] 1 WLR 1373 is authority for the proposition that natural justice does not apply to the discharge of legislative functions. The court held that a failure to consult prior to exercising powers to create delated legislation, in the absence of any statutory requirements to do so, could not invalidate the process on the ground that there had been any breach of the rules of natural justice – they simply did not apply.

Preliminary procedures

There are a number of authorities suggesting that natural justice will not apply where action is merely preparatory to the making of a decision, or 'purely administrative' as it is sometimes described.

In both *Furnell* v *Whangarei High Schools Board* [1973] AC 660 and *Herring* v *Templeman* [1973] AC 660 it was held that an individual had no right to be heard by a sub-ordinate body instructed to prepare a report for a disciplinary body. Only when the charges were put to the individual concerned did the right to be heard apply.

Similar reasoning was adopted in *Norwest Holst Ltd* v *Secretary of State for Trade* [1978] Ch 201, where it was held that the company had no right to be heard prior to the appointment of inspectors to investigate the company's affairs. Such appointments were 'purely administrative' decisions. See also *Lewis* v *Heffer* [1978] 3 All ER 354.

'Mere applicants'

As has been seen, Megarry V-C in *McInnes* v *Onslow-Fane* (above) held that the mere applicant has no right to be heard as such, in ordinary situations such as licensing. This sentiment has been echoed in other decisions. In *Central Council for Education and Training in Social Work* v *Edwards* (1978) The Times 5 May it was held that an applicant for a place on a polytechnic course had no right to a hearing, or for the reasons for being denied a place. If, on the other hand, an interview was granted it had to be conducted fairly.

Similarly, in *R* v *Gaming Board for Great Britain, ex parte Benaim and Khaida* [1970] 2 QB 417, an application for a gaming licence had been refused by the Board without reasons being given or the applicants being notified of the evidence against them. The applicants sought certiorari to quash the refusal and an order of mandamus to compel the Board to give sufficient information for the applicants to be able to know the case against them. In confirming the decision at first instance not to grant the orders sought, Lord Denning MR considered what natural justice required in such cases. His Lordship turned to *Re HK (an infant)* (above) for guidance and stated that the approach recommended in that case by Lord Parker CJ was applicable, and quoted with approval his dictum that:

'... even if an immigration officer is not acting in a judicial or quasi-judicial capacity, he must at any rate give the immigrant an opportunity of satisfying him of the matters in the subsection, and for that purpose let the immigrant know what his immediate impression is so that the immigrant can disabuse him. That is not, as I see it, a question of acting or being required to act judicially, but of being required to act fairly.'

Lord Denning MR felt that these words could be applied equally to the Board in the present case. It should let the applicants know its impressions of their case so that they could put forward further evidence to put the record straight if necessary. It was held that the Board was not required to divulge the evidence upon which it proposed to act because much of it had been given in confidence by police informers.

Further, in *Breen* v *AEU* [1971] 1 All ER 1148, Lord Denning stated, obiter, that:

'If a man seeks a privilege to which he has no particular claim ... then he can be turned away without a word. He need not be heard. No explanation need be given ...'

Holders of existing rights

As the decisions in *Ridge* v *Baldwin* and *McInnes* v *Onslow-Fane* illustrate, individuals who are subject to decision-making processes affecting rights recognised by the courts can usually complain if the rules of natural justice are not complied with.

Where public servants such as teachers are concerned, there may be some difficulty in deciding whether they are holders of office or dismissible at pleasure: see *Malloch* v *Aberdeen Corporation* [1971] 2 All ER 1278, where the House of Lords held that a schoolteacher who was 'dismissible at pleasure' could not be dismissed without a hearing. Similarly, in *Stevenson* v *United Road Transport Union* [1977] 2 All ER 941, the Court of Appeal held that a union official had been unfairly dismissed, having been kept in ignorance of the case against him and refused a legitimate request for an adjournment of his hearing. The Court of Appeal accepted that as Stevenson was an 'officer' of the union he had some status which took him out of the 'master and servant' category.

'Domestic' bodies

While administrative law is primarily concerned with the actions of public bodies (to the extent to which such a definition is possible), it should be borne in mind that the rules of natural justice can apply to 'private law' situations as well. The courts will generally be reluctant to 'over-judicialise' the proceedings of domestic bodies by laying down too many procedural requirements, but will be mindful that where a body exercises disciplinary functions, and can take decisions affecting the ability of an individual to pursue his livelihood, the requirements of fairness should be observed.

The Court of Appeal decision in *Currie* v *Barton* (1988) The Times 12 February illustrates, however, that where factors such as livelihood are not involved, the courts are inclined to adopt a 'hands-off' approach. The plaintiff had been chosen as a reserve player in a county tennis match. His response was to walk off the court and refuse to take part. He wrote a long letter to the Essex County Lawn Tennis Association Committee explaining his actions. The committee resolved to suspend the plaintiff from playing for the county team for three years. The plaintiff sought a declaration that the suspension was in breach of natural justice because he had not been granted a hearing before the committee. In dismissing his appeal, O'Conner LJ expressed the view that the courts should not intervene in the affairs of 'domestic' bodies unless such bodies were in a contractual relationship with those affected by their decisions, or their decisions affected the ability of an individual to pursue his/her livelihood. In the present case, the committee was concerned with amateur sport; consequently there was 'less at stake'. In any event, there had been no need for the plaintiff to appear before the committee in person. Its members had been aware of his side of the matter and he knew that a suspension was a distinct possibility as a result of the hearing.

14.4 Legitimate expectation cases

Increasingly the courts are recognising that there are groups of individuals who while not being 'mere applicants' do have a legitimate expectation of being dealt with in accordance with the rules of natural justice. This expectation arises not simply because some property right or status is being threatened; it can also arise because a previous course of conduct on the part of the decision-making body or a previous statement leads the individual or group to believe that it will be consulted, notified or heard before action affecting it is taken.

Predictably, the requirements of natural justice in legitimate expectation cases vary enormously depending upon the context, but usually the legitimate expectation is of being heard. As suggested by reference to the Vice-Chancellor's classification in *McInnes* v *Onslow-Fane* (above), the individual seeking to renew a licence he has held for some time would come within this class. In *Schmidt* v *Secretary of State for Home Affairs* [1969] 2 Ch 149, two Scientology students were refused an extension of their permission to remain in the country when their right to remain had expired. They complained that they had not been granted a hearing. The Court of Appeal held that there had been no breach of natural justice. Lord Denning stated that, as they had no right to remain in the country, the students had no legitimate expectations of being granted a hearing. The situation might have been different if their right to stay had been revoked before its expiry. In *Cinnamond* v *British Airports Authority* [1980] 1 WLR 582 Lord Denning MR held that taxi-cab drivers who were prohibited by an order from entering Heathrow Airport other than as legitimate passengers had no legitimate expectation of being heard before the order was made because they had long records of convictions, with fines outstanding, for unlawfully plying their trade in the vicinity of the airport. On the other hand:

'... suppose that these car-hire drivers were of good character and had for years been coming into the airport under an implied licence to do so. If in that case there was suddenly a prohibition order preventing them from entering then it would seem only fair that they should be given a hearing and a chance to put their case.'

Departure from a published policy

In *R* v *Secretary of State for the Home Department, ex parte Khan* [1985] 1 All ER 40, the Home Office had published a circular indicating the criteria that would be applied when persons in the United Kingdom wished to adopt a child from abroad. The applicant wished to adopt a relative's child who lived in Pakistan. He applied for an entry clearance certificate for the child which was refused by the Secretary of State, applying criteria other than those set out in the circular. The applicant applied for judicial review of the Secretary of State's refusal, contending that he had a legitimate expectation, arising out of the circular, that the procedure therein set out would be followed. The Secretary of State claimed that his discretion in such matters was unfettered.

The court held that, provided the circular did not conflict with the Minister's statutory duty, he was under a duty to apply the criteria therein stated. He could only resile from the provisions of the circular if there was an overriding public interest that he should so act, and interested persons were first afforded a hearing. In the circumstances the Secretary of State had acted unfairly and unreasonably in deciding the applicant's case after applying criteria different from those set out in the circular.

Departure from express assurances

In *Attorney-General of Hong Kong* v *Ng Yuen Shiu* [1983] 2 AC 629 the Hong Kong government had made public its changed policy towards illegal immigrants, stating that each one, if he or she came forward, would be interviewed, and although no guarantee would be given that they would not subsequently be removed, each case would be treated on its merits. The respondent, who had entered Hong Kong illegally in 1976, was interviewed by an immigration officer and subsequently detained pending the making of a removal order. The respondent's appeal to the immigration appeal was dismissed without a hearing. The Court of Appeal of Hong Kong granted the respondent an order of prohibition preventing his removal, pending a proper hearing of his case. The Attorney-General of Hong Kong appealed to the Privy Council. In dismissing the appeal, the Privy Council substituted an order of certiorari for the order of prohibition.

The reasoning behind the decision is an illuminating example of the growth of the importance of the 'legitimate expectation' doctrine. The Privy Council held that, assuming there was no general right in an alien to have a hearing in accordance with the rules of natural justice before the making of a removal order against him, a person was nevertheless entitled to a fair hearing before a decision adversely affecting his interests was made by a public official or body if he had a legitimate or reasonable expectation of being accorded such a hearing. Such an expectation might be based on some statement or undertaking by, or on behalf of, the public authority which had the duty of making the decision if the authority had through its officers, acted in a way which would make it unfair or inconsistent with good administration to deny the person affected an inquiry into his case. That principle was as much applicable where the person affected was an alien as where he was a British subject, because a public authority was bound by its undertaking as to the procedure it would follow, provided those undertakings did not conflict with its statutory duty. It followed that the government undertaking that each case would be treated on its merits had not been implemented since the respondent had been given no opportunity to explain the humanitarian grounds on which he might have been allowed to remain in Hong Kong, in particular that he was a partner in a business which employed a large number of workers.

In *R* v *Secretary of State for the Home Department, ex parte Ruddock* [1987] 2 All ER 518, which involved an allegation by the applicant that the Secretary of State had not, as promised, followed the required procedures before authorising the tapping of the applicant's telephone, Mr Justice Taylor observed that the doctrine of legitimate expectation was not limited to those cases involving a legitimate expectation of a hearing before some right was affected. It extended to situations where no right to be heard existed, but fairness required a public body to act in compliance with its public undertakings and assurances. In the present case the Secretary of State had repeatedly confirmed, between 1952 and 1982, that the criteria for authorising 'phone taps' would be complied with, and that gave rise to a legitimate expectation that he would in fact comply with such criteria. In short, the legitimate expectation was that the Secretary of State would act fairly.

In *R* v *Brent London Borough Council, ex parte MacDonagh* (1989) The Times 22 March the applicants sought judicial review of the local authority's decision to evict the gypsies from a site without first giving them advance notice. In accordance with its statutory duty under the Caravan Sites Act 1968, Brent London Borough Council. had provided a site for gypsies but on a number of occasions had evicted them from it in order to repair services and ensure that it was sanitary. In March 1987, 33 gypsies on the site were each served with a letter indicating that they would not be evicted from the site in future unless the local authority provided suitable alternative accommodation. In 1988, in the light of the extent to which conditions on the site had deteriorated, the local authority took the decision to evict. The Divisional Court granted an order of certiorari, quashing the decision to evict, and an injunction to prevent the local authority from revoking its consent to the occupation of the site without consultation with the gypsies. The letters sent to the 33 gypsies, and the previous conduct of the local authority, gave rise to a legitimate expectation that they would not be evicted without some alternative accommodation being made available.

Where the assurance given is based on a mistake by the promisor as to the promisee's legal rights, the courts will not hold that a legitimate expectation has arisen in favour of the promisor, not least because the court might be in danger of extending the promisor's power in a manner not permitted by statute: see generally 18.3. In *R* v *Secretary of State for the Home Department, ex parte Silva and Another* (1994) The Times 1 April, the applicants, prisoners originally from Colombia, serving prison sentences for drugs offences, were informed of the Home Secretary's intention to deport them in a letter that erroneously referred to the applicants being permitted a right to appeal against the decision. The mistake was subsequently rectified and the applicants were notified that they were to be deported pursuant to s3(6) of the Immigration Act 1971, which did not provide for any right of appeal. Considering the application for judicial review of the Home Secretary's decision to order deportation, on the ground that his initial letter had given rise to a legitimate expectation that the deportation would be ordered under s3(5)(b) of the 1971 Act, which did permit a right of appeal, the Court of Appeal held that applicants' reliance on *Ng Yuen Shiu* (above) was misguided, as they had not shown that it would be unfair or detrimental to the principles of good administration for the Home Secretary to depart from his initial decision.

Departure from a previous course of conduct

In *Council of Civil Service Unions* v *Minister for the Civil Service* [1984] 3 All ER 935 the Prime Minister, acting under prerogative powers, had issued a directive prohibiting membership of trade unions at the government's communications headquarters in Cheltenham. The unions applied for a declaration that the action was in breach of natural justice, because they had not been consulted prior to the directive being issued. The House of Lords held, inter alia, that the previous regular practice of consultation between the Minister and the unions on matters relating to conditions of service, gave the unions a legitimate expectation of being consulted on this occasion before union membership was prohibited. In this case, however, such legitimate expectation was displaced by considerations of national security.

Legitimate expectation of what?

Some of the case law on legitimate expectation suggests that the expression 'legitimate expectation' can be used in respect of the procedure that an applicant expects the public body to follow, eg consultation before decision-making. In others there are suggestions that the phrase relates to an expectation as to what the substantive decision would be, for example that the applicant would be granted a licence. Given that natural justice is concerned with the legality of the procedure adopted by the decision-making body, legitimate expectation should, properly understood, only apply in the former situation. Where an applicant expects to have a substantive decision made in his favour, and a public body later makes a contrary decision, his only grounds of challenge might be that the decision was unreasonable, or possibly that the public body is estopped from denying him the privilege he expected to obtain. The issue was considered by the Divisional Court in *R* v *Secretary of State for Transport, ex parte Richmond-Upon-Thames London Borough Council* [1994] 1 WLR 74, where a number of local authorities successfully challenged proposed changes to the regulations governing night flights at London's airports. Inter alia, the applicants had contended that they had a legitimate expectation that any revision to the regulations would not result in an increase in noise from night flights. Laws J recognised that the expression 'legitimate expectation' could be used in two situations: first, in relation to what he described as the 'procedural expectation', where a public authority provides that it will give certain persons a hearing before arriving at a decision on a particular matter, and secondly, where a public body had adopted a policy and, by promise or past practice, indicated that this would be its *continuing* policy. In such cases the court might intervene where it considered the public body to be acting unfairly where it changed the policy without giving those affected a hearing. Some commentators had described such cases as involving 'substantive expectations', but Laws J expressed the view that:

> '... the putative distinction between procedural and substantive rights in this context has little, if any utility; the question is always whether the discipline of fairness, imposed by the common law, ought to prevent the public authority ... from acting as it proposes'.

Significantly, he rejected any contention that there could be, in public law, a legitimate expectation that a particular policy would not be changed even though those affected had been consulted. Such a contention, he said:

> '... would impose an obvious and unacceptable fetter upon the power, and duty, of a responsible public authority to change its policy when it considered that that was required in fulfilment of its public responsibilities'.

He further added that in his view:

> '... the law of legitimate expectation, where it is invoked in situations other than one where the expectation relied on is distinctly one of consultation, only goes so far as to say that there may arise conditions in which, if policy is to be changed, a specific person or class of persons affected must first be notified and given the right to be heard'.

Note that following this decision the Secretary of State sought to introduce new night flying restrictions in a more acceptable form. The revised restrictions were, however, successfully challenged in a subsequent application, *R v Secretary of State for Transport, ex parte Richmond-upon-Thames London Borough Council and Others* (1994) The Times 29 December, where Mr Justice Latham identified two grounds of illegality in the procedure followed by the Secretary of State. First, the consultation paper produced by his department contained material errors concerning the calculation of overall noise levels, hance the consultation process that followed from it was fundamentally flawed. Secondly, the Secretary of State had not expressly conceded that the new arrangements for night flights would involve a material departure from his previously stated policy that there would be an overall reduction in noise levels from night flights, or at best no increase in noise levels. Whilst he was free to depart from his previously stated policy he was required to recognise that he had done so.

14.5 Consequences of a breach of natural justice

What happens once a decision has been taken in breach of natural justice? Is it void, or voidable? Can the individual ignore the decision with impunity and rely on its invalidity as justification? Can a breach of natural justice at first instance be cured by a valid hearing on appeal?

In theory, an intra vires decision is valid, but an intra vires decision vitiated by an error of law is voidable, in the sense that it continues in force as a valid decision unless and until it is quashed by an order of certiorari, and an ultra vires decision is void, of no effect; it is as if no decision was ever taken.

While this approach may have the advantage of simplicity, how is an individual to know if a decision is in breach of natural justice, and therefore ultra vires? It would be rather dangerous, for example, where a market trader's licence has been revoked, for him to assume on his own, or even his legal adviser's, judgment that because there had been a breach of natural justice the revocation was void, and he could therefore continue legally to trade.

Many aspects of judicial review only make sense if one adopts the approach that actions that are ultra vires are void. For example, the reasoning in *Anisminic Ltd* v *Foreign Compensation Commission* (see Chapter 21 below) proceeds on the basis that the 'ouster' clause is of no effect because the Commission's determination was ultra vires, and therefore void.

In *Ridge* v *Baldwin* (above) the House of Lords made it clear that there are no 'degrees of nullity'; an ultra vires decision is void. As Lord Reid commented:

> '... there was considerable argument whether in the result the watch committee's decision is void or merely voidable. Time and again in the cases I have cited it has been stated that a decision given without regard to the principles of natural justice is void and that was expressly decided in *Wood* v *Wood* (1874) LR 9 Exch 190. I see no reason to doubt these authorities. The body with the power to decide cannot lawfully proceed to make a decision until it has afforded to the person affected a proper opportunity to state his case.'

A better approach to the problem is that propounded by H W R Wade who suggests that decisions should be regarded as voidable, where there is an error of law; 'void', where there appears to be evidence that the body has acted ultra vires, but this is yet to be confirmed by the courts, and void where a decision has been declared to be such by the courts and its effects can safely be ignored. The danger of describing an ultra vires decision as void in any absolute sense until declared to be such by the courts is illustrated by those decisions which, after the expiry of a time limit, become unchallengeable in the courts. It would be odd to say that an 'absolutely void' decision had nevertheless to be observed because of the partial 'ouster' clause.

A more difficult problem is posed by questioning the validity of acts done in reliance on a 'void' order, which is subsequently declared absolutely void by the courts. For example, could Charles Ridge have resumed activities as Chief Constable of Brighton in place of his successor?

Invalidity and appeals

The problem considered here is the extent to which breaches of natural justice at an initial hearing can be cured at a subsequent appeal. On the one hand, there is the logical difficulty created by the fact that a hearing in breach of natural justice is a nullity, and there cannot be an appeal from a nullity; on the other hand an appeal, unlike judicial review, does involve a complete rehearing of a case and is in effect the decision being taken all over again. The problem has been considered on a number of occasions.

In *Leary* v *National Union of Vehicle Builders* [1970] 2 All ER 713 Megarry J stated:

> 'If the rules and the law combine to give the member the right to a fair trial and the right of appeal, why should he be told that he ought to be satisfied with an unjust trial and a fair appeal? … As a general rule … I hold that a failure of natural justice in the trial body cannot be cured by a sufficiency of natural justice in an appellate body.'

This statement of the law has, however, been considered to be too wide. The leading authority, the Privy Council decision in *Calvin* v *Carr* [1979] 2 All ER 440, considered the claim of a jockey to the effect that a hearing of his case before the stewards, which resulted in his disqualification, was in breach of natural justice and could not, therefore, be remedied by a properly conducted appeal hearing before an appellate committee of the Australian Jockey Club. The Privy Council dismissed the jockey's appeal, but suggested a classification that could be used as a guide to determining when an invalid first hearing could be cured by a valid appeal. Lord Wilberforce explained the approach as follows:

> 'First there are cases where the rules provide for a rehearing by the original body, or some fuller or enlarged form of it … It is not difficult in such cases to reach the conclusion that the first hearing is superseded by the second …
>
> At the other extreme are cases where, after examination of the whole hearing structure, in the context of the particular activity to which it relates (trade union membership, planning, employment etc) the conclusion is reached that a complainant has the right to nothing less than a fair hearing both at the original and at the appeal stage.'

Lord Wilberforce continued by describing a third, intermediate, situation where the possibility of defects at an initial hearing being remedied on appeal would depend on the circumstances. His Lordship stated that:

> '… it is for the court, in the light of the agreements made, and in addition having regard to the course of proceedings, to decide whether, at the end of the day, there has been a fair result, reached by fair methods, such as the parties should fairly be taken to have accepted when they joined the association. Naturally there may be instances when the defect is so flagrant, the consequences so severe, that the most perfect of appeals or rehearings will not be sufficient to produce a just result.'

15

What Are the Requirements
of a Fair Hearing?

15.1 Introduction

15.2 Prior notice of decision-making

15.3 The right to make representations

15.4 The right to legal representation

15.5 The giving of reasons

15.6 The rule against bias

15.1 Introduction

This chapter is concerned with the procedures that have to be observed by an inferior body to comply with the requirements of natural justice. The previous chapter attempted to deal with the question of when natural justice applies, and it will be recalled that some situations seem to require the full panoply of 'judicial' type safeguards, whilst in others there is only a duty to act fairly. The problem is that the extent to which natural justice applies to a situation, and if it does what procedural requirements must be observed, will necessarily vary from one situation to another, depending upon context, subject matter and the rights of those affected.

All that can be said with any certainty is that if the situation is one to which natural justice/duty to act fairly does not apply, such as purely administrative functions, then the contents of this chapter will be largely irrelevant. If, on the other hand, the situation is one that requires some compliance with natural justice or the duty to act fairly, then the precedural requirements detailed here will have to be followed to a degree.

15.2 Prior notice of decision-making

A basic requirement of a fair administrative process is that those likely to be affected by decisions are given adequate notice that they are going to be made. Adequate

208

notice allows an individual to prepare his case properly and conduct his affairs accordingly. Note that in some situations the administrative process denies an individual any notice that a decision affecting him has been taken. For example, in the sphere of town and country planning, property owners are given no official warning that their properties are about to be 'listed', a designation bringing with it considerable restrictions on the rights of owners to deal with their properties as they choose. The justification for what would otherwise be a clear breach of natural justice is expediency. Many property owners, on being informed that their properties are about to be listed, would simply have them demolished rather than have on their hands a building, over which they have restricted rights, and this would clearly frustrate the whole purpose of listing.

The case law illustrates situations where the courts will intervene. In *Cooper* v *Wandsworth Board of Works* (1863) 14 CBNS 180, the plaintiff succeeded in an action against the Board for trespass on the grounds that it failed to notify him of its decision or to consider any representations he might have to make.

As Viscount Haldane LC stated in *Local Government Board* v *Arlidge* [1915] AC 120, 132:

> 'My Lords, when the duty of deciding an appeal is imposed, those whose duty it is to decide it must act judicially. They must deal with the question referred to them without bias, and they must give to each of the parties the opportunity of adequately presenting the case made.'

In *Willis* v *Childe* (1851) 13 Beav 117 it was held that a schoolmaster who was informed a few hours before a meeting of the trustees was due to take place that they would be considering representations from him on their decision to dismiss him had been given inadequate notice of the meeting, and its subsequent proceedings were of no effect.

In *R* v *Thames Magistrates' Court, ex parte Polemis* [1974] 2 All ER 1219 the applicant, the master of a ship moored on the Thames from which it was alleged that oil had been discharged, received a summons to attend trial at the magistrates' court at 10.30 am on the day that his ship was due to sail. His solicitor applied unsuccessfully for an adjournment. The applicant was eventually convicted and fined £5,000, and successfully sought an order of certiorari to quash the conviction on the ground that he had not had reasonable time to prepare his defence, with a consequent breach of natural justice. In granting relief Lord Widgery CJ rejected the 'futility of giving proper notice' argument, observing:

> 'It is again absolutely basic to our system that justice must not only be done but must manifestly be seen to be done. If justice was so clearly not seen to be done, as on the afternoon in question here, it seems to me that it is no answer to the applicant to say: "Well, even if the case had been properly conducted, the result would have been the same." That is mixing up doing justice with seeing that justice is done, so I reject that argument.'

Similarly, in *Glynn* v *Keele University* [1971] 1 WLR 487, a breach of natural justice was held to have occurred where a student was fined by the university without first being told the reasons why or being granted a hearing, although relief was denied on other grounds. Note, however, that the requirements of giving notice may be relaxed somewhat where the case is straightforward and the issues well known to the parties.

In *R v Brent London Borough Council, ex parte Assegai* (1987) The Times 18 June a school governor was dismissed without being given notice of the decision, and without being given the opportunity to reply in writing to complaints that had been made against him. Although he was unsuccesful in applying for judicial review of the local authority subcommittee decision to dismiss him, the court held that natural justice required him to be given some notice of the proceedings because his appointment was supported by legislation, had a public law element, and was in the nature of a status or office. Woolf LJ observed that the only possible relationships in which all the requirements of natural justice were excluded were ones in which there was no element of public employment or service, nor support by statute, and nothing in the way of an office or status which was capable of protection. See also *R v Chief Constable of Thames Valley Police, ex parte Stevenson* (1987) The Times 22 April.

Statutory requirements

The requirement of notice is sometimes incorporated in procedural requirements specified in statutes or delegated legislation, for example, the Town and Country Planning (Inquiries Procedure) Rules 1992 where specified parties must be given 42 days' notice, in writing, of the holding of an inquiry.

Failure to comply with a statutory requirement as to the giving of notice will usually result in any consequent action being invalidated: see *R v Swansea City Council, ex parte Quietlynn* (1983) The Times 19 October. Where there has been substantial compliance with the requirement of giving notice, however, action may still be valid: see *Coney v Choice* [1975] 1 WLR 422.

Changes in nature of the hearing

Where natural justice requires some notice to be given of an impending decision, it also requires the decision-making body to provide some information as to the nature of the hearing, what is being determined etc. If this were otherwise, giving notice of the decision being taken would be pointless as the individual would not be able to prepare his case properly. The logical extension of this line of reasoning is that if a decision-making body informs an individual that a hearing is to be held to consider 'X' and once at the hearing, the individual finds that the decision-making body has decided to deal with 'Y', there will have been a breach of natural justice because the decision-making body will not have kept to the terms of the notice given. In *Andrews v Mitchell* [1905] AC 78 a member of a friendly society appeared before its disciplinary body on a charge of misconduct punishable by way of a fine. At the conclusion of the hearing the disciplinary body decided to expel him on a different charge under a different rule. This was held to be a clear breach of natural justice.

15.3 The right to make representations

It is frequently assumed that, if natural justice or a duty to act fairly applies to a procedure, then an individual automatically has a right to be heard. This is not necessarily the case. Where a person's livelihood is at stake, or allegations have been made which amount to an attack on an individual's integrity, then representations will almost certainly have to be allowed. In *R v Wear Valley District Council, ex parte Binks* [1985] 2 All ER 699, the respondent authority terminated the applicant's oral contractual licence to sell take-away food from a caravan. The business was her only source of livelihood. She was given no notice of the decision, and four weeks' notice to remove her caravan. On an application for judicial review, Taylor J held that the local authority was obliged to comply with the rules of natural justice in terminating the licence, and that this required that the applicant should be given an opportunity to be heard before the decision was taken, and should be given reasons for the decision. The court regarded as significant the fact that the applicant's licence was one which permitted her to trade in a public place, and that it was her sole means of livelihood. On the other hand, as Megarry V-C indicated in *McInnes v Onslow-Fane* [1978] 1 WLR 1520, there may be cases where a person applies for an award, or a licence, of some sort, and cannot be said to have any legitimate expectation of being heard. The applicant for a place at a university or polytechnic would be in this position.

Must representations be oral?

It is again sometimes wrongly assumed that if natural justice requires a person to be allowed to make representations, these must take the form of an oral hearing. In fact, an oral hearing is the exception, not the rule. In many cases an individual can put all necessary evidence before a decision-making body in the form of written representations.

Certainly an investigative body can act fairly where it collects written evidence instead of hearing witnesses orally: see *Selvarajan v Race Relations Board* [1976] 1 All ER 12. Where the facts are well known and accepted by both sides, or the individual concerned admits to some wrongdoing and merely seeks to make a plea in mitigation, written representations may be adequate: see *Brighton Corporation v Parry* (1972) 70 LGR 576 and *R v Aston University Senate, ex parte Roffey* [1969] 2 QB 538. The gravity of the matters under consideration as regards the applicant will clearly be a factor weighing heavily with the court. As Lord Mustill observed in *R v Secretary of State for the Home Office, ex parte Doody and Others* [1993] 3 WLR 154, in relation to whether or not a prisoner sentenced to mandatory life imprisonment should be given the opportunity to make representations prior to the Home Secretary's determination of the minimum period to be served:

> 'What does fairness require in the present case? My Lords I think it unnecessary to refer
> by name or to quote from, any of the oft-cited authorities in which the courts have

explained what is essentially an intuitive judgment. They are far too well known. From them, I derive the following. (1) Where an Act of Parliament confers an administrative power there is a presumption that it will be exercised in a manner which is fair in all the circumstances. (2) The standards of fairness are not immutable. They may change with the passage of time, both in the general and in their application to decisions of a particular type. (3) The principles of fairness are not to be applied identically by rote in every situation. What fairness demands is dependent on the context of the decision, and this is to be taken into account in all its aspects. (4) An essential feature of the context is the statute which creates the discretion, as regards both its language and the shape of the legal and administrative system within which the decision is taken. (5) Fairness will very often require that a person who may be adversely affected by the decision will have an opportunity to make representations on his own behalf either before the decision is taken with a view to producing a favourable result, or after it is taken, with a view to procuring its modification, or both. (6) Since the person affected cannot usually make worthwhile representations without knowing what factors may weigh against his interests fairness will very often require that he is informed of the gist of the case that he has to answer.'

A leading authority on this issue is now the decision of the House of Lords in *Lloyd and Others* v *McMahon* [1987] 2 WLR 821, a case concerning the surcharging of councillors who refused to set a lawful rate within the required time limit, causing consequent financial loss to the authority of which they were members. The appellants were notified by the district auditor that they could make representations in writing before he reached a final decision, and they responded collectively with documentary evidence explaining that they had delayed setting a rate pending any decision by central government to increase its grant support for the council. During the hearing of their appeal against certification the Divisional Court invited the councillors to give oral evidence in support of their case but they declined to do so. Dismissing their further appeals, the House of Lords held that there was clear evidence of wilful misconduct by the councillors, and that the district auditor had not acted unfairly in refusing to allow them an oral hearing prior to his issuing of the certificate under the 1982 Act. As Lord Keith stated (at 872):

'It is easy to envisage cases where an oral hearing would clearly be essential in the interests of fairness, for example where an objector states that he has personal knowledge of some facts indicative of wilful misconduct on the part of a councillor. In that situation justice would demand that the councillor be given an opportunity to depone to his own version of the facts. In the present case the district auditor had arrived at his provisional view upon the basis of the contents of documents, minutes of meetings and reports submitted to the council from the auditor's department and their own officers ... No facts contradictory of or supplementary to the contents of the documents were or are relied on by either side. If the appellants had attended an oral hearing they would no doubt have reiterated the sincerity of their motives from the point of view of advancing the interests of the inhabitants of Liverpool. It seems unlikely, having regard to the position adopted by their counsel on this matter before the Divisional Court, that they would have been willing to reveal or answer questions about the proceedings of their political caucus. The sincerity of the appellants' motives is not something capable of justifying or excusing failure to carry out a statutory duty, or of making reasonable what is otherwise an unreasonable delay in carrying out such a duty. In all the circumstances I am of opinion that the district auditor did not act unfairly, and that the procedure which he followed did not involve any prejudice to the appellants.'

The requirements of a fair hearing are not, of course, fixed, but will vary with the circumstances of the case, as the above extract indicates. Compare the factors that led Lord Keith to deny the need for an oral hearing in the *Lloyd* case with those persuading the court in *R v Army Board of the Defence Council, ex parte Anderson* [1991] 3 All ER 375 to conclude that the hearing given there had been inadequate. Anderson had complained to the Council that he had been the victim of racial discrimination whilst a serving soldier. The Council, which acted as a forum of last resort in respect of soldiers' complaints, subject only to the possibility of judicial review, wrote to the applicant stating that his request for redress of grievance had been denied. In allowing his application for review of the Council's decision Taylor LJ took the *Lloyd* case as authoritative. His Lordship indicated that relevant factors in the case before him were the statutory framework within which the Council operated, the kind of decision it had to take, and the nature of the decision–making body itself. The fact that the legislation in question provided for a particular procedure did not mean that the courts would not imply further requirements where it was necessary to do so to ensure fairness. A crucial factor in the present case was that the Council was a tribunal of last resort. As such it was required to do more than simply act bona fides, without bias or caprice. His Lordship then summarised what he regarded as the correct approach to ensure fairness in hearings such as the present, where the tribunal was not merely making an administrative decision, but was exercising a disciplinary function. First, he felt that members of the Council had to meet together to consider the evidence rather than reach conclusions in isolation from each other. Secondly, an oral hearing was not essential to fairness but was probably required where there were substantial differences on issues of fact which could not be resolved on the papers. It was clear that the Council was not entitled to adopt as an inflexible policy the approach that oral hearings would never be permitted. The question of whether evidence should be tested by cross-examination stood or fell with the question of whether or not an oral hearing should be granted. Thirdly, even if an oral hearing was not granted, a complainant should be given the opportunity to respond to the Council's findings of fact following its investigations, subject to public interest immunity.

Even where the rules of natural justice would normally require some form of consultation with the person affected by a decision, the court may disregard them in order to achieve a wider policy goal. For example in *R v Life Assurance Unit Trust Regulatory Organisation Ltd, ex parte Ross* [1991] NLJ 1001, where the applicant had not been consulted by LAUTRO prior to its decision to instruct leading companies not to deal with his company, Mann LJ expressed the view that the most important factor was that LAUTRO should be able to protect investors effectively. He stated:

'The achievement of that purpose must on occasion require action which has urgently to be taken, and the entertainment of representations may not be compatible with urgency ...
In my judgment once it is recognised, as inevitably it must be, that a self-regulating organisation may have to act with urgency in order to achieve its purpose, then it would

be undesirable to encumber it with the necessity to make a judgment as to whether time admits of an opportunity to make representations ...'

Hearing denied on grounds of futility

It has been argued from time to time that there is no right to be heard where the hearing would make no difference to the outcome, or would be a 'useless formality'.

In *Glynn* v *Keele University* (above) the court refused to invalidate disciplinary action taken in respect of the student concerned, despite the fact that he had been denied a hearing on the **ground that nothing he could have said would have made any difference to the outcome**. Similarly, in *Cinnamond* v *British Airports Authority* [1980] 1 WLR 582, **Lord Denning MR** stated that orders issued by the defendant authority banning the plaintiffs from entering Heathrow Airport, otherwise than as bona fide passengers, were not invalid on the ground that the plaintiff taxi-drivers had not been granted a hearing prior to the orders being made. His Lordship took the view that a **hearing was unnecessary here and, by implication, that it would have been pointless**, especially as the plaintiffs knew exactly why the banning orders had been made. For earlier evidence of Lord Denning MR's robust approach to such cases, see *Ward* v *Bradford Corporation* (1972) 70 LGR 27.

Despite the above, it is submitted that the **conventional wisdom is that futility will not suffice as a general ground for refusing a hearing**. As Lord Reid observed in *Ridge* v *Baldwin* [1964] AC 4:

> 'It may be convenient at this point to deal with an argument that, even if as a general rule a watch committee must hear a constable in his own defence before dismissing him, this case was so clear that nothing that the appellant could have said could have made any difference. It is at least very doubtful whether that could be accepted as an excuse. But even if it could the watch committee would in my view fail on the facts. It may well be that no reasonable body of men could have reinstated the appellant. But as between the other two courses open to the watch committee the case is not so clear. Certainly on the facts as we know them the watch committee could reasonably have decided to forfeit the appellant's pension rights, but I could not hold that they would have acted wrongly or wholly unreasonably if they had in the exercise of their discretion decided to take a more lenient course.'

In *Malloch* v *Aberdeen Corporation* [1971] 1 WLR 1578, Lord Reid again warned against adopting a too generalised approach to the denial of a hearing on grounds that it would serve no purpose. Under the Education (Scotland) Act 1946, as amended, every teacher employed by an education authority was required to be registered with the General Teaching Council (a statutory body). Mr Malloch declined to register. The Aberdeen Education Authority was advised that it had no option but to dismiss him. Subsequently Mr Malloch was informed that a meeting of the education committee was to be held in order to initiate steps to dismiss him. He was not allowed to make representations to the committee even though he wished to. The committee passed a resolution to dismiss him. Mr Malloch sought to impugn the resolution being passed on the ground that it was contrary to natural justice.

The House of Lords allowed Mr Malloch's appeal (by a majority). Lord Reid said:

> 'Then it was argued that to have afforded a hearing to the appellant before dismissing him would have been a useless formality because whatever he might have said could have made no difference. If that could be clearly demonstrated it might be a good answer. But I need to decide that because there was here, I think, a substantial possibility that a sufficient number of the committee might have been persuaded not to vote for the appellant's dismissal. The motion for dismissal had to be carried by a two-thirds majority of those present, and at the previous meeting of the committee there was not a sufficient majority to carry a similar motion. Between these meetings the committee had received a strong letter from the Secretary of State urging them to dismiss the teachers who refused to register. And it appears that they had received some advice which might have been taken by them to mean that those who failed to vote for dismissal might incur personal liability. The appellant might have been able to persuade them that they need not have any such fear.'

Note that in the course of the above passage Lord Reid does seem to countenance the possibility of a hearing being denied in very clear cases. See further *R v Chief Constable of Thames Valley Police, ex parte Stevenson* (above).

Evidence at the hearing

The strict rules of evidence one would expect to see applied in a court of law are not binding on statutory tribunals, and even less so in the case of domestic bodies.

An adjudicator may be allowed to act on his own knowledge, provided he puts those points to the parties before him and invites representations thereon. In *Wetherall* v *Harrison* [1976] QB 773 the prosecutor appealed against the justices' ruling that the case against the defendant, who had been charged with failing to supply a specimen for the purposes of a 'drink driving' offence, should be dismissed on the basis that his failure had arisen from a genuine fit induced by the prospect of a blood sample being taken. The justices had been persuaded to their conclusion in the light of the expert knowledge of one of their number, a doctor. The court held that it was acceptable for a tribunal member to rely on his own personal knowledge when coming to a decision provided he used it as a means of interpreting the evidence given in court and not as a replacement for it.

As Lord Widgery CJ observed:

> 'Laymen ... considering a case which has just been heard before them lack the ability to put out of their minds certain features of the case. In particular, if the justice is a specialist, be he a doctor, or an engineer or an accountant, or what you will, it is not possible for him to approach the decision in the case as though he had not got that training, and indeed I think it would be a very bad thing if he had to. In a sense, the bench of justices are like a jury, they are a cross section of people, and one of the advantages, which they have is that they bring a lot of varied experience into the court room and use it.'

Natural justice usually requires an individual to be informed of the evidence upon which a decision is being made. This would not perhaps be so in 'mere applicant' cases where there is no 'case against' the individual as such, but might apply where refusal of a licence cast a slur on the applicant's character. The purpose of revealing to an applicant evidence possessed by the decision-making body that might count against him is that it may provide an opportunity for him to refute some of the allegations, correct mistakes, or explain away otherwise damaging evidence.

In *Re Pergamon Press Ltd* [1971] Ch 388 it was held that inspectors investigating a company's affairs had to give an outline of the charges against the company and provide it with a fair opportunity of correcting or criticising the evidence. This did not necessarily extend to providing transcripts of evidence. Similarly in *Maxwell* v *Department of Trade and Industry* [1974] QB 523 it was held to be sufficient for inspectors to put to the plaintiff any substantially prejudicial points that had been made against him.

In *R* v *Department of Education and Science, ex parte Kumar* (1982) The Times 18 November the applicant, who had been employed to teach for a probationary period, had not been shown a number of reports prepared by the inspectors and relied upon by the Secretary of State in deciding that the applicant was not suitable for further employment as a teacher. In a letter to the applicant the Department of Education stated that it regarded the reports as confidential. The reports had been prepared after a number of visits had been made by the inspectors to the school where the applicant was serving his probationary period. Examples of conduct and occurrences were given which had caused the author of the report to form a highly adverse opinion of the applicant's teaching ability, but because the reports had not been shown to the applicant he had had no opportunity to deal with their contents. This situation appeared to the court to produce a result falling below the standard of fairness required by the rules of natural justice. Even though the department regarded the reports as confidential, the applicant should have been given an opportunity to comment on the allegations which they contained. While it could not be said that the Secretary of State's decision would have been any different, it might have been, and there was accordingly a risk of injustice. The decision of the Secretary of State was quashed and the matter remitted to him for further consideration, during which period the applicant was to be given the opportunity of making further representations in the light of the reports now made available to him.

Cross-examination at the hearing

As a rule, if an individual is afforded the right to make oral representations he will normally be allowed the right to cross-examine those giving evidence against him. The purpose of cross-examination, it should be remembered, is to test the veracity of evidence. In *University of Ceylon* v *Fernando* [1960] 1 All ER 631 the Privy Council held it was not a breach of natural justice for an inquiry into allegations of misconduct at examinations not to inform the plaintiff of his right to cross-examine a witness, but it might have been if the plaintiff had been denied permission to cross-examine the witness.

Public inquiries present a particular problem here. Participants will seek to destroy the credibility of the opponent's evidence by cross-examination, but it must be borne in mind that inquiries are not courts of law. In *Nicholson* v *Secretary of State for Energy* (1978) 76 LGR 693 the plaintiff was not allowed to cross-examine witnesses from local authorities at a public inquiry into an application to carry out open cast mining. The court had no option but to quash the minister's grant of permission to carry out the works in the light of the breach of natural justice. The relevance of the local authority evidence to the plaintiff's case may have been a deciding factor. Compare this with the House of Lords' decision in *Bushell* v *Secretary of State for the Environment* [1981] AC 75, where it was held not to be a breach of natural justice for an inquiry inspector to refuse objectors the right to cross-examine representatives of a government department on the accuracy of traffic flow predictions, upon which the policy of building motorways was based. Lord Diplock expressed the view that cross-examination on such a topic would achieve no useful result, as the purpose of an inquiry was to prepare a report for the information of the minister it was not like civil litigation where the party that best proved its case and destroyed its opponent's would win.

Adjournment of the hearing

Refusal of an adjournment may result in a breach of natural justice if, as a result, the applicant is unable to continue with a proper presentation of his case. In *Priddle* v *Fisher & Sons* [1968] 3 All ER 506, an industrial tribunal considering the appellant's claim for redundancy payments against his former employer proceeded to deal with the case despite the fact that it had been informed that the appellant himself was unable to attend because of severe weather conditions, and that his representative had fallen ill and was therefore unable to conduct the case on his behalf. The Court of Appeal held that the tribunal possessed a discretion as to when to allow an adjournment and had erred in law by not exercising that discretion in the instant case.

Lord Parker CJ commented that in his judgment:

'... the exercise of a judicial discretion on wrong principles does amount to a point of law, and accordingly this court has jurisdiction to deal with the matter ... The matter can be put in many ways, but the way in which it appeals to me is that a tribunal is acting wrongly in law if, knowing that an appellant has all along intended to attend and give evidence in support of his claim, and being satisfied, as they must have been, that he was unable for one reason or another to attend, they refuse to adjourn merely because he had not asked expressly for an adjournment. Before deciding to continue the tribunal should be satisfied that he was inviting them to continue in his absence. The matter is even more clear when one realises here that the burden is on the employers and the appellant has a right to cross-examine them to show, if he can, that the reason given for dismissal was a disguise for a dismissal on the ground of redundancy.'

Similar views were expressed in *R* v *South West London Supplementary Benefit Appeal Tribunal, ex parte Bullen* (1976) 120 Sol Jo 437. The interests of fairness may, in certain circumstances, have to give way to administrative expediency, however. In the context of a public inquiry, the granting of an adjournment may cause great inconvenience to other participants. In *Ostreicher* v *Secretary of State for the Environment* [1978] 3 All ER 82, the applicants unsuccessfully sought an adjournment of an inquiry into objections to a clearance order on the ground that the inquiry would coincide with the Jewish Passover period. Lord Denning MR observed that in any given case the court simply had to consider what was fair to the parties concerned, but sought to draw a distinction between an administrative inquiry and judicial proceedings before a court. He stated:

> 'An administrative inquiry has to be arranged long beforehand. There are many objectors to consider as well as the proponents of the plan. It is a serious matter to put all the arrangements aside on the application of one objector out of many. The proper way to deal with it, if called upon to do so, is to continue with the inquiry and hear all the representatives present: and then, if one objector is unavoidably absent, to hear his objections on a later day when he can be there. There is ample power in the rules for the inspector to allow adjournments as and when reasonably required.'

Note that under the Town and Country Planning (Inquiries Procedure) Rules 1992, an inspector may proceed with an inquiry in the absence of any person entitled to attend (r.14(9)), and may adjourn the inquiry from time to time (r.14(11)).

The courts will not look kindly on the ineptitude of those representing the applicant, even if this involves punishing the applicant for the failings of his advisers. In *Al-Mehdawi* v *Secretary of State for the Home Department* [1989] 3 All ER 843, the House of Lords considered an application for certiorari to quash a decision of an immigration adjudicator who had ordered the deportation of the applicant. The applicant had been invited to attend before the hearing of his appeal against the deportation, but due to the ineptitude of his solicitors notification did not reach him in time, and the appeal proceeded in his absence. The applicant then sought to quash the adjudicator's dismissal of his appeal on the basis that he had been denied a hearing in breach of natural justice. The House of Lords held that certiorari would not lie to quash the decision as the unfairness did not result from the actions of the adjudicator.

15.4 The right to legal representation

When considering this aspect of natural justice it is important to distinguish between cases where an individual has been refused the right to be legally represented, and cases where the right exists, but the individual has not availed himself of it. That legal representation is an acknowledged aspect of a fair procedure is evidenced by the fact that nearly all tribunals permit applicants to have legal representation if they so wish. That absence of legal representation does not, of itself, invalidate a hearing, is evidenced by the number of unrepresented defendants convicted in the magistrates' courts. The principal concern here is with cases where representation is denied.

Much may depend on what is at stake for the individual concerned as a result of the tribunal's decision. In *Maynard* v *Osmond* [1977] QB 240 the Court of Appeal held that statutory regulations governing police disciplinary proceedings, which provided that a police constable could conduct his own defence or be represented by another officer, did not entitle a constable to representation by a lawyer. The regulations had excluded a right, that might have existed at common law, to legal representation. The fact that legal representation was allowed to more senior officers was held to be evidence that Parliament had not intended it to be available to more junior ranks, who in any event had less to lose than their more senior colleagues.

Rules of private associations excluding the right of legal representation before disciplinary committees have generally been upheld. In *Enderby Town FC* v *FA Ltd* [1971] Ch 591 the Court of Appeal upheld the validity of the Football Association's decision prohibiting legal representation in cases before it. As Lord Denning MR observed:

> 'In many cases it may be a good thing for the proceedings of a domestic tribunal to be conducted informally without legal representation. Justice can often be done in them better by a good layman than by a bad lawyer. This is especially so in activities like football and other sports, where no points of law are likely to arise, and it is all part of the proper regulation of the game. But I would emphasise that the discretion must be properly exercised. The tribunal must not fetter its discretion by rigid bonds. A domestic tribunal is not at liberty to lay down an absolute rule: "We will never allow anyone to have a lawyer to appear for him." The tribunal must be ready, in a proper case, to allow it.'

Where an individual's reputation or livelihood is at stake there may be a much stronger argument in favour of legal representation: see *Pett* v *Greyhound Racing Association* [1969] 1 QB 125.

In *Fraser* v *Mudge* [1975] 3 All ER 78, the Court of Appeal held that prisoners subjected to the disciplinary regime of the prison did not have full rights of legal representation. In certain circumstances, however, such hearings can have serious consequences for those concerned, such as loss of significant amounts of remission, and the importance of such hearings has now been recognised by the courts, as evidenced by decisions such as *R* v *Secretary of State for the Home Department, ex parte Tarrant* [1984] 1 All ER 799, where it was held that although a prisoner appearing before a Board of Visitors on a disciplinary charge did not have an automatic right to legal representation, the Board did have a discretion to permit it. In that case it had been a breach of natural justice to deny the prisoner legal representation, given the grave nature of the charge and the consequences for the prisoner of his being found guilty.

In *R* v *Board of Visitors of Swansea Prison, ex parte McGrath* (1984) The Times 21 November, however, it was held that apart from exceptional cases the Board of Visitors was under no duty to consider exercising its discretion to grant legal representation to a prisoner, unless the prisoner so requested. Furthermore, in *R* v *Board of Visitors of the Maze Prison, ex parte Hone* [1988] 1 All ER 321, where the applicants were prisoners charged with serious offences against prison discipline who had not been permitted legal representation at the hearing of their cases by the prison Board of Visitors, and who contended that there had, therefore, been breaches of natural justice, the House of Lords held that simply because the charge facing a prisoner was one which, if he were a defendant in a criminal court, would automatically entitle him to legal representation, this did not mean that he had an automatic right under the rules of natural justice to legal representation when appearing before the prison Board of Visitors on a corresponding charge against prison discipline. Boards of Visitors had a discretion to allow legal representation, and this would depend on the facts of each case.

15.5 The giving of reasons

Citizens will normally expect reasons for a decision to be given by a public body, particulary where the decision is one adverse to their interests. For a significant range of tribunals the giving of reasons, where requested, is not a matter of discretion but a duty imposed by s10 of the Tribunals and Inquiries Act 1992, provided that the tribunal in question is one listed in Sch 1 to the Act. As regards other decision-makers, it is rather less clear whether or not a duty to give reasons exists at common law. While an unreasoned decision is the exception rather than the norm, the absence of reasons will not necessarily lead the courts to invalidate a decision on that basis alone. As Lord Keith commented in *Lonrho plc* v *Secretary of State for Trade and Industry* [1989] 1 WLR 525 at 539:

> 'The only significance of the absence of reasons is that if all other known facts and circumstances appear to point overwhelmingly in favour of a different decision, the decision-maker who has given no reasons cannot complain if the court draws the inference that he had no rational reason for his decision.'

Traditionally the law has taken the view that those coming within the category of 'mere applicants' for a particular privilege, and particularly prisoners seeking to challenge decisions made in respect of 'executive sentencing', have had little or no right to be told of the reasons for decisions. In *R* v *Gaming Board for Great Britain, ex parte Benaim and Khaida* [1970] 2 QB 417, where the applicants had been refused consent to apply for a gaming licence by the Board, which had refused to give reasons for its decision, the Court of Appeal held that the Board was not obliged to disclose the sources of the information upon which it had acted. Apart from the fact that much of the evidence had been supplied in confidence, the Board was not obliged to state the reasons for the refusal as, in any event, the applicants were being denied a privilege, not a right. Lord Denning MR reiterated this view in *Breen* v *AEU* [1971] 2 QB 175. Megarry V-C in *McInnes* v *Onslow-Fane* [1978] 1 WLR 1520 suggested that a mere applicant would only be entitled to reasons for a decision where, for example, the refusal of a licence involved a slur on his reputation. In many such cases there was 'no case against' the applicant as such; the decision-making body simply considered him to be unsuitable. Megarry V-C said:

'... in the absence of anything to suggest that the [members of the tribunal] have been affected by dishonesty or bias or caprice, or that there is any other impropriety, I think that [they] are fully entitled to give no reasons for their decision, and to decide the application without any preliminary indication to the plaintiff of those reasons.'

Perhaps the high water mark of the 'executive minded' approach was exemplified by the decision of the Court of Appeal in *Payne* v *Lord Harris* [1981] 1 WLR 754, where it was held that a prisoner was not entitled to know the reasons for the rejection of his application to be released on licence. Lord Denning MR stated:

'No doubt it is the duty of all those concerned – to act fairly. That is the simple precept which now governs the administrative procedure of all public bodies. But the duty to act fairly cannot be set down in a series of propositions. Each case depends on its own circumstances. Sometimes fairness may require that the man be told of the outline of the case against him. At other times it may not be necessary to have a hearing or even to tell the man the case against him, because it must be obvious to him.'

In particular he felt that there was a danger that reasons, if given, would tend to become short and stereotyped rather than full and informative. He continued:

'If [the reasons] were full and informative, they would give the prisoner an opening with which he could challenge the refusal. He could lodge an application for judicial review, complaining that the Board took things into account which they should not have done – or that their decision was unreasonable. If he were refused judicial review he would harbour a grievance which would become obsessive – just as much as if he is refused parole without reasons being given.'

As will be seen, the courts have since moved away from this conservative approach to executive accountability, but note the significance of this restrictive approach for litigants; without the reasons for a decision it may be impossible to substantiate the grounds for an application for review, such as error of law, or failure to take into account relevant considerations. The approach advocated by Lord Denning MR in respect of the Parole Board would have effectively made judicial review of such determinations impossible.

The trend now is towards greater openness in decision-making, the courts approaching the issue on the basis of requiring reasons unless there are some compelling public policy reasons for their not being provided. In *R* v *Civil Service Appeal Board, ex parte Cunningham* [1991] 4 All ER 310 the applicant, who had been employed as a prison officer, was accused of assaulting a prisoner and dismissed. On appeal, the Civil Service Appeal Board found his dismissal to have been unfair and recommended his reinstatement, but this was not accepted by the Home Office. The Board thereupon awarded him £6,500 for the loss of his position but declined to give reasons for the level of the award. The applicant regarded the award as being far too low, and applied to the courts for an order that the Board should supply the reasons for its decision. Otton J, for the Divisional Court, held that the Board would be ordered to provide the reasons sought. Although in his Lordship's view there was no general duty at common law requiring administrative bodies to give reasons for their decisions, and despite the fact that he was unwilling to infer (in this particular case) that the absence of reasons necessarily meant that there were no good reasons for the decision, there was no evidence to suggest that the proper working of the Board would be undermined by its having to supply a short statement of reasons, simply to put the applicant's mind at rest. The Court of Appeal upheld this ruling. It is, perhaps, not without significance that the applicant was unable, as a prison officer, to take his case before an industrial tribunal which would have been required to give reasons for its decisions. The aim of the Civil Service Pay and Conditions Code is to ensure that Crown servants are in no less a favourable position than other employees. Where reasons are given they should be adequate in the sense of being intelligible and indicative of the basis for the decision: see *R* v *Criminal Injuries Compensation Board, ex parte Cummins* (1992) The Times 21 January.

The trend to openness has been confirmed by the House of Lords' decision in *R* v *Secretary of State for the Home Office, ex parte Doody and Others* [1993] 3 WLR 154. The Secretary of State, acting under s61 of the Criminal Justice Act 1967, had the power to determine the first date upon which prisoners who had received mandatory life sentences for murder might be considered for release (that is, the point at which the 'penal element' of the sentence would expire). The procedure adopted involved the Secretary of State obtaining the views of the trial judge and the Lord Chief Justice prior to informing a prisoner of the first date for review of his continued detention. The effect was that a prisoner would then be aware of his minimum period of imprisonment. The applicants, each of whom was a prisoner serving a life sentence following conviction for murder, sought to challenge the decision of the Secretary of State in respect of the date set for review as regards their own cases. Inter alia they each sought a declaration to the effect that the Secretary of State should inform a prisoner of his reasons for departing from the judicial recommendation if this was what he intended to do. The House of Lords held that the Secretary of State was obliged to give reasons for departing from the period recommended by the judiciary as regards the 'penal element' of the sentence.

Lord Mustill, while confirming that there was no general legal duty to give reasons for an administrative decision, went on to observe that it was important that there should be 'an effective means of detecting the kind of error which would entitle the court to intervene' should a decision as to sentencing be wrong in law. In His Lordship's view, a requirement that reasons be given for departing from a judicial recommendation as to the minimum term could provide evidence of any such errors. Lord Mustill regarded *Payne* v *Lord Harris of Greenwich* (above) as reflecting an outmoded view of the duty to give reasons. In particular he felt that in the 13 years since that decision the perception of society's obligation towards persons serving prison sentences had changed noticeably, and that the trend in administrative law was now firmly towards openness in decision-making. He observed:

> 'There is no true tariff, or at least no tariff exposed to the public view, which might give the prisoner an idea of what to expect. The announcement of his first review date arrives out of thin air, wholly without explanation. The distant oracle has spoken and that is that

... I doubt whether in the modern climate of administrative law such an entirely secret process could be justified.'

This discernable trend towards 'transparent' decision making where individual liberty is at stake has been promoted further by decisions such as that in *R* v *Secretary of State for the Home Department, ex parte Duggan* [1994] 3 All ER 277, where the Divisional Court held that a prisoner who had been classified as a category 'A' risk, and thus subject to greater restrictions, was entitled to be provided with the gist of the reports compiled for the category A section, so that he could comment upon them, and should be provided, subject to the constraints required by public interest immunity, with the reasons for any subsequent decision. As Rose LJ observed:

'... to my mind the authorities show an ever-increasing variety of situations where, depending on the nature of the decision and the process by which it is reached, fairness requires that reasons be given'.

His Lordship added that if the principles of natural justice applied to a prison governor adjudicating upon infractions of prison discipline (per Lord Oliver in *Leech* v *Parkhurst Prison Deputy Governor* [1988] AC 533 at 578) then, a fortiori they applied to a decision that impacted upon the ultimate date on which a prisoner would be released.

Sitting as a Deputy High Court Judge in *R* v *Lambeth London Borough Council, ex parte Walters* (1993) The Times 6 October, Louis Blom-Cooper QC, asserting that there was now at least a general duty to give reasons at common law, suggested that the true position was now one where it was:

'... hard to envisage any situation, except possibly where the giving of reasons would reveal some aspect of national security, or unintentionally disclose confidential information or invade privacy, where an individual should not know the reasons for the decision which had been made'.

It may yet be too early to claim that this is in fact an entirely accurate summary of the law. A more structured and, with respect, more helpful approach is that advocated by Sedley J in *R* v *Higher Education Funding Council, ex parte Institute of Dental Surgery* [1994] 1 All ER 651. In refusing to invalidate a decision of the respondent's on the ground that it had not supplied reasons for downgrading the research rating of the applicant institution, he offered the following summary:

'1. There is no general duty to give reasons for a decision, but there are classes of case where there is such a duty.
2. One such class is where the subject matter is an interest so highly regarded by the law – for example personal liberty – that fairness requires that reasons, at least for particular decisions, be given as of right.
3. (a) Another such class is where the decision appears aberrant. Here fairness may require reasons so that the recipient may know whether the aberration is in the legal sense real (and so challengeable) or apparent.

(b) It follows that this class does not include decisions which are in themselves challengeable by reference only to the reasons for them. A pure exercise of academic judgment is such a decision.

(c) Procedurally, the grant of leave in such cases will depend upon prima facie evidence that something has gone wrong. The respondent may then seek to demonstrate that it is not so and that the decision is an unalloyed exercise of an intrinsically unchallengeable judgment. If the respondent succeeds, the application fails. If the respondent fails, relief may take the form of an order of mandamus to give reasons, or (if a justiciable flaw has been established) other appropriate relief.'

It is submitted that if the above summary is correct there will still be a swathe of administrative decision-making immune from any duty to give reasons, eg the rejection by a university of an application for a place on a degree course, or the decision to transfer a prisoner to separate detention under rule 43(1) of the Prison Rules (SI 1964 No 388): see *R* v *Deputy Governor of Parkhurst Prison, ex parte Hague* (1990) The Times 22 June. See further *Leech* v *Deputy Governor of Parkhurst Prison* [1988] AC 533 and *R* v *Secretary of State for the Home Department, ex parte Gunnell* (1984) The Times 7 November.

15.6 The rule against bias

The rule against bias is a common law doctrine which provides that no man should be a judge in his own cause. It is frequently referred to as one of the two 'rules' of natural justice, the other being the right to a fair hearing. In reality the rule against bias is an aspect of fair procedure. If the applicant has a right to a fair hearing, then, by definition, the tribunal should be free from bias.

An applicant rarely has to, or is indeed able, prove actual bias on the part of the tribunal. Appearances are everything. Provided that there is a real likelihood of bias the decision may be vitiated.

Apparent bias – pecuniary interest

In the majority of cases, pecuniary interest by a decision-maker in a matter subject to his influence is sufficient to invalidate any resulting determination. The leading case is *Dimes* v *Grand Junction Canal Proprietors* (1852) 3 HL Cas 759, where Lord Cottenham LC had affirmed decrees made by the Vice-Chancellor in litigation between Dimes and the canal proprietors. Dimes discovered that, despite the fact that the Lord Chancellor had for a long period held shares in the canal company both in his own right and as trustee, he had continued to hear matters arising out of the litigation, relying on the advice of the Master of the Rolls who sat with him. Dimes appealed to the House of Lords against all the decrees made by the Lord Chancellor on the ground that he was disqualified by interest. The House of Lords set aside the decrees issued by the Lord Chancellor on the ground of pecuniary interest. In the course of his speech Lord Campbell stated:

'No one can suppose that Lord Cottenham could be, in the remotest degree, influenced by the interest that he had in this concern; but, my Lords, it is of the last importance that the maxim that no man is to be a judge in his own cause should be held sacred. And that is not to be confined to a cause in which he has an interest. Since I have had the honour to be Chief Justice of the Court of Queen's Bench, we have again and again set aside proceedings in inferior tribunals because an individual, who had an interest in a cause, took a part in the decision. And it will have a most salutary influence on these tribunals when it is known that this High Court of last resort, in a case in which the Lord Chancellor of England had an interest, considered that his decree was on that account a decree not according to law, and was set aside. This will be a lesson to all inferior tribunals to take care not only that in their decrees they are not influenced by their personal interest, but to avoid the appearance of labouring under such an influence.'

Despite the strictness with which the rule against pecuniary interest is applied, it is subject to a remoteness principle to the effect that where the pecuniary interest is so minimal, or indirect as to be of negligible significance, it will not be used as justification for invalidating a decision. In *R v Rand* (1866) LR 1 QB 230, the court was asked to quash a certificate issued by justices permitting Bradford Corporation to take water from a certain reservoir. The justices were trustees of institutions which held Bradford Corporation bonds, and it was contended that this interest disqualified them from acting, and invalidated the certificate granted. The court refused to quash the certificate, holding that any pecuniary interest on the part of the justices was more theoretical than real.

The operation of the rule against pecuniary interest may be excluded, to a degree, by statute; see the Licensing Act 1964 s193, as applied in *R v Barnsley County Borough Licensing JJs, ex parte Barnsley and District Licensed Victuallers' Association* [1960] 2 QB 167. Conversely it may be bolstered by legislation; for example ss94–98 of the Local Government Act 1972 provide that it is a criminal offence for a councillor to participate in any discussion or vote on a matter in which he has a direct or indirect pecuniary interest. This prohibition extends even to a councillor voting against his own interests: see further *R v Hendon Rural District Council, ex parte Chorley* [1933] 2 KB 696.

Apparent bias – professional links

In *R v Sussex JJ, ex parte McCarthy* [1924] 1 KB 256 a solicitor who was representing a client against McCarthy in a motoring accident also worked as a clerk to the Sussex justices who were trying McCarthy on a criminal charge arising out of the same motoring incident. When the justices retired to consider their verdict, the clerk retired with them and they convicted the defendant of dangerous driving. Quashing the conviction on the ground that the appearance of bias was fatal, Lord Hewart CJ uttered his famous dictum to the effect that justice not only had to be done but had to be seen to be done. Similarly, in *R v Altrincham JJ, ex parte Pennington* [1975] QB 549 the conviction of the defendant for selling underweight quantities of vegetables to various schools was quashed on discovery that the chairman of the court was also a co-opted member of the local authority's education committee.

The principle has been extended to administrative agencies such as tribunals. In *Metropolitan Properties Co* v *Lannon* [1968] 3 All ER 304 a number of tenants applied to the rent officer to fix a fair rent for their flats. The landlord objected to the rent officer's decision and appealed to the rent assessment committee, the chairman of which was a solicitor who lived with his father, who was himself a tenant of the company which was associated with the landlord in the present case. The chairman's firm had from time to time acted for his father's fellow tenants against the associated company on matters similar to the ones in issue here; the chairman himself had assisted his father in writing to the rent officer. The committee fixed rents for the flats below that assessed by the experts and below that asked for by the tenants themselves. The Court of Appeal held that the committee's decision was vitiated by the fact that bias on the part of the committee might reasonably have been suspected, although there was some uncertainty as to precisely how the test should be formulated. Note that in *R* v *Holderness Borough Council, ex parte James Roberts Developments Ltd* (1992) The Times 22 December, a case where a refusal of planning permission was upheld despite the fact that the planning committee had a local builder and developer as one of its members, Simon Brown LJ expressed the view that even if the test laid down in *Lannon* was to be applied, it was going too far to say that merely because a member of the committee was a local builder he was for that reason alone to be disqualified, and any decision made by the committee vitiated. Butler-Sloss LJ added that if a builder were to be disqualified in such a case, it was likely that a solicitor or surveyor involved in local developments would be similarly disqualified, and consequently such a prohibition would be too wide. Dillon LJ, dissenting, felt that in the light of what he saw as the great dangers of bribery and corruption in local government, particularly where planning matters were concerned, it was vital that justice should be seen to be done.

Apparent bias – intermingling of functions: first instance and appeal

Difficulties may arise where, for example, disciplinary action is taken by a subordinate body and has to be approved by an appellate or executive body, and members of the disciplinary body are also members of the appellate or executive body. Such 'intermingling of functions' may result in a decision being invalidated on grounds of bias. Clearly the fear is that those who make a decision at first instance are unlikely to disagree with their own decisions if they sit in judgment on them on an appellate body. In *Hannam* v *Bradford Corporation* [1970] 1 WLR 937, the plaintiff was a teacher who had gone absent without leave from the school at which he taught. The school governors met and decided to sack him. The staff subcommittee of the local authority met to consider this decision (note that this hearing was not an appeal by Hannam). The subcommittee had the power to prohibit the dismissal, but decided not to exercise this power. Three of the ten subcommittee members were also governors of the school at which Hannam had taught, but they had not attended the meeting of governors at which the decision to dismiss him had been taken. The subcommittee's decision was subsequently ratified by the full council. Hannam brought an action for breach of contract, claiming that the question of his dismissal should have been determined by a properly constituted tribunal. The Court of Appeal held that as the staff subcommittee, when considering the plaintiff's dismissal, was exercising a quasi-judicial function, its decision to allow the dismissal to stand was invalid. The three governors on the subcommittee were sitting in judgment on a decision of a body to which they belonged. The fact that they had taken no part in the original decision was irrelevant. As Sachs LJ observed, the governors did not, on donning their subcommittee hats, cease to be an integral part of the body whose action was being impugned. The quorum for the subcommittee was three. What if the only members had been the governors? In his view, no one could seriously suggest that their decision would have been allowed to stand. In the event the plaintiff's action for breach of contract failed on other grounds.

Similarly, in *R* v *Kent Police Authority, ex parte Godden* [1971] 2 QB 662, where the applicant, who had been a Chief Inspector in the Kent Police, was moved in 1969 to administrative duties. He complained of malpractices by his superiors an inquiry was held, but nothing was found to justify his allegations. In 1970 his desk was searched and erotic material was discovered. Godden was seen by the force's chief medical officer, declared paranoid and placed on sick leave. Following examination by his own doctor he was declared to be perfectly normal. In early 1971 the Kent Police appointed the same chief medical officer to determine whether Godden should be permanently retired, whereupon Godden applied for prohibition and mandamus, on the basis that any such examination by the force's own medical officer would be vitiated by bias. The Court of Appeal held that his application should succeed. It was the view of Lord Denning MR that a doctor examining a man to determine whether he should be retired was undoubtedly acting in a judicial capacity. The chief medical officer was disqualified from acting because of his earlier diagnosis of Godden. In effect he would be sitting on an appeal from his own earlier decision.

It should not always be assumed, however, that procedural irregularity will of itself persuade the court to intervene. In *Ward* v *Bradford Corporation* (1972) 70 LGR 27 a local disciplinary committee decided to expel a student teacher living in college accommodation because she had allowed a man to remain in her hall of residence room overnight, the committee's decision being approved by a governing body, three of whose members were also members of the committee. Despite the obvious potential for the intermingling of function, the Court of Appeal upheld the validity of the expulsion, holding that the governing body had acted fairly throughout, and noting that the three members of the committee entitled to sit on the governing body had not done so. Lord Denning MR took the view that the complainant had not 'lost anything' even if there had been bias, as she clearly would never have made a good teacher.

There may be situations where the intermingling of functions is an unavoidable consequence of the scheme approved by Parliament, in which case the courts are most unlikely to overturn any decisions arrived at as a result of complying with the statutory procedure: see *Franklin* v *Minister of Town and Country Planning* [1948] AC 87.

Apparent bias – intermingling of functions: investigator and prosecutor

In *R* v *Barnsley Metropolitan Borough Council, ex parte Hook* [1976] 1 WLR 1052 the applicant, a market trader licensed by the local authority, was seen urinating in the street by two council workmen. The applicant had done this because the council lavatories were shut. Heated words were exchanged, and the incident was reported to the market manager, who wrote to the applicant revoking his licence. The applicant appealed unsuccessfully to two council committees, the market manager having been present whilst these committees had deliberated on the outcome of these appeals. The Divisional Court refused to grant certiorari on the ground that the revocation was merely an administrative act. The Court of Appeal held that the relief sought would be granted, on the basis that in revoking a trader's licence the council was under a duty to act judicially, the duty being inferred from the fact that the decision was one affecting the applicant's livelihood. The decision had been vitiated by the market manager's presence throughout the committees' proceedings, as this amounted to the prosecutor being present, in the absence of the accused, when the adjudicators were making their decisions.

Apparent bias – intermingling of functions: previous knowledge of the issues or individual concerned

In *R* v *Board of Visitors of Frankland Prison, ex parte Lewis* (1985) The Times 7 November the applicant, a prisoner who had been found guilty of an offence against prison discipline by the prison's Board of Visitors, subsequently discovered that the chairman of the Board had also been involved in a consideration of his application to the parole board, and hence had knowledge of his background, in particular his previous convictions. Considering his application for judicial review of the Board's finding of guilt on the basis that it was vitiated by bias, the court held that although prison Boards of Visitors were under a duty to act judicially when considering disciplinary hearings, a member was not disqualified from acting simply because he had acquired information about the prisoner in a different administrative capacity. Woolf J felt that it was inevitable that members of Boards of Visitors would know more about those appearing before them than, for example, magistrates because of the administrative duties which they frequently performed, such as considering the suitability of prisoners for release on parole. A Board of Visitors always had a discretion not to proceed with a hearing if it was of the opinion that, because of the way in which it was constituted at that time, it would be improper for it to do so. It had to be borne in mind that Parliament had constituted these bodies to act on the basis of their special knowledge of the prison system. Members should not be too ready to regard a general background knowledge of the prisoner as a ground for not adjudicating. In this case his Lordship felt that a reasonable and fair-minded person would not have regarded the chairman as disqualified.

A similar decision was made in *R v Oxford Regional Mental Health Review Tribunal, ex parte Mackman* (1986) The Times 2 June, where the applicant, a patient at Broadmoor, appeared before the Mental Health Review Tribunal on 16 January 1985, unsuccessfully seeking an order for his discharge. Renewing his application in November 1985, only to find that the president of the tribunal on this occasion was the same person who had presided over, and refused, his earlier application, the applicant unsuccessfully sought an adjournment so that the application might be heard by a differently constituted tribunal. The subsequent request for a discharge was refused. In refusing the application for (inter alia) certiorari to quash the decision, McNeill J pointed out that there was no statutory requirement that a tribunal member should not sit on successive applications. A reasonable and fair-minded person sitting in court and knowing of the facts would not have had a reasonable suspicion that the applicant would not have had a fair hearing.

It would appear that a distinction can be drawn in this matter between courts of law on the one hand and tribunals on the other, in that, in some areas, it may be inevitable that a tribunal member is going to be involved in dealing with more than one case involving an individual, especially when the tribunal deals with a somewhat specialised subject matter. In magistrates' courts there is arguably greater scope for a magistrate declining to sit in a particular case, and being replaced by a colleague. This distinction is supported by the decision of the Divisional Court in *R v Downham Market Magistrates' Court, ex parte Nudd* (1988) The Times 14 April, where the applicant appeared before the same chairman of justices in respect of three separate offences in a space of 13 months. The applicant successfully sought judicial review of the third conviction on the basis of bias, in that the chairman of the bench already knew of the applicant's antecedents; the court held that the chairman should not have sat in this case, given his prior experience of the applicant's background and in the light of the fact that the conviction complained of turned on a conflict of evidence between the applicant and a police officer. The court felt that members of the public might have had a reasonable suspicion that the chairman could have been unduly influenced by his prior knowledge of the applicant and thus have been unable to give him a fair hearing. See further *R v Board of Visitors of Walton Prison, ex parte Weldon* (1985) The Times 6 April.

Apparent bias – politics and preferences

It some cases allegations of bias will arise because an adjudicator makes his committed views on a relevant topic known in such a manner that the resulting appearance of bias disqualifies him from exercising his discretion. In a sense the decision maker can be regarded as acting unreasonably since by definition he is taking into account irrelevant considerations, ie he is motivated by factors unconnected with the merits of the case. A striking example of this problem is provided by *R* v *Inner West London Coroner, ex parte Dallaglio and Others* [1994] 4 All ER 139. The applicants were relatives of those who had died as a result of the *Marchioness* disaster in August 1989 when a pleasure boat sank as a result of a collision with another vessel on the Thames. The inquests into the deaths had been opened, but subsequently adjourned following the intervention of the DPP. A newspaper article concerning the conduct of the inquest suggested that there might have been some form of official cover-up, particularly in light of the fact that some relatives had been denied sight of the bodies of those killed. The coroner met with journalists in an attempt to rectify what he saw as misrepresentations by the press. In the course of his discussions he alleged that one of the applicants had been 'unhinged' by grief following her son's death, and that others were 'mentally unwell'. He subsequently resisted the applicants' demands that the inquest be reopened on the basis that the majority of relatives now wanted to treat the event as closed. The applicants, initially unsuccessful in applying for judicial review of the coroner's refusal to remove himself from the inquest on the grounds of apparent bias, and his refusal to reopen the inquest, succeeded before the Court of Appeal, where the coroner's comments were described as injudicious, insensitive and gratuitously insulting and, on the basis of *R* v *Gough* (considered below), undoubtedly gave rise to an appearance of bias. Earlier cases that would also now presumably fall foul of the test for bias advocated in *Gough* include *R* v *Halifax Justices, ex parte Robinson* (1912) 76 JP 233 (licensing justice who declared that he would have been a traitor to the strict temperance sect of which he was a member, if he voted in favour of granting a liquor licence); *R* v *Bingham JJs, ex parte Jowitt* (1974) The Times 3 July (chairman of the bench had stated that he would always believe the evidence of a police officer in preference to that of a member of the public). An obvious point to be noted about all these examples is that the issue of bias may not have been aired but for the 'confession' by the decision maker as to his strongly held views: see further *R* v *Nailsworth Licensing JJs, ex parte Bird* [1953] 1 WLR 1046.

It may be the case that a more relaxed view is taken where the decision-making body is exercising a more administrative role, as opposed to the judicial or quasi-judicial functions encountered in the examples considered above. In *R* v *Amber Valley District Council, ex parte Jackson* [1984] 3 All ER 501, a company applied to the council for planning permission to develop an amusement park on a site in its area. The applicant sought an order of prohibition to prevent the council from considering the matter on the basis that the council was Labour controlled, and the Labour group was, as a matter of policy, in favour of the development, and could not therefore make an unbiased decision on the application. The court held a publicly stated policy preference did not disqualify the councillors from adjudicating on the planning application, provided they observed their duty to act fairly and take into account all material considerations, including objections.

The test for bias

Historically the courts have applied one of two tests for bias. The lower of the two, in the sense that it is the more easily satisfied, is the reasonable suspicion test, applied in *R* v *Sussex Justices, ex parte McCarthy* (above) where Lord Hewart CJ stated:

> 'Nothing is to be done which creates even a suspicion that there has been an improper interference with the course of justice.'

This has been more recently applied in *R* v *Liverpool City Justices, ex parte Topping* [1983] 1 WLR 119, the Divisional Court holding that the test to be applied was whether a reasonable and fair-minded person sitting in court and knowing all the facts would have a reasonable suspicion that a fair trial for the applicant was not possible.

The alternative test, and one which has generally placed a heavier evidential burden on the applicant, is that of 'real likelihood' of bias. In *Metropolitan Properties Co* v *Lannon* (above) Lord Denning MR appeared to lend support to the view that this was the test to be preferred where he stated:

> 'It brings home this point; in considering whether there was a real likelihood of bias, the court does not look at the mind of the justice himself or at the mind of the chairman of the tribunal ... It does not look to see if there was a real likelihood that he would, or did, in fact favour one side at the expense of the other ... the court looks at the impression which would be given to other people ... If right-minded persons would think that, in the circumstances, there was a real likelihood of bias on [the part of the adjudicator] then he should not sit.'

The confusion may have been resolved by the House of Lords' decision in *R* v *Gough* [1993] 2 WLR 883. The appellant and his brother were charged with conspiracy to rob. The case against the appellant's brother was dropped before it reached the trial stage, but the appellant was tried and convicted. When the verdict was announced, the appellant's brother caused a disturbance in the courtroom, whereupon one of the members of the jury recognised him as her next-door neighbour. The trial judge declined to act on this new evidence, on the basis that he was functus officio. The House of Lords dismissed the appeal, but in the course of so doing attempted to clarify the issue as to the test to be applied where allegations of bias were raised by identifying three categories of case. Where actual bias was alleged, the proceedings would be invalidated upon proof of bias. Where the allegation of bias rested upon a pecuniary or proprietary interest, the proceedings would be invalidated upon proof of the pecuniary or proprietary interest. In cases of apparent bias, where there was no pecuniary or proprietary interest, the correct test was that of whether or not there was a real danger of bias. The 'real danger' test was seen as being equally applicable to arbitrators and members of inferior tribunals. The decision has potentially far-reaching effects, in that it appears to sweep away the real likelihood/reasonable suspicion dichotomy. It may prove to be the case that there is simply one test for cases of apparent bias, thus scotching the distinction drawn between judicial and administrative procedures in *Steeples* v *Derbyshire County Council* [1984] 3 All ER 468, although this authority is not referred to in their Lordships' speeches. Lord Goff criticised the emergence of the 'reasonable suspicion' test in judicial cases as being a misinterpretation of the decision in *R* v *Sussex Justices JJ, ex parte McCarthy* [1923] All ER Rep 233. He preferred the approach adopted in *R* v *Camborne Justices, ex parte Pearce* [1954] 2 All ER 850, which rejected 'reasonable suspicion' on the grounds that it presented too low a threshold for challenge, opening up the possibility of appeal on the flimsiest of pretexts.

Lord Goff went on to explain that the question of whether or not there was a real danger of bias in any particular case was to be assessed by the court in the light of the evidence before it. He rejected the notion of an objective 'reasonable man' test on the basis that:

> '... it is difficult to see what difference there is between the impression derived by a reasonable man to whom such knowledge has been imputed and the impression derived by the court, here personifying the reasonable man.'

The term 'real danger' was preferred to 'real likelihood' because of the desire to emphasise that the possibility of bias should be enough to impugn the validity of proceedings, as opposed to proof of probability.

Is the application of the rule gradual or absolute?

It has been noted previously that the rules of natural justice and the duty to act fairly apply in varying degrees to different situations. Sometimes what is at stake requires the full panoply of justice to be provided before a decision can be made; in other cases, a body is required to do little more than act in good faith.

Unlike the right to a fair hearing, the rule against bias by its very nature must be more absolute in its operation. A decision is either vitiated by bias or it is not. The rule against bias either applies or it does not. If one assumes that the rule against bias definitely applies to 'judicial' proceedings, or to those hearings where significant rights are at stake, the question arises as to whether there is a cut-off point in the application of the rule as one moves towards the more 'administrative' type of decision or towards the 'mere applicant' type of case. In *R* v *Secretary of State for Trade, ex parte Perestrello* [1981] QB 19 the applicant owned a company that was being investigated by the Department of Trade. A company that he had formerly owned had also been the subject of such an investigation, which had led to the previous company being wound up. The searches in the present case involved demands for the production of documents under the terms of s109 Companies Act 1967. The same inspectors who had carried out the searches in respect of the previous company were carrying out the searches in respect of the applicant's present company. The court dismissed his application on the basis that bias had not been made out, and that even if it had been this was not a situation where that would provide a valid ground of challenge. Officers carrying out an investigation under s109 were in the position of potential prosecutors in so far as their function was to ascertain whether the suspicions that had prompted the investigation were justified by what they found. They had to act fairly, but their actions could not be attacked on the basis of bias. The decision is, therefore, supportive of the view that the rule against bias may be inapplicable in the case of preliminary or purely administrative functions.

Even where the function in question is classified as being 'quasi-judicial' the courts may be slow to hold that the rule against bias applies. In *R* v *Chief Constable of South Wales, ex parte Thornhill* (1987) The Times 1 June, the applicant was a police officer against whom disciplinary proceedings had been brought for failing to disclose a business interest as required by Police Regulations. The Chief Constable had found the allegations proved and had determined to dismiss the applicant. Whilst the Chief Constable had been considering his decision, the Deputy Chief Constable, who acted as a 'prosecutor' in this matter, had visited the Chief Constable in his office. The applicant contended that this gave rise to an appearance of bias. The Court of Appeal dismissed his application for review, Stocker LJ commenting that, although it was an important principle that justice must be seen to be done, it also had to be borne in mind that where the courts were reviewing procedures that were not 'judicial' in the strict sense, a more flexible approach had to be adopted. Given that the proceedings in the instant case were 'quasi-judicial', if a satisfactory explanation could be given for the events that gave rise to the appearance of bias, the courts would not intervene.

It is submitted that, notwithstanding the above, the minimum requirement of the duty to act fairly is that the body in question should be free from bias. Support for this view is provided by Megarry V-C's judgment in *McInnes* v *Onslow-Fane* [1978] 1 WLR 1520, where he states that even in a 'mere applicant' type of case the decision-making body should act honestly, without caprice and without bias. The practical difficulty in such cases will, of course, lie in obtaining evidence of bias.

16

Reasonableness and Proportionality

16.1 Introduction

16.2 Unreasonableness

16.3 Proportionality

16.1 Introduction

The purpose of this and the following chapter is to consider the grounds upon which the courts will intervene to quash a decision, or declare it to be invalid, because there has been an abuse of power by a decision-making body. 'Abuse of power' is a very wide term. It can include assuming jurisdiction one does not have; knowingly flouting a statutory procedural requirement; adopting an overrigid policy, or illegally delegating functions.

In the context of this chapter, and the one which follows it, the phrase 'abuse of power' is being used in a narrower sense, encompassing what are sometimes referred to as the 'implied limits' on power, meaning that they are not expressed in an inferior body's enabling Act, but are 'read in' by the courts.

Two warnings should be noted at the outset. First, the topic 'abuse of power' is immense and the case law considerable. Rather than attempt to provide an exhaustive account of every relevant decision, this chapter attempts to highlight the relevant, illustrative and useful authorities.

Secondly, the topic, as will be seen, is approached, in the interests of ease of comprehension, as a succession of heads of review, such as 'unreasonableness', or 'failing to take into account relevant considerations'. It must be remembered that these divisions are to some extent artificial and far from watertight; many major decisions can as easily be placed under one heading as another.

Before one turns to consider the topic, a number of important concepts need to be reconsidered in outline.

Source of power

When considering the actions of an administrative agency, consider first the source of its power. Usually this will be an enabling Act, but it may be an Order in Council issued under the Prerogative, or Royal Charter.

It is this source of power that must be considered in trying to identify the limits of the inferior body's jurisdiction. As has been seen the obvious limits are the express words of the statute which will relate what the inferior body is empowered to do. The enabling Act may also lay down the procedure to be followed by the body when exercising its powers. Where the tribunal in question has, like the Panel on Take-overs and Mergers, no obvious means of legal support, there will clearly be no statute, contract or legally binding constitution to refer to in order to assess the scope of its powers. In such cases the courts appear, nevertheless, to be willing to proceed on the basis that they will recognise an abuse of power when they see it; see the comments of Lord Donaldson MR in *R* v *Panel on Take-overs and Mergers, ex parte Guinness plc* [1989] 2 WLR 863, considered at 11.4.

Types of power

Depending upon the degree of flexibility intended by the legislature, the powers of an inferior body may be tightly or loosely worded. The body may be given powers to decide an issue, but only after taking certain matters into account. For example, under the Town and Country Planning Act 1990, local planning authorities must have regard to matters such as the development plans for their areas before exercising their discretion to grant planning permission. Failure to have regard to these matters could invalidate a decision.

Powers may be worded in such a way as to appear to leave all discretion in the decision-making body: so-called subjectively worded powers. Typically these appear in the formulation: 'Awards shall be made ... as the Minister thinks fit.'

Prima facie it appears very difficult to see how a court could intervene to control the exercise of such a power, as the only criterion set by the legislature is that the minister should be satisfied that an award should be made. In *Liversidge* v *Anderson* [1942] AC 206 a majority of the House of Lords held that, as the Defence Regulation under consideration empowered the Home Secretary to detain a person if he had reasonable cause to believe him to be of hostile origin or associations, the Minister's order detaining Liversidge could only be challenged on the ground of bad faith. The majority were unwilling to inquire into whether the Home Secretary had reasonable grounds for his belief. Even allowing for the fact that the decision was made during wartime, and involved issues that might have had a bearing upon national security, it was unsatisfactory in terms of its constitutional implications, raising as it did the prospect of the Minister only having to satisfy himself that he had reasonable cause to believe that detention was necessary before authorising it.

This 'hands-off' approach to the exercise of subjectively worded powers by ministers and other administrative bodies no longer pertains. In *IRC* v *Rossminster Ltd* [1980] AC 952, the House of Lords considered the effect of a provision under which an officer was entitled to seize any material which he had reasonable cause to believe might be required as evidence. The Inland Revenue accepted that the courts could inquire into whether there were reasonable grounds for that belief. Lord Scarman stated that:

> 'The ghost of *Liversidge* v *Anderson* ... casts no shadow ... (and) I would think it need no longer haunt the law ... It is now beyond recall.'

Lord Wilberforce expressed the point somewhat more prosaically:

> 'Parliament by using such phrases as "is satisfied", "has reasonable cause to believe" must be taken to accept the restraint which the courts in many cases have held to be inherent in them.'

Context

Notwithstanding the more dynamic approach now adopted by the judiciary in reviewing the exercise of even subjectively worded powers, one general consideration remains paramount and that is context. Remember that judicial review lies at the discretion of the courts. The judiciary have at times shown themselves reluctant to question the validity of government policy, believing this to be a matter on which ministers answer to Parliament under the doctrine of ministerial responsibility, or ultimately the electorate at a general election. Furthermore, the courts are slow to question ministers' actions in respect of deportation, extradition or emergency powers matters, generally adopting the view that the minister is in a better position to judge what is required in the national interest than the court.

16.2 Unreasonableness

Introduction

Very few enabling Acts stipulate that an inferior body must act reasonably. This limitation is usually implied by the reviewing court on the basis that Parliament cannot have intended the inferior body to have had the power to act unreasonably; or that Parliament only contemplated the delegated powers being used reasonably. An unreasonable exercise of power will be beyond that intended by Parliament and will, therefore, render administrative action ultra vires.

The problem

The difficulty with unreasonableness is that it is such a subjective concept. Opinions can obviously vary widely on whether a particular decision is reasonable or not. Judicial review is supposed to be concerned with the legality of decisions not their merits. Thus an administrative body can make a 'bad' decision with which people may disagree, but that does not necessarily mean it is an ultra vires decision. Determining the reasonableness of a decision, however, invariably involves questioning its merits, thus when one introduces unreasonableness as a ground of review, one is immediately asking judges to make value judgments about the quality of the decisions made by inferior bodies. At this point merits and legality become intertwined. As will be seen, the courts purport to apply an objective test to determine reasonableness, but in the final analysis these judgments are made by men, not machines, and so some personal element is inevitably introduced into what is supposed to be an evaluation of legality.

The 'Wednesbury' test

The established test for reasonableness in administrative law is derived from the Court of Appeal's decision in *Associated Provincial Picture Houses* v *Wednesbury Corporation* [1948] 1 KB 223. The local authority had the power to grant permission for the opening of cinemas, subject to such conditions as it saw fit to impose. The plaintiff sought a declaration that a condition imposed on a grant of permission to open one of its cinemas, namely that no child under 15 was to be allowed in without an adult, was ultra vires.

Lord Greene MR outlined the principles upon which the authority's decision might be open to attack. These were: not directing itself properly in law; not taking into account relevant considerations, or conversely taking into account irrelevant consideration; acting unreasonably; acting in bad faith; or acting in disregard of public policy.

As regards the condition imposed by the defendant authority, Lord Greene MR thought it important to bear in mind that Parliament had entrusted the local authority with the discretion to impose conditions because of its knowledge of the area's needs, and (impliedly) because having been elected it reflected the views of the area's inhabitants. The courts should, therefore, be slow to intervene to quash a condition imposed by such a body, but would do so where a condition was seen to be unreasonable. This meant that the condition would have to be one that was so unreasonable that no reasonable authority would have imposed it, and to prove a case of that kind would require compelling evidence.

Manifest unreasonableness

In some cases action will be so outrageous that little difficulty arises in persuading a court that it is unreasonable. The term 'manifest absurdity' is sometimes used to describe the radical departure from the proper use of power that is involved. A few examples will suffice. In *Williams* v *Giddy* [1911] AC 381 the Public Service Board of New South Wales awarded a retiring civil servant a gratuity of one penny per year of service. Not only was the award unreasonable but, the Privy Council noted, it was tantamount to a refusal to exercise discretion. A famous illustration was provided by Warrington LJ in *Short* v *Poole Corporation* [1926] Ch 66, when he stated that it would be totally unreasonable simply to dismiss a teacher because she had red hair. Note that this decision could also be invalidated for taking into account irrelevant considerations. Other instances include *Backhouse* v *Lambeth London Borough Council* (1972) 116 Sol Jo 802, where a local authority increased the rent payable on a council property to £18,000 per week (this was part of a campaign against the Conservative Government's 'Fair Rents' legislation). The court declared the action to be manifestly unreasonable – clearly it was a rent increase that no reasonable authority would have sanctioned. A more recent illustration is provided by *R* v *Secretary of State for the Home Department, ex parte Cox* (1991) The Times 10 September. The applicant, who had been convicted of murder in 1971 and released on licence in 1983, was charged during 1989 with making threats to kill a neighbour, and his licence was revoked, although the charges were eventually dismissed. It was decided to release the applicant on licence again on 21 September 1990, but on 15 September he was arrested driving a car with an invalid tax disc and found to be in possession of a small quantity of cannabis. The Secretary of State cancelled the decision to release the applicant on the ground that he presented a risk of danger to the public. The Divisional Court quashed the Secretary of State's decision on the ground that it was unreasonable in the *Wednesbury* sense, bordering on the perverse.

Identifying unreasonableness

To be 'unreasonable' an act must be of such a nature that no reasonable person could possibly entertain such a thing. This is a stringent test that leaves the ultimate discretion with the judges; they decide what they believe a reasonable man might think. As Lord Hailsham observed in *Re W (An Infant)* [1971] AC 682 at 700, in the course of illustrating the difficulty of sustaining an allegation that action is unreasonable, two reasonable persons can come to opposite conclusions on the same set of facts without forfeiting their title to be regarded as reasonable. Caution should therefore be exercised before attaching the adjective 'unreasonable' to executive action. As Lord Ackner stated in referring to *Wednesbury* unreasonableness in *R* v *Secretary of State for the Home Department, ex parte Brind*:

> 'This standard of unreasonableness ... has been criticised as being too high. But it has to be expressed in terms that confine the jurisdiction exercised by the judiciary to a supervisory, as opposed to an appellate, jurisdiction. Where Parliament has given to a minister or other person or body a discretion, the court's jurisdiction is limited, in the absence of a statutory right of appeal, to the supervision of the exercise of that discretionary power, so as to ensure that it has been exercised lawfully. It would be a wrongful usurpation of power by the judiciary to substitute its, the judicial, view on the merits and on that basis to quash the decision. If no reasonable minister properly directing himself would have reached the impugned decision, the minister had exceeded his powers and thus acted unlawfully and the court in the exercise of its supervisory role will quash that decision. Such a decision is correctly, though unattractively, described as a "perverse" decision. To seek the court's intervention on the basis that the correct or objectively reasonable decision is other than the decision which the minister has made is to invite the court to adjudicate as if Parliament had provided a right of appeal against the decision – that is, to invite an abuse of power by the judiciary.'

The task of determining whether the Secretary of State or the local education authority was proposing to act unreasonably fell to the House of Lords in *Secretary of State for Education* v *Tameside Metropolitan Borough Council* [1977] AC 1014. In 1974 the Labour Party controlled the local education authority and decided to convert the state schools to the 'comprehensive' system of education. After the local elections in May 1976 the Conservative Party won control of the education authority and decided to retain the grammar/secondary school system. Section 68 of the Education Act 1944 gave the Secretary of State power to issues directions to a local education authority:

> '... if ... satisfied ... that any local education authority ... have acted or are proposing to act unreasonably with respect to the exercise of any power conferred or the performance of any duty imposed by or under this Act'.

The Secretary of State directed the newly elected Conservative authority to retain the 'comprehensive' system. The authority refused and the Secretary of State sought an order of mandamus to compel compliance, on the basis that, in her view, it would not be possible for the authority to revert to a selective system of schooling before the commencement of the new academic year without ensuing chaos. When the case was before the Court of Appeal, Lord Denning (echoing the comment of Lord Hailsham, above) observed that:

> '... two **reasonable persons** can reasonably come to opposite conclusions ... No one can properly be labelled as being unreasonable unless he is not only wrong but unreasonably wrong, so wrong that no reasonable person could sensibly take that view ...'

His Lordship held that the Secretary of State must have misdirected herself on the interpretation of 'unreasonableness', as there was no evidence on which the Secretary of State could declare herself satisfied that the council was proposing to act unreasonably; in other words he was satisfied that the authority could manage the change in the time available. The House of Lords upheld the Court of Appeal's decision. Although the case appears to involve a choice between competing concepts of reasonableness, it is submitted that it could be seen as a case where the Secretary of State had no jurisdiction to make an order under s68 as the evidence that had to exist as a precondition for the exercise of that power was not before the court.

Generally, the current trend would appear to be for the courts not to intervene in relation to decisions of local authorities on matters of social policy that are within the authorities' control. As Lord Brightman commented in *R* v *Hillingdon London Borough Council, ex parte Puhlhofer* [1986] AC 484:

> 'Where the existence or non-existence of a fact is left to the judgment and discretion of a public body and that fact involves a broad spectrum ranging from the obvious to the debatable to the just conceivable, it is the duty of the court to leave the decision of that fact to the public body to whom Parliament has entrusted the decision-making power save in a case where it is obvious that the public body, consciously or unconsciously, are acting perversely.'

This passage was cited with approval by **Ralph Gibson LJ** in *West Glamorgan County Council* v *Rafferty* [1987] 1 WLR 457. Following the decision of the House of Lords in *Council of Civil Service Unions* v *Minister for the Civil Service* [1984] 3 All ER 935, there has been a tendency to use the expression 'irrationality' to describe what has traditionally been regarded as *Wednesbury* unreasonableness. The use of this alternative expression can be attributed to the speech of Lord Diplock in which he stated (at 951):

> 'By "irrationality" I mean what can by now be succinctly referred to as "*Wednesbury* unreasonableness" ... It applies to a decision which is so outrageous in its defiance of logic or of accepted moral standards that no sensible person who had applied his mind to the question to be decided could have arrived at it. Whether a decision falls within this category is a question that judges by their training and experience should be well equipped to answer, or else there would be something badly wrong with our judicial system ... "Irrationality" by now can stand on its own feet as an accepted ground on which a decision may be attacked by judicial review.'

Proving unreasonableness

Generally, the courts appear no more ready to invalidate a decision on the grounds of irrationality than on the basis of *Wednesbury* unreasonableness. Two examples can be given of the evidential difficulties in establishing the degree of irrationality which will justify intervention by the courts. In *R* v *Great Yarmouth Borough Council, ex parte Sawyer* (1987) The Times 18 June the applicant, the chairman of the local Taxi Proprietors' Association, sought judicial review of the respondent's decision to increase the number of hackney carriage licences granted. The Court of Appeal, dismissing the application, held that there was a very heavy burden indeed resting upon any applicant who sought to show that a public body, in the exercise of its discretion, had acted irrationally. Woolf LJ explained that it could not be said in this case that the decision of the local authority – to allow market forces to determine the granting of licences – was perverse in the sense that no reasonable authority would have come to it. It was not for the court to usurp the function of the authority simply because it disapproved of the decision. It could only intervene if it could be shown that the authority had arrived at its decision unlawfully. It is significant to note the importance attached by the courts to the purpose behind the relevant legislation. For a similar approach, albeit in a somewhat different context (a decision not to re-let council properties to families on the council's waiting list), see *R* v *Hammersmith and Fulham London Borough Council, ex parte Beddowes* [1987] 2 WLR 263.

In *Re Walker's Application* (1987) The Times 26 November the applicant for review was a mother whose child urgently needed a heart operation. The health authorities in Birmingham had already postponed the operation five times due to a shortage of trained nursing staff. The basis of the application was the alleged failure of the authority to provide an adequate service. The Court of Appeal held, in rejecting the application, that while the health authorities were clearly public bodies amenable to review, the rationing of resources was a matter for them and not for the courts. Only if it could be shown that the allocation of funds by the authority was unreasonable in the *Wednesbury* sense, or if there were breaches of public law duties, would the courts be prepared to intervene. The decision perhaps begs the question as to how bad the provision of a public service has to become before the courts would be willing to label an allocation of resources as perverse; see further *R* v *Camden London Borough Council, ex parte Gillan* (1988) The Times 12 October.

Application of the unreasonableness/irrationality principle

The doctrine of unreasonableness propounded in the *Wednesbury* case, and developed as irrationality in the *GCHQ* case, has been applied in every conceivable aspect of administrative law as one of the guiding principles of judicial intervention. The areas include town and country planning; see *Hall & Co Ltd* v *Shoreham by Sea Urban District Council* [1964] 1 WLR 240: unreasonable to use the power to impose conditions on a grant of planning permission to the effect that the developers should construct a road for public use without any compensation); challenges to bye-laws and delegated legislation; ministerial discretion generally. For example, in a written reply to a parliamentary question in 1985 the Home Secretary revealed that, although he would consult the relevant members of the judiciary with a view to establishing a 'tariff' of terms of imprisonment for prisoners convicted of certain serious offences, this consultation process would not begin until a prisoner had served at least three or four years of the sentence that had been imposed, and furthermore he would be prepared to proceed on the basis of his own views in preference to those of a trial judge, where he thought fit. It was held in *R* v *Secretary of State for the Home Department, ex parte Handscomb* (1988) 86 Cr App Rep 59 that it would be irrational for the Minister never to refer cases to the trial judges for their comments until prisoners sentenced by them had served three years of their sentences, Watkins LJ observing that no satisfactory explanation was given by the Minister for this delay. The court regarded the Minister's decision to act upon his own views in preference to those of a trial judge as 'clearly irrational.' If the Minister was not to accept the trial judge's view of the case, whose was he to follow?

16.3 Proportionality

In the course of his speech in *Council of Civil Service Unions* v *Minister for the Civil Service* [1985] AC 374, at 410, Lord Diplock stated:

> '... one can conveniently classify under three heads the grounds upon which administrative action is subject to control by judicial review. The first ground I would call "illegality", the second "irrationality" and the third "procedural impropriety". That is not to say that further development on a case by case basis may not in course of time add further grounds. I have in mind particularly the possible adoption in the future of the principle of "proportionality" which is recognised in the administrative law of several of our fellow members of the European Economic Community ...'

As the above extract indicates, **proportionality as a ground of challenge** is well established in the jurisprudence of the EEC: see *Buitoni SA* v *Fonds d'Orientation et de Regularisation des Marches Agricoles* [1979] 2 CMLR 655. There are, in fact, English decisions that predate *GCHQ* where the courts seem to have acted on the basis that the action taken by a public body was disproportionate to that required by the circumstances of the case: see *R* v *Barnsley Metropolitan Borough Council, ex parte Hook* [1976] 1 WLR 1052 (market trader's licence revoked in response to allegations that he had urinated in the street). Following the *GCHQ* case there was some evidence of proportionality succeeding as a ground for review. In *R* v *Brent London Borough Council, ex parte Assegai* (1987) The Times 18 June a school governor was dismissed following complaints made about him, banned from attending meetings, and banned from entering local authority premises. In justifying the court's decision to grant the application for judicial review, Woolf LJ pointed out that the punishment imposed on the applicant was out of all proportion to the nature of the complaints made. **Whether or not proportionality can yet be cited as anything more than a species of unreasonableness is, it is submitted, doubtful.**

In the decision of the House of Lords in *R* v *Secretary of State for the Home Department, ex parte Brind* [1991] 2 WLR 588, the Home Secretary, acting pursuant to powers conferred upon him by s29(3) of the Broadcasting Act 1981 in regard to the IBA, and clause 13(4) of the licence and agreement with the BBC, ordered both organisations to refrain from broadcasting interviews with members and representatives of certain named terrorist organisations. The applicants were journalists who sought a declaration that the restrictions were ultra vires the Minister's powers, inter alia on the grounds that they were out of all proportion to the problem that the Minister sought to deal with. In the course of dismissing the appeal to the House of Lords, Lord Ackner recognised that while a decision by a minister which suffered from a total lack of proportionality would be regarded as *Wednesbury* unreasonableness, being a decision which no reasonable minister could make, the test of proportionality propounded on behalf of the applicants in the present case was a more strict test. His Lordship expressed the view that to import it into English law would inevitably result in a blurring of the distinction between the courts' proper supervisory role and an improper appellate role.

Lord Lowry was yet more forthright in his refusal to import what he saw as a 'European' concept into judicial review (at 609):

'In my opinion proportionality and the other phrases are simply intended to move the focus of discussion away from the hitherto accepted criteria for deciding whether the decision-maker has abused his power and into an area in which the court will feel more at liberty to interfere. The first observation I would make is that there is *no* authority for saying that proportionality in the sense in which the appellants have used it is part of the English common law and a great deal of authority the other way. This, so far as I am concerned, is not a cause for regret for several reasons: (1) The decision-makers, very often elected, are those to whom Parliament has entrusted the discretion and to interfere with that discretion beyond the limits as hitherto defined would itself be an abuse of the judges' supervisory jurisdiction. (2) The judges are not, generally speaking, equipped by training or experience, or furnished with the requisite knowledge and advice, to decide the answer to an administrative problem where the scales are evenly balanced, but they have a much better chance of reaching the right answer where the question is put in a *Wednesbury* form. The same applies if the judges' decision is appealed. (3) Stability and relative certainty would be jeopardised if the new doctrine held sway, because there is nearly always something to be said against any administrative decision and parties who felt aggrieved would be even more likely than at present to try their luck with a judicial review application both at first instance and on appeal. (4) The increase in applications for judicial review of administrative action (inevitable if the threshold of unreasonabless is lowered) will lead to the expenditure of time and money by litigants, not to speak of the prolongation of uncertainty for all concerned with the decisions in question, and the taking up of court time which could otherwise be devoted to other matters. The losers in this respect will be members of the public, for whom the courts provide a service.'

See further *R* v *General Medical Council, ex parte Colman* [1990] 1 All ER 489, *R* v *Secretary of State for Health, ex parte United States Tobacco International Inc* [1991] 3 WLR 529 and *NALGO* v *Secretary of State for the Environment* (1992) The Times 2 December, where the court observed that it could not quash the Local Government Officers (Political Restrictions) Regulations (SI 1990/851) on the ground of proportionality in the absence of clear House of Lords authority that such a ground of review now existed, as on the basis of the *Wednesbury* test the regulations were reasonable.

17

Relevant and Irrelevant Factors

17.1 Getting the balance right

17.2 Relevant factors

17.3 Acting on no evidence

17.4 Bad faith

17.1 Getting the balance right

Administrative action can be declared ultra vires where it is shown that the decision-maker has acted on the basis of **irrelevant considerations, or** where it can be shown that **relevant considerations have been** ignored. Arguably, to do either of these things might also constitute **acting unreasonably.** A failure to advert to relevant considerations could mean that a decision-maker acts without the necessary evidence to justify his decision; similarly, where a decision-maker seeks to achieve some **ulterior goal** by **using a power not intended for the purpose, he can be described as acting upon an irrelevant consideration.** The basic principles under consideration were stated by **Lord Esher MR** in *R v St Pancras Vestry* (1890) 24 QBD 371 at 375, where he observed:

> '[The decision-making body] must **fairly consider** [the case before them] **and not take into account any reason for their decision which is not a legal one.** If people who have to exercise a public duty by exercising their discretion take into account matters which the courts consider not to be proper for the exercise of their discretion, then in the eye of the law they have not exercised their discretion.'

The courts recognise that administrators are frequently involved in the difficult task of balancing one set of considerations against another. It is submitted that judicial review should not be granted unless there is evidence that the decision-making body has carried out the 'balancing act' unreasonably.

The matter was addressed by **Lord Donaldson MR** in *R v Secretary of State for Social Services, ex parte Wellcome Foundation* [1987] 2 All ER 1025, where the applicants sought to challenge the issuing of an importation licence by the Secretary of State. They alleged that he was wrong in his contention that the possible infringement of their trade mark that might result from the importation of certain

244

medicinal products under the licence was an irrelevant consideration in the exercise of his power. The Court of Appeal held that the Secretary of State had exercised his discretion lawfully, on the basis that the main considerations governing the discretion granted to the Minister by the legislation were those relating to public health and safety. The possible infringement of a trade mark was an irrelevant consideration. His Lordship observed:

> 'Good policy-making, administration and decision-making involve studying problems from all angles. It is a practical process and must never be allowed, and still less induced, to become a theoretical and legalistic exercise. For my part I can find nothing whatsoever to criticise in the approach of a decision-maker which involves him in saying to himself, "I do not know whether, as a matter of law, factor A is or is not a relevant consideration. This is, or may be a difficult question, but I do not need to consider it further, because I am quite satisfied that other factors, which are admittedly relevant, are of such comparative weight, that my decision will be the same whether or not I take account of factor A."'

This decision was subsequently upheld on appeal to the House of Lords.

17.2 Relevant factors

Aims and objects of the legislation

One consideration that a decision-making body should always bear in mind when exercising its discretion is the purpose of the enabling Act from which it derives its powers. This is sometimes expressed in terms of the inferior body having to bear in mind the 'aims and objects' of the primary legislation when exercising its discretion.

In *Padfield* v *Minister of Agriculture* [1968] AC 997 the Minister was empowered to order an investigation into complaints relating to the administration of the Milk Marketing Scheme as he thought fit. The litigation arose out of the Minister's refusal to refer the plaintiff's complaint to a committee of inquiry, and the evidence indicated that the Minister had been motivated by a fear that an inquiry might prove politically embarrassing. The House of Lords, by a majority, held that the Minister was abusing his discretion so as to frustrate the aims and objects of the parent Act, the Agricultural Marketing Act 1958. The Minister may have been given widely drafted powers, but these were not to be used to thwart the policy behind the legislation. While the decision is of incomparable constitutional significance, confirming as it does the power of the judiciary to control the exercise of executive discretion at the highest level, it also arguably exposes the futility of challenging administrative action in the courts. The complaint was eventually referred to a committee of inquiry which upheld the complainant's case, but the Minister refused to take any further action on the matter. It serves as a reminder that administrative law is primarily concerned with the proper procedures being followed, and not with the execution of policy where those procedures are valid.

Ulterior motives

A decision-maker purporting to exercise a discretion while in reality pursuing some ulterior goal will be abusing his power, in the sense that he is flouting the aims and objects of the enabling Act and acting on irrelevant considerations. In short, power given for one purpose cannot be used for another, even where the decision-maker may be acting from the best of intentions. A leading example of invalidity under this head is *Sydney Municipal Council* v *Campbell* [1925] AC 388, where the Privy Council held that compulsory purchase powers vested in a local authority were not to be used for speculating in property, even if the profit made was used to offset the rates. Similarly in *R* v *Hillingdon London Borough Council, ex parte Royco Homes Ltd* [1974] QB 720 the respondent authority granted outline permission for houses, subject to conditions requiring that they should be designed so as to provide space and heating to the standards required by the government for council housing; that they should be constructed at a cost per dwelling not exceeding the limits normally allowed for council housing, to receive government subsidies; that they should be first occupied by persons on the authority's housing waiting list; and that they should for ten years from the first occupation be occupied by a person under the protection of the Rent Act 1968.

Lord Widgery summarised Royco's arguments in this way:

> '... these four conditions were imposed to suit an ulterior purpose, a purpose ulterior to the duty of the council as planning authority ... their purpose was to ensure that, if a private developer was allowed to develop this land, he should have to use it in such a way as to relieve the council of a significant part of its burden as housing authority to provide houses for the homeless ... they are ultra vires and bring the whole planning permission down.'

The Divisional Court held that the local planning authority could not use powers granted for 'planning purposes' to relieve the housing shortage in the area over which it had jurisdiction. In any event, the court regarded the conditions as so unreasonable that no reasonable planning authority would have imposed them. See further on this point *Newbury District Council* v *Secretary of State for the Environment* [1981] AC 578.

Where, in the exercising of a power, some incidental benefit accrues to the authority concerned, the courts will not declare the action ultra vires simply because of the benefit. It may be a matter of looking for the dominant purpose in the exercise of the power. For example in *Westminster Corporation* v *London and North Western Railway Co* [1905] AC 426 the local authority, which was empowered to build public conveniences but not subways, constructed an underground convenience that effectively formed a subway under a particular street. The railway company argued that a power to build lavatories was being used to build subways. The House of Lords held that this was merely an incidental benefit arising from a legitimate use of the authority's powers.

It is an important constitutional issue that an authority cannot levy a tax or otherwise raise revenue without there being an express statutory power for the purpose. The courts will thus invalidate the exercise of discretion, even where this is a side-effect of the decision: see *Sydney Municipal Council* v *Campbell* (above). A leading example is provided by the Court of Appeal's decision in *Congreve* v *Home Office* [1976] QB 629. The Secretary of State announced that the cost of a colour television licence was to be increased from £12 to £18, the increase taking effect on 1 April 1975. Congreve, along with 20,000 other licence holders, applied for a new licence shortly before the date set for the increase, even though his own licence had not expired, because he would still make an overall saving. Contemplating a substantial loss of revenue if this practice was allowed, the Secretary of State adopted a policy of revoking any new 'overlapping' licences after eight months if the extra £6 was not paid by the holder. The Minister purported to act under s1(2) of the Wireless Telegraphy Act 1949 which states that a licence may be revoked by a notice in writing served on the holder. Congreve sought a declaration that the Minister's action was unlawful. The Court of Appeal held that the Secretary of State had acted unlawfully in using his statutory power of revocation for a purpose for which it was never intended, namely, the raising of revenue. Citing *Padfield* as authority, Lord Denning MR spoke of the courts having a duty to correct a misuse of power where a minister exercised discretion for reasons that were bad in law. The Master of the Rolls also adverted to the issue of taxation:

> 'There is yet another reason for holding the demands for £6 to be unlawful. They were made contrary to the Bill of Rights. They were an attempt to levy money for the use of the Crown without the authority of Parliament: and that is quite enough to damn them: see *Attorney-General* v *Wilts United Dairies Ltd* (1921) 37 TLR 884.'

See further *R* v *Bowman* [1898] 1 QB 663.

Local government finance

Despite the fact that the lion's share of local government income is supplied directly by central government grant, the courts will nevertheless expect local authorities to exercise discretion properly as regards spending. In particular, local authorities will have to show that they have paid sufficient regard to the interests of those who contribute to locally raised revenue. Formerly these would have been ratepayers. Since April 1993, following the abolition of the Community Charge, which in turn had replaced the old rating system, the basis for local taxation has been the Council Tax. Presumably the case law relating to the use of ratepayers' money is equally applicable to the exercise of discretion in spending monies raised via the Council Tax.

A leading authority on judicial control of local government spending is *Roberts* v *Hopwood* [1925] AC 578. Poplar Borough Council, acting under statutory powers to pay its workers such wages as it thought fit, resolved to pay its male and female workers a wage of £4 per week. The payments made in pursuance of this resolution were challenged by the District Auditor as being contrary to law, and this contention was eventually approved by the House of Lords. First, the local authority had taken into account irrelevant considerations in wishing to set an example as a 'model' employer; it had relied, wrongly, on considerations of 'socialist philanthropy, and feminist ambition'. Secondly, it had failed to take into account the fact that during this period the cost of living was actually falling and therefore wages should have been reduced, not increased. Thirdly, the authority had failed to give sufficient regard to the interests of its ratepayers, who would in part have to finance the increases. The House of Lords took the view that the authority was at least under a fiduciary duty to spend ratepayers' money wisely.

The courts have sought to apply the principles enunciated in *Roberts* v *Hopwood* in a number of cases involving disputes as to the legality of local authority spending where the allegation has been of a failure to take into account relevant considerations, usually the fiduciary duty owed to rate payers. In *Prescott* v *Birmingham Corporation* [1955] Ch 210 a scheme to provide pensioners with free bus travel at the expense of local authority ratepayers was struck down by the courts. The authority was obliged to provide transport on business principles, and under the scheme was effectively making a gift to one section of the travelling public at the expense of ratepayers. Although viewed strictly the case involved a finding that the authority had breached the terms of a 'trust' upon which it held ratepayers' money, the decision can be viewed on wider terms as one where action was invalidated for failure to give due weight to the ratepayers' interest in securing value for money.

Similarly, in *Bromley London Borough Council* v *Greater London Council* [1983] 1 AC 768, the House of Lords invalidated a proposed scheme of fare cuts which the GLC had intended to introduce. The scheme, if put into effect, would have resulted in a substantial increase in the level of rates due from ratepayers. The GLC argued, inter alia, that its controlling Labour group had been elected with a mandate to reduce fares by 25 per cent and was simply proposing to carry out the policy on which it had won the election. Among the grounds upon which the action of the GLC was held to be unlawful was the point that it had failed to have sufficient regard to the effect of the scheme on its ratepayers, and had placed too much emphasis on its election promises to cut fares.

Pickwell v *Camden London Borough Council* [1983] 1 All ER 602 is a good illustration of the difficulties that the courts face in deciding between competing political philosophies in such cases. Following a protracted national strike of local authority manual workers, Camden London Borough Council, concerned about the effect of refuse not being collected and so on, entered into an agreement with its manual workers to increase their wages, as a result of which the strike ended in Camden. Some weeks later a national settlement was reached where lower wage increases were agreed to by the rest of the country's local authority manual workers. A year later Camden London Borough Council, in line with other authorities, increased the wages of its manual workers again. The District Auditor sought a declaration that this second increase in wages amounted to unlawful expenditure by the local authority which, it was argued, should not have raised wages again but have left them as they were so that wages in the rest of the country could rise to the same level. The court declined to declare the expenditure illegal, holding that the local authority had, quite legitimately, been concerned with the effect of the strike on its area. The authority had not, in fixing wage levels above the national average, been taking into account irrelevant considerations such as those of Poplar Borough Council in *Roberts* v *Hopwood*, of desiring to set an example as a model employer. The court placed great emphasis on the fact that the local authority was in the best position to judge the necessity of getting its refuse workers back to work. If its policies were unpopular the local electorate could show its displeasure at the next local elections.

Local government mandates

In both *Bromley* v *Greater London Council* (above) and *Secretary of State for Education* v *Tameside Metropolitan Borough Council* (above) the issues raised involved discussion of the significance to be given to the fact that a local authority may be voted into power having promised to implement a particular policy.

In *Tameside* the Conservative majority had given an undertaking to voters that, if elected, it would preserve grammar schools in the area. In holding that the local authority was not purporting to act unreasonably, Lord Wilberforce laid much emphasis on the fact that it was an elected body, and that those who voted for the reversal of educational policy advocated by the Conservatives must be taken to have accepted some degree of disruption as a result of the implementation. His Lordship went on to suggest that having stood on a platform of ending comprehensivisation Conservative councillors were in a sense bound to implement the policy once in power.

This is to be contrasted with his Lordship's approach to the same argument when relied upon by the GLC as justifying the implementation of a 25 per cent cut in London Transport fares, with a consequent rise in rates. The 'election mandate' argument was rejected by Lord Wilberforce in this latter case because, he argued, in *Tameside* a power existed to restore grammar schools, and an election mandate to do so was a relevant factor in determining whether the exercise of that power was reasonable. In the *Greater London Council* case, no power to order London Transport to operate deliberately at a loss existed in the first place – the wishes of the electorate therefore became irrelevant. An election mandate could not give the GLC a power it did not otherwise possess.

Local government politics

In *R* v *Board of Education* [1910] KB 165 Farwell LJ took the view that allowing political considerations to influence decision-making would necessarily invalidate the process: They were, to his mind, 'pre-eminently extraneous'. Today such a view seems to be untenable. Local government is always dominated by party politics, and to that extent resolutions passed by majority groupings are bound to be motivated by adherence to one political viewpoint or another. See *Tameside* (above) and *Cardiff Corporation* v *Secretary of State for Wales* (1971) 22 P & Cr 718.

Decisions such as *Pickwell* v *Camden* (above), *R* v *Amber Valley District Council, ex parte Jackson* [1984] 3 All ER 501 and *R v Waltham Forest London Borough Council, ex parte Waltham Forest Ratepayers' Action Group* [1988] 2 WLR 257, all indicate a more realistic and pragmatic approach being adopted by the courts to the decisions of local authorities. They reflect a willingness to accept the inevitability of local government being highly politicised, and an acknowledgement that the correct procedure for resolving disputes on policy is the democratic process of local elections.

Inevitably, however, there are limits to what the courts are willing to permit in terms of local authorities pursuing overtly political objectives, and these were exceeded in *R v Ealing London Borough Council and Others, ex parte Times Newspapers Ltd* (1986) The Times 6 November. A number of local authorities had resolved that the libraries under their control should not stock publications produced by Times Newspapers and others while the publishers were in dispute with sacked employees of the newspapers. The purpose of the ban was to show solidarity with the dismissed workers. The publishers, and a number of residents of each authority, applied for judicial review of the ban. It was held that the authorities had acted unlawfully. Watkins LJ recognised that the authorities had a discretion as to how they carried out their duties under the Public Libraries and Museums Act 1964, and that as a result it was not for the courts to usurp that function readily. His Lordship also observed that local government was a political arena and that it was not proper for the courts to adjudicate between one political philosophy and another. Neither of these factors, however, gave authorities an untrammelled discretion to come to decisions purely on the basis of political considerations. The ban imposed by the authorities was clearly related to an ulterior purpose, ie involvement in an industrial dispute. No rational authority could have thought that this was a proper way of discharging its duties under the 1964 Act. There was an alternative remedy available by way of s10 of the Act, under which the Minister had certain default powers, but the courts would not be prevented from granting a remedy themselves where, as in the present case, there was a glaring example of abuse. See also *R v Liverpool City Council, ex parte Secretary of State for Employment* (1988) The Times 12 November and *R v Derbyshire County Council, ex parte Times Supplements Ltd* [1990] NLJ 1421.

Race relations

Given that local authorities are under a statutory duty to promote good race relations within their areas (s71 of the Race Relations Act 1976), to what extent should they be permitted to take this into account in exercising statutory discretion? The question is particulary important given the 'dynamic ' approach of some local authorities on this issue, evidenced by the adoption of high profile 'anti-racist' policies ranging from the eviction of council tenants found guilty of racial harassment to campaigns against apartheid. In *Wheeler* v *Leicester City Council* [1985] 2 All ER 1106, the House of Lords considered the validity of a local authority resolution banning a rugby football club from using a council recreation field because of the club's connections with South Africa. The local authority specifically objected to the fact that a number of club members had played in South Africa, something that the club had no power to prevent. Their Lordships held the ban to be unreasonable, not least because the club had not been guilty of any wrongdoing. It is noteworthy, however, that their Lordships did consider the promotion of good race relations a relevant factor in the exercise of the local authority's power, particularly in the light of the large number of individuals of Afro-Caribbean and Asian origin living in its area. Similarly, in *R v London Borough of Lewisham, ex parte Shell UK Ltd* (1987) The Times 23 November Lewisham London Borough Council had approved a resolution that stated, inter alia, that it would boycott the products of Shell UK Ltd, provided that alternative products were available at reasonable prices. The company applied for judicial review of the resolution, seeking: a declaration that the resolution, and the campaign waged by the authority to dissuade other local authorities from using the company's products, were ultra vires; orders of certiorari to quash the resolution; and an injunction to stop the authority implementing the resolution. Despite the council's reliance on s71 of the Race Relations Act 1976, the court held that it could not use its contracting power to punish a company in relation to activity which was not prohibited by English law.

Neill LJ, commenting on the council's actions, observed:

'For my part, I do not accept ... that it was obligatory for the council to adduce evidence from ratepayers or others to prove that there was a body of public opinion in favour of the action taken by the council ... having regard to the fact that this is a multi-racial borough, the council was entitled to decide on the basis of its own experience and perception that it was in the interests of good race relations that trading with a particular company should cease because of its links with apartheid. I shall therefore assume, though on the present evidence the matter must be very near the line, that the council's decision not to continue to trade with Shell UK, unless in effect it was obliged to do so, could not be successfully attacked as being unreasonable in a *Wednesbury* sense ... It seems to me to be quite clear, however, ... that the purpose of the decision was not merely to satisfy public opinion in the borough or to promote good race relations in the borough, but was in order to put pressure on Shell UK and Shell Transport to procure a withdrawal of the Shell group from South Africa ... It is to be remembered that neither Shell UK nor any of the other UK Shell companies was acting in any way unlawfully. Nor is there any suggestion whatever that Shell UK or any of the other UK companies was in any way in breach of the contract compliance scheme devised by the Commission for Racial Equality. The attitude which Shell UK and Shell Transport adopted was a responsible one. The council, and indeed a great many other people, may strongly disagree with the policy adopted by the Shell group and as to the efficacy of this policy in bringing about any change in the South African regime, but I find it impossible in the light of the authorities to escape from the conclusion that by seeking to bring pressure on Shell UK to change the Shell policy towards South Africa, the council was acting unfairly and in a manner which requires the court to intervene.'

As a result the court concluded that the wish to change the Shell policy towards South Africa was inextricably tied up with the desire to improve race relations in the borough, and had the effect of vitiating the decision as a whole. The court also noted that, as a result of its decision on this point, the council's participation in a campaign to persuade other local authorities effectively to boycott trade with Shell UK and its associated companies was also **ultra vires**.

'Green' politics

Given the political changes in South Africa since the above cases were considered by the courts, councillors seeking a moral reference point from which to launch a programme of activism have increasingly turned to so-called 'green politics', issues such as opposition to blood sports and the promotion of animal rights. Although the focus for campaigning shifts, the legal issues remain constant. If a local authority exercises its discretion having taken into account the opposition to blood sports, or the transport of live animals for export, has it acted unlawfully? Much turns on the wording of the power pursuant to which the action is taken. In *R v Somerset County Council, ex parte Fewings and Others* (1994) The Times 10 February, the respondent local authority purported to ban stag hunting on land held under s122 of the Local Government Act 1974 'for the benefit, improvement and development' of the area. The authority based its decision on the fact that the majority of its members found such blood sports morally offensive. The ban was successfully challenged by representatives of the Quantock Staghounds on the basis that the authority, unlike a private landowner, was not entitled to be guided in the exercise of its discretion regarding land use by moral or ethical preferences. In essence, unless activities such as blood sports, the transportation of live animals, or circuses making use of animals for exhibitionistic purposes contravene the criminal law, local authorities have no right to prohibit the use of municipal facilities to those promoting such activities on the ground that they affront the moral preferences of councillors.

As Laws J succinctly put it in the *Somerset* case:

'A public body has no rights except those required to vindicate the better performance of the duties for whose fulfilment it existed. It had no axe to grind beyond its public responsibility: a responsibility which defined its purpose and justified its existence.'

17.3 Acting on no evidence

Acting on no evidence has, arguably, only begun to be more widely recognised as a ground for review in the past 30 years or so. In a sense it is a case of 'old wine in new bottles' because review under this head can be seen as dealing with a species of unreasonableness, in that no reasonable body would come to a decision unsupported by evidence. Equally the existence of evidence might be regarded as a jurisdictional precondition, in that there must be evidence before a body has the power to proceed with the making of a decision. In any event there is a growing body of case law reflecting the view that to act without evidence is to act ultra vires.

Authorities from the first half of this century indicate a willingness on the part of the courts to recognise the existence of some evidence, objectively assessed, as a prerequisite for the exercise of power. In *Burgesses of Sheffield* v *Minister of Health* (1935) 52 TLR 171 the owners of land subject to a compulsory purchase order issued by the local authority sought to challenge its confirmation by the Minister on the ground that, contrary to the requirements of s3 of the Housing Act 1930, there was insufficient evidence that the acquisition was 'reasonably necessary for the purpose of securing a cleared area of convenient shape and dimensions, and ... for the satisfactory development or user of the cleared area'. Mr Justice Swift, while satisfied that the necessary evidence existed in the instant case, explained the role of the court thus:

> 'If [the local authority] go to the Minister asking for powers to buy land compulsorily which is not reasonably necessary for the satisfactory development of the land in the cleared area, they will not get those powers; the Minister would simply say to them: "This is not reasonably necessary." Even if the Minister gave them the powers asked for, the Court, should the matter come before it, could quash the order if satisfied that there was no material on which it could be said that the land was reasonably required or was reasonably necessary for the satisfactory development of the cleared area. It is for the corporation in the first place to say whether it is reasonably necessary or not; it is for the Minister in the second place to say whether it is reasonably necessary or not; and it is for the Court, if the matter is brought before it, to say whether there is any material on which the Minister could have come to the conclusion that it was reasonably necessary. If the Court comes to the conclusion that there is no such material, then it will not hesitate to quash the Minister's order ...'

The modern equivalent is, perhaps, *Coleen Properties* v *MHLG* [1971] 1 WLR 433, in which the Court of Appeal quashed a ministerial order confirming a slum clearance scheme after no evidence supporting it had been offered at a public inquiry, and the inspector had recommended against it. As there was no new evidence justifying the Minister's departure from the inspector's conclusions, his order was thus quashed. In a different area, but acknowledging the same principles, the House of Lords, in *R* v *Home Secretary, ex parte Zamir* [1980] AC 930, held that an immigration officer, who has power to refuse leave to enter the country if satisfied of certain facts, is, on 'normal principles', not at liberty to refuse it if there is no evidence to support his decision.

The absence of evidence was also held to be fatal to the validity of the action challenged in *R* v *Derbyshire County Council, ex parte Times Supplements Ltd* (above). The applicants published articles about the activities of the respondent council leader, considered by the controlling Labour group to be libellous. The respondents resolved not to place any advertisements in publications owned by the applicants. A meeting of its education committee also resolved to withdraw all future advertisements for teaching posts from the educational supplements published by the applicants. The committee's decision was later endorsed by a full meeting of the council. The Divisional Court found that the authority had acted in bad faith and for an improper purpose. Given that there was no evidence that, prior to the publication by the applicants of articles concerning the activities of the council leader, the respondents had been in anyway dissatisfied by the service provided by the applicants in advertising council posts, the court concluded that there was no valid grounds for the authority's decision. Watkins LJ expressed his view that the 'educational' grounds put forward by the councillors who gave evidence (that advertising in *The Times*'s educational supplements was no longer as effective as advertising in the *Guardian*) were implausible. He felt that the Labour grouping had taken the decision in bad faith (as to which see below), and had then sought to produce some 'evidence' to justify it in the hope that the court would be persuaded that this was a lawful consideration. Costs were awarded against the respondents on an indemnity basis, as it was felt that there had been an attempt to mislead the court. See further *Secretary of State for Education* v *Tameside Metropolitan Borough Council* [1977] AC 1014, *R* v *Commission for Racial Equality, ex parte Hillingdon London Borough Council* [1981] 3 WLR 520 and *R* v *Secretary of State for the Home Department, ex parte Khawaja* [1983] 2 WLR 321.

As a ground for review, acting on no evidence has the attraction that it depends less on the idiosyncrasies of individual judges, and their conceptions of reasonableness, or relevant considerations, and more on the establishment of objective criteria that have to be satisfied before powers can be exercised. In this sense, the no evidence rule straddles the boundary between substantive ultra vires and jurisdictional fact.

The sense in which the 'no evidence' rule straddles the boundary between substantive ultra vires and jurisdictional fact is well illustrated by the Divisional Court's ruling in *R* v *Secretary of State for Foreign Affairs, ex parte World Development Movement Ltd* (1994) The Times 27 December. In July 1991 the Foreign Secretary, in the exercise of his discretion under s1(1) of the Overseas Development and Co-operation Act 1980, made a grant to the Malaysian government for the building of the Pergau Dam. In April 1994, despite concerns about the funding of the project, the Foreign Secretary refused to withhold outstanding payments. The applicants, a pressure group concerned with abuses of overseas aid, successfully challenged the legality of both the original decision to grant aid, and the later decision not to withhold outstanding payments, on the ground that the Foreign Secretary had known that the aid was not being granted for a sound economic development. Rose LJ indicated that affidavit evidence of the respondent revealed that the contemplated development, in the form of the Pergau Dam project, was so economically unsound that no economic argument in its favour could be constructed. The fact that Parliament had not limited the power under the 1980 Act by expressly specifying that it had to be exercised for a sound development purpose did not mean that it could, therefore, be used to promote unsound development. The court recognised that the respondent would have to take into account wider political and diplomatic considerations when deciding whether or not to honour a pledge to grant overseas aid, but those factors only became relevant once a proper purpose for granting aid arose under the 1980 Act. It could not be left to the respondent himself to determine whether or not a grant of aid under the 1980

Act would be lawful. In short, the provision of evidence justifying the investment was a precondition to the valid exercise of discretion.

17.4 Bad faith

In many ways acting in bad faith represents an extreme example of taking into account irrelevant considerations. Here the administrator deliberately sets out to harm the interests of another person, knowing that he does not have the power to act in this way. In this sense it could be argued that bad faith is not, in reality, an independent ground for invalidity, at least to the extent that an applicant for review can succeed in establishing ultra vires action without having to go as far as establishing bad faith on the part of a decision-maker. The significance of establishing bad faith may lie in respect of the availability of damages. A classic example is provided by the Canadian case of *Roncarelli* v *Duplessis* (1959) 16 DLR (2d) 689, where the premier of Quebec purported to revoke a liquor licence because the holder had regularly provided sureties for Jehovah's Witnesses who had been arrested by the police. The premier was clearly exercising a power he did not possess, and was motivated by a desire to affect the interests of the citizen adversely. The courts have consistently pointed out that there is an enormous evidential burden resting upon anyone attempting to establish bad faith, and the English courts have been slow to allow such challenges to succeed: see *Davies* v *Bromley Corporation* [1908] 1 KB 170, *Cannock Chase District Council* v *Kelly* [1978] 1 All ER 152 and *R* v *Secretary of State for the Home Department, ex parte Ruddock* [1987] 2 All ER 518.

Bad faith – liability in tort

As indicated above, perhaps the real significance of bad faith lies not so much in the fact that it can provide the basis for an application for review as in the fact that malicious abuse of power is a tort in its own right.

In theory, any individual suffering loss as a result of deliberate ultra vires action can issue a writ against the relevant officer of the public body concerned, claiming damages. In *Smith* v *East Elloe Rural District Council* [1956] AC 736, the House of Lords, while refusing to allow the plaintiff to challenge a compulsory purchase order that had been made in respect of her property because she was out of time, did suggest that if she felt that the order had been made in bad faith she could proceed with an action for malicious abuse of power against the officer concerned. Acting upon this advice, Mrs Smith subsequently brought such an action against the clerk to the council in *Smith* v *Pywell* (1959) 173 Estates Gazette 1009. The action failed on its merits, however.

A difficulty in this area has been the question of whether or not a plaintiff must actually establish 'malice' or 'ill-will' on the part of a public officer in order to succeed. In *Asoka Kumar David* v *MAMM Abdul Cader* [1963] 3 All ER 579, the Privy Council considered a claim for damages brought by the proprietor of a cinema in Ceylon, who contended that he had been refused a cinema licence because of malice towards him on the part of the chairman of the licensing authority. Viscount Radcliffe stated:

> 'The presence of spite or ill-will may be insufficient in itself to render actionable a decision which has been based on unexceptionable grounds of consideration and has not been vitiated by the badness of the motive. But a "malicious" misuse of authority, such as is pleaded by the appellant in his plaint, may cover a set of circumstances which go beyond the mere presence of ill-will, and in their Lordships' view it is only after the facts of malice relied on by a plaintiff have been properly ascertained that is possible to say in a case of this sort whether or not there has been any actionable breach of duty.'

Against this suggestion that 'malice' or 'ill-will' must be established, the decision of the Court of Appeal in *Bourgoin SA* v *Minister of Agriculture, Fisheries and Food* [1985] 3 All ER 585 should be considered. The United Kingdom government imposed a ban on the importation of turkeys from countries where particular methods of dealing with disease amongst turkeys were in use. One consequence of this was that French turkey producers were unable to export to the United Kingdom. The plaintiffs claimed that the import ban was in breach of the Treaty of Rome, and could not be justified on public health grounds. In 1982 the European Court of Justice ruled that the importation ban was in breach of Art 30 of the Treaty of Rome, and the ban was removed by the United Kingdom government. The plaintiffs sought damages in the English courts to compensate them for the economic loss that they had suffered. The claim was based on allegations that the Minister had either been in breach of his statutory duty in imposing the ban, or had been guilty of misfeasance. At first instance, Mr Justice Mann found that both grounds of challenge were made out and that damages were consequently available. In dealing with the Minister's appeal the Court of Appeal held (Oliver LJ dissenting) that the appropriate remedy for breach of statutory duty in a case such as this was by way of an application for judicial review. Damages would be available, however, in respect of an action for the tort of misfeasance, provided that the plaintiff could show that a public officer knew that the action he was taking was ultra vires, and that the action would adversely affect the interests of the plaintiff. It was not necessary to prove actual malice on the part of the public officer.

Note that the court here referred to 'misfeasance', not 'malfeasance' or 'malicious abuse of power'. It is submitted that nothing of substance turns on the use of differing terminology. As Wade points out:

> 'There is thus a tort which has been called misfeasance in public office, and which includes malicious abuse of power, deliberate maladministration, and perhaps other unlawful acts causing injury.' (Administrative Law 6th ed p777)

Is negligence enough?

On the basis of *Bourgoin*, for a successful claim for malicious abuse of power to be made out, the public officer concerned must be shown to have known that he was acting ultra vires. Confirmation of this view is to be found in subsequent decisions such as *Bennet* v *Commissioner of Police of the Metropolis* (1994) The Times 28 December where the plaintiff's claim for damages for, inter alia, public misfeasance, in respect of the time he had spent in detention between his arrest in February 1991 and his eventual release without trial in July 1993, was struck out because he had failed to establish an essential ingredient of the tort, ie an intent to injure on the part of the Home Secretary. See further *Dunlop* v *Woollahra Metropolitan Council* [1982] AC 158; *Rowling* v *Takaro Properties Ltd* [1988] 1 All ER 163 and *An Bord Bainne Co-operative Ltd v Milk Marketing Board* (1987) Financial Times 26 November.

Which procedure?

A plaintiff can proceed with an action for damages for misfeasance against a public officer by way of writ, despite *O'Reilly* v *Mackman* [1983] 2 AC 237. Such actions could be regarded as coming within the scope of one of Lord Diplock's exceptions, in that the public law issue involved arises as a collateral matter: see further *Davy* v *Spelthorne Borough Council* [1984] AC 262. A plaintiff could, however, proceed by way of an application for judicial review, and add a claim for damages on the basis that damages would have been available as a remedy had the action started by way of writ. See RSC O.53 r.7, and *Jones* v *Swansea City Council* [1989] 3 All ER 162.

18

Fettering Discretion – Delegation and Policy

18.1 Introduction

18.2 The rule against delegation

18.3 Fettering discretion by adoption of a policy

18.1 Introduction

As the heading suggests, this chapter deals with those situations where an inferior body acts ultra vires by failing to exercise its power. This statement should be qualified by pointing out that we are concerned here with the reasons why power is not exercised. For convenience, it is traditional to group the cases under the four headings of policy, delegation, contract and estoppel, although as with abuse of power none of these categories is intended to be 'watertight'.

18.2 The rule against delegation

Introduction

The basic principle is that where Parliament delegates a function to an inferior body, and bestows upon it the powers necessary for it to perform that function, the inferior body should not delegate that function to any other body. There are a number of reasons for this rule, which is sometimes expressed as the Latin maxim delegatus non potest delegare. The individual has the right to have decisions affecting his position made by the body empowered to do so. In selecting an inferior body to perform a particular function, Parliament will have had regard to its suitability and expertise. It would be thwarting the intention of Parliament to permit the function to be carried out by some other body. If a function is being discharged by a tribunal other than that authorised by the enabling Act, the tribunal purporting to act must be assuming a jurisdiction that it does not in fact have, and therefore must be acting ultra vires.

258

A classic example of unlawful delegation is provided by the case of *Ellis* v *Dubowski* [1921] 3 KB 621, where a local authority with statutory powers to licence cinemas issued licences subject to the condition that only films approved by the British Board of Film Censors could be shown. The local authority was held to have unlawfully delegated its function of licensing films for public display as it had completely abdicated the function. Compare this with the later decision in *Mills* v *London County Council* [1925] 1 KB 213 where a similar delegation of powers was upheld, the difference being that, regardless of the view of the Board, the LCC had taken care in its resolution to reserve to itself the ultimate choice as to whether a film should be shown or not. In effect it had retained a power to review the decisions of the British Board of Film Censors. The rule against delegation has also been applied to central government. In *H Lavender & Sons Ltd* v *MHLG* [1970] 3 All ER 871, the company applied for planning permission in order to extract certain minerals from an agricultural holding. Most of the holding was within a reservation area (ie was high quality agricultural land). The planning authority refused permission and the company appealed to the Minister under s23 of the Town and Country Planning Act 1962. In dismissing the appeal the Minister of Housing and Local Government stated his reasons, inter alia, as follows:

> 'It is the Minister's present policy that land in the reservations should not be released for mineral working unless the Minister of Agriculture, Fisheries and Food is not opposed to working. In the present case the agricultural objection has not been waived, and the Minister has therefore decided not to grant planning permission for the working of the appeal site.'

The company applied to the High Court under s179 of the Town and Country Planning Act 1962 for the Minister's decision to be quashed. The court held the abdication of power by the Ministry to be ultra vires. It could not defer to the views of another government department when exercising its discretionary powers. Note that the case could also be regarded as one involving the fettering of discretion by the adoption of an over-rigid policy, in this case the policy of referring all such applications to the Ministry of Agriculture.

Government departments

Given the huge work load of many government departments, it is inconceivable that any minister should personally exercise all the powers and functions bestowed upon him or her by Parliament. This reality has to be reconciled with the theory, already expounded above, that power once delegated should not be delegated further.

The courts have accepted that, except where a statute expressly requires a Secretary of State to act personally, his powers are frequently going to be exercised on his behalf by senior civil servants. The safeguard, and presumably the reason why the courts are willing to countenance such a practice, is that constitutionally the actions of civil servants are the actions of the minister, for which the minister is responsible to Parliament. Further, the fact that discretionary powers are exercised by a civil servant and not the minister does not prevent judicial review from operating in the event of illegality.

In *Carltona Ltd* v *Commissioners of Works* [1943] 2 All ER 560, the appellant's food factory was requisitioned by the Commissioners acting under Regulation 51(1) of the Defence (General) Regulations 1939 which provided that:

> 'A competent authority, if it appears to that authority to be necessary or expedient so to do in the interests of the public safety, the defence of the realm or the efficient prosecution of the war, or for maintaining supplies and services essential to the life of the community, may take possession of any land, and may give such directions as appear to the competent authority to be necessary or expedient in connection with the taking of possession of that land.'

On 4 November 1942 a Mr Morse signed the requisition notice on behalf of the Commissioners (in effect the Minister of Works and Planning). The appellants sought a declaration that the notice was invalid because of unlawful delegation of the Minister's functions to Mr Morse. The Court of Appeal rejected the claim of the appellants and made clear the principle that functions given to a 'minister' or 'secretary of state' were exercisable on his behalf by his department. As Lord Greene MR stated:

> 'It cannot be supposed that this regulation meant that, in each case, the minister in person should direct his mind to the matter. The duties imposed upon ministers and the powers given to ministers are normally exercised under the authority of the ministers by responsible officials of the department. Public business could not be carried on if that were not the case. Constitutionally, the decision of such an official is, of course, the decision of the minister. The minister is responsible. It is he who must answer before Parliament for anything that his officials have done under his authority, and, if for an important matter he selected an official of such junior standing that he could not be expected competently to perform the work, the minister would have to answer for that in Parliament. The whole system of departmental organisation and administration is based on the view that ministers, being responsible to Parliament, will see that important duties are committed to experienced officials. If they do not do that, Parliament is the place where complaint must be made against them.'

In *Point of Ayr Collieries Ltd* v *Lloyd-George* [1943] 2 All ER 546 a challenge to an order requisitioning a coal mine was challenged on grounds similar to those raised in *Carltona*. In upholding the order, Lord Greene commented that it might have been more appropriate for the Minister himself to sign the order, but this was not required as a matter of law. Further support for this position has been supplied in *Re Golden Chemical Products* [1976] 2 All ER 543, where officers acting for the Secretary of State for Trade presented a petition under s35 of the Companies Act 1967 for the winding up of Golden Chemical Products Ltd. The company opposed the petition on the grounds that the power under s35 could only be exercised by the Secretary of State personally. The court rejected this argument, holding that it was established departmental practice that such functions be discharged by officials of the department. Brightman J stated that the fact that a s35 petition could have devastating effects for the company did not compel the conclusion that only the Minister could authorise such action.

The application of the rule against delegation within government departments may depend to a certain extent on the nature of the function being delegated. It has been suggested that where personal liberty is affected, the minister himself should act. The contention was considered in *R* v *Skinner* [1968] 2 QB 700, where the court considered the validity of using a breath-testing machine designed to measure blood alcohol levels of motorists suspected of driving with excess alcohol. Reliance on the readings produced by the machine was challenged when it became known that its use had been authorised by a senior civil servant on behalf of the Home Secretary, and not by the Home Secretary personally. The Court of Appeal had no doubt that the Minister's function could be discharged by a senior official. The court pointed out that in certain circumstances it might be impolitic for the Minister not to be seen to intervene personally, but whether or not he should do so was a matter for the Minister: see *R* v *Governor of Brixton Prison, ex parte Enahoro (No 2)* [1963] 2 QB 455 and *Liversidge* v *Anderson* [1942] AC 206.

The question of what factors the court should consider when assessing the legality of the delegation of ministerial functions, in the absence of any express statutory restriction, was reviewed by the House of Lords in *R* v *Secretary of State for the Home Department, ex parte Oladehinde* [1990] 3 WLR 797. The applicants had been served with notices of intention to deport by immigration officers. The officers had been acting under the instructions of immigration inspectors to whom the function of making decisions to deport had been delegated by the Secretary of State. After appealing unsuccessfully to the adjudicator and the Immigration Appeal Tribunal, the applicants sought judicial review of the deportation decisions on the ground (inter alia) that the Secretary of State acted unlawfully in delegating his power of deportation under s3(5)(a) of the Immigration Act 1971 to immigration inspectors. The Divisional Court granted the application for review, quashing the deportation orders, on the grounds that it had been the intention of Parliament that the immigration officers should have a distinct function, that of controlling entry to the country, while the Secretary of State was to be concerned with decisions relating to the right to remain and deportation. The Court of Appeal allowed the Secretary of State's appeal. The House of Lords, dismissing the appeals, held that there was nothing in the wording of s3(5)(a) which appeared expressly or impliedly to limit the Secretary of State's power to delegate his function of ordering deportations. In the absence of any such statutory restrictions, the factors to which the court would have regard were the seniority of the officers to whom the power had been delegated, the possibility of any conflict with their other statutory duties, and whether they had fully considered the applicant's cases. In all these respects it was established that the Secretary of State had acted lawfully. Note that the Secretary of State had been careful to avoid any allegation of 'intermingling of functions' on the part of civil servants in the immigration service, by ensuring that the officials entrusted with the task of making the deportation orders had not been involved in the same cases as immigration officers.

Subject to a challenge on the grounds of irrationality, it is difficult to see how the delegation of functions by a secretary of state, even in relation to matters such as sentencing, could now be shown to be ultra vires. With regard to the task of reviewing the release date for prisoners serving life sentences, the House of Lords in *R v Secretary of State for the Home Office, ex parte Doody and Others* [1993] 3 All ER 92 expressly approved the comments of Staughton LJ. Noting that the Home Secretary had to deal, on average, with 130 mandatory life sentence cases each year, Staughton LJ rejected the contention that it would be improper for him delegate such a function. He observed:

> 'Parliament must be well aware of the great burden that is placed on senior ministers who not only take charge of their departments but also speak for them in Parliament, attend meetings of the Cabinet and its committees, and see to their constituency affairs ... I can see nothing irrational in the Secretary of State devolving [the consideration of minimum periods to be served by convicted murderers] upon junior ministers. They too are appointed by the Crown to hold office in the department, they have the same advice and assistance from departmental officials as the Secretary of State would have, and they too are answerable to Parliament.'

Local authorities have an increasingly large number of functions to perform, and the problems of having to deal with all matters at full council meetings is recognised by s101 of the Local Government Act 1972 which permits local authorities to arrange for the discharge of their functions by officers, committees, and even other local authorities, provided they reserve to themselves the right to exercise their powers if they so choose.

Even where the statutory power to delegate has not been invoked, the courts adopt an indulgent attitude to delegation by local authorities. In *Provident Mutual Life Assurance Association* v *Derby City Council* [1981] 1 WLR 173, the appellants challenged the validity of a rating notice issued by the respondent authority on the ground that it had been made by the authority's principal rating assistant, and not its Treasurer. In rejecting the appellant's contentions, Lord Roskill stated:

> 'My Lords, the statutory conditions precedent to the imposition of a fiscal liability must obviously be properly complied with ... but Parliament has conferred very wide powers on local authorities, and Parliament plainly contemplated that the actual machinery of enforcement and collection would not be operated personally by some senior local government official but would be so operated by the relevant senior official's staff.'

Administrative functions

To the extent that such classifications continue to be important, it can generally be said that the courts adopt a liberal approach to the delegation of administrative functions, typically preparatory work, because at that stage of the administrative process no rights are directly affected.

In *Jeffs* v *New Zealand Dairy Production and Marketing Board* [1967] 1 AC 551, the Privy Council held that the Board, which was concerned with determining applications for permission to grow produce in zoned areas, could delegate to a committee the function of collecting evidence relating to how it should act, at least where the credibility of witnesses was not in question; this was essentially an administrative matter.

Similarly, in *Selvarajan* v *Race Relations Board* [1976] 1 All ER 12 it was held that the investigative functions of the Board could be delegated to a committee, especially in the light of the fact that it was a body with a large number of members, and it would be unrealistic to expect it to discharge such functions at a full meeting.

In *Attorney-General, ex rel McWhirter* v *IBA* [1973] QB 621, the court accepted that, even though the Authority was under a statutory duty to satisfy itself that programmes were suitable for broadcast within the terms of its enabling Act, it was entirely proper for the task of viewing programmes to be carried out by its staff.

Judicial functions

It is with regard to judicial functions, more than any other type of activity, that the rule against delegation is strictly applied. Note that in *Jeffs* v *New Zealand Dairy Production and Marketing Board* (above) the Privy Council held that the actual determination of applications for zoning was a judicial function that could not be delegated.

Barnard v *National Dock Labour Board* [1953] 2 QB 18 provides a classic illustration of the principle being applied. Under the Dock Workers (Regulations) Order 1947 a National Dock Labour Board was established with the duty, inter alia, of delegating the administration of as many aspects of the scheme as possible to local boards. Among the functions delegated was the operation of a disciplinary code. Dock workers in London, who had been dismissed following a dispute about the unloading of raw sugar, sought a declaration that the dismissals were unlawful. Following discovery of documents it emerged that the local board had delegated its power of dismissal to the port manager. The Court of Appeal, granting the declaration sought, held that disciplinary functions, being judicial in nature because they affected persons' rights, could not be delegated. Lord Denning MR stated the matter thus:

> 'While an administrative function can often be delegated, a judicial function rarely can be. No judicial tribunal can delegate its functions unless it is enabled to do so expressly or by necessary implication.'

This decision was subsequently approved by the House of Lords in *Vine* v *National Dock Labour Board* [1957] AC 488, where similar disciplinary powers had been delegated by the local board to a disciplinary committee. Their Lordships emphasised that in determining the legality of delegation of functions, the court should consider the nature of the duty in question and the characteristics of the body on whom it is put.

A more recent reiteration of this principle was provided by *R* v *Gateshead Justices, ex parte Tesco Stores Ltd* [1981] 2 WLR 419. Under Rule 3 of the Justices' Clerks Rules 1970, the issuing of Court summonses could be delegated from a single justice to the justice's clerk. Tesco Stores applied for an order of certiorari to quash a summons issued against it on the ground that the justice's clerk in question had unlawfully delegated this function to court officers. The Divisional Court granted the applications for certiorari, holding that there was no power to delegate a judicial function and therefore, since under the Rules of 1970 only a clerk to the justices could exercise the judicial function of a justice of the peace to consider an information, the informations had not been laid before a person who was authorised to consider them, and the convictions would be quashed. As Donaldson LJ stated:

> '... the requirement that a justice of the peace or the clerk to the justices as a justice of the peace shall take personal responsibility for the proprietory of taking so serious a step as to require the attendance of a citizen before a criminal court, is a constitutional safeguard of fundamental importance. We have no doubt that this function is judicial.'

See further *R* v *DPP, ex parte Association of First Division Civil Servants* (1988) The Times 26 May.

18.3 Fettering discretion by adoption of a policy

Introduction

Inferior bodies vested with statutory powers are, in theory, supposed to consider each use of discretion in its own right, bearing in mind all relevant considerations. The price paid for giving such bodies discretion is inconsistency. The exercise of discretion is not governed by a system of precedent, so that a claimant denied a discretionary award cannot argue that in a previous similar application an award was made.

As a result, very many inferior bodies develop policies as to how discretion is to be exercised, thus promoting the twin goals of consistency and fairness because like cases are treated alike. A policy can be advertised in advance so that applicants will know what criteria are important, and tailor their cases accordingly.

Ideally, decision-makers following a particular policy should be willing to recognise those situations where an exception needs to be made and the policy departed from. It is by this means that a policy evolves, through application and experience. Although failure to comply with a stated policy is not necessarily unlawful (see *R* v *Avon County Council, ex parte Rexworthy* (1988) The Times 30 December), persons affected may have a legitimate expectation that a policy will be followed.

Further, a body may have to deal with numerous applications, and this task is made easier where cases can be processed by following policy guidelines. Problems arise, however, when a policy becomes a rule; that is, the inferior body regards itself rigidly bound by its own policy, and refuses to depart it from it.

Application of the rule

The leading decision is that of *R* v *Port of London Authority, ex parte Kynoch Ltd* [1919] 1 KB 176, where Kynoch Ltd applied to the Port of London Authority for a licence (under the Port of London Act 1908 s7 and the Thames Conservancy Act 1894 s10) to construct a deep-water wharf and other works on land they owned, on the bank of the Thames. The PLA rejected the application 'on the ground that the accommodation applied for is of the character of that which Parliament has charged the Authority with the duty of providing in the port'. Under the Port of London Act 1908 s2 the PLA was under a duty to take into consideration the state of the river and the accommodation and facilities afforded in the Port of London and, subject to the provisions of the Act, to take such steps as it considered necessary for improvement. Under s2(2) the PLA had power (inter alia) to 'construct, equip, maintain, or manage any docks, quays, wharves and other works in connection therewith.' Kynoch Ltd appealed to the Board of Trade against the PLA's decision but subsequently withdrew the appeal and applied instead for mandamus to compel the Authority to exercise its discretion according to law. The evidence included an affidavit showing that the merits of the application had been fully considered by two committees and the Authority itself.

The court held that the PLA acted lawfully in rejecting the application, because it had fully considered the arguments raised by Kynoch Ltd and rejected them on their merits. The vital point, in the view of Banks LJ, was that the decision-making body must not 'shut its ears' to an applicant who has something new to say. As he observed:

> 'There are on the one hand cases where a tribunal in the honest exercise of its discretion has adopted a policy, and without refusing to hear an applicant, intimates to him what its policy is, and that after hearing him it will in accordance with its policy decide against him, unless there is something exceptional in his case ... if the *policy* has been adopted for reasons which the tribunal may legitimately entertain, no objection could be taken to such a course. On the other hand there are cases where a tribunal has passed a *rule*, or come to a determination, not to hear any application of a particular character by whomsoever made. There is a wide distinction to be drawn between these two classes.'

In *British Oxygen Co Ltd* v *Minister of Technology* [1971] AC 610 the House of Lords introduced more flexibility into Banks LJ's dictum by pointing out that the legality of adopting a rule to govern the exercise of discretion would vary with the context within which decisions were made. A rule could be adopted provided that the decision-making body was still willing to listen to someone with something new to say. Lord Reid stated:

> 'I do not think there is any great difference between a policy and a rule ... What the authority must not do is refuse to listen at all. But a Ministry or large authority may have had to deal already with a multitude of similar applications and then they will almost certainly have evolved a policy so precise that it could well be called a rule.
>
> There can be no objection to that, provided the authority is always willing to listen to anyone with something new to say.'

An important factor in the House of Lords' decision was the large number of applications dealt with by the Ministry. In some ways the decision is contradictory, because on the one hand inferior bodies are allowed to have policies to help speed up their administrative processes while on the other they will still have to consider every case to see whether any applicant has anything new to say.

The correct way to approach the application of a policy to the exercise of discretion would be to ask two questions. First, has the inferior body listened to applicants with something new to say? If no, then it is acting *ultra vires*; if yes, then the second question must be asked: is the policy that has been applied *intra vires*? This would involve consideration of whether it was reasonable, based on relevant consideration, and so on.

See further *R* v *Tower Hamlets London Borough Council, ex parte Khalique* (1994) The Times 16 March, wherein the respondent authority's policy of regarding applications for housing from those more than £500 in arrears with payments of rent to the council as 'non-active', was declared unlawful on the basis that it went far beyond what was permissible in the adoption of a policy as considered in *British Oxygen*, not only because it prevented the applicant from putting his case, but also because the existence of rent arrears was extraneous to the discharge of the statutory duty to provide secure accommodation.

The importance of context

Under s1(1) Children and Young Persons Act 1963, local authorities were placed under a duty to promote children's welfare by providing advice, guidance and assistance in order to diminish the need to receive children into care under the Children Act 1948. The social services committee of a local authority passed a resolution that in cases where the housing department of the authority had determined that a family with young children were intentionally homeless, and the family subsequently approached the social services department, assistance with accommodation would not be provided under the provisions of the 1963 Act, although considerations would be given to receiving the children into care if the circumstances warranted it.

In *Attorney-General v Wandsworth London Borough Council, ex rel Tilley* [1981] 1 All ER 1162, the Attorney-General, in a relator action brought on behalf of a ratepayer and a member of the local authority's council, sought a declaration that the local authority resolution was invalid, as it amounted to a fetter on the discretion exercisable by the authority under s1(1) of the 1963 Act. The Court of Appeal, upholding the decision at first instance to grant the declaration sought, thought a strict policy was inappropriate where the welfare of children was at stake.

Templeman LJ stated:

'... a local authority, dealing with individual children, should not make a policy or an order that points towards fettering its discretion in such a way that the facilities offered to the child do not depend on the particular circumstances of that child or of its family but follow some policy which is expressed to apply in general cases.'

Similarly, in *Findlay* v *Secretary of State for the Home Department* [1984] 3 All ER 801 the House of Lords upheld the Home Secretary's policy of not considering certain categories of prisoner for parole unless they had served at least 20 years of their sentences. The House of Lords held that he was entitled to have a policy regarding the exercise of his discretion to grant parole, since it would be difficult for him to manage the complexities of his statutory duties in regard to parole without a policy. Furthermore, consideration of an individual case was not excluded by a policy which provided that exceptional circumstances or compelling reasons had to be shown for parole because of the weight attached to the nature of the offence, the length of the sentence and the factors of deterrence, retribution and public confidence, all of which it was the duty of the Secretary of State to consider. Accordingly, the new policy was lawful.

Natural justice

An interesting development is the link between fettering discretion by adoption of an over-rigid policy and denial of a fair hearing. The equation is a simple one; by refusing to consider representations from an individual who may have something new to say, the decision-making body has denied him the right to be heard.

An example is provided by *R* v *Secretary of State for the Environment, ex parte Brent London Borough Council* [1982] 2 WLR 693, where the Divisional Court held that the Secretary of State had acted ultra vires in refusing to hear representations from local authorities who were about to suffer a significant loss of rate support grant as a result of his policy on 'overspending' authorities. In refusing to hear what they might have to say, he was denying the authorities a fair hearing on a matter of considerable importance to them. Consider, on the same approach, *John* v *Rees* [1970] Ch 345 and *R* v *Police Complaints Board, ex parte Madden* [1983] 2 All ER 353.

19

Fettering Discretion – Contract and Estoppel

19.1 Fettering discretion by contract

19.2 Estoppel

19.1 Fettering discretion by contract

Introduction

Many statutory bodies like local authorities have to be able to enter into contracts in order to function properly. Every contract entered into will, to some small degree, fetter the freedom of the body concerned, because it then commits it to a particular course of action, and invariably involves the allocation of limited resources to finance the contract. Given that every contract, therefore, involves some fetter on discretion, the problem is a matter of degree. To what extent can a body contract not to use its powers in a particular way?

A second problem is one of incompatibility. Certain contractual undertakings will be inconsistent with the purposes for which the body was set up, and for that reason ultra vires.

A contract found to be ultra vires a local authority is unenforceable. Section 9 of the European Communities Act 1972 does not apply to statutory authorities.

The problem of incompatibility

When trying to discern whether or not a contractual undertaking is incompatible with the status of a statutory body, regard must be had to the aims and objects of the enabling Act.

In *Ayr Harbour Trustees* v *Oswald* (1883) 8 App Cas 623, the Trustees were appointed under the Ayr Harbour Act 1879 for the management and improvement of the harbour and were empowered to take certain lands (including Oswald's) for this purpose. In order to reduce the amount of compensation payable to Oswald on taking this land the trustees agreed that the conveyance of the land should restrict their use of it so as not to interfere with access from Oswald's remaining land to the harbour. Oswald did not agree with this course of action and brought an action for a declaration that the trustees had to purchase the land absolutely. The House of Lords, affirming the decision of the Court of Session, held that the trustees had the power under the Act of 1879 then or at any time in the future to modify the land taken so as to destroy any access from Oswald's land to the harbour and that the trustees were not competent to dispense with the future exercise of their powers by themselves or their successors. The trustees had been given the powers of compulsory purchase so that they might be able to develop the harbour and surrounding land in the public interest, without having to defer to the private interests of individuals. An agreement to grant access to the land being acquired would be totally incompatible with the purpose for which the trustees had been vested with these powers. By contrast, in *Stourcliffe Estates* v *Bournemouth Corporation* [1910] 2 Ch 12 the defendant local authority unsuccessfully tried to argue that it was not bound by a covenant, entered into when it purchased park land from the plaintiffs, to the effect that it would not carry out any building work on the land. The plaintiffs applied for an injunction to prevent the local authority from building public conveniences on the land, and the Court of Appeal held the covenant to be valid. The situation was unlike the *Ayr Harbour Trustees* case, as it could not be said that a promise not to build on land was contrary to the purpose for which the local authority had been created; its functions were many and varied. For a more contemporary version of the *Ayr Harbour* problem, see *Triggs* v *Staines Urban District Council* [1969] 1 Ch 10 where the court held that an agreement by a local authority not to use its powers of compulsory purchase in respect of a particular piece of land for a specified period was clearly incompatible with the authority's duty to retain its full planning powers to be used in the public interest.

Where a public body enters into what is essentially a normal commercial contract, the courts will not permit that body to plead the fettering of discretion principle in order for it to be released from its obligations. The decision of the House of Lords in *Birkdale District Electric Supply Co Ltd* v *Southport Corporation* [1926] AC 355 is instructive. In 1901 the company, a statutory body, took over the local electricity supply from Birkdale Urban District Council and agreed, under seal, that the prices charged by it to private customers should not exceed those charged in an adjoining area by Southport Corporation. In 1911 Birkdale Urban District Council became a part of Southport Corporation. The company continued to supply electricity to the area. In 1923, the Corporation applied for an injunction to restrain the company from charging prices in excess of the Southport prices. The company argued that since it had a statutory power to charge what it wished, within certain limits, the 1901 agreement was invalid as an unlawful fetter on the exercise of this discretion. The House of Lords held that, far from being an unlawful fetter on the statutory body's discretion, the agreement was of a type that was commonly entered into by commercial bodies. The case could only begin to be equated with *Ayr Harbour Trustees* v *Oswald* if the statutory body had, for example, entered into a contract not to generate electricity. In *Dowty Boulton Paul Ltd* v *Wolverhampton Corporation*

[1971] 1 WLR 204 the local authority, having leased land to the plaintiff company in 1935 for 99 years, decided in 1970 that it wanted to repossess the land in order to build housing. The plaintiff company argued that the lease was a valid contractual undertaking by which the local authority was bound. The court agreed, describing the suggestion of the local authority that the lease was subject to an implied condition enabling it to determine the lease at will as 'startling'.

A local authority may not be bound by a commercial undertaking which, while not being incompatible with its other functions, goes too far in committing it to a particular course of action. In *York Corporation* v *Henry Leetham & Sons Ltd* [1924] 1 Ch 557 the plaintiff Corporation was entrusted by statute with the control of navigation in parts of the rivers Ouse and Foss, with power to charge such tolls, within limits, as the Corporation deemed necessary to carry on the two navigations in which the public had an interest. The Corporation made two contracts with the defendants under which they agreed to accept, in consideration of the right to navigate the Ouse, a regular annual payment of £600 per annum in place of the authorised tolls. The agreements, which were perpetually renewable at the request of the defendants, were held by Russell J to be ultra vires, and thus void, because they purported to disable the Corporation, whatever emergency might arise, from exercising its statutory powers to increase tolls as from time to time might be necessary.

Furthermore, a local authority cannot, by means of a commercial contractual undertaking, be prevented from exercising its legislative powers in the public interest. In *William Cory & Sons Ltd* v *London Corporation* [1951] 2 KB 476, the authority had entered into an agreement with the plaintiff company under which refuse would be transported in barges down the Thames. When the contract still had twenty years to run, the Corporation passed new bye-laws introducing more rigorous hygiene controls over refuse carried in open barges. The effect was to make the contract less profitable because modifications had to be made to the barges used by the plaintiffs in performance of the contract. The court held that it could not imply a term into the agreement to the effect that the Corporation would refrain from enacting legislation making the contract more onerous to perform. Such a term would have clearly been ultra vires.

Ultimately the courts are engaged in a balancing exercise, weighing the aims and objects of the relevant legislation, on the one hand, with the need to ensure that public bodies have sufficient freedom to act as they think fit on the other. *R* v *Hammersmith and Fulham London Borough Council, ex parte Beddowes* [1987] 2 WLR 263 provides an excellent example of how controversial the courts' assessment of where the balance lies can be. The Court of Appeal upheld, by a majority, negative covenants entered into by the council which prevented it from re-letting council flats to council tenants when they fell empty. The purpose of the covenants was to encourage owner-occupation of blocks of flats on derelict council estates. Fox LJ stated that the council's housing duty had to be considered in the light of the 'right to buy' legislation that had recently been introduced. His Lordship felt that this legislation indicated that a local authority might discharge its housing function by encouraging owner-occupation as well as by acting as a landlord, and that the courts had to be sympathetic to the efforts of a local authority attempting to take radical action to deal with a 'problem estate'. Hence the court held that the covenants did not amount to an unlawful fetter on the council's discretion, in that they were not incompatible with its housing powers and duties.

19.2 Estoppel

Reliance on estoppel to prevent a statutory body from exercising its public law powers gives rise to a particular difficulty in administrative law. An inferior body makes a promise to act in a particular way. The promisee relies on this statement and in most cases acts to his detriment on the strength of it. It is then discovered that what has been promised is beyond the power of the inferior body. The choice for the courts is a stark one between adherence to the ultra vires principle and unfairness to the promisee on the one hand, and holding that the inferior body is estopped from going back on its promise and in fact ordering it to act beyond its powers on the other.

Two situations may arise, both variants on the same theme: the first where the administrative body purports to exercise a power it simply does not possess, and the second where the body does possess the power, but promises to use it in a manner that would be ultra vires.

Where no power exists

The basic principle here is that estoppel cannot operate so as to enable an authority to do that which it lacks the power to do, otherwise inferior bodies could acquire limitless jurisdiction by making promises to carry out acts beyond their powers.

In *Balbir Singh* v *Secretary of State for the Home Department* (1978) Imm AR 204, it was held that an immigrant did not acquire the right to appeal against a tribunal's decision simply because the Secretary of State's statement said that such a right existed. The right of appeal could only be provided by statute, and it was clearly beyond the powers of the Minister to confer such a right. Similarly in *Islington Vestry* v *Hornsey Urban District Council* [1900] 1 Ch 695, a local authority which had permitted a neighbouring authority to use its sewers, despite the absence of any power to allow this, was not estopped from terminating this use, despite the reliance of the plaintiffs.

Where power does exist

The alternative problem arises where an inferior body does possess a power (eg to grant planning permission) but promises to use that power in a manner that would

be ultra vires. *Southend-on-Sea Corporation* v *Hodgson (Wickford) Ltd* [1962] 1 QB
416 provides an example. The company wished to buy land for use as a builders'
yard, and after making inquiries was assured by the local authority surveyor that
planning permission was not needed for such a use because of existing use rights.
The company purchased the land, and started to use it as a builders' yard, only to
be served with an enforcement notice ordering it to stop such use, the local planning
authority claiming that planning permission had not been granted. The Divisional
Court held that the local authority could not be estopped from issuing an
enforcement notice by the surveyor's assurances, as this would be to prevent it from
using its powers for the benefit of its inhabitants generally. The decision represents
the traditional approach of strict adherence to the ultra vires principle. The
unauthorised representation of an official cannot bind an inferior body to act beyond
its powers, or to refrain from performing a statutory duty or exercising its discretion
in the public interest.

Notwithstanding the clear statement of principle that the decision represented, a
number of decisions during the late 1960s and 1970s suggested a more indulgent
approach. For example, in *Wells* v *MHLG* [1967] 2 All ER 1041 the plaintiff applied
for planning permission, and received a letter from the local authority's surveyor stating
that permission was not required for the development proposed. The building work
was carried out by Wells, and evoked complaints from neighbours about its effect on
the area. The local authority thereupon served an enforcement notice upon Wells
claiming that he did not have planning permission for the works. The Court of Appeal
held that although the precise statutory procedure had not been followed, the letter
from the surveyor amounted to a determination by the authority that planning
permission was not necessary under s53 Town and Country Planning Act 1971. The
decision is clear authority for the view that a statutory body cannot waive minor
procedural requirements, and then claim that it is not obliged to abide by its
undertakings because precise statutory procedural requirements have not been followed.

In *Lever Finance Ltd* v *Westminster (City) London Borough Council* [1971] 1 QB
222 the company was granted planning permission to build a group of houses which,
according to the plans, showed the development as being at least 40ft away from the
nearest existing building. During the course of construction, minor modifications
were made to the plans, and on each occasion the local authority planning officer
gave his approval 'on the nod' (ie informally). When the development was nearing
completion it became obvious that the sum total of the 'minor' modifications was
considerable. The new houses were now only 23ft away from the nearest existing
buildings. Neighbours complained, and the company was advised to apply for formal
planning permission for the changes. This was refused by the local authority. The
company sought a declaration that it was entitled to continue with the work, the
local authority being estopped by the actions of its planning officer. The Court of
Appeal held that in the light of the fact that it was common practice for the
planning officers to agree minor modifications to planning permission already

granted, and that the company had acted to its detriment on the strength of his statement, the local authority would be bound by its officer's decision. The Court of Appeal clearly considered it unfair that a member of the public might not otherwise be able to rely on statements made by council officers within the scope of their ostensible authority. But consider also the damage done to the interests of neighbouring landowners. By upholding an estoppel, the Court of Appeal prevented the local authority from exercising its planning powers in the best interest of its area and inhabitants.

The present position

For the moment, the correct position as regards the issue of estoppel and statutory bodies is provided by the Court of Appeal decision in *Western Fish Products Ltd* v *Penwith District Council* [1981] 2 All ER 204. In April 1976 the plaintiffs purchased a site that had previously been used for food processing, intending to develop the site for similar purposes. The chairman of the plaintiff company, in reply to his enquiries, received a letter from a planning officer of the defendant authority stating that the site had existing use rights for the various food processes the plaintiffs intended to carry out. As a result the plaintiff company carried out extensive work on the site, renovating and modifying the factory buildings thereon. Some months later the plaintiffs were asked to apply for planning permission for this work. At a full council meeting this application was rejected, and enforcement notices were issued. The plaintiffs then sought declarations that the defendant authority was not entitled to issue the enforcement notices in the light of its planning officer's statement. The Court of Appeal upheld the decision of the court below to dismiss the action.

In the course of his decision Megaw LJ confirmed that the council's officers could not bind the authority by purporting to take decisions that only the council itself could take. To hold otherwise would be to run counter to the accepted principle that an estoppel could not be raised to prevent the exercise of a statutory discretion or to prevent or excuse the performance of a statutory duty. A local authority could, by s101 Local Government Act 1972, arrange for the discharge of its functions by, inter alia, its officers, but this had to be formally agreed within the authority. In the *Western Fish* case, the function of determining applications for planning permission had not been delegated to planning officers, and his Lordship saw no reason why the plaintiffs should ever have thought that the council's planning officer could bind the authority by anything said or written in this regard. Where a planning officer acts within the scope of the power properly delegated to him his actions will bind the authority for whom he acts, but beyond that it could not be said that an authority would be bound by the actions of its officers, simply because they acted within the scope of their ostensible authority (that is to say, the officers appeared to be entitled to take such decisions). In his Lordship's view, for estoppel to arise in this situation:

'... there must be some evidence justifying the person dealing with the planning officer for thinking that what the officer said would bind the planning authority. Holding an office, however senior, cannot, in our judgment, be enough by itself.'

The evidence required could be of a previous course of conduct whereby officers had in the past carried out functions on behalf of the local authority, with the authority's knowledge and approval, despite the formal delegation of functions not having been carried out. In the case of Penwith District Council, there was no evidence to suggest that the planning officer could determine applications for planning permission.

One other situation in which an estoppel may be upheld arises where, for example, a planning authority waives a (directory) procedural requirement. As in *Wells* v *MHLG* (above), the authority will not be allowed to claim later that a grant of permission, or other determination, is invalid on these grounds. See further the House of Lords' decision in *Gowa* v *Attorney-General* [1985] 1 WLR 1003, where the Crown was estopped from denying the applicant's status as a British citizen even though it had been granted in error by a colonial governor empowered to deal with such matters, and see *Minister of Agriculture and Fisheries* v *Hulkin* (unreported), cited in *Minister of Agriculture and Fisheries* v *Matthews* [1950] KB 148 at 153–154.

While the courts have been willing to recognise the operation of estoppel in only a very limited range of situations in public law, an applicant may seek to attack the procedure adopted on the grounds of breach of natural justice. In *R* v *Liverpool Corporation, ex parte LTFOA* [1972] 2 QB 299 Lord Denning MR was of the view that a local authority should be bound by a public undertaking given to taxi drivers within its area to the effect that only a limited number of new taxi licences would be granted, regarding the obligation to abide by the undertaking as virtually contractual. While there is, in reality, no contractual relationship, it might now be contended that to depart from a publicly declared course of action, without first consulting those likely to be affected would be unlawful. In short, the issue of legitimate expectation may need to be considered; see the Privy Council decision in *Attorney-General of Hong Kong* v *Ng Yuen Shiu* [1983] 2 AC 629 and comments of Taylor LJ in *R* v *Secretary of State for Health, ex parte United States Tobacco International Inc* [1991] 3 WLR 529.

20

Remedies

20.1 Introduction

Prior to the introduction of O.53 and the application for judicial review, litigants seeking to challenge the decisions of public bodies would have had to proceed by way of action in order to obtain a declaration, an injunction or damages, or would have had to apply for one of the public law remedies, the prerogative orders of mandamus, prohibition or certiorari. One of the major changes introduced by the reforms of 1977 was that, for the first time, all six remedies became available to an applicant seeking judicial review of administrative action. In theory, even after 1977, a litigant could chose between proceeding by way of action for a declaration that a public body had acted unlawfully, and applying for judicial review under O.53. As has been explained in Chapter 11, however, the effect of *O'Reilly* v *Mackman* has been to force litigants to use the application for judicial review where the respondent is a public body and the issue in the case is primarily one of public law. The purpose of this chapter is, therefore, to examine both the availability of the six remedies on an application for review and what those remedies can achieve.

When considering the issue of remedies by way of judicial review, it is important to bear in mind that the court has an enormous discretion as regards the granting of relief. Even if a prima facie case of ultra vires action has been made out, the court may be reluctant to act if it is of the view that the applicant is 'undeserving' (*Ward* v *Bradford Corporation* (1972) 70 LGR 27; *Cinnamond* v *British Airports Authority* [1980] 1 WLR 582), has delayed unduly before coming to the court (*Glynn* v *Keele University* [1971] 1 WLR 487) or if Parliament has provided a statutory procedure for the provision of remedies. In *R* v *Chief Adjudication Officer, ex parte Bland* (1985) The Times 6 February, Taylor J held that judicial review would not be available as an alternative to a specialised statutory system of appeals unless special reasons for not using the statutory procedure were advanced: see further *R* v *Paddington Valuation Officer, ex parte Peachey Property Corporation* [1966] 1 QB 380 at 400 and *R* v *Epping and Harlow General Commissioners, ex parte Goldstraw* [1983] 3 All ER 257.

20.2 Injunction

An injunction is an order of the court directed at a defendant or respondent, ordering that party not to proceed with a particular action or, in the case of a mandatory injunction, to act in a particular way. In private law proceedings it is an equitable remedy that will only be granted where damages would not provide sufficient relief. Subject to the provisions of s21 of the Crown Proceedings Act 1947, considered in Chapter 4, an injunction is available against the servants of the Crown acting in a personal capacity, where the plaintiff seeks to protect some private law right: see *Raleigh* v *Goschen* [1898] 1 Ch 73 and *Ellis* v *Earl Grey* (1833) 6 Sim 214. Given that proceedings under O.53 must involve a public body and an issue of public law, the question arises as to when, if ever, an injunction would be available against a minister of the Crown on an application for review. Although the term 'injunction' is used here to refer to a final order of the court, it will be appreciated that in proceedings for review the applicant will probably be seeking interlocutory relief, in the form of an interim injunction, to prevent the minister from taking executive action, pending the determination of the issue by the court. As regards final conclusive orders, an order of prohibition would have the same effect as a traditional injunction, and an order of mandamus the same effect as a mandatory injunction. The matter has caused considerable difficulty and has been considered recently on two occasions by the House of Lords: in *Factortame Ltd* v *Secretary of State for Transport* [1989] 2 WLR 997 (and when considering a reference back by the European Court of Justice in *Factortame Ltd* v *Secretary of State for Transport (No 2)* [1990] 3 WLR 818) and *M* v *Home Office* [1993] 3 All ER 537. Although the later of these two cases now represents the law, it is instructive to examine both in order to understand how the issue arose.

Factortame

As part of its common fisheries policy, fishing quotas were introduced by the EC to prevent over-fishing. The United Kingdom Parliament enacted the Merchant Shipping Act 1988 (Part II) to protect British fishing interests by restricting the number of vessels whose catch could be counted against the British quota. The Secretary of State for Transport issued regulations under the Act that required any vessel wishing to fish as part of the British fleet to be registered under the 1988 Act. Registration was contingent upon a vessel's owner being a British citizen or domiciled in Britain. Where the vessels were owned by companies, the shareholders would have to meet these requirements. The applicants were British registered companies operating fishing vessels in British waters. These companies now found it impossible to obtain registration because their shareholders and directors were Spanish. The applicants contended that the regulations effectively prevented them from exercising their rights under Community law to fish as part of the British fleet. The Secretary of State contended that Community law did not prevent the United Kingdom from introducing domestic legislation determining which companies were 'British nationals' and which were not.

The applicants sought judicial review of the Minister's decision that their registration should cease, of his determination that their vessels were no longer 'British' ships, and of the relevant parts of the Act and Regulations which would have the effect of preventing them from fishing. As to remedies, the applicants sought, inter alia, an interim injunction suspending the operation of the legislation pending the ruling of the European Court of Justice as to its compatibility with EC law. As regards the interpretation of Community law, the Divisional Court requested a preliminary ruling under Art 177 of the Treaty of Rome so that the questions relating to the applicants' rights could be resolved. Pending that ruling, the court granted the applicants interim relief in the form of an injunction to suspend the operation of the legislation by restraining the Minister from enforcing it, thus enabling the applicants to continue fishing. The Secretary of State challenged the order for interim relief, which was set aside by the Court of Appeal. The applicants appealed unsuccessfully to the House of Lords, their Lordships holding that an English court had no power to grant interim relief to prevent the operation of a statute passed by Parliament.

Lord Bridge put forward two grounds for denying the remedy. First, if the ultimate decision of the European Court of Justice went against the applicants they would have enjoyed approximately two years' (the length of time it would take for that court to resolve the matter) unjust enrichment by being allowed to continue fishing. On that basis no interim relief would be given, unless it was shown that there was some overriding principle of Community law which provided that Member States should provide some form of relief to litigants who claimed that their rights were being interfered with, pending a decision of the European Court of Justice. Secondly, Lord Bridge sought to deny the availability of the relief sought by reference to ss21(2) and 23(2)(b) of the Crown Proceedings Act 1947, holding that these provisions preserved what had been the common law position, that is, that such relief was not available in judicial review proceedings on the Crown side. Lord Bridge expressed the view that it was not surprising that the Crown Proceedings Act 1947 did not expressly state that injunctions were not available in proceedings on the Crown side of the Queen's Bench Division; they had not been before 1947, so why should the statute have bothered to re-state the existing law? His Lordship drew support for his analysis from the fact that the Law Commission, in its *Report on Remedies in Administrative Law* (Law Com No 73) (Cmnd 6407), had looked at the problem of obtaining an interim injunction by way of an application for judicial review, and had assumed that, given s21 of the 1947 Act, such an order would not be possible. The Law Commission had drafted an amended s21 which it appended to its Report, but as O.53 was concerned with procedure and practice it would have been outside the jurisdiction of the Rules Committee to institute such a far-reaching change by way of delegated legislation, and the change was therefore not adopted. In arriving at these conclusions Lord Bridge expressly rejected the reasoning in two earlier decisions, *R* v *Secretary of State for the Home Department, ex parte Herbage* [1987] 1 QB 872 and *R* v *Licensing Authority, ex parte Smith Kline & French Laboratories Ltd (No 2)* [1990] 1 QB 574. The question of whether or not EC law required the provision of such an interim form of relief was referred by the House of Lords to the European Court of Justice under Art 177.

By way of response, the European Court of Justice held that Community law did require the courts of Member States to give effect to the directly enforceable provisions of Community law, such Community laws rendering any conflicting national law inapplicable. A court which would grant interim relief but for a rule of domestic law should set aside that rule of domestic law in favour of observing Community obligations. When the matter returned to the House of Lords, therefore, the question for consideration was no longer that of whether or not relief was available in principle, but that of whether or not it should be granted in this particular case. The House took the view that the determining factor should be not the availability of damages as a remedy but the balance of convenience, taking into account the importance of upholding duly enacted laws. It noted that damages were not available against a public body exercising its powers in good faith, and expressed the view that a domestic court should not restrain a public authority from enforcing an apparently valid law unless it was satisfied, having regard to all the circumstances, that the challenge to the validity of the law was, prima facie, so firmly based as to justify so exceptional a course being taken. As regards the Spanish trawlermen, it was felt that the applicants did have a strong case for relief being granted, particularly with regard to the provisions requiring residence and domicile of owners. The balance of convenience was found to favour the granting of such relief.

The effect of the ruling would seem to be that the courts can now effectively prevent the application of the provisions of an Act of Parliament, where adherence to it appears to result in a violation of rights protected by Community law, by granting orders to prohibit ministers from exercising powers necessary to implement the legislation. Some care should be exercised in drawing the distinction between the courts preventing a minister from exercising his statutory powers, which is effectively the result of the relief granted in the present case, and the invalidation of an Act of Parliament, which would be quite a different matter. Where the European Court of Justice finds domestic legislation to be inconsistent with Community law, it is for the legislature to take the necessary remedial steps if it so wishes.

As matters stood following the two House of Lords' rulings in *Factortame*, therefore, an applicant seeking to challenge a right protected under Community law would be able to obtain interim injunctive relief against a minister, but, according to Lord Bridge, s21 of the Crown Proceedings Act would prohibit the granting of such relief if the case was one solely concerned with domestic law.

M v Home Office

In *M* v *Home Office* [1992] 2 WLR 73 the applicant, M, had arrived in the United Kingdom from Zaire seeking political asylum, but was not granted permission to remain following the Home Secretary's finding that M had not established the required 'well grounded fear of persecution' in Zaire. M was due to be returned to Zaire on 1 May 1991, the flight leaving London at 6.30pm. Judicial review proceedings to challenge the Secretary of State's decision on asylum were heard on 1 May, and at 5.55pm Garland J indicated that, as in his view there was an arguable case to be considered, M should not be removed from the country until there had been a full hearing of the case. Counsel for the Home Office indicated that the department would seek to prevent M's removal from the country, although he had not been instructed to give an undertaking that M's removal would be prevented. M did depart on the flight to Zaire, and later that evening the judge granted a mandatory order compelling the Home Office to ensure the return of M to the United Kingdom. The Home Secretary declined to obey the order and instead challenged its validity in the courts. During these proceedings Garland J accepted that he did not have the power to issue what amounted to mandatory injunctions against ministers, but suggested that he had been seeking to ensure compliance with the earlier undertaking given by counsel for the Secretary of State to the effect that the judicial review proceedings would not be rendered otiose by M's removal from the jurisdiction. M brought proceedings for contempt against the Secretary of State based on his failure to comply with the court's order while it had been in force. The applicant's motion was dismissed at first instance, but he was partly successful before the Court of Appeal. The House of Lords held, inter alia, that s31 of the Supreme Court Act 1981 empowered the courts to grant coercive orders against a minister of the Crown acting in his official capacity. In particular, RSC O.53 r.3(10) empowered the court to grant an interim injunction against a minister. To this extent the decision goes some way to resolving the confusion generated by *Factortame* regarding the availability of injunctive relief against ministers.

Lord Woolf, in a closely argued speech, found himself unable to agree with the reasoning that had led Lord Bridge to conclude that interim injunctive relief was, subject to the demands of Community law, not available in respect of ministers of the Crown acting in an official capacity because of s21 of the 1947 Act. He expressed the view that the purpose of s21 had been to prevent any extension of the availability of injunctive relief against the Crown to circumstances where it had not been available prior to 1947. The 1947 Act did not affect the right of an individual to seek injunctive relief against an individual Crown servant, acting in his official capacity. In particular, he was persuaded by the argument that, by virtue of s38(2) of the 1947 Act, s21 had not been intended by Parliament to apply to proceedings on the Crown side of the Queen's Bench Division, and proceedings for the prerogative orders were brought on the Crown side. The prerogative orders had never been available against the Crown, so when s31(2) of the Supreme Court Act 1981 extended the prerogative jurisdiction to include the granting of injunctions, including interim injunctions, by way of judicial review proceedings it was not creating a conflict with s21 of the 1947 Act (that is it did not create the possibility of injunctions being granted against the Crown where previously they had not been). Even prior to 1947, however, it had been recognised that the prerogative orders were available in respect of a minister of the Crown acting in an official capacity. Hence the effect of s31(2) was to make injunctive relief available in situations where there was jurisdiction to grant a prerogative order, although in Lord Woolf's view the power to do so should be exercised sparingly. Furthermore, there was no serious doubt as to the availability of declaratory relief by way of O.53 against a minister acting his official capacity. If a declaration was now available in such cases it would be curious if an (interim) injunction was not.

As indicated in Chapters 3 and 4, some doubt may still surround the availability of injunctive relief where what is challenged is an exercise of (delegated) prerogative power. Traditionally the relief granted in such cases has been declaratory, on the basis that it would be incongruous to grant a prerogative order against the Crown. Lord Woolf specifically relies on the argument that, since injunctions and the prerogative orders are now available via the same procedure, the courts should have the jurisdiction to grant an injunction wherever they have the jurisdiction to grant a prerogative order. If, therefore, the courts have declined in the past to grant prerogative orders in respect of the exercise of prerogative power, congruity would suggest that the courts would also decline to grant injunctive relief. Lord Woolf comments in *M* v *Home Office* that, in the light of the *GCHQ* case:

> '... a distinction probably no longer has to be drawn between duties which have a statutory and those which have a prerogative source'.

Note that in the *GCHQ* case, however, the applicants originally sought an order of certiorari to quash the Prime Minister's instruction on union membership, but at the first hearing this was amended to become a request for declaratory relief. The remedy sought in both *R* v *Criminal Injuries Compensation Board, ex parte Lain* [1967] 2 QB 864 and *R* v *Secretary of State for the Foreign and Commonwealth Office, ex parte Everett* [1989] 2 WLR 224 was an order of certiorari, but it could be contended that both cases involved the exercise of delegated prerogative power, where the decision-maker has to act within the terms of the delegation. If a minister exercising prerogative power is to be regarded as being amenable to the prerogative orders, it raises the question of when, if ever, action is taken by the Crown as such. The Crown, other than when the monarch acts in person, can only act via its ministers.

The issue is not entirely academic, as difficulties could arise with regard to a challenge to the creation of regulations by way of Order in Council. Would the courts be willing to grant interim relief to prevent this exercise of prerogative power?

Apart from the issue of injunctive relief, the courts may, in any event, be able to achieve much the same result by granting a stay of proceedings. In *R* v *Secretary of State for Education and Science, ex parte Avon County Council* [1991] 2 WLR 702 the Court of Appeal expressed the view that, under O.53 r.3(10)(a), the term 'proceedings' should be construed widely so as to encompass the procedures by which administrative bodies arrived at their decisions: see further *R* v *Secretary of State for the Home Department, ex parte Muboyayi* [1992] QB 244 and *R* v *Inspectorate of Pollution, ex parte Greenpeace Ltd* [1994] 4 All ER 321.

20.3 Declaration

A declaration is an order of the court stating the legal position between two parties, and can be sought to provide some clarification on a disputed point of law: see *Attorney-General* v *Able* [1984] 1 All ER 277. Although it has no coercive force, and refusal to act in accordance with a declaration will not be a contempt, a public body is most unlikely to ignore the implications of any declaratory relief granted by the courts: see *Webster* v *Southwark London Borough Council* [1983] QB 698. The declaration is a particularly flexible remedy as regards the challenging of executive action. In theory it permits the citizen to question proposed executive action rather than wait for it to happen and attempt to have it quashed. In *Dyson* v *Attorney-General* [1911] QB 410 and [1912] 1 Ch 158 the court held that it was permissible for the plaintiff to question the validity of tax assessment notices (on the ground that they were ultra vires the enabling Act) prior to the notices being issued, rather than having to dispute the claim for tax when made: see further *Gillick* v *West Norfolk and Wisbech Area Health Authority* [1986] AC 112. Reliance on a declaration in a case involving a challenge to the exercise of prerogative powers might also avoid the problems adverted to above, as to whether or not the prerogative orders are available in respect of such action. Any doubt as to whether declaratory relief can be obtained in situations where prerogative orders cannot has been resolved by the House of Lords' decision in *R* v *Secretary of State for Employment, ex parte Equal Opportunities Commission and Another* [1994] 2 WLR 409. The Commission made representations to the Secretary of State to the effect that existing domestic law relating to redundancy and unfair dismissal was contrary to EC law as it indirectly discriminated against female employees by offering reduced protection to part-time workers. The Secretary of State rejected these assertions, whereupon the Commission thereupon applied for judicial review (seeking a declaration and an order of mandamus) of the Secretary of State's decision not to act in this matter, with a view to challenging the differential in the qualifying dates for redundancy compensation and a declaration and order of mandamus in respect of Secretary of

State's failure to amend the law to take into account an earlier period of full-time employment in calculating the amount of redundancy payment due. A majority of their Lordships held that even though the case was not one where the court would have been empowered to grant a prerogative order, as there was no 'decision' of the Secretary of State to quash, reference to the *Factortame* series of cases confirmed that the Commission was entitled to apply for a declaration as to the extent to which the provisions of the 1978 Act relating to redundancy and compensation for unfair dismissal were compatible with Community law. Such an application would not involve a declaration that the United Kingdom or the Secretary of State was in breach of Community obligations, as the Commission's purpose could be served simply by a declaration confirming the incompatibility of domestic law and Community law. Lord Browne-Wilkinson in particular charted the history of declaratory relief, and observed that if the availability of declaratory relief was co-terminus with the availability of the prerogative remedies litigants would have been seriously disadvantaged by decisions such as *O'Reilly* v *Mackman*. As he stated:

> '... under O.53 any declaration as to public rights which could formerly be obtained in civil proceedings in the High Court can now also be obtained in judicial review proceedings. If this were not so, the effect of the purely procedural decision in *O'Reilly* v *Mackman*, requiring all public law cases to be brought by way of judicial review, would have had the effect of thenceforward preventing a plaintiff who previously had locus standi to bring civil proceedings for a declaration as to public rights (even though there was no decision which could be the subject of a prerogative order) from bringing any proceedings for such a declaration. No statutory provision has ever removed the right to seek such a declaration ... O.53 r.1(2) does not say that a declaration is only to be made in lieu of a prerogative order. All it requires is that the court should have regard to "the nature of the matters in respect of which" prerogative orders can be made.'

Availability

In theory the applicant for a declaration need not have any subsisting cause of action, but as Lord Diplock observed in *Gouriet* v *Union of Post Office Workers* [1978] AC 435:

> '... the jurisdiction of the court is not to declare the law generally or give advisory opinions; it is confined to declaring contested legal rights, subsisting or future, of the parties represented in the litigation before it'.

Thus in *Malone* v *Metropolitan Police Commissioner* [1979] Ch 344, where the plaintiff sought a declaration that the tapping of his telephone by the police constituted an invasion of his right to privacy, as enshrined in the European Convention of Human Rights, the Vice-Chancellor refused to grant the declaration sought because, in his view, the case did not raise any issues concerning rights protected by English law. He expressed the view that it would have been an unwarranted usurpation of the functions of the legislature for him to have laid down any legal principles applicable to this matter. In *Gillick* v *West Norfolk Area Health Authority* (above), Lord Bridge observed that the court should exercise the 'utmost restraint' in granting a remedy by way of a declaration. It should certainly not exercise its jurisdiction to grant the remedy if there was some other equally convenient remedy available to the applicant. This reasoning was cited with approval by Woolf J in *R* v *Secretary of State for the Environment, ex parte Greater London Council* (1985) The Times 30 December, where his Lordship expressed the view that the power to grant declarations should not be used merely as a means of improving the reasoning for decisions of administrative bodies where a decision itself was unobjectionable.

A declaration will not be granted where there is no longer a live issue in the case. In *Williams* v *Home Office (No 2)* [1982] 1 All ER 1151 a prisoner who had been transferred to a special control unit sought a declaration that his transfer had been in breach of natural justice, as he had not committed any offences against prison discipline, and had not been told of the reasons for the transfer. By the time the matter reached the court, however, the prisoner had been returned to his usual cell. The court refused to grant the declaration sought on the basis that the matter was now only of 'academic' interest. In the same spirit, the courts will refuse a declaration if the issues involved do not raise the possibility of any legal consequence. Hence in *Maxwell* v *Department of Trade and Industry* [1974] QB 523 a declaration that departmental inspectors had acted in breach of natural justice in compiling a report was refused because the report alone could not produce any legal consequences, it was merely preparatory to further action.

A declaration will not be granted where the effect would be to provide a 'second opinion' in respect of a matter that an administrative body has already lawfully dealt with. Hence in *Healey* v *Minister of Health* [1955] 1 QB 221, where the plaintiff sought a declaration that he was a 'mental health officer' and thus entitled to a certain level of superannuation, the Court of Appeal refused to grant declaratory relief. The Minister, who was designated under the relevant Act to determine such matters, had already announced his decision to the contrary. The plaintiff was not alleging any ultra vires act on the part of the Minister, or error of law, so that, even if the court granted the declaration sought, it would not affect the Minister's decision. The court saw no purpose in simply producing two conflicting decisions. Similarly, in *Punton* v *Ministry of Pensions and National Insurance* [1963] 1 All ER 275, a declaration that the plaintiff was 'not a person directly interested in a trade dispute' was refused, because it would simply have resulted in a decision conflicting with that already made by the National Insurance Commissioner. A declaration cannot quash a decision that the applicant seeks to overturn. In such cases an order of certiorari must be requested.

20.4 Damages

Subject to the exceptions considered in Chapter 4 (Crown liability in contract and tort), and Chapter 10 (liability of local authorities and other statutory corporations), damages may be awarded against public bodies in actions commenced by way of writ in respect of the normal range of private law liabilities. Following the introduction of O.53 in 1977, it has become possible for an applicant for judicial review to add a claim for damages. Order 53 r.7 provides:

'On an application for judicial review the court may ... award damages to the applicant if ... the court is satisfied that, if the claim had been made in an action begun by the applicant at the time of making his application, he could have been awarded damages.'

It was not the purpose of these reforms to create a new right to damages as a remedy in administrative law. Damages will only be available if the applicant can show that they would have been available in an action started by way of writ. While a private law action for damages might lie against a public body in respect of its giving negligent advice, it seems very doubtful whether an action will succeed on the basis that the public body has negligently acted ultra vires. In *Dunlop* v *Woollahra Municipal Council* [1982] AC 158 Lord Diplock went so far as to doubt whether any private law duty of care is owed by a public authority when exercising its statutory discretion. Similar doubts were raised by the Privy Council in *Rowling* v *Takaro Properties* [1988] 1 All ER 163. It would appear that the only remedy in such cases is to apply for judicial review to have the ultra vires decision quashed; see further *R* v *Knowsley Borough Council, ex parte Maguire* [1992] NLJ 1375. The litigant is caught in a vicious circle as he will not be able to add a claim for damages to his application for review, as he would not have been able to claim damages for the ultra vires action in proceedings commenced by way of writ. On the basis of *Bourgoin SA* v *Ministry of Agriculture, Fisheries and Food* [1985] 3 All ER 585, it would appear that damages are available by way of action where a public officer deliberately acts ultra vires (malicious abuse of power); hence if the litigant wanted to proceed by way of an application for review a claim for damages could be made.

Other matters are still uncertain. How, for example, should a litigant pursue an action for breach of statutory duty, where there appears to be a right to a remedy by way of damages? Presumably if the litigant has the option of proceeding by way of writ he will not go out of his way, given the need to obtain leave within three months etc, to seek judicial review instead. In *R* v *Northavon District Council, ex parte Palmer* (1993) The Times 17 August the applicant, who had been incorrectly refused housing by the respondent authority, applied for judicial review of the decision, seeking, inter alia, damages for breach of its housing duty. While the matter was adjourned the authority reconsidered her case and determined it properly in her favour. The applicant thereupon amended her claim and requested a declaration that she had been wrongly denied housing and damages. The Divisional Court held that, even though the application for prerogative relief had become redundant, the claim for a declaration would be allowed to proceed since it provided a basis on which the court could consider the claim for damages. If the application were struck out, the applicant would be forced to pursue her claim for damages by way of action, thus running the risk that her writ might be struck out as an abuse of process, since her claim was founded on a public law issue.

20.5 Certiorari and prohibition

The prerogative orders of certiorari, prohibition and mandamus are only available by way of an application for judicial review under O.53 of the Rules of the Supreme Court, which has been placed on a statutory footing by s31 of the Supreme Court Act 1981. Order 53 r.1 states:

'1(1) An application for –
a) an order of mandamus, prohibition or certiorari ... shall be made by way of an application for judicial review ...
1(2) An application for a declaration or an injunction ... may be made by way of an application for judicial review, and on such an application the court may grant the declaration or injunction claimed if it considers that, having regard to –
a) the nature of the matters in respect of which relief may be granted by way of order of mandamus, prohibition or certiorari,
b) the nature of the persons and bodies against whom relief may be granted by way of such an order, and
c) all the circumstances of the case,
it would be just and convenient for the declaration or injunction to be granted on an application for judicial review.'

Order 53 r.2 further provides that:

'On an application for judicial review any relief mentioned in rule 1 may be claimed as an alternative or in addition to any other relief so mentioned if it arises out of or relates to or is connected with the same matter.'

Certiorari

The effect of an order of certiorari is to quash the decision of an inferior body on the basis that the decision is either ultra vires or vitiated by an intra vires error of law. The effect of quashing a decision in this way is to render it null and void. Given that judicial review is concerned with the legality of the decision-making process, and not with the substantive merits of a decision properly arrived at, the court in granting an order of certiorari will not be substituting its own decision for that of the inferior body. Order 53 r.9(4) provides, however, that where the relief sought is an order of certiorari, and the court is satisfied that there are grounds for quashing the decision to which the application relates, the court may, in addition to quashing it, remit the matter to the court, tribunal or authority concerned with a direction to reconsider it and reach a decision in accordance with the findings of the court.

Availability of certiorari

The starting point for any examination of the availability of certiorari is the dictum of Atkin LJ in *R* v *Electricity Commissioners, ex parte London Electricity Joint*

Committee Co (1920) Ltd [1924] 1 KB 171 (hereinafter the *Electricity Commissioners* case). As he observed:

> 'The operation of the writs [of prohibition and certiorari] has extended to control the proceedings of bodies which do not claim to be and would not be recognised as courts of justice. Whenever any body of persons having legal authority to determine questions affecting the rights of subjects, and having the duty to act judicially, act in excess of their legal authority, they are subject to the controlling jurisdiction of the King's Bench Division exercised in these writs.'

As will be seen from the above passage, there are essentially three criteria that must be satisfied for certiorari to issue. First, the decision-making body must act with legal authority. Historically this has meant that certiorari has been available in respect of bodies exercising statutory power, typically local authorities, tribunals and ministers, as opposed to decisions of domestic tribunals, or private companies registered under the Companies Acts 1948: see *R v BBC, ex parte Lavelle* [1983] 1 All ER 241 and *Law v National Greyhound Racing Club Ltd* [1983] 3 All ER 300. It is now clear that the exercise of prerogative power falls within the scope of judicial review but, as outlined above, there may still be uncertainty as to the suitability of the prerogative orders as the appropriate form of relief. In *ex parte Lain*, Diplock LJ observed that the Criminal Injuries Compensation Board's jurisdiction to discharge the quasi-judicial function of awarding compensation was not derived from any agreement between the Crown and applicants for compensation:

> '... but from instructions by the executive government, that is, by prerogative act of the Crown. The appointment of the board and the conferring upon it of jurisdiction ... and ... authority to make payments ... are acts of government, done without statutory authority but nonetheless lawful for that.'

Regardless of the position in relation to prerogative power, however, the scope of certiorari as a remedy has been significantly widened by the Court of Appeal's decision in *R v Panel on Take-overs and Mergers, ex parte Datafin* [1987] 2 WLR 699. The court held that the remedy would be available against a body lacking statutory or prerogative powers (in fact lacking any de jure power) on the basis that its decisions were nevertheless of great significance and affected the public – those dealing in companies quoted on the Stock Exchange. A key factor, it is submitted, was the fact that there was no other means of legal challenge to the Panel's decisions. It confirms that the court will be less concerned with the source of a body's power and more with the effect of its decisions.

The second criterion is that the decision-making body must be empowered to deal with questions affecting the rights of subjects. The issue here is in determining the nature of the rights that fall to be protected by the courts on an application for review. In *R v Hull Prison Board of Visitors, ex parte St Germain* [1979] QB 425, the Court of Appeal held that certiorari was available to quash a decision of the Board because it adjudicated upon rights of prisoners that fell to be protected by public law. The Board's contention that no question of rights arose, because its decisions only effected remission, was rejected, the court taking the view that the Board's decisions were effectively punishments, and that a prisoner, therefore, had the right to be dealt with in accordance with the rules of natural justice: see further *R* v *Board of Visitors of Blundeston Prison, ex parte Fox Taylor* [1982] 1 All ER 646.

In *R* v *Criminal Injuries Compensation Board, ex parte Lain* (above), it had been argued by the Board that certiorari was not available to quash its decisions because its determination gave rise to no enforceable rights, all awards being discretionary. The Divisional Court held that this was too narrow an interpretation of the Atkin dictum, which was not simply limited to enforceable rights but would apply to decisions taken as a step towards the creation of legally enforceable rights.

The applicant should only fail in his bid to establish that his public law rights are affected by the decision being challenged if the court concludes that the case raises primarily private law issues. Lord Parker CJ in *ex parte Lain* observed:

> '... the exact limits of ... certiorari have never been and ought not to be specifically defined. They have varied from time to time being extended to meet changing conditions. At one time the writ only went to an inferior court. Later its ambit was extended to statutory tribunals determining a lis inter partes. Later again it extended to cases where there was no lis in the strict sense of the word but where immediate or subsequent rights of citizens were affected. The only constant limits throughout were that it was performing a public duty. Private ... tribunals have always been outside the scope of certiorari ... We have as it seems to me reached the position when the ambit of certiorari can be said to cover every case in which a body of persons of a public as opposed to a purely private or domestic character has to determine matters affecting subjects provided always that it has a duty to act judicially.'

As will have been seen in Chapter 11, making the distinction between public law rights and private law rights is far from straight forward. In *R* v *Barnsley Metropolitan Borough Council, ex parte Hook* [1976] 1 WLR 1052 (revocation of a market trader's licence) it was held that certiorari would be granted because, although the relationship between the parties was essentially contractual, the matter also involved a public law element, the regulation of a public market. In *R* v *Basildon District Council, ex parte Brown* (1981) 79 LGR 655, however, a completely contrary conclusion was arrived at, certiorari being refused on the ground that the relationship between the market trader and the local authority as a licensing agency was contractual, and did not therefore raise any public law issues. Consider in addition the decisions in *R* v *East Berkshire Health Authority, ex parte Walsh* [1984] 3 WLR 818, and *R* v *Secretary of State for the Home Department, ex parte Benwell* [1985] QB 554.

The third criterion for the granting of certiorari, namely that the decision-making body must being under a duty to act judicially, was one of the chief causes of the restricted development of natural justice prior to *Ridge* v *Baldwin* [1964] AC 40. It was thought that only courts, or administrative bodies deciding a dispute between two parties concerning rights traditionally protected by law, were under a duty to act judicially and therefore amenable to certiorari. In *Ridge* v *Baldwin* Lord Reid changed the course of the law's development by holding that in order to determine whether there existed a duty to act judicially the court should have regard to the nature of the power being exercised, and the rights thereby affected. The change in emphasis to what is at stake for the applicant has significantly widened the scope of the remedy. Hence in *R* v *Barnsley Metropolitan Borough Council, ex parte Hook* (above) some members of the Court of Appeal inferred the duty to act judicially from the fact that the local authority was a statutory body having the power to determine the rights of others.

Alternative remedy available

Certiorari, like the other prerogative orders, is a discretionary remedy; in particular it will not be granted if a more suitable alternative remedy exists. In *R* v *Peterkin, ex parte Soni* (1972) Imm AR 253 certiorari was refused when an application was made to quash the determination of an immigration adjudicator, because an appeal lay from his decision to an immigration appeal tribunal. Lord Widgery pointed out that the courts should normally allow statutory appellate machinery to work, where it had been provided, in preference to granting certiorari. The prerogative orders were not to be used as an alternative form of appeal. The courts, before deciding to grant or refuse certiorari, will consider the suitability of the alternatively remedy. In *R* v *Chief Immigration Officer, Gatwick Airport, ex parte Kharrazi* [1980] 3 All ER 373, the applicant sought an order of certiorari to quash the decision refusing him entry as he would have had to return to Iran in order to invoke the appeal procedure provided by statute. As Lord Denning MR observed:

> 'If there is a convenient remedy by way of appeal to an adjudicator, then certiorari may be refused: and the applicant left to his remedy by way of appeal. But it has been held on countless occasions that the availability of appeal does not debar the court from quashing an order by prerogative writs ... It depends on the circumstances of each case. In the present case the remedy by way of appeal is useless. This boy's education – indeed, his whole future – will be ruined if he is sent off by plane to Tehran. Rather than his future be ruined, it is better to quash the refusal – and let the Home Secretary reconsider the case.'

See also *R* v *Paddington Valuation Officer, ex parte Peachey Property Corporation* [1966] 1 QB 380.

Prohibition

Prohibition is a prerogative order directed at an inferior body, compelling it to refrain from a course of action: in effect the public law equivalent of an injunction. Non-observance of an order of prohibition by an inferior body amounts to contempt of court. The criteria for the granting of prohibition are essentially the same as those for the granting of certiorari, as laid down in the *Electricity Commissioners* case (above) in which it was one of the remedies sought. By its very nature, it is only of use where an individual is able to produce evidence that an inferior body proposes to act beyond its jurisdiction. In *R* v *Liverpool Corporation, ex parte Liverpool Taxi Fleet Operators' Association* [1972] 2 QB 299, the applicants sought an order of prohibition to prevent the local authority from reneging on a public undertaking that the number of licensed cab drivers in the city would not be increased. In granting the relief sought, Lord Denning MR stated:

'We have considered what the actual relief should be. On the whole we think it is sufficient in this case to let prohibition issue. The order should prohibit the corporation or their committee or sub-committee from acting on the resolutions of 16th November 1971, 8th December 1971 and 22nd December 1971; in particular, from granting any further number of licences pursuant to s37 of the Town Police Clauses Act 1847 over and above the 300 currently existing, without first hearing any representations which may be made by or on behalf of any persons interested therein, including the applicants in this case and any other matters relevant thereto, including the undertaking recorded in the two clerk's letters of 11th August 1971. If prohibition goes in those terms, it means that the relevant committees, sub-committees and the corporation themselves, can look at the matter afresh. They will hear all those interested and come to a right conclusion as to what is to be done about the number of taxi cabs on the streets of Liverpool. I would say that the trouble has arisen because the corporation was advised that this undertaking was not binding on them, whereas it certainly was binding unless overridden by some imperative public interest. I am sure that all concerned have been acting as best they can, but nevertheless prohibition in my view should issue so as to prevent the corporation committee acting on those resolutions.'

20.6 Mandamus

Mandamus is a prerogative order directed at an inferior body, compelling it to act in accordance with duties to which it is subject. It will only lie against a public body, in relation to public law duties. A court will not grant an order of mandamus compelling the exercise of discretion in a particular way, since judicial review is concerned with the legality of actions, not with their merits. If, for example, a tribunal is given the power to award licences to whomever it thinks fit, the court will not compel it by mandamus to award a licence to a particular person. What the court will order such a body to do, however, is to exercise its discretion according to law, for example by taking into account relevant considerations, or providing reasons for its decisions. Mandamus will lie, therefore, in respect of statutory duties and implied common law duties, such as the duty to exercise power according to law. The most significant example of the latter is provided by *Padfield* v *Minister of Agriculture* [1968] AC 997, where mandamus was granted against the Minister, compelling him to consider a complaint about the milk marketing scheme, according to law, despite the fact that the enabling Act appeared to leave the holding of an inquiry to his discretion. Simply because a duty has been expressly stated in an enabling Act does not mean that mandamus will necessarily issue to compel its performance. Certain statutory duties are drafted in such wide, vague terms that they are not amenable to orders of mandamus. The courts will not grant the remedy unless compliance with the order can be supervised. Without supervision it would be impossible to know whether the order was being complied with, and hence whether any contempt was being committed. In short, the courts will not act in vain; mandamus will not be granted unless something can be achieved by making the order.

Lack of funds on the part of a public body will generally not be accepted as justification for failing to comply with a public law duty. In *R v Poplar Borough Council, ex parte London County Council (No 2)* [1922] 1 KB 95 mandamus was issued to compel a London borough to pay the precept due to the London County Council, despite its arguments that due to the poverty of the borough it was unable to pay. As Younger LJ observed:

> '[The Councillors of Poplar are] by law left with no discretion as to their action in this matter ... If the rate directed be excessive in its amount, or burdensome in its incidence on Poplar, that is a justification for an alteration in the law, but it is no justification for disobedience to the law before it is altered. If the appellants will not carry out the duties they have undertaken by accepting election to this body, it is their duty to make way for others who will. Deliberate disobedience to this order cannot, in my judgment, be overlooked or excused.'

Where the failure to perform a statutory duty appears to be motivated by the desire to make a political point, the courts are unlikely to restrain themselves from ordering that the duties be discharged. This view is supported by the decision of the Divisional Court in *R v Camden London Borough Council, ex parte Gillan and Others* (1988) The Times 12 October. The Housing Act 1985 imposed a duty upon Camden London Borough Council (the authority) to hear and adjudicate upon applications for accommodation from homeless persons. The evidence submitted by the applicants indicated that the authority was providing only very limited opportunities for such applications to be made. The authority's homeless persons unit was not attended at night or over weekends, and homeless persons could not talk to housing officers face to face, but only via the telephone. Further evidence suggested that telephones in the unit were either constantly engaged or left unanswered. The applicants sought judicial review of the authority's discharging of its duties under the 1985 Act, and in particular sought orders of mandamus to compel the authority to comply with the requirements of the Act. The authority contended that rate-capping imposed by central government had left it without the funds to provide a better service to the homeless. Allowing the applications, and granting the remedies sought, the court held that the impecuniosity of the authority, whether arising from a reduction in income from rates or any other source, could not excuse the cavalier fashion in which it had failed to discharge its duties to the homeless under the 1985 Act. The court was of the opinion that in an area with as high a population density as Camden the local authority should be providing a 24-hour service.

While the decision has its encouraging aspects it begs the question of how effectively the court was able to supervise the authority's compliance with the order of mandamus. Compare this with the approach of the court in *R v Secretary of State for Social Services, ex parte Hincks* 1980 (unreported) where, although the Secretary of State was under a duty to provide certain welfare services, the court rejected out of hand any argument that he was, as a consequence, under a duty to secure from Parliament sufficient funds to provide adequate welfare services. What the authorities do confirm is that if the court perceives the public body to be doing its best, in good faith, to discharge a duty that is not absolute in nature, it may give it the benefit of the doubt and not intervene. In *R* v *Bristol Corporation, ex parte Hendy* [1974] 1 WLR 498 the local authority, acting under s39(1) of the Land Compensation Act 1973, offered the applicant temporary accommodation following the closing order that had been made in respect of his flat. The applicant sought an order of mandamus to compel the authority to comply with its duty under s39 to provide him with 'suitable alternative residential accommodation on reasonable terms'. Refusing the order of mandamus, Scarman LJ stated:

> 'If there is evidence that a local authority is doing all that it honestly and honourably can to meet the statutory obligation, and that its failure, if there be failure, to meet that obligation arises really out of circumstances over which it has no control, then I would think it would be improper for the court to make an order of mandamus compelling it to do that which either it cannot do or which it can only do at the expense of other persons not before the court who may have equal rights with the applicant.'

Alternative remedy available

As with certiorari, mandamus will not be granted where it appears that Parliament has supplied a more suitable alternative remedy: in particular, default powers vested in a minister. In *Pasmore* v *Oswaldtwistle Urban District Council* [1898] AC 387 the court held that it was not open to an individual to seek an order of mandamus compelling the local authority to comply with its duty to provide sewers, because statutory default powers had been vested in the Minister and he was the correct person to apply for such an order. In *Watt* v *Kesteven County Council* [1955] 1 QB 408 it was held that the existence of ministerial default powers which could be used in the event of a local education authority failing to provide sufficient schools for its area militated against mandamus being available at the suit of a private individual to compel performance of the duty. There was a similar situation in *R* v *ILEA, ex parte Ali* (1990) The Times 21 February, where the applicant sought an order of mandamus to compel the local education authority to provide an adequate number of primary school places in Tower Hamlets. Despite the fact that the Minister had refused to exercise his statutory powers to intervene, the court refused to grant the relief sought. The statutory duty in question was not regarded as being absolute but merely one that required ILEA to do its best. The court appreciated that the authority might be at the mercy of unforeseen circumstances, such as teacher shortages. Furthermore, although the Minister's default power under s99 of the Education Act 1944 did not oust the jurisdiction of the court to order mandamus, until such ministerial directives were issued and ignored it was difficult to see how mandamus could issue, given the wide nature of the duties in question. In the final analysis it was felt that an order of mandamus added nothing to ILEA's duties, nor did it clarify them, as that body fully accepted what they were. Given the imminent demise of ILEA, an order of mandamus would have been, in any event, somewhat redundant.

Mandamus inappropriate

There have been situations where, despite mandamus clearly being available, the courts, in the exercise of their discretion, have refused to grant it on the ground that it would be inappropriate for the court to intervene. In *R v Metropolitan Police Commissioner, ex parte Blackburn* [1968] 2 QB 118, the Court of Appeal refused to grant mandamus to compel the Metropolitan Police Commissioner to prosecute persons involved in illegal gaming, although it was stated, obiter, that a policy decision not to enforce a particular law would be challengeable in the courts. Lord Denning MR commented that:

> '... it is for the Commissioner of Police of the Metropolis, or the chief constable, as the case may be, to decide in any particular case whether inquiries should be pursued, or whether an arrest should be made, or a prosecution brought. It must be for him to decide on the disposition of his force and the concentration of his resources on any particular crime or area.'

Similarly, in *R v Chief Constable of Devon and Cornwall, ex parte Central Electricity Generating Board* [1981] 3 WLR 967, in refusing to grant mandamus to compel the Chief Constable to clear protesters from the proposed site of a nuclear power station, Lord Denning MR observed:

> '... I would not give any orders to the chief constable or his men. It is of the first importance that the police should decide on their own responsibility what action should be taken in any particular situation ... The decision of the chief constable not to intervene in this case was a policy decision with which I think the courts should not interfere ... I hope he will decide to use his men to clear the obstructors off the site or at any rate help the board to do so.'

See further the reluctant refusal of mandamus in *Chief Constable of the North Wales Police v Evans* [1982] 3 All ER 141.

21

Exclusion of Review

21.1 Introduction

21.2 Finality clauses

21.3 'No certiorari' clauses

21.4 'As if enacted' clauses

21.5 'Shall not be questioned' clauses

21.6 Partial ouster clauses

21.1 Introduction

From time to time Parliament enacts legislation containing provisions which purport to exclude judicial review, or perhaps any legal challenge to a particular determination of a public body. The rationale for such provisions is usually pragmatic: a tribunal has a finite fund of money to distribute and Parliament seeks prevent any challenge once the fund has been allocated; planning decisions need to be settled and beyond any legal challenge before development can safely take place. The constitutional implications of such clauses are, however, stark. Without recourse to the courts how is the rule of law to be maintained? To seek to prevent judicial review runs counter to the development of public law in the post-war era. Despite the fact that where access to the courts is excluded some other form of administrative control is sometimes provided, the courts have not been altogether willing to take such legislative provisions at face value. As will be seen, despite Parliament's efforts, ouster clauses have only been permitted a very limited range of operation.

21.2 Finality clauses

Some statutes have attempted to prevent decisions from being challenged by declaring them to be 'final'. The courts have interpreted this to mean that, while an appeal on merits cannot be sought, review on grounds of illegality is still possible. The leading case is *R* v *Medical Appeal Tribunal, ex parte Gilmore* [1957] 1 QB 574.

The applicant sought to quash the decision of a medical appeal tribunal. Section 36(3) of the National Insurance (Industrial Injuries) Act 1946, provided that 'any decision of a claim or question ... shall be final'. He applied for certiorari on the ground of a manifest error of law on the face of the record. The Divisional Court refused leave to apply for certiorari. The decision was reversed by the Court of Appeal. During the hearing before the Court of Appeal it was conceded that the tribunal's decision was wrong in law.

Denning LJ explained that the remedy of certiorari could only be excluded by the use of very clear words. In his Lordship's view the words 'shall be final' were not enough, and the decision could still be quashed for error of law, even though it might be final as regards the facts.

21.3 'No certiorari' clauses

Parliament has attempted to exclude review by expressly providing in legislation that a decision is not to be subject to an order of certiorari. Rather like finality clauses, this has been rendered ineffective by the courts. The clearest explanation of this is provided by a passage from Denning LJ's judgment in *R* v *MAT, ex parte Gilmore* (above):

> 'In contrast to the word "final" I would like to say a word about the old statutes which used in express words to make away the remedy by certiorari by saying that the decision of the tribunal "shall not be removed by certiorari". Those statutes were passed chiefly between 1680 and 1848, in the days when the courts used certiorari too freely and quashed decisions for technical defects of form. In stopping this abuse the statutes proved very beneficial, but the court never allowed those statutes to be used as a cover for wrongdoings by tribunals. If tribunals were to be at liberty to exceed their jurisdiction without any check by the courts, the rule of law would be at an end. Despite express words taking away certiorari, therefore, it was held that certiorari would still lie if some of the members of the tribunals were disqualified from acting: see *R* v *Cheltenham Commissioners* (1841) 1 QB 467, where Lord Denman CJ said (ibid at p 474): "The statute cannot effect our right and duty to see justice executed." So, also, if the tribunal exceeded its jurisdiction: see *ex parte Bradlaugh* (1878) 3 QBD 508; or if its decision was obtained by fraud: see *R* v *Gillyard* (1848) 12 QB 527, the courts would still grant certiorari. I do not pause to consider those cases further, for I am glad to notice that modern statutes never take away, in express words, the right to certiorari without substituting an analogous remedy. This is probably because the courts no longer use it to quash for technical defects but only in case of a substantial miscarriage of justice. Parliament nowadays more often uses the words "final" or "final and conclusive" or some such words which leave intact the control of the Queen's courts by certiorari.'

In this regard, note s12 of the Tribunals and Inquiries Act 1992 set out at Chapter 7.

21.4 'As if enacted' clauses

The courts cannot question the validity of primary legislation; therefore, in theory, if a ministerial order is deemed, by the enabling Act, to have been enacted as part of the enabling Act, it cannot be invalidated by the courts. This theory was accepted by the House of Lords in *Ministry of Health* v *R, ex parte Yaffe* [1931] AC 494, but was limited to the extent that an invalid (ultra vires) order would still be challengeable because the enabling Act could only have contemplated the making of valid orders; therefore any invalid order would be ultra vires the enabling Act.

21.5 'Shall not be questioned' clauses

Anisminic v *FCC*

Anisminic owned property in Egypt valued at approximately £4m. During the Suez crisis the Egyptian authorities seized the property, and Anisminic entered into a contract to sell the property to an Egyptian company for a fraction of its true value. After the cessation of hostilities the United Kingdom government received £27.5m by way of compensation and the task of distributing the fund was given to the Foreign Compensation Commission. The Commission rejected Anisminic's claim on the erroneous basis that the successor in title to the expropriated property should have been of British nationality at a specific date. Anisminic sought a declaration that the determination of the Commission was a nullity because it had misconstrued the terms of the relevant statutory Order. Section 4(4) of the Foreign Compensation Act 1950 Act provided that no determination of the Commission was to be called into question in any court of law. The House of Lords, in *Anisminic* v *Foreign Compensation Commission* [1969] 2 AC 147, held, by a majority, that the determination was ultra vires; in basing its decision on a matter which it had no right to take into account, or in making an inquiry which the Order did not empower it to make, the Commission had exceeded its powers, and so the declaration sought would be granted. The rationale for the decision can be constructed in the following way:

1. The Commission was a statutory body with jurisdiction to consider claims for compensation.
2. In rejecting Anisminic's claim it had misconstrued the terms of an Order in Council, something that would normally be regarded as an error of law and, although intra vires, reviewable by way of error of law on the face of the record.
3. The clause excluding the jurisdiction of the courts referred to 'determinations' of the Commission. The House of Lords interpreted this as meaning 'valid determinations'. A valid determination was one that was intra vires. An ultra vires decision would only be a 'purported' determination, and therefore not protected by the exclusion clause (or 'ouster clause').
4. Returning to the Commission's decision, if it was only an error of law that vitiated its decision, it was an intra vires decision and therefore 'valid', and therefore protected by the exclusion clause.
5. The House of Lords (by a majority) avoided this conclusion by holding that what the Commission had committed was not an 'ordinary', intra vires, error of law but an error of law going to jurisdiction: in short an ultra vires error of law.

6. The result was then predictable. As the error of law took the Commission beyond its jurisdiction, its decision was ultra vires, therefore it was only a 'purported' determination, and therefore not one protected by the exclusion clause.

The consequences of Anisminic *v* FCC

The immediate response of many commentators in the wake of *Anisminic* was to sound the death knell of review for error of law on the face of the record. If one could now argue that an error of law was one resulting in a decision being ultra vires, why bother with the more limited remedy of review of an intra vires error?

Responsible in many ways for fostering this view was the Court of Appeal's decision in *Pearlman* v *Keepers and Governors of Harrow School* [1979] QB 56, in which the leading judgment was that of Lord Denning. Mr Pearlman had sought a county court declaration that the installation of central heating in his property was a 'structural alteration' with the result that the rateable value of his property should be reduced. The county court refused the declaration, finding that the works carried out did not constitute a 'structural alteration'. By statute the decision of the county court judge was declared to be 'final and conclusive'. Mr Pearlman appealed to the Court of Appeal where Lord Denning held that the error of law made by the trial judge was one going to his jurisdiction and therefore not protected by the exclusion clause, that is, an ultra vires error of law. In any event, in Lord Denning's view, the distinction between intra vires errors of law and those going to jurisdiction was so fine that it ought to be discarded. In his view the correct approach was to say that no inferior tribunal had the jurisdiction to make a mistake of law upon which its decision depended.

If this view had prevailed in subsequent decisions, then error of law on the face of the record would have become redundant all such errors would simply have been ultra vires. The dissenting judgment of Geoffrey Lane LJ in *Pearlman*, however, struck a much more cautious note, his view being that there was still scope for errors of law that could be intra vires.

In *South East Asia Firebricks Sdn Bhd* v *Non-Metallic (etc) Union* [1981] AC 363 the Privy Council reasserted the distinction between jurisdictional errors and other types of error by holding that the decision of the Industrial Court of Malaysia was protected by the relevant ouster clause. In the course of his speech, Lord Fraser referred to Lord Denning's approach to the problem in *Pearlman*:

'... if the inferior tribunal has merely an error of law which does not affect its jurisdiction, and if its decision is not a nullity for some reason such as breach of the rules of natural justice then the ouster clause will be effective. In *Pearlman* Lord Denning MR suggested that the distinction between an error of law which affected jurisdiction and one which did not, should now be 'discarded'. Their Lordships do not accept that suggestion. They consider that the law was correctly applied to the circumstances of that case in the dissenting opinion of Geoffrey Lane LJ when he said:

"... the only circumstances in which this court can correct what is to my mind the error of the County Court judge is if he was acting in excess of his jurisdiction as opposed to merely making an error of law in his judgment by misinterpreting the meaning of 'structural alteration ... or addition'."'

The current position

The situation has been resolved to some extent by the House of Lords' decision in *Re Racal Communications Ltd* [1981] AC 374. An application was made to a High Court judge for an order authorising inspection of a company's books on the grounds that reasonable cause existed to believe that a person, while an officer of the company, had committed certain offences. The High Court judge declined to grant the order, on the basis that he did not think the individual alleged to be involved in illegal activities was an 'officer' of the company, and he did not think the wrongdoings alleged were of the sort that justified the making of the order sought. By the statute in question the judge's decision was stated as being 'non-appealable'.

The Court of Appeal nevertheless reversed this decision, holding that the judge at first instance had wrongly declined to exercise his jurisdiction, and that this constituted an error of law going to jurisdiction; the decision was therefore ultra vires and not protected by the ouster clause. The Court of Appeal granted the Order requested. Note that the leading judgment in the Court of Appeal was that of Lord Denning, relying heavily on his own previous decision in *Pearlman*.

The House of Lords unanimously reversed the decision of the Court of Appeal on a number of grounds: first, that it was only sensible to talk of errors 'going to jurisdiction' when dealing with an inferior body, the jurisdiction of which was limited by an enabling Act. High Court judges have unlimited common law jurisdiction, which makes it illogical to describe them as making errors going to jurisdiction. Secondly, the Court of Appeal was purporting to exercise a reviewing function in stating the judge's decision to be ultra vires. This was an error, as the Court of Appeal had no inherent power of review; it was a statutory body with jurisdiction to hear certain types of appeals only.

Lord Diplock sought to explain the circumstances in which the courts would regard an error of law as one going to jurisdiction, and therefore reviewable. He drew a distinction between decisions of 'administrative' bodies, such as the Foreign Compensation Commission, and judicial bodies, such as county court judges. The former had no expertise in law, so the courts would be more likely to intervene to deal with an error of law committed by such a body, notwithstanding the existence of an ouster clause. Judicial bodies were more likely to have expertise on matters of law, and the courts would be slow to interfere with their decisions. That is why the decision in *Anisminic* was still good law, and the decision of the majority in *Pearlman* was not. In *O'Reilly* v *Mackman* [1983] 2 AC 237 Lord Diplock referred to the significance of *Anisminic* in the following terms:

'The breakthrough that *Anisminic* made was the recognition by the majority of this House that if a tribunal whose jurisdiction was limited by statute or subordinate legislation mistook the law applicable to the facts as it had found them, it must have asked itself the wrong question, ie one into which it was not empowered to enquire and so had no jurisdiction to determine. Its purported "determination", not being a "determination" within the meaning of the empowering legislation, was accordingly a nullity.'

He went on to describe the effect of *Anisminic* as having been to:

'... virtually abolish the distinction between errors within jurisdiction that render voidable a decision that remained valid until quashed, and errors that went to jurisdiction and rendered a decision void ab initio ...'

The distinction between courts of law and administrative bodies was assessed as regards coroners' courts in *R* v *Greater Manchester Coroner, ex parte Tal* [1984] 3 All ER 240. The families of two prisoners who, along with a third prisoner, had died in custody sought judicial review of the verdicts returned by a coroner's court that had indicated that there was a possibility that the third prisoner's death had been caused by the other two. The court held that the application for review would be refused on the basis that no allegation of unlawfulness had been substantiated, but rejected the contention that such decisions might be unreviewable. Robert Goff LJ explained that *R* v *Surrey Coroner, ex parte Campbell* [1982] QB 661 (where the *Anisminic* principle was held not to apply to the decision of a coroner's court) was incorrect. In his view Lord Diplock had not intended that the *Anisminic* principle should only be applicable to administrative bodies. Inferior courts, such as coroners' courts, were amenable to judicial review for error of law going to jurisdiction in the same way that tribunals were.

Conclusive evidence clauses

In *R* v *Registrar of Companies, ex parte Esal (Commodities) Ltd (in liquidation)* [1985] 2 All ER 79 the court had to consider the effect of s98(2) of the Companies Act 1948, which provided:

'The registrar shall give a certificate under his hand of the registration of any charge registered in pursuance of this Part of this Act, stating the amount thereby secured, and the certificate shall be conclusive evidence that the requirements of this part of this Act have been complied with.'

A bank wished to register a charge in respect of the company's assets. Paperwork was submitted to the registrar on 29 February 1984, but it was incorrectly filled in, and certain details were lacking. On 29 March 1984 the paperwork was resubmitted in its proper form and the charge was registered without the company's knowledge. On 7 November 1984 the company was made the subject of a winding-up order, and its creditors sought judicial review of the registrar's decision to register the bank's charge on the basis that he had lacked jurisdiction to do so. Inter alia, it was alleged that the registrar had erred in law in regarding the original paperwork as 'prescribed paperwork' within the Act. The registrar relied on s98(2), arguing that his certificate had to be regarded as conclusive in the interests of commercial certainty.

The court held that, despite s98(2), the registrar's certificate was reviewable in the courts. He was a person amenable to judicial review, in the sense that he exercised statutory powers affecting the rights of others, and the decisions of public officials had to be amenable to scrutiny by way of judicial review for either error of law or breach of natural justice. The need to promote commercial certainty was to some extent protected by the time limits in applying for judicial review.

21.6 Partial ouster clauses

The only type of clause purporting to exclude review to have been granted effectiveness by the courts is that allowing a period during which a decision can be challenged before the ouster clause takes effect.

In *Smith* v *East Elloe Rural District Council* [1956] AC 736, the plaintiff sought to challenge the validity of a compulsory purchase order which had been made in respect of her property some five years earlier. Under the Acquisition of Land (Authorisation Procedure) Act 1946, a court could quash an order where it appeared to be beyond the powers of the enabling Act, or where the procedural requirements of the enabling Act had not been complied with, causing the applicant substantial prejudice. Applications to the High Court to challenge compulsory purchase orders under the Act had to be submitted within six weeks of the order being made. The House of Lords held, by a majority, that the ouster clause prevented challenge on any ground beyond the six-week time limit. Lord Reid, dissenting, said that the order must remain challengeable at any time for bad faith; he could not accept that it was the intention of Parliament to protect such decisions.

An almost identical provision fell to be considered by the Court of Appeal in *R* v *Secretary of State for the Environment, ex parte Ostler* [1977] QB 122. The applicant sought leave to apply for an order of certiorari to quash a stopping-up order under the Highways Act 1959 and a compulsory purchase order under the Acquisition of Land (Authorising Procedure) Act 1946 (whose wording was identical to that considered in the *East Elloe* case). A preliminary objection was taken by the Secretary of State that, whatever the facts (and in this case the applicant alleged bad faith which amounted to fraud), any attack on the validity of the orders was barred in any legal proceedings whatsoever because the statutorily prescribed six-week period had expired. The Divisional Court considered that the speeches in *Anisminic* v *FCC* (above) undermined the reasoning in *Smith* v *East Elloe Rural District Council*. The Secretary of State appealed to the Court of Appeal on this question as a preliminary point of law. The Court of Appeal held that the clause was still effective to exclude challenge outside the six-week time limit. Lord Denning sought to explain why the decision of the House of Lords in *Anisminic Ltd* v *FCC* could not be taken to have reduced the authority of *Smith* v *East Elloe Rural District Council*. First, in *Anisminic* the ouster clause was complete; here it was partial. Secondly, in *Anisminic* the House of Lords was considering the determination of a judicial body (a view subsequently contradicted by Lord Diplock in *Re Racal Communications*); in *East Elloe* the courts were considering an administrative decision which affected the rights of third parties, ie the general public. Thirdly, *Anisminic* concerned an actual determination, whereas *East Elloe* concerned the validity of the process by which a decision was reached.

Ex parte Ostler and *East Elloe* have since been reaffirmed by the Court of Appeal in *R v Secretary of State for the Environment, ex parte Kent* [1990] JPL 124, and *R v Cornwall County Council, ex parte Huntington and Another* [1994] 1 All ER 694. In *ex parte Kent* the court refused to allow a challenge outside the statutory six-week time limit where a local authority had failed to notify a planning application to persons likely to be affected by the proposed development with the result that objectors had not been able to make representations to the local authority or the Secretary of State. Regarding the case as indistinguishable from *ex parte Ostler*, Parker LJ indicated the reluctance with which he had arrived at his conclusion, but trusted that there would be very few cases such as this where an objector was denied the right of legal challenge through no fault of his own.

In *ex parte Huntington* the applicants sought to challenge the decisions of local authorities with respect to the amendment of definitive maps and statements regarding the making of right of way orders under the Wildlife and Countryside Act 1981. The Act provided for notice to be given of the making of an order by the local authority, the holding of a public inquiry into objections, and publication of the Secretary of State's decision following the inquiry. Paragraph 12 of Sch 15 to the 1981 Act provided for any challenge to such an order, on the grounds specified in that paragraph, to be made within 42 days with the proviso that:

> 'Except as provided by this paragraph, the validity of an order shall not be questioned in any legal proceedings whatsoever.'

The applicants, who were awaiting the outcome of the public inquiry, applied unsuccessfully for leave to apply for judicial review to quash the right of way order on the grounds that in making it the local authority had acted ultra vires. Although the matter was technically obiter (no legal challenge was possible until the orders had been confirmed, therefore the court did not have jurisdiction to entertain any challenge prior to confirmation), Simon Brown LJ cited with approval the comments of Mann LJ, at first instance, to the effect that:

> 'The intention of Parliament when it uses an *Anisminic* clause is that questions as to validity are not excluded ... [W]hen paragraphs such as those considered in *Ex p Ostler* are used, then the legislative intention is that questions as to invalidity may be raised on the specified grounds in the prescribed time and in the prescribed manner, but otherwise the jurisdiction of the court is excluded in the interests of certainty.'

22

The Parliamentary Commissioner for Administration

22.1 Background

22.2 The Parliamentary Commissioner Acts 1967 and 1994. The Parliamentary and Health Service Commissioners Act 1987

22.3 Parliamentary control of the Parliamentary Commissioner for Administration

22.4 Judicial control

22.5 The work of the Parliamentary Commissioner for Administration

22.6 The other 'ombudsmen'

22.7 Criticisms

22.8 Advantages over judicial review

22.1 Background

The concept of an independent officer to investigate complaints against the administration is not new. Scandinavian countries had appointed such persons, known popularly as 'ombudsmen', as early as 1809. The appointment of such an officer in the United Kingdom is, however, a comparatively recent development, dating from 1967.

Previously, the traditional methods by which complaints against government departments would be pursued were either to complain to a member of Parliament, or to seek what is now referred to as judicial review of the decision complained of. Both courses of action had their limitations. Members of Parliament could not mount a very effective investigation into the workings of government departments, and largely had to limit themselves to asking questions of ministers in the House of Commons. Judicial review could only be invoked by those with locus standi, and was limited to dealing with ultra vires action. The need for some form of central investigative agency to inquire into instances of unsatisfactory executive action gradually became more obvious, given the rapid growth of state involvement in everyday life, and the very considerable powers being vested in ministers.

A dramatic illustration of these problems was provided by what became known as 'the Crichel Down Affair'. Land had been compulsorily acquired by the Ministry of Defence shortly before the Second World War, and an undertaking had been given to the owner at the time of acquisition that, if the land was found to be surplus to requirements, he would be given the opportunity to repurchase. After the war the Ministry of Defence ceased to have any use for the land, and it was transferred to the Ministry of Agriculture. The land was then offered for sale in an auction, and a bid from the son-in-law of the pre-war owner, who now farmed land adjoining that which had been compulsorily purchased, was rejected. Following complaints, an inquiry was set up to discover what had happened. It discovered evidence of serious improprieties on the part of civil servants involved, who had determined for personal reasons that the land should not be resold to the original owner's family at any price. The matter was eventually debated in the House of Commons, resulting in the resignation of the incumbent minister, Sir Thomas Dugdale. The whole affair is typical of the sort of matter that would now be the subject of an investigation by the Parliamentary Commissioner for Administration (PCA).

The second factor giving considerable impetus to the creation of the PCA was the 'Justice' report in 1961, known popularly as the Whyatt Report, which strongly advocated the creation of an ombudsman along Scandinavian lines, to investigate complaints of maladministration in central government departments.

There was at the time considerable opposition to the concept, principally for two reasons. The first was the fear that it would undermine the doctrine of ministerial responsibility, and the second that it would be a threat to the traditional role of Members of Parliament in receiving complaints from their constituents and questioning ministers on the matters raised during question time in the House of Commons – a fear that is a factor in the continued existence of the 'MP filter' created by the 1967 legislation.

22.2 The Parliamentary Commissioner Acts 1967 and 1994. The Parliamentary and Health Service Commissioners Act 1987

Constitution, appointment, and tenure

These matters are dealt with in ss1 and 3 of the 1967 Act. Section 1 provides:

'1(1) For the purpose of conducting investigations in accordance with the following provisions of this Act there shall be appointed a Commissioner, to be known as the Parliamentary Commissioner for Administration.
(2) Her Majesty may by Letters Patent from time to time appoint a person to be the Commissioner, and any person so appointed shall (subject to the subsection (3) of this section) hold office during good behaviour.
(3) A person appointed to be the Commissioner may be relieved of office by Her Majesty at his own request, or may be removed from office by Her Majesty in consequence of Addresses from both Houses of Parliament, and shall in any case vacate office on completing the year of service in which he attains the age of sixty-five years.'

The 1987 Act amends s1 by providing for the removal of a commissioner of grounds of incapacity.

Staffing arrangements are governed by s3 which provides:

'3(1) The Commissioner may appoint such officers as he may determine with the approval of the Treasury as to numbers and conditions of service.

(2) Any function of the Commissioner under this Act may be performed by any officer of the Commissioner authorised for that purpose by the Commissioner. [The 1987 Act provides also for delegation to officers of the Health Service Commissioners].

(3) The expenses of the Commissioner under this Act, to such amount as may be sanctioned by the Treasury, shall be defrayed out of moneys provided by Parliament.'

The 1987 Act provides for the appointment of 'acting Commissioners' where necessary.

Recent PCAs have been lawyers. The present PCA is William Reid, who succeeded Andrew Barrowclough. A previous PCA, Sir Cecil Clothier, heads the Police Complaints Authority.

Jurisdiction

The PCA cannot investigate instances of maladministration of his own volition; he can only respond to complaints from members of the public.

The government departments subject to investigation by the PCA are listed in Sch 2 to the 1967 Act as amended by the 1987 Act. Not surprisingly the schedule includes all the major government departments, and one of the major changes introduced by the 1987 Act was the extension of the Parliamentary Commissioner's jurisdiction to 'quangos'. Not all such bodies are included, however. Bodies subject to control by the Council on Tribunals are still excluded, as are bodies performing only advisory functions, charitable bodies under the control of the Charity Commissioners, the nationalised industries, and professional bodies. The result is that bodies such as the Criminal Injuries Compensation Board and the Civil Aviation Authority are excluded on the basis that they are, in reality, tribunals. Similarly, the Boundary Commission and the Monopolies and Mergers Commission are excluded on the basis that they perform a purely advisory role. Any action taken on the basis of advice given by these bodies is itself the subject of ministerial responsibility. The schedule remains alterable by way of statutory instrument. Note that reference to a government department includes reference to ministers, members and officers of the department.

Section 110(1) of the Courts and Legal Services Act 1990 added a new subsection (6) to s5 so as to extend the jurisdiction of the Parliamentary Commissioner to 'administrative functions exercisable by any person appointed by the Lord Chancellor as a member of the *administrative* [emphasis added] staff of any court or tribunal'. The Parliamentary Commissioner Act 1994 goes further by adding a new subsection (7) which extends jurisdiction to the administrative functions of the administrative staff of any 'relevant tribunal' where those members of staff are appointed by, or with the consent of, a governemnt department or other desiganted authority. The relevant tribunals are those listed in Sch 4 to the 1967 Act (added by the 1994 Act) and include tribunals set up under the Vaccine Damage Payment Act 1979, the Child Support Act 1991, and ss41, 43 and 50 of the Social Security Administration Act 1992.

Section 5(3) of the Act prohibits the PCA from investigating any of the matters referred to in Sch 3 to the Act. These include action taken in matters certified by a secretary of state or other minister of the Crown to affect relations or dealings between the government of the United Kingdom and any other government or any international organisation of states or governments.

Also excluded are the following:

1. 'Action taken in connection with the administration of the government of any country or territory outside the United Kingdom which forms part of Her Majesty's dominions or in which Her Majesty has jurisdiction.'
2. 'Action taken by the Secretary of State under the Extradition Act 1870 or the Fugitive Offenders Act 1881.'
3. 'Action taken by or with the authority of the Secretary of State for the purposes of investigating crime or of protecting the security of the State, including action so taken with respect to passports.'
4. 'The commencement or conduct of civil or criminal proceedings before any court of law in the United Kingdom, of proceedings at any place under the Naval Discipline Act 1957, the Army Act 1955 or the Air Force Act 1955, or of proceedings before any international court or tribunal.'
5. 'Any exercise of the prerogative of mercy or of the power of a Secretary of State to make a reference in respect of any person to the Court of Appeal, the High Court of Justiciary or the Courts-Martial Appeal Court.'
6. Action taken on behalf of the Minister of Health or the Secretary of State by a (Regional Health Authority, an Area Health Authority, a District Health Authority, a special health authority except the Rampton Hospital Review Board, a Family Practitioner Committee, a Health Board or the Common Services Agency for the Scottish Health Service) or by the Public Health Laboratory Service Board. Action taken by any person appointed by the Lord Chancellor as a member of the administrative staff of any court or tribunal, so far as that action is taken at the discretion, or on the authority of any person acting in a judicial capacity or in his capacity as a member of the tribunal. Similarly, any action taken by any member of the administrative staff of a relevant tribunal.
7. 'Action taken in matters relating to contractual or other commercial transactions, whether within the United Kingdom or elsewhere, being transactions of a government department or authority to which this Act applies or of any such authority or body as is mentioned in paragraph (a) or (b) of subsection (1) of s6 of this Act as not being transactions for or relating to –

   a. the acquisition of land compulsorily or in circumstances in which it could be acquired compulsorily;

   b. the disposal as surplus of land acquired compulsorily or in such circumstances as aforesaid.'

8. 'Action taken in respect of appointments or removals, pay, discipline, superannuation or other personnel matters, in relation to –

   a. service in any of the armed forces of the Crown, including reserve and auxiliary and cadet forces;

   b. service in any office or employment under the Crown or under any authority listed in Schedule 2 of this Act; or

   c. service in any office or employment, or under any contract for service, in respect of which power to take action, or to determine or approve the action to be taken, in such matters is vested in Her Majesty, any Minister of the Crown or any such authority as aforesaid.'

9. 'The grant of honours, awards or privileges within the gift of the Crown, including the grant of Royal Charters.'

10. Under s110 of the Courts and Legal Services Act 1990, s5 and Sch 3 of the 1967 Act are amended to exclude from the ombudsman's jurisdiction action taken by any person appointed by the Lord Chancellor as a member of the administrative staff of any court or tribunal, so far as that action is taken at the direction of any person acting in a judicial capacity, or in his capacity as a member of the tribunal.

As regards those departments subject to his investigation, the PCA is limited by s5(1) to investigating:

> '... any action taken by or on behalf of a government department or other authority to which this Act applies, being action taken in the exercise of administrative functions of that department or authority'.

The effect of this is that he cannot carry out any investigation of complaints relating to the exercise of legislative functions, such as the preparation or creation of delegated legislation, although he could investigate complaints into the way in which a scheme set up by way of delegated legislation was actually being administered.

   Section 12(3) of the Act provides:

> 'It is hereby declared that nothing in this Act authorises or requires the Commissioner to question the merits of a decision taken without maladministration by a government department or other authority in the exercise of a discretion vested in that department or authority ...'

Despite earlier views to the contrary (see Sir Edmund Compton's approach), this section is now seen as meaning that the PCA cannot actually question the merits of a decision taken without maladministration. He can still investigate maladministration in administrative processes and the decisions resulting therefrom.

Who may complain?

This is governed principally by s6 of the 1967 Act, which provides:

> '6(1) A complaint under this Act may be made by any individual, or by any body of persons whether incorporated or not, not being –
>
> a) a local authority or other authority or body constituted for purposes of the public service or of local government or for the purposes of carrying on under national ownership any industry or undertaking or party of an industry or undertaking;
>
> b) any other authority or body whose members are appointed by Her Majesty or any Minister of the Crown or government department, or whose revenues consist wholly or mainly of moneys provided by Parliament.
>
> (2) Where the person by whom a complaint might have been made under the foregoing provisions of this Act has died or is for any reason unable to act for himself, the complaint may be made by his personal representative or by a member of his family or other individual suitable to represent him; but except as aforesaid a complaint shall not be entertained under this Act unless made by the person aggrieved himself.'

The 'hurdles'

A person wishing to have a complaint considered by the PCA must first clear a number of procedural and jurisdictional hurdles, as follows:

1. Each complaint must be in writing.
2. Complaints must be submitted in the first instance to a Member of Parliament. This is the so-called 'MP filter' which is supposed to serve two functions. First, it provides the Member with an opportunity to deal with the complaint if he sees fit; secondly, it is a means by which clearly inappropriate or unmeritorious complaints can be rejected before reaching the PCA, thus reducing his workload. In reality Members of Parliament are reluctant to reject complaints in this manner for fear of appearing unhelpful to their constituents.
3. Complaints must be of injustice sustained in consequence of maladministration. Maladministration is nowhere defined in the Act, but the so-called 'Crossman's catalogue' is frequently cited as an example of its meaning.
4. A complainant will not have his complaint investigated if it appears that it is:

> ' – any action in respect of which the person aggrieved has or had right of appeal, reference or review to or before a tribunal constituted by or under any enactment or by virtue of Her Majesty's prerogative; or
>
> any action in respect of which the person aggrieved has or had a remedy by way of proceedings in any court of law.
>
> Provided that the Commissioner may conduct an investigation notwithstanding that the person aggrieved has or had such a right or remedy if satisfied that in the particular circumstances it is not reasonable to expect him to resort or have resorted to it.'
> (Section 5(2))

In *Congreve* v *Home Office* [1976] QB 629 Mr Congreve successfully applied for a declaration that the Home Office had acted illegally in revoking the television licences of those who had renewed their licences early to avoid paying the new higher fee. In fact, the action of the Home Office had already been condemned in a special report by the PCA, illustrating the overlap between the powers of the courts, and the role of the PCA in policing maladministration.

5. Complaints are subject to a time limit, as s6(3) indicates:

> 'A complaint shall not be entertained under this Act unless it is made to a member of the House of Commons not later than twelve months from the day on which the person aggrieved first had notice of the matters alleged in the complaint; but the Commissioner may conduct an investigation pursuant to a complaint not made within that period if he considers that there are special circumstances which make it proper to do so.'

6. Complaints must be resident in the United Kingdom, or the action complained of must have taken place in relation to him whilst he was present in the United Kingdom. Complaints may be accepted in relation to the actions of consular staff abroad, provided the aggrieved person is a United Kingdom citizen. See s6(5).

Investigative procedure

By s5(5):

> 'In determining whether to initiate, continue or discontinue an investigation under this Act, the Commissioner shall, subject to the foregoing provisions of this section, act in accordance with his own discretion; and any question whether a complaint is duly made under this Act shall be determined by the Commissioner.'

Presumably the PCA's discretion is not unlimited, but the courts have shown themselves unwilling to question his decisions as to whether to investigate a complaint or not: see *Re Fletcher's Application* [1970] 2 All ER 527.

It should be noted that the PCA adopts an investigatory approach to complaints, if possible promoting a friendly settlement between the private individual and government department. The basic procedure is outlined by s7 of the Act, which states:

> '7(1) Where the Commissioner proposes to conduct an investigation pursuant to a complaint under this Act, he shall afford to the principal officer of the department or authority concerned, and to any other person who is alleged in the complaint to have taken or authorised the action complained of, an opportunity to comment on any allegations contained in the complaint.
> (2) Every such investigation shall be conducted in private, but except as aforesaid the procedure for conducting an investigation shall be such as the Commissioner considers appropriate in the circumstances of the case; and without prejudice to the generality of the foregoing provision the Commissioner may obtain information from such persons and in such manner, and make such inquiries, as he thinks fit, and may determine whether any person may be represented, by counsel or solicitor or otherwise, in the investigation.'

The PCA has powers similar to those of the High Court as regards securing the presence of witnesses and the production of documents. Section 8 states:

> '8(1) For the purposes of an investigation under this Act the Commissioner may require any Minister, officer or member of the department or authority concerned or any other

person who in his opinion is able to furnish information or produce documents relevant to the investigation to furnish any such information or produce any such document.

(2) For the purposes of any such investigation the Commissioner shall have the same powers as the Court in respect of the attendance and examination of witnesses (including the administration of oaths or affirmations and the examination of witnesses abroad) and in respect of the production of documents.

(3) No obligation to maintain secrecy or other restriction upon the disclosure of information obtained by or furnished to persons in Her Majesty's service, whether imposed by any enactment or by any rule of law, shall apply to the disclosure of information for the purposes of an investigation under this Act; and the Crown shall not be entitled in relation to any such investigation to any such privilege in respect of the production of documents or the giving evidence as is allowed by law in legal proceedings.'

Note that subs4 excludes the production of Cabinet or Cabinet Committee papers.

The PCA is protected in the conduct of his investigations by the laws relating to contempt of court: see s9(1).

The PCA is empowered to reimburse complainants and witnesses for their expenses, and pay compensation for the time they have given up to help his investigation: see s7(3).

Reports

On completing his investigations, the PCA must report on his findings to the Member of Parliament who referred the complaint to him, and to the principal officer of the government department against whom the complaint was made: see s10(3).

Enforcement

Put simply, the PCA cannot have any of his recommendations put into effect by force of law. If he conducts an investigation and concludes that maladministration has occurred, and that the complainant has suffered injustice as a result, he can lay a special report on the matter before both Houses of Parliament.

Everything is then left to the doctrine of ministerial responsibility, the assumption being that the minister will be asked questions about the matter, and will have to taken some appropriate action. In reality such reports are not often necessary, because a mutually agreed settlement can be reached.

22.3 Parliamentary control of the Parliamentary Commissioner for Administration

By s10(4) of the 1967 Act:

'The Commissioner shall annually lay before each House of Parliament a general report on the performance of his functions under this Act and may from time to time lay before each House of Parliament such other reports with respect to those functions as he thinks fit.'

Such annual reports are always referred to the relevant Select Committee for consideration, and comment where appropriate. Since 1967 the Select Committees have made a number of suggestions as to the way in which the PCA should carry out his functions, such as the correct approach to s12(3) of the 1967 Act, and the widening of his powers to deal with the actions of United Kingdom consular officials. At present the PCA lays quarterly reports of selected cases, and occasionally reports of special interest. Reports do not identify complainants, ministers or civil servants.

Some disquiet was expressed at the eight-month delay in the reappointment of the Select Committee following the 1992 election. In February 1993 the Committee announced that it was to undertake a far-reaching inquiry into the jurisdiction and procedures of the Parliamentary and Health Service Commissioners.

22.4 Judicial control

The PCA is a creature of statute and therefore can be classified with other administrative bodies of limited jurisdiction. He is amenable to judicial review but, as stated above, the courts are yet to intervene to invalidate any of his actions. In *R v Local Commissioner for Administration for the North and East Area of England, ex parte Bradford Metropolitan County Council* [1979] QB 287 the court refused to grant an order of prohibition to prevent the Local Government Commissioner from conducting an investigation, but note that in *R v Local Commissioner for Administration for the South (etc), ex parte Eastleigh Borough Council* [1988] 3 WLR 113, the Court of Appeal held (the Master of the Rolls dissenting) that the local government ombudsman had exceeded his powers in making certain reports, because it had not been established that the complainant had suffered injustice in consequence of maladministration. See also *R v Commissioner for Local Administration, ex parte Croydon London Borough Council* [1989] 1 All ER 1033.

In *R v Parliamentary Commissioner, ex parte Dyer* [1994] 1 WLR 621 the applicant had complained to the PCA in relation to the mishandling of her claim for invalidity benefit and other related welfare benefits. Subsequent to his investigation the Department of Social Security agreed to offer the applicant an apology and an ex gratia payment of £500 plus her expenses. The PCA reported to the applicant's MP, and the department, that he considered this a satisfactory outcome. The applicant sought judicial review of the PCA's alleged failure to investigate all of her complaints, his failure to seek her comments on the settlement, and his view that he was precluded from reopening the complaint. The PCA contended that either his decisions were unreviewable, as he was answerable to Parliament for the discharge of his functions, or they could only be reviewed in the exceptional case where he had abused his discretion. While noting that, in theory, the PCA's decisions were reviewable, in practice, given the wide discretion vested in him by the 1967 Act, any court would be reluctant to intervene. Consequently the PCA's decision only to select certain of the applicant's complaints for investigation would not be overturned. His practice of submitting a draft report to the department being investigated but not to the complainant was not contrary to natural justice, given that it was the department being investigated that would have to defend its action if it was found to have been guilty of maladministration. Having submitted his report to the relevant government department and to the relevant MP the PCA had no remaining power to re-open the complaint as he was functus officio.

22.5 The work of the Parliamentary Commissioner for Administration

The PCA provides details of the range of his investigations, and of his more significant cases, in the annual report that is presented to Parliament. Among the PCA's more notable successes was his investigation into what became known as 'the Sachsenhausen case'.

Under an Anglo-German Agreement of 1964 the German Government provided £1m for compensating UK citizens who had suffered from Nazi persecution during the Second World War. Distribution of this money was left to the discretion of the UK Government and in 1964 the then Foreign Secretary, R A Butler, approved rules for the distribution. Later the Foreign Office withheld compensation from 12 persons who claimed to be within these rules because of their detention within the Sachsenhausen concentration camp. Pressure from many MPs failed to get this decision reversed, a complaint of maladministration was referred to the PCA. By this time the whole of the £1m had been distributed to other claimants. After extensive investigations the PCA reported that there were defects in the administrative procedures by which the Foreign Office reached its decisions and subsequently defended them, and that this maladministration had damaged the reputation of the claimants. When this report was debated in the Commons, the then Foreign Secretary, George Brown, assumed personal responsibility for the decisions of the Foreign Office, which he maintained were correct. He nonetheless made available an additional £25,000 in order that the claimants might receive the same rate of compensation as successful claimants on the fund.

Similarly high-level investigations have included Sir Cecil Clothier's report on the failure of the Home Office to review the convictions of over 1,500 prisoners who had been convicted on the strength of the discredited evidence of Home Office forensic scientist Dr Alan Clift. The Home Office was criticised in the PCA's report for its 'serious failure' to act more quickly in the light of what he described as an 'unprecedented pollution of justice'. The PCA was also involved in obtaining compensation (over £150m) for those who had lost money through investing in Barlow Clowes, following the licensing of the company by the DTI, and £600,000 was made available to compensate poultry farmers following the handling of the salmonella in eggs scare by the MAFF.

Many of the complaints investigated have resulted in modest levels of compensation being paid, but they are nevertheless important in providing the individual concerned with an assurance that his concerns are taken seriously, and can result in improvements in the way that the executive conducts its business. For example, where Customs officials had advised that a car could be temporarily imported into the United Kingdom without payment of purchase tax, but on arrival the owner was made to pay the £167 purchase tax which was in reality due, the PCA persuaded the Department, which had refused any concession, to refund the full amount. Similarly where a complainant had been encouraged by the Board of Trade to suppose that his company would be eligible for an investment grant if it installed a grain-processing plant. The plant was ruled ineligible after it had been installed and the expenditure had been incurred. The PCA persuaded the Board to pay compensation of £950.

While the reports of the PCA are usually acted upon by ministers, there have been instances where they have been ignored, most notably in the case of the collapse of the Court Line holiday company, where he criticised the Minister concerned for leading the public into believing that the company was sound and that they should continue to book holidays with it. Many members of the public suffered financial loss when the company went into liquidation, but the government department denied any fault on its part.

The government department attracting the highest number of complaints is usually the Department of Social Security, closely followed by the Inland Revenue. This does not reflect on the quality of staff in these departments but illustrates the point that these are areas where difficulties are likely to be encountered by the individual dealing with the administrative.

The PCA's report for 1992 reveals that 945 cases were referred to him; of these 103 were upheld in full and 74 in part, while 661 were deemed by the PCA to be beyond his jurisdiction.

22.6 The other 'ombudsmen'

The Local Government Act 1974

The 1974 Act established two Commissions for Local Administration, one for England and one for Wales. A similar Commission was created for Scotland.

The Commission for Local Government (CLG) investigates complaints of maladministration in connection with the execution of administrative functions performed by a local authority. Normally complaints must be in writing and submitted in the first instance to a member of the authority against whom the complaint is made, although the CLG can accept direct complaints if he sees fit. Under s26(6) Local Government Act 1974, the local government ombudsman is not permitted to entertain a complaint in relation to any issue in respect of which the complainant has a viable remedy before the courts. See *R v Commissioner for Local Administration, ex parte Croydon London Borough Council* [1989] 1 All ER 1033.

In the event that a local authority is found guilty of maladministration the CLG will issue a report, copies of which must be kept available by the local authority concerned for public inspection. If an authority fails to respond to criticisms made in a CLG report, there is little he can do except make a further report. His findings are unenforceable, as is the case with the PCA, the vital difference being the absence of any equivalent of ministerial responsibility at local government level to cajole councils into action. Note that any matter which affects all or most of the authority's inhabitants is outside the jurisdiction of the CLG.

The refusal of some local authorities to comply with the findings of the CLG has become the subject of increasing concern. In *Administrative Justice: Some Necessary Reforms*, published by 'Justice' in 1988, the authors observe that:

'The local commissioners are treated contemptuously by some local authorities and the public are repeatedly being made aware of their inability to achieve results.'

The report goes on to point out that of the 160 reports issued by the local government commissioners up to 31 March 1986, 120 had failed to produce a satisfactory conclusion.

Northern Ireland

In 1969 the 'ombudsman' principle was extended to the Province, and it should be noted that the Commissioner for Complaints Act (Northern Ireland) 1969 provides for decisions of the Northern Ireland Parliamentary Commissioner for Administration to be enforceable by way of a complainant applying to the county court for damages, injunction or other appropriate order.

The Health Service Commissioners

The National Health Service Reorganisation Act 1973 and National Health Service (Scotland) Act 1972 created three Health Service Ombudsmen (one each for England, Wales and Scotland respectively). The relevant statutory provisions were subsequently re-enacted in the National Health Service Act 1977 and the National Health Service Act (Scotland) 1978, and have now been consolidated in the Health Service Commissioners Act 1993.

The Health Service Commissioners are appointed by the Queen on the advice of the Prime Minister, and hold office during good behaviour, retiring at the age of sixty-five. It has been past practice for the same person to occupy all four posts (Parliamentary Commissioner and Health Service Commissioners).

The Health Service Commissioner for England can investigate complaints made against Regional Health Authorities, District Health Authorities, specified Special

Health Authorities, NHS Trusts, Family Health Service Authorities, the Dental Practice Board and the Public Health Laboratory Service Board. The provisions for Wales and Scotland are broadly similar. A complaint must allege that a person has sustained injustice or hardship in consequence of: a failure in a service provided by a health service body; the failure of such a body to provide a service that it was a function of that body to provide; maladministration connected with any other action taken by or on behalf of such a body. As with the Parliamentary Commissioner, the Health Service Commissioners are not authorised to question the merits of a decision taken without maladministration by a health service body in the exercise of a discretion vested in that body (s3).

A complaint can be made by an individual or organisation, whether incorporated or not, provided that the complainant is not a 'public authority' as defined in s8(2). Complaints must be made in writing, normally within a year of the matter complained of being made aware to the complainant, and the body that is the subject of the complaint must normally have been given an opportunity to respond to it before the commissioner acts. In contrast to the procedure to be followed in respect of the Parliamentary Commissioner, the health Service Commissioners have the power to accept complaints directly from members of the public and organisations.

Investigations are conducted in private, with the health body concerned being given an opportunity to comment on the allegations. The exact procedure to be adopted is largely within the discretion of the relevant commissioner. Health service bodies under investigation, and any other person who may be able to assist the investigation can be compelled to produce evidence, and those who obstruct the inquiry can be subject to punishment for contempt of court.

The Health Service Commissioners cannot normally entertain complaints where the complainant has the right to obtain redress in respect of the matter complained of before a court or tribunal. Under s5 of the 1993 Act the commissioners are specifically excluded from investigating complaints that relate to the diagnosis of illness or the care or treatment of a patient, where, in the opinion of the commissioner, the action complained of was taken solely in consequence of the exercise of clinical judgment.

On completion of his investigation the commissioner will send a copy of his report to (inter alia) the complainant, any MP involved in the making of the complaint, and the health service body concerned.

22.7 Criticisms

Criticisms, and suggestions as to how the various Commissioners could function more effectively, have come from academics, Select Committees and the Commissioners themselves. The main points made are as follows.

Procedure

The continued existence of the 'MP filter' has been subject to criticism. It is possible that some Members of Parliament have adopted a policy of automatically referring complaints, and it serves to distance the PCA from the public, which is not seen as desirable. A previous PCA, Sir Cecil Clothier, received many complaints directly from the public, and responded not by rejecting them but by submitting them to Members of Parliament so that they could be re-submitted to him.

It has been argued that the PCA should be able to launch investigations on his own initiative.

Jurisdiction

The PCA should also be allowed to investigate the preparation and making of delegated legislation, which he is at present unable to do, being restricted to 'administrative' functions.

The PCA should also be allowed to investigate complaints concerning personnel matters in the civil service, government contracts, and the activities of nationalised industries (the latter being within the jurisdiction of his French counterpart, the Médiateur).

Enforcement

At local government level, a major weakness of the CLGs is the absence of any effective methods of enforcing recommendations contained in reports. An improvement would be an extension of the Northern Ireland system whereby complainants can obtain court orders to compel local authorities to act.

22.8 Advantages over judicial review

Jurisdictional

Judicial review is, with the exception of error of law, limited to ensuring that public bodies act intra vires, yet there are many forms of maladministration which can cause problems for the public without amounting to ultra vires action. These may be beyond the control of the courts, but matters such as delay, incompetence, stupidity, rudeness and loss of documents fall squarely within the ambit of the PCA. In short, the PCA can reach problems of administration beyond the reaches of judicial review.

Many of the matters dealt with would not warrant litigation even if they were within the scope of judicial review, but are nevertheless a problem to those affected. For example, a complaint may result in a form being made more comprehensible, or a process being speeded up.

Practical

A complaint to the PCA costs the price of a postage stamp! All other costs are borne by the taxpayer, which compares favourably with judicial review. As will have been noted, the PCA can even award complainants out-of-pocket expenses.

As the investigation is conducted by the PCA, no effort is required on the part of the complainant to prepare a prima facie case, unlike the application for judicial review.

The time limit for bringing a complaint, 12 months, is more liberal than the three months allowed under RSC O.53.

As the PCA procedure is conciliatory as opposed to adversarial, the dispute is unlikely to be exacerbated by his investigation, and those called to give evidence are less likely to be defensive, given that their anonymity is assured.

Remedies

The PCA works towards an amicable settlement between the complainant and the government department. The result of this settlement may be something that could not have been obtained on an application for judicial review, and ranges from an ex gratia payment (remember damages are not available for ultra vires action) or the reversal of a decision (judicial review can only quash a decision, not substitute a new one) to the alteration of an administrative process (some court decisions about improper administrative processes are simply not implemented).

Decisions by courts on applications for judicial review only directly effect the case of individual litigants involved; a wider significance can only be obtained if the decision is widely reported and followed by administrators. Where, by contrast, the PCA investigates and reports that a particular administrative process is improper, the department concerned may well agree to amend its procedures in future cases: the so-called 'ripple effect'. The finding in relation to one complaint may affect the treatment of hundreds or thousands of similar cases where no complaint has actually been made.

23

Recent Cases

23.1 Prerogative power

23.2 Liabilities of local authorities

23.3 Introduction to judicial review

23.1 Prerogative power

R v *Secretary of State for the Home Department, ex parte Fire Brigades Union and Others* (1994) The Times 10 November Court of Appeal (Sir Thomas Bingham MR, Hobhouse and Morritt LJJ)

Use of prerogative power in preference to statutory scheme – whether lawful

Facts

A scheme existed for allocating public funds by way of compensation for the victims of crime. The scheme, which was administered by the Criminal Injuries Compensation Board, was created under the prerogative. Sections 108–117 of the Criminal Justice Act 1988 sought to codify this scheme and place it on a statutory basis, leaving the quantum of any funds awarded to be determined by application of common law principles. Section 171(1) empowered the Secretary of State to bring the scheme into effect on a day to be announced. In November 1993, in the exercise of his prerogative powers, the Secretary of State announced a new tariff scheme under which set amounts would be payable to the victims of crime, depending upon how their claims were categorised. The effect of this new tariff scheme was that much lower awards would be made in the future, resulting in a halving of the cost of the criminal injuries compensation scheme by the year 2000. The applicants applied for judicial review of:

1. the Secretary of State's failure to implement the statutory scheme under the 1988 Act; and
2. his exercise of prerogative power in introducing the revised tariff for awards.

The application was dismissed at first instance, and the applicants appealed.

Held

The appeal was allowed (in part). Whilst the Secretary of State was under no duty to introduce the statutory scheme, it was an abuse of his common law prerogative powers to introduce a compensation scheme other than that contained in the 1988 Act. The Master of the Rolls dissented on the first issue and Hobhouse LJ on the second.

On the first issue Hobhouse and Morritt LJJ took the view that the Secretary of State was under no duty to bring the statutory compensation scheme into effect, and thus could not be forced to do so by the courts, ie he could delay introduction indefinitely. It was the view of Hobhouse LJ that Parliament could have restricted this discretion and had chosen not to do so. Sir Thomas Bingham MR (dissenting) expressed the view that the Secretary of State had a discretion under s171(1) regarding the date for the introduction of the statutory scheme and thus had the power to delay its introduction where there were proper grounds for doing so, eg the need to prepare legislation or the cost to the exchequer. In his view, however, the Secretary of State could not be permitted to say that he need never bring the provisions into force as this would call into question why Parliament had ever enacted the scheme.

On the second issue, Sir Thomas Bingham MR and Morritt LJ expressed the view that the Secretary of State could not exercise his prerogative power to introduce a new tariff scheme when a power to introduce such a scheme existed under statute. The relevant provisions of the 1988 Act would have to be repealed before the exercise of prerogative power in this sphere could be permitted.

23.2 Liabilities of local authorities

West Wiltshire District Council v *Garland and Others* [1994] NLJ 1733
Court of Appeal (Balcombe, Butler-Sloss and Leggatt LJJ)

District auditors – whether duty owed – breach of statutory duty

Facts

The plaintiff local authority had commenced proceedings against a number of its own senior council officers for breach of contract and fiduciary duty, alleging that they had procured the making of payments by the local authority in breach of its procedures. The defendants issued third party notices against the Audit Commission's district auditors alleging that the auditors had negligently advised the defendants in respect of payments, and that in doing so they had been in breach of their duty to give proper advice to the local authority and its officers. It was contended that the auditors were liable either to contribute to any award of damages made in favour of the local authority, or should indemnify the defendants in respect of any damages awarded. At first instance, an application by the auditors to have the third party notices set aside and the proceedings against them dismissed was allowed in part on the basis that, whilst it cannot have been the intention of Parliament that the duty should be owed to the council officers, the auditors were under a duty, vis-à-vis the local authority, to conduct an audit properly. As a consequence, the court ordered that the third party notices be amended, so as to sever the claims based on any duty owed towards the individual council officers, or any common law duty of care owed to the local authority, leaving the possibility of liability for breach of statutory duty as regards the local authority. The auditors appealed against this ruling.

Held

The appeal (so far as it related to the auditors' duty to the authority) was dismissed.

Adopting the principles set out by Lord Bridge in *Hague* v *Deputy Governor of Parkhurst Prison* [1991] 3 All ER 733 in assessing whether or not the existence of an actionable breach of statutory duty would create a right to sue for damages, the Court of Appeal held that the questions to consider were:

1. Was the auditing duty created by the Local Government Finance Act 1982 owed to a class including the local authority and its officers?
2. If the answer to this was 'Yes', had Parliament intended to give such persons an enforceable right of action under the legislation?

On this basis the auditing body owed a statutory duty to the body being audited, and breach of that duty was actionable at the suit of that authority. Further, the right to sue for damages for breach of statutory duty did not preclude a common law duty enforceable by an action in negligence.

It would not be proper, however, to conclude that the District Auditor could be personally liable in negligence to the very officers it was his duty to criticise if he believed there had been irregularities. Alternatively, the denial of a common law duty of care owing to the officers could be rationalised on the grounds of 'proximity'. Short of being the subject of an action for bad faith, public policy required that the district auditor must be uninhibited in the discharge of his functions and his criticism of individual officers.

M v *Newham London Borough Council and Others; X (Minors)* v *Bedfordshire County Council* [1994] 2 WLR 554 Court of Appeal (Sir Thomas Bingham MR, Staughton and Peter Gibson JJ)

Breach of statutory duty towards child – whether local authority liable in damages

Facts

In the first appeal, the child plaintiff M had been made a ward of court following interviews in which she had named her mother's boyfriend as the person responsible for sexually abusing her. When M's mother eventually saw the transcript of her daughter's evidence she was able to point out that the person her daughter had identified as the perpetrator of the abuse was in fact a cousin, who had lived with M and her mother some time previously. The local authority took steps to rehabilitate M with her mother. M, her mother, and the mother's boyfriend sought damages in respect of the distress caused by these events, alleging that the local authority, the health authority, and the psychiatrist employed by the health authority, had failed to take reasonable care to investigate the allegations of sexual abuse properly. The action was struck out as disclosing no cause of action and the plaintiffs appealed. In the second appeal the local authority delayed for over two years before seeking care orders in respect of the infant plaintiffs, despite evidence from the NSPCC, schools, the police and neighbours that the children were living in dreadful conditions, were malnourished and at risk of sexual abuse. The action brought against the local authority was struck out and the plaintiffs appealed.

Held

1. Dismissing the appeals, no action for breach of statutory duty lay in respect of the actions of the local authorities.
2. (Sir Thomas Bingham dissenting) no action would lie at common law for negligence.

Extracts from judgments

On the issue of breach of statutory duty Sir Thomas Bingham MR observed:

'The courts are very regularly called upon to consider whether the imposition of a duty by a particular statute impliedly givers a right of action to a person injured by reason of a breach of that duty. I myself share the regret voiced by Lord du Parcq in *Cutler* v *Wandsworth Stadium Ltd* [1949] AC 398, 410:

"Parliament has not by now made it a rule to state explicitly what its intention is in a matter which is often of no little importance, instead of leaving it to the courts to discover, by a careful examination and analysis of what is expressly said, what that intention may be supposed probably to be."

But the proper approach of the courts to their task of examination and analysis has been clearly and authoritatively laid down, and has not been the subject of debate before us. The governing principles were very helpfully summarised by Lord Jauncey of Tullichettle in *R* v *Deputy Governor of Parkhurst Prison, ex parte Hague* [1992] 1 AC 58, 168G–171A, and we must apply them.

It is very clear, from the statutes to which brief reference has been made and other statutes not mentioned, that protection of the interests and welfare of children has for many years been a prime object of parliamentary concern. The framework of protection has been developed and refined over the years. Local authorities have increasingly become the primary instrument for giving effect to the intentions of Parliament. To that end, and no doubt in recognition of the very sensitive and difficult questions which are bound to arise, the responsibility for judging what ought or ought not to be done in the case of any given child is in the first instance entrusted to them. There can in this case be no doubt about the class for whose protection the legislation was enacted. Nor can there be doubt about Parliament's intention that the duties imposed upon local authorities should (despite all the inherent difficulties) be competently and conscientiously performed. But I can detect nothing in any of the legislation which persuades me that Parliament intended to confer a right of action on any person who could show, without more, a breach of any of these statutory duties injurious to him. It seems to me fatal to the plaintiffs' contentions (1) that the duties imposed on local authorities were framed in terms too general and unparticular to lend themselves at all readily to direct enforcement by individuals; and (2) that the local authorities were accorded so large an area for the exercise of their subjective judgment as to suggest that direct enforcement by individuals was not contemplated.'

Regarding the availability of damages for breach of statutory duty, Staughton LJ observed:

'When we speak of the intention of Parliament we may often mean, in effect, the intention of the government department which sponsored a bill, or of the parliamentary draftsman who wrote it, or of members who prepared amendments. But in any case it is an objective assessment, founded on the language of the statute and the terms of its other provisions, and on an assessment of the reasons which would have motivated the legislature to confer, or not to confer, a right to damages for breach.

In *Cutler* v *Wandsworth Stadium Ltd* [1949] AC 398, 410 Lord du Parcq said:

"To a person unversed in the science or art of legislation it may well seem strange that Parliament has not by now made it a rule to state explicitly what its intention is ... There are no doubt reasons which inhibit the legislature from revealing its intention in plain words. I do not know, and must not speculate, what those reasons may be."

One can, I think, legitimately infer that it might have been politically embarrassing to insert in the Children Act 1989 a section reading "No local authority shall be liable to a child for negligence in performing its duties under this Act, or in failing to do so." Some members might have hesitated to vote for so explicit a disclaimer. Would there have been embarrassment and hesitation if instead the section had said that the local authority *was* to be liable? One cannot tell [as Lord du Parcq implied], and must not speculate.

For a number of reasons which I shall consider later, it would appear that in recent times there has been some slight hardening of the courts' approach, against finding a remedy in damages for breach of statutory duty.'

He continued:

'There may be a number of reasons for the tend against enforcement in private law, if such it be. It is of course no new phenomenon that statutes enact duties on public officials which may impinge on the lives of every citizen. That happens in education, in the health service, and in child care itself since 1889. But it can certainly be said that there has been no decrease in the process. By contrast it has, in recent times, become all too clear that the private enforcement of civil rights is only available on a somewhat capricious basis. Disregarding corporate plaintiffs, only the very rich or the very poor among private individuals can accord to bring a civil action. It is unlikely that Parliament is primarily concerned with enforcement only by those two classes when it enacts legislation.

There are, of course means of enforcement other than a civil suit when a duty is enacted by statute. Take for example section 17(1) of the Children Act 1989: "It shall be the general duty of every local authority ... (a) to safeguard and promote the welfare of children within their area who are in deed; ..." In the first place, the members and employees of a local authority will know of that section; it is to be hoped that they will enforce it upon themselves. Secondly, if they do not, the Secretary of State or Members of Parliament or the National Society for the Prevention of Cruelty to Children can draw their attention to the duty and any specific need for it to be observed. Newspapers can do the same; and there is the sanction of severe criticism by the press or a public inquiry when an error is made. There is the local government ombudsman. There are also the remedies of public law. These are invoked, for example, in relation to statements under section 7 of the Education Act 1981, which deal with the special educational needs of particular children. Finally the Children Act 1989 itself contains its own remedies. Section 26(3) provides that every local authority shall establish a procedure for considering representations and complaints. By section 84 the Secretary of State may declare a local authority to be in default if it has failed to comply with any duty under the Act, and give directions to ensure compliance.

I bear in mind that the cause of action in the *Newham* case is said to have arisen in 1987 and 1988, before the Children Act 1989 was passed; and that the *Bedfordshire* case covers a period before and after it came into force in October 1991. For that very reason counsel for Bedfordshire did not rely on alternative remedies in the statute. Nevertheless it is, as it seems to me, open to serious question whether Parliament ever envisaged that the various statutes with which we are concerned would be enforced by a private civil suit, as opposed to the other remedies which I have mentioned. In my judgment the statutory duties relied on in these appeals are in the nature of public law functions, the expressions used by Lord Bridge of Harwich in *Cocks* v *Thanet District Council* [1983] 2 AC 286, 292, and adopted by Otton J in *E (A Minor)* v *Dorset County Council*, 7 April 1993. They involve to a large extent an exercise by the local authority of its own judgment or discretion, with a view to invoking the assistance of the courts (or not doing so).

For all these reasons I conclude that the statutory provisions in question here do not give rise to a private law remedy in damages.'

Stovin v *Wise; Norfolk County Council (Third Party)* [1994] 1 WLR 1124 Court of Appeal (Nourse, Kennedy and Roch LJJ)

Failure by a highway authority to make junction safe – whether principles of negligence applicable

Facts

The plaintiff motorcyclist was injured in a collision with a car being driven by the defendant. The plaintiff's visibility at the junction where the collision occurred had been obscured by a raised bank of earth to his left. The local highway authority was aware of the dangerous nature of the junction and the fact that a number of accidents had occurred there in the recent past. Efforts had been made to secure the agreement of the landowner to the levelling of the ground to improve visibility at the junction, but by the time of the plaintiff's accident no response had been received. The plaintiff's action against the defendant was settled, but the defendant joined the highway authority as a third party alleging that it was to blame for not having taken more steps to improve safety at the junction. At first instance the court ruled that the highway authority had breached its common law duty of care and that it was 30 per cent to blame for the collision. The authority appealed.

Held

The appeal was dismissed.

Extracts from the judgments

Kennedy LJ summarised the position at common law, by reference to *Anns* v *Merton London Borough Council* [1978] AC 728, *Sheppard* v *Glossop Corporation* [1921] 3 KB 132 and *East Suffolk Rivers Catchment Board* v *Kent* [1941] AC 74, and continued:

'In the present case the distinction between the policy and operational area of the statutory power never arose, because the highway authority never got to the point of deciding whether or not to use the statutory power, but as Lord Wilberforce [in *Anns*] makes clear the existence of a power may create an obligation to consider whether or not to exercise it. Having referred to the *East Suffolk* case he said, at p755:

"... to say that councils are under no duty to inspect, is not a sufficient statement of the position. They are under a duty to give proper consideration to the question whether they should inspect or not. Their immunity from attack, in the event of failure to inspect, in other words, though great is not absolute. And because it is not absolute, the necessary premise for the proposition 'if no duty to inspect, then no duty to take care in inspection' vanishes."

Lord Wilberforce may have had in mind action against a council by way of judicial review, but, at pp756–757, he set out what he considered to be two significant points about the *East Suffolk* case: first, the operational activity at the breach in the wall was still within a discretionary area, and secondly only Lord Atkin considered the case in relation to a duty of care at common law. That, to my mind, emphasises how difficult it is for the highway authority in the present case to derive any assistance from the *East Suffolk* case. In *Anns'* case Lord Salmon, at p765G, was "not at all sure what point of law the *East Suffolk* case is said to decide" and, at p766G, expressed his agreement with Lord Atkin's dissenting decision. Lord Atkin had spoken of the general obligation of a citizen to some persons in some circumstances to conduct himself with reasonable care so as not to injure those persons likely to be affected by his want of care.

Mr Stow's first submission to us [for the highway authority] was that even if *Anns'* case was correctly decided in relation to physical damage, as opposed to economic loss, the highway authority was not liable in law to contribute to the plaintiff's damages. Once it is clear how the case is put against the highway authority at common law it seems to me that the decision in *Anns'* case although not directly relevant does offer some support for the judge's decision. What I cannot accept is Mr Stow's submission that the decision in the *East Suffolk* case affords a simple and reliable approach to the issue of common law liability in the present case, or his alternative submission, said to be based on Lord Salmon's support of Lord Atkin, that no common law duty could have arisen until the statutory power was exercised.'

As to the impact of the House of Lords' decision in *Murphy* v *Brentford District Council* [1991] 1 AC 398, he observed:

'... the House of Lords, departing from *Anns*, held that the local authority in exercising its functions was not under a common law duty to safeguard a subsequent purchaser of a house from economic loss. So, in the context of the present case, it is, as it seems to me, important to recognise two things: first, that the decision in *Murphy's* case is confined to economic loss, more than one of their Lordships indicating that the position might be different if foreseeable personal injury were sustained. Lord Oliver of Aylmerton, for example, said, at p487:

> "The infliction of physical injury to the person or property of another universally requires to be justified. The causing of economic loss does not. If it is to be categorised as wrongful it is necessary to find some factor beyond the mere occurrence of the loss and the fact that its occurrence could be foreseen."

Second, the decision was concerned with the wide-ranging common law duty to which local authorities had been held to be subject as a result of their limited involvement in the erection of buildings which later turned out to be defective. On any view there was not the close link between alleged breach of duty and damage which there is when a road accident is found to be due in part to an obstruction to visibility which a highway authority charged with the duty of maintaining the highway had decided ought to be removed, and had been in a position to carry that decision into effect before the relevant accident occurred. ... Here the highway authority did not simply fail to act. It decided positively to proceed by seeking agreement from British Rail, and its failure to pursue that course is not an omission on which it can rely to escape liability, any more than a car driver could escape liability simply because his breach of duty consisted in a failure to apply the brakes. In each case the particular omission could properly be regarded as a negligent method of performing a task which gave rise to obligations, the task in the case of the highway authority being that of obtaining consent from British Rail, and in the case of the car driver, driving his vehicle.

In *Lonrho plc* v *Tebbit* [1942] 4 All ER 280 Dillon LJ recognised that in *Rowling* v *Takaro Properties Ltd* [1988] AC 473, 501 Lord Keith had cast doubt on the usefulness of the distinction between policy and operational decisions. In the *Lonrho* case this court was being urged to strike out a claim against the Secretary of State, who it was alleged had negligently failed to release an undertaking as soon as it ceased to be in the public interest to maintain it. Dillon LJ, having reminded himself of the incremental approach to the development of the tort of negligence now favoured by the House of Lords, said, at p287:

> "... the private interest of Lonrho in having the undertaking released as soon as it was no longer needed in the public interest is obvious. It does not therefore appal me that it should be suggested that, if the Secretary of State imposes the restrictions of the undertaking on Lonrho in the public interest, the Secretary of State should thereby assume a private law duty to Lonrho to release the undertaking when it is no longer needed and the restriction on Lonrho's freedom to conduct its business no longer has a rationale. There is an arguable case for Lonrho, therefore, against which may have to be set the sort of considerations militating against the imposition of liability which Lord Keith rehearses in *Rowling* v *Takaro Properties Ltd*."

The facts in the present case are a long way from those of the *Lonrho* case, but if the highway authority in the present case could really escape liability on the basis that all it did was fail to act, the same defence ought to have been of assistance to the Secretary of State in the *Lonrho* case.'

His Lordship concluded:

'Having considered all the authorities to which are attention has been invited I am satisfied that the judge was right to find that the highway authority was in breach of duty at common law for the reasons which he gave, expanded by Mr Nelson in the way that I have indicated earlier in this judgment. The highway authority alone had responsibility for the maintenance of the roads where the accident occurred. Many of its duties and powers, including the power in section 79, had as their principal object the promotion of the safety of road users. In this case the highway authority became aware of a dangerous restriction of visibility which it, and in reality it alone, had the physical and financial resources to eliminate, and because it judged the danger to be serious it decided to devote those resources to that end. In those circumstances it seems to me to be entirely in line not only with the *Anns* approach but also with the incremental approach to liability to say that in this case once the highway authority decided to seek the co-operation of British Rail it owed a duty of care to road users to press forward with its proposal with reasonable expedition. It was in breach of that duty, and as a result it contributed to the injury which the plaintiff sustained.

Finally it may be worth saying that the decision in this case should not lead to a flood of litigation against highway authorities for failing to improve visibility. The circumstances were probably unique. The danger was significant, it was known to the authority, and subject to a landowner's agreement the authority had actually decided to act at its own expense long before the relevant accident occurred. However, we are not directly concerned with the fate of other cases or other claimants. For the reasons which I have given I am satisfied that this appeal should be dismissed.'

23.3 Introduction to judicial review

R v *Secretary of State for Employment, ex parte Equal Opportunities Commission and Another* [1994] 2 WLR 409 House of Lords (Lords Keith, Jauncey, Lowry, Browne-Wilkinson and Slynn)

Availability of judicial review – declaratory relief – locus standi

Facts
The Equal Opportunities Commission made representations to the Secretary of State to the effect that existing domestic law relating to redundancy and unfair dismissal was contrary to EC law as it indirectly discriminated against female employees by offering reduced protection to part-time workers. The Secretary of State rejected these assertions. The Equal Opportunities Commission thereupon applied for judicial review (seeking a declaration and an order of mandamus) of the Secretary of State's decision not to act in this matter, with a view to challenging the differential in the qualifying dates for redundancy compensation. It was joined in its application by D, a part-time worker, who had been made redundant shortly before the day on which she would have become eligible for a redundancy payment. The Equal Opportunities Commission also made an application for judicial review (seeking a declaration and an order of mandamus) of the Secretary of State's failure to amend the law to take into account an earlier period of full-time employment in calculating the amount of redundancy payment due. At first instance the application was refused. The Commission and D appealed unsuccessfully to the Court of Appeal, where it was held, inter alia, that D's application did not have a sufficient public law element to warrant consideration by way of judicial review and should be pursued before an industrial tribunal. Furthermore (Dillon LJ dissenting), there were other

means by which questions as to the extent to which domestic law was compatible with EC law could be resolved. The Secretary of State could not be compelled by the courts to introduce amending legislation. The Secretary of State's letter did not, in any event, raise any justiciable issues, as it did not affect any individual's legal rights or duties, and in the light of these points, the Equal Opportunities Commission lacked locus standi to pursue its applications. D and the Commission appealed to the House of Lords.

Held

1. D's appeal was dismissed, as it did not raise a matter suitable for determination by way of judicial review, and ought not to have been advanced against the Secretary of State as he was not her employer and would not be liable to compensate her in the event of her case succeeding.

2. The Commission's appeal was allowed, as the Secretary of State had not discharged the burden of showing that the indirect discrimination against women resulting from the threshold provisions of the Employment Protection (Consolidation) Act 1978 was objectively justified, and not an infringement of article 119 of the EC Treaty.

3. Even though the case was not one where the court would have been empowered to grant a prerogative order, as there was no 'decision' of the Secretary of State to quash, reference to the *Factortame* series of cases confirmed that the Commission was entitled to apply for a declaration as to the extent to which the provisions of the 1978 Act relating to redundancy and compensation for unfair dismissal were compatible with Community law. Such an application would not involve a declaration that the United Kingdom or the Secretary of State was in breach of Community obligations, as the Commission's purpose could be served simply by a declaration confirming the incompatibility of domestic law and Community law.

4. (Lord Jauncey dissenting) The Commission did have locus standi, as the litigation concerned the extent to which the legislation ensured equality of treatment of employees. Lord Keith observed:

> '... it would be a very retrograde step now to hold that the EOC has no locus standi to agitate in judicial review proceedings questions related to sex discrimination which are of public importance and affect a large section of the population. The determination of this issue turns essentially upon a consideration of the statutory duties and public law role of the EOC as regards which no helpful guidance is to be gathered from decided cases ...'

Comment

The significance of the decision may lie in the extent to which it encourages statutory bodies to adopt a dynamic role in applying for declarations concerning the compatibility of domestic and EC law, rather than waiting for a suitable case to arise as a vehicle for such a challenge.

R v *Secretary of State for Health, ex parte Furneaux* [1994] 2 All ER 652
Court of Appeal (Butler-Sloss, Mann and Peter Gibson LJJ)

Delay in applying for judicial review – grounds for denying relief sought

Facts

The applicants were doctors who had applied for permission to provide pharmaceutical services from their group practice surgery. Outline permission was granted but, following objections, an appeal was considered by the Secretary of State who, without informing the applicants of all of the evidence upon which he proposed to act, allowed the appeal and refused the permission sought. The Secretary of State's decision was made in July 1991. In December 1992 the applicants sought judicial review of his refusal and it was agreed by the parties that the refusal ought to be quashed and the matter remitted for reconsideration by the Secretary of State. In the autumn of 1991, acting on the basis of the Secretary of States's refusal to grant the applicants permission to provide pharmaceutical services at their surgery, Elmfield Drugs Ltd had purchased the only pharmacy in the locality. The company was subsequently granted leave to intervene in the review proceedings and applied for the application to be dismissed on the ground of delay. At first instance the company's application was dismissed on the basis that no link had been established between the delay on the part of the doctors in applying for review and the prejudice to the interests of a third party, the company. The company appealed.

Held

The appeal was allowed and the application for judicial review dismissed. The judge at first instance had erred in ruling that a causal link had to be established between the delay and the prejudice to third parties. Mann LJ relied upon the dictum of Ackner LJ in *R* v *Stratford-on-Avon District Council, ex parte Jackson* [1985] 3 All ER 769, to the effect that wherever there was a failure to act promptly, or at least within three months, in applying for judicial review there was, viewed objectively, undue delay. Hence, regardless of any 'good reasons' for delay, the court retained a discretion to refuse an application or the relief sought, if it was of the view that to do so would be likely to cause substantial hardship to, or substantially prejudice the rights of, any person, or would be detrimental to good administration. The correct approach was to identify a connection between prejudice and the grant of relief sought.

Glossary of Terms

Administrative Agency

See Administrative Body.

Administrative Body

A body, usually created by statute, but sometimes by prerogative powers, to carry out a particular task, such as the resolution of disputes or promotion of central government policy.

Appeal

Appeal only exists where statute so provides. On appeal an appellate body can substitute its own decision for the original. An appeal can be launched against the merits of a decision – compare with judicial review.

Audi Alteram Partem

One of the two limbs of natural justice, the rule that no man shall be denied a fair hearing – otherwise described as the right to be heard.

Certiorari

One of the prerogative orders, only available by way of judicial review against a public body having the power to determine questions affecting rights. Has the effect of quashing an ultra vires decision, or intra vires decision vitiated by error of law on the face of the record.

Declaration

Originally only available as a private law remedy, now available on an application for judicial review. Simply states the court's view of the law on the issues raised. Has no coercive force.

Delegated Legislation

A generic term for orders made by bodies given the powers to do so by Parliament. Includes statutory instruments and bye-laws. Not all matters actually described as delegated legislation are actually legislative in effect.

Directory Requirements

Statutory procedural requirements that should normally be followed, however failure to do so will not necessarily be fatal to consequent action.

Enabling Act

The primary Act that gives an inferior body the powers to act, and consequently lays down the limits of its power, eg the Civil Aviation Act 1971 is the enabling Act of the Civil Aviation Authority.

Estoppel

An estoppel arises where A makes a promise or representation to B, upon which B acts to his detriment. A may then be estopped from going back on his promise. In public law an estoppel will not normally be upheld against a public body where it would result in that body acting ultra vires, or where it would conflict with that body's public duty.

Express Limits on Power

The wording of the enabling Act detailing the limits of an inferior body's power.

Fettering Discretion

Where a body refuses to use its powers as Parliament contemplated. The fettering may arise from a contract, policy, delegation of power, or estoppel.

Implied Limits

Limits placed on the powers of inferior bodies by the courts, as opposed to the enabling Act, eg that a body must act reasonably.

Inferior Body

A body of limited jurisdiction, and therefore capable of acting ultra vires and being reviewed by the courts; see Administrative Body.

Intra Vires

Within the powers delegated to an inferior body. Intra vires actions are not normally reviewable, save for error of law on the face of the record.

Judicial Activism

Where the judiciary have decided to create new grounds for reviewing administrative action previously thought unreviewable, eg *Padfield* v *Minister of Agriculture*; *Ridge* v *Baldwin*.

Judicial Review

Supervision of inferior bodies by the courts. Concerned only with the legality of their actions not the merits. Reviewing court cannot substitute a new decision for the one reviewed. Procedure under O.53 must be used.

Jurisdiction

Power to act. Jurisdiction will be laid down in a body's enabling Act. Acting beyond jurisdiction is ultra vires.

Jurisdictional Error

Where a body makes a mistake on a matter of fact or law upon which its jurisdiction depends.

Justices

Magistrates – who frequently perform licensing functions.

Justiciable Matter

An issue upon which the courts are competent to pronounce, as opposed to non-judiciable matters such as defence policy, or the conduct of foreign affairs.

Locus Standi

An applicant for judicial review must have locus standi – meaning he has sufficient interest in the matter to which his application relates. The standing requirements are to prevent applications from persons with no connection to the issue.

Mandamus

One of the three prerogative orders, compels a public body to perform its duties.

Mandatory Requirements

Procedural requirements laid down in an inferior body's enabling Act which must be complied with. Failure to comply renders subsequent action ultra vires.

Ministerial Orders

Includes codes, guidance, and directives. See delegated legislation.

Nemo Judex in Causa Sua

One of the two rules of natural justice, that no man should be a judge in his own cause. Also referred to as the rule against bias.

Ombudsman

Formally referred to as the Parliamentary Commissioner for Administration (PCA).

Order 53

The rule of Supreme Court procedure governing the process by which applications for judicial review must be made.

Ouster Clause

A statutory provision purporting to exclude recourse to the courts by an individual wishing to challenge the decision of an inferior body.

Parent Act

See Enabling Act.

Petition of Right

The pre Crown Proceedings Act procedure by which action against the Crown in contract were proceeded with.

Prerogative Order

The public law remedy available by way of judicial review to deal with ultra vires action. They are available at the discretion of the court. Being prerogative orders they are clearly not available against the Crown. See certiorari, mandamus, or prohibition.

Prerogative Power

The power still remaining in the Crown, ie not now transferred to statute eg the power to declare war, or sign treaties.

Primary Act

See Enabling Act.

Prohibition

One of the prerogative orders, intended to stop an inferior body from acting ultra vires.

Public Body

A body created by statute having public law functions.

Public Corporation

A body created by statute to perform a particular function, either commercial or regulatory.

Statutory Corporation

See Public Body, or Public Corporation.

Subordinate Body

See Inferior Body.

Subordinate Legislation

See Delegated Legislation.

Ultra Vires

Acting beyond jurisdiction; outside the express and implied limits on power.

Void

Of no effect – as a result of being declared ultra vires by the court.

Void ab Initio

Void retrospectively, ie never of any effect.

Voidable

A decision that is effective, but could be invalidated because of some vitiating factors such as an error of law.

Index

HLT Publications

HLT books are specially planned and written to help you in every stage of your studies. Each of the wide range of textbooks is brought up-to-date annually, and the companion volumes of our Law Series are all designed to work together.

You can buy HLT books from your local bookshop, or in case of difficulty, order direct using this form,

The Law Series covers the following modules:

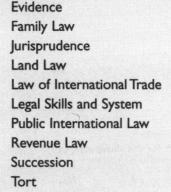

Administrative Law	Evidence
Commercial Law	Family Law
Company Law	Jurisprudence
Conflict of Laws	Land Law
Constitutional Law	Law of International Trade
Contract Law	Legal Skills and System
Criminal Law	Public International Law
Criminology	Revenue Law
English Legal System	Succession
Equity and Trusts	Tort
European Union Law	

The HLT Law Series:
A comprehensive range of books for your law course, and the legal aspects of business and commercial studies.

Each module is covered by a comprehensive six-part set of books

● Textbook

● Casebook

● Revision Workbook

● Suggested Solutions, for:
● 1985-90
● 1991-94
● 1995

Module	Books required	Cost
To complete your order, please fill in the form overleaf	Postage	
	TOTAL	

Prices (including postage and packing in the UK):
Textbooks £19.00; Casebooks £19.00; Revision Workbooks £10.00; Suggested Solutions (1985-90) £9.00, Suggested Solutions (1991-94) £6.00, Suggested Solutions (1995) £3.00.

For Europe, add 15% postage and packing (£20 maximum). For the rest of the world, add 40% for airmail (£35 maximum).

ORDERING

By telephone to 01892 724371, with your credit card to hand

By fax to 01892 724206 (giving your credit card details).

By post to:

HLT Publications,
The Gatehouse, Ruck Lane, Horsmonden, Tonbridge, Kent TN12 8EA

When ordering by post, please enclose full payment by cheque or banker's draft, or complete the credit card details below.

We aim to dispatch your books within 3 working days of receiving your order.

Name

Address

Postcode

Telephone

Total value of order, including postage: **£**

I enclose a cheque/banker's draft for the above sum, or

charge my   ☐ Access/Mastercard   ☐ Visa   ☐ American Express

Card number

☐☐☐☐   ☐☐☐☐   ☐☐☐☐   ☐☐☐☐

Expiry date

☐☐☐☐

Signature

Date

Publications from **The Old Bailey Press**

Cracknell's Statutes

A full understanding of statute law is vital for any student, and this series presents the original wording of legislation, together with any amendments and substitutions and the sources of these changes.

Cracknell's Companions

Recognised as invaluable study aids since their introduction in 1961, this series summarises all the most important court decisions and acts, and features a glossary of Latin words, as well as full indexing.

Please telephone our Order Hotline on 01892 724371, or write to our order department, for full details of these series.